ALSO BY CHARLES MOORE

The Place of Houses
(with Donlyn Lyndon and Gerald Allen)

Dimensions
(with Gerald Allen)

Body, Memory and Architecture
(with Kent Bloomer)

Home Sweet Home: American Domestic Vernacular Architecture
(with Peter Becker and Kathryn Smith)

THE
CITY OBSERVED:
LOS ANGELES

THE CITY OBSERVED: LOS ANGELES

A GUIDE TO ITS ARCHITECTURE AND LANDSCAPES

CHARLES MOORE
PETER BECKER
REGULA CAMPBELL

PHOTOGRAPHY BY REGULA CAMPBELL

VINTAGE BOOKS
A DIVISION OF RANDOM HOUSE NEW YORK

FIRST VINTAGE BOOKS EDITION, JUNE 1984

Text Copyright © 1984 by Charles Moore, Peter Becker, and Regula Campbell
Photos Copyright © 1984 by Regula Campbell

Library of Congress Cataloging in Publication Data.

Moore, Charles Willard, 1925–
The city observed: Los Angeles

1. Architecture—California—Los Angeles.   2. Los
Angeles (Calif.)—Buildings.   I. Becker, Peter, 1946–
II. Campbell, Regula.   III. Title.
[NA735.L55M66   1984b]   917.94′940453   83-40544
ISBN 0-394-72388-0 (pbk.)

Manufactured in the United States of America

Cartography by David Lindroth
Designed by Carole Lowenstein

This book is dedicated to David Gebhard
and Robert Winter, without whose excellent volume,
A Guide to Architecture in Los Angeles and Southern California,
we would have been lost before we started

CONTENTS

FOREWORD

There is no one who understands Los Angeles better than Charles Moore. A blunt statement, I know, and sure to offend someone, but I will hold to it after reading this book. Indeed, I will go one better—there is no one who understands Los Angeles better and communicates that understanding with more ease, literacy and sheer grace than Charles Moore. It is a joy to read his words on the city; his enthusiasm is infectious, yet it never comes at the price of a clear critical sense.

I am especially pleased that, in association with Peter Becker and Regula Campbell, Charles Moore has produced this latest volume of *The City Observed* series. It is to him that I owe much of my own knowledge of that extraordinary landscape called Los Angeles; his essay of 1965 in the Yale journal *Perspecta,* "You Have to Pay for the Public Life," awakened many students and scholars, myself included, to the significance of Southern California's vernacular architecture and to the design lessons of Disneyland in particular. I do not have to turn back to that essay to remember Charles Moore's observation that Disneyland "is not just some sort of physical extension of Mickey Mouse," but a real urban place—the closest thing Southern California has, in fact, to a traditional urban experience. That it is also all make-believe does not deny its validity—it just tells us a great deal more about Southern California.

The City Observed books, of which this is the third to be published, were intended as personal architectural guides to American cities, each with a clear point of view. The clarity of the critical stance cannot be questioned here—it is one of respect for the flamboyant, stage-set qualities of Los Angeles, and for the emotional, even sensual, potential of architecture. But to leave it at that somehow seems to suggest that Charles Moore's standards are a bit soft, and that is not true at all. His eye is as sure and his words as sharp as any critic's; he may love the unexpected, but by no means does he love all of it.

There is no large city that is easy to capture in a single book, and Los Angeles is particularly difficult. Where does it begin? Where does it end? Is it really a city anyway, once you get past downtown? *The City Observed: Los Angeles* pays relatively little heed to the first two questions—which is fine, since they matter little—but it brings us to a certain conclusion on the third. Though Charles Moore makes much of the differences between Anaheim and Bel Air, between Wilshire Boulevard and Sunset Boulevard, between the beaches by the sea and the canyons and valleys of the mountains, in the end he does even more to show us how these things all come together. It is all one place, this wild, exuberant Eden, this end of the American road, and it is a place with more of an identity, in its way, than most other cities. The real achievement of this book, then, is not just to discourse at length on the parts—it is to say some important things about the whole, and to give the diverse landscape of Los Angeles coherence.

PAUL GOLDBERGER

INTRODUCTION

RIDES IN RAMONALAND

This book is part of a series of cities observed: it describes a spread-out city, mostly new, altogether different from the compact old centers of Manhattan and Boston, and in need of an altogether different plan of attack. We can't easily call a halt at the city limits of Los Angeles, wide as those extend; nor does it seem proper to go all the way northwest to Santa Barbara, east to Palm Springs or south to San Diego. Those places share Southern California with Los Angeles, but they have their own identities. Rather, we look from Malibu on the west to the San Fernando Valley on the north, to Riverside on the east to San Juan Capistrano on the south, the area describable as metropolitan Los Angeles. We can't set it up for walking tours, even for the most ferociously athletic. So we have arranged chapters on places like Downtown, Disneyland, Beverly Hills, Westwood, Hollywood, Pasadena and Santa Catalina Island, where one can often walk but sometimes might still better ride. And when it seems more interesting or clear or useful, we have organized our places along a route like the famous 66, by way of which generations of Americans arrived at the promised land; or the route of the Padres, by way of which Spaniards and Mexicans came earlier; or Wilshire Boulevard or Sunset or Western Avenue or Ventura Boulevard, all of which stretch for miles across the Los Angeles plain.

Unlike most cities, Los Angeles is not organized as a set of places or neighborhoods. It is so big that it must be seen, for the most part, as a set of very long streets or freeways or rides, and the places of interest as events along the way. Although the events in each chapter are arranged, loosely, along a certain route, the order of the chapters themselves might appear arbitrary because it mostly is, a consequence of the famous sprawl. Downtown does come first, however, because it was here first, and for many it remains at least the city's symbolic heart. And Disneyland comes second, though for some of us it belongs at the beginning, for it is now the real heart of Los Angeles. Together, the Downtown and Disneyland chapters offer as good an introduction as any to life in Southern California. The next two chapters follow something of a historical sequence: the Route of the Padres was Los Angeles' first road, and Route 66 was the one most newcomers, most poignantly in the 1930s, came in on. Although some of the remaining chapters manage to pick up where previous ones left off, there is no particular order to them. Santa Catalina Island is off by itself and very special, so we put it next to last. Other Continuing Attractions takes us through a number of places rather similar to Disneyland to become a kind of ride of rides. If Los Angeles, as we'll try to demonstrate, is really a collection of theme parks, here are a group of them conflated, as fitting a terminus as any for our ride.

Along the way we betray our prejudices, in favor of the fanciful Spanish colonial architectural legacy rich in reminiscences of early California as well as of a handful of architects who struck out in non-Spanish directions: the two Viennese, Rudolph Schindler and Richard Neutra, the Argentine Cesar Pelli, the Canadian Frank Gehry and a few others. Other prejudices will emerge: a general preference for the 1920s over the 1930s, for the '30s over the '40s, the '40s over the '50s, and for just about anything over the '60s. There is most often a partiality for the intimate over the grand, and special delight when the grand encapsulates the intimate. We have tried to include only places the visitor can see without special permission; therefore, houses and other private places are described only if enough is visible from public ground to make mention worthwhile.

Another prejudice, in this city of gardens, is in favor of the view that the whole environment, indoors or out, built or planted or ridden on, is the province of a book like this. In Southern California the part that is planted is very likely to be more sophisticated and more delightful than the part that is built. Just remember that very little is very old, and almost nothing is original. The native flora, called chaparral, has survived; but almost all the rest of the landscape is foreign, like us. The native fauna, Indians and bears, have fared less well. Some of the new people brought with them their old traditions of building houses and gardens and highways; but more notably, the new arrivals who built here have devised their own traditions out of pages of the local romance.

For a couple of generations during the Golden Age of the movies, Los Angeles was everybody's Hometown. The L.A. movie lot, with corner drugstore, Main Street and Andy Hardy's neighborhood, as well as the more dangerous hideaways of Raymond Chandler's Hollywood, were almost as familiar as our own backyards. Most of the movies are made elsewhere now, where labor is cheaper, but TV production goes on and a little bit of L.A. seems to have made an immense impression on people across the globe. Once, in Kashmir, halfway around the world, a young clerk noticed my Los Angeles address and excitedly recounted that he had been in L.A. the year before on his honeymoon, and had seen ... Lion Country Safari, Orange County's drive-through wildlife theme park.

It was a little unsettling that this young Indian had found so much excitement, ten thousand miles away, in a made-up replica of something people used to go to his country to experience. Some years ago Noël Coward noticed that phenomenon too; this is what he said of L.A.: "There is always something so delightfully real about what is phony here. And something so phony about what is real." And, I confess, a part of my own excitement in writing about the place is to push around notions of the limits of reality. Attitudes about reality—left us by the polemicists of Modern Architecture, from "form follows function" to "ornament is crime"—now seem narrow and needlessly restrictive or even misleading and wrong. It should be instructive to examine a place where romance repeatedly seduces reality, and only new arrivals cry "Rape!"

Los Angeles piles up paradoxes about reality almost into a new art form. For instance, the social reformers/environmental designers of the early twentieth century told us that the neighborhood unit was supposed to incubate a community of interest which would build a new organic, humane society. Well, L.A. has neighborhood units with a vengeance, and now the press is fussing that they're too independent to get together to address the civic urgencies. And if

L.A. has ever had a real civic hero, surely he is Walt Disney. Ray Bradbury calls him "the greatest avant-garde shaker and mover of the twentieth century." Walt Disney gave us the Theme Park, the multilayered parfait of civic realities, which saved the public realm in Southern California when it was otherwise at the edge of extinction. He replaced the downtowns, civic amenities, public parks and other urban infrastructure, already unimpressive in Southern California, with a made-up, hoked-up, highly energized and extremely attractive Magic Kingdom. Now, when Southern Californians want a model for their urban arrangements, they often look to Disney's Theme Park, and it does not stretch credulity very far to see Southern California's rather ephemeral public realm as a concentration of Theme Parks.

Many of these parks should probably be called Ramonaland, after the romantic heroine of Helen Hunt Jackson's 1881 novel that turned the moist eyes of the world toward Southern California before there were movies. As almost everyone used to know, *Ramona* concerns a beautiful girl brought up in a hacienda near Los Angeles during California's passage from Mexican to Yankee sovereignty in the mid-nineteenth century. She turns out, after many guarded disclosures, to be half Indian and runs off with a noble, handsome, gentle young Indian named Alessandro. Together they suffer a full sampling of the indignities being heaped on the Indians by their new Yankee overlords. One of these proves fatal to Alessandro, another to their child, but a kind of mauve-shaded latter-day happiness is devised for Ramona, presumably on account of her (partially) non-Indian blood. She marries her Spanish Don of a foster brother, who is weak but kind and wise and not bad-looking, though not a patch on Alessandro's proud machismo. The foster brother can afford to take her off to Mexico City for a long and fulfilling life, so far away that her California girlhood fades into an Arcadian dream.

The power and poignancy of these images were staggering, and the romantic attraction of Ramona's Southern California Garden of Eden has, with some help from the climate, magnetized generations of Americans toward this earthly paradise. But some have smelled a rat.

The genocidal Yankees described by Mrs. Jackson were awful, all right, but they did no more than continue the tradition begun when the Spanish arrived in 1781. The Spanish introduced slavery, squalor and syphilis to the Indians, which quickly killed off half of their 150,000 population. Even their spiritual leader, the sainted Padre Junipero Serra, was reported by his contemporary, Governor Fages, to enjoy too much the whipping of the Indian neophytes. The settlers who arrived after California fell into Yankee hands in 1848 merely exterminated the Indians who were left.

While the sentimental literature of an idyllic early California has largely been discredited, the romantic "Spanish" architecture it inspired has survived. This pervasive style has given the buildings and landscapes of Southern California a special character, recalling an imaginary past in an altogether synthetic manner. Though this book will display an abiding enthusiasm for them, these Hispanic styles don't really have the status of a tradition; the designer or the builder, inspired by a Southern California that never was, has *decided* each time whether to make a simple white-walled Mission or Spanish building. Unlike Greek-island builders, whose tradition told them how to structure, how to fenestrate, even what color blue to paint the trim, the Californians have had to choose among four separate Spanish persuasions.

The first, popular before the turn of the twentieth century, was the Mission Style, which took its cues from the string of California missions that the Spanish padres had founded a century before. This style relies generally on massive undecorated masonry walls and thin, simple wooden details. The Arts and Crafts vocabulary of details is replete with everything from little domed towers to rustic handcrafted wooden furniture.

After two decades of a passionate vogue, the Mission Style gave way to a couple of idioms closer to the Spanish source. One, Spanish Colonial Revival (the key word is Colonial), has proven amazingly enduring. It also depends for its effect on massive white walls and low-pitched roofs, usually tile, but it substitutes for the rustic Arts and Crafts detailing a touch of curvilinear ironwork for emphasis or relief. The other, introduced by the renowned Bertram Grosvenor Goodhue (the architect of the L.A. Public Library) for the San Diego World's Fair of 1915, was more fancifully decorated, more flamboyantly Spanish, inspired by the frenzies of seventeenth-century Spanish Baroque; the style curiously became termed Churrigueresque after the Spanish architect brothers Churriguerra, though those sober worthies never actually reached the point of designing in that exuberant style.

Finally, by the end of the 1920s, the planes of Spanish Colonial Revival and the wiggles of Churrigueresque had both been crisply pleated into an Art Deco–inspired Modern, an idiom that David Gebhard and others have further subdivided into a straight-lined "Zigzag Moderne" and a round-cornered "Streamline Moderne."

These four romantic, made-up new traditions have helped make-believe Los Angeles to become a city of theme parks, from Disneyland to Knott's Berry Farm to the historicized downtown of the City of Orange—gardens of Eden where Ramona might have found solace, and where now an honest dollar can be made. Of course, there is some architecture in Eden, but it hardly ever carries the story. The point usually seems to be to *feel* the place, not just look at it.

Looking at most cities involves seeing a lot of buildings. Looking at Los Angeles involves experiencing a lot of *rides*. It's hard to avoid experiencing a ride with your whole body, not just your eyes, whether the ride is on a roller coaster or a toy train or a full-size monorail or a boat in a lagoon or on a track or a chute or a freeway interchange—or even if the ride is on foot, like the tour at the Gamble House in Pasadena. Even the strictly architectural sights of Los Angeles are experienced more than seen, often in carefully controlled time. They are theater as much as architecture, ephemeral as often as architectonic, make-believe as often as real; and the result is a greater reality, the delightful reality of Noël Coward's phony.

Still, great numbers of people come to visit this paradoxical place where the real is phony and the buildings are rides and the monuments are often freeways. They see the flaws, too: gorgeously bronzed inhabitants seem too often flawed by the blank stare in their beautiful eyes, and the sunny climate seems as flawed by smog as the history is by genocide.

A hundred years ago Los Angeles was thought best ignored, and a California guide of 1873 suggests that visitors not bother with Los Angeles and the south unless their stay is so long (well over sixty days) that time hangs heavy. A century later that advice is seldom given, and people keep coming. Some love it, and feel at once at home—I have, since I was a small child. Others, often New Yorkers, would feel more at ease on an Aztec chopping block. Still others, who might enjoy the rides, are so disoriented by the spread of it all that they despair.

Fate has put the enormous spread of Los Angeles in the same state as San Francisco, which, notably among American cities, displays its urban structure in dramatic ways. San Francisco's two regular grids crash into each other in a satisfying, action-inducing way at Market Street. They drape over the hills of the peninsula and reveal themselves much better than if they were stretched out flat. Moreover, there is high urban drama when the grids' authority is challenged by obstacles, especially by the city's steep hills and cliffs, and some accommodation is made, to the greater glory of perceptible order.

It is only partly fatuous, on the other hand, to cast aside despair and regard Los Angeles' layout as a kind of molecular physicist's or a Zen order of overlapping probabilities and nets and clouds. The clouds in L.A., unfortunately, often include suspended particulate, carbon monoxide, ozone, sulfate, lead, nitrogen dioxide and sulfur dioxide; but there *are* patterns underneath, layer on layer.

The first layer is the plain (Figure 1): The city of Los Angeles covers 451 square miles, the largest area of any municipality in the world. It lies on a flat stretch roughly 35 miles square that is bounded on the south and west by the ocean, and on the north and east by high mountains, which normally keep the cold air out, though nowadays they can keep the bad air in as well. Across this plain flow three rivers: the Los Angeles, the San Gabriel and the Santa Ana, huge during winter rains, but dry most of the year, allowing Mark Twain to think it bizarre that he had fallen into the Los Angeles River and come out dusty.

When the Spaniards first arrived from the south, the Los Angeles plain was a kind of coastal desert, with Indians living where there were streams or springs, in delicate balance with the bears, who lived everywhere else. The Indian villages were of brush, rendered sanitary by periodic burning. The native desert ground cover, chaparral, renews itself by burning too. Almost explosive in its summer-dry state, it has in the more recent past caused a series of disastrous brushfires that have cremated expensive homes. Then, as now, floods from the seasonal rains ravaged the plain. The Spaniards, like the Americans after them, were particularly dismayed by the frequent shaking of the ground. But where there was water, between shakes it was paradise. Like the Indian villages, the population at the Spanish missions was located where the water was plentiful. The local missions still exist at San Juan Capistrano, San Gabriel and San Fernando, three in the string of twenty-one connected by El Camino Real, the Royal Road, which runs from the Mexican border to Sonoma, north of San Francisco.

Settlement during the sixty-seven years after the Spanish arrival in 1781 became more concentrated, though there were fewer people. By 1848, at the end of the Mexican War, when the territory was ceded to the victorious United States, the remaining Indians were worked by only five thousand Spaniards. But then the waves of Yankees came: a thick new layer of settlement in 1870, another in 1876, and then especially in the late 1880s. After a pause, they came again in what is called the "long boom," from 1893 to 1914. There were new waves from 1919 to 1925; there was a desperate one in the 1930s when droughts in Oklahoma and elsewhere drove west the poor people celebrated in John Steinbeck's *Grapes of Wrath;* and then there was the biggest one of all during World War II and after, when servicemen introduced to paradise came back for more. These American waves of immigrants brought better technology to find and distribute water, which left them not so closely tied to rivers, so the Yankees could settle where they deemed it particularly healthy or particularly attractive. The valley between Los Angeles and San Bernardino, fifty miles to the east, was especially favored for its view of snow-capped peaks above the orange groves that came to grow there.

After 1902 a network of fast interurban streetcars (Figure 2) ran on tracks

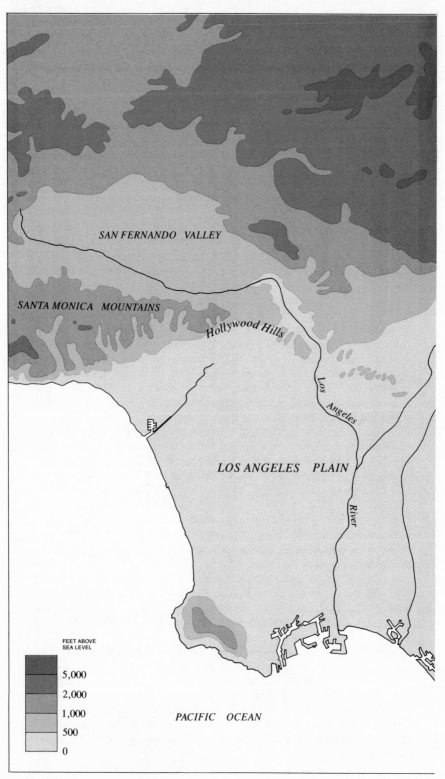

FIGURE 1 · LOS ANGELES PLAIN

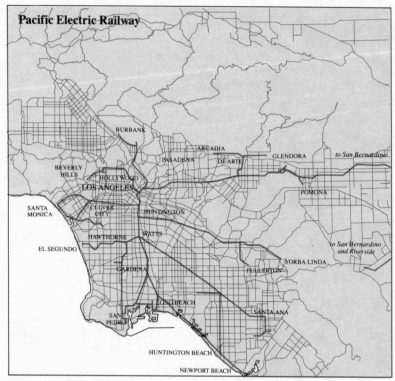

FIGURE 2 · PACIFIC ELECTRIC RAIL SYSTEM

with a special right of way separate from the street, crisscrossing the Los Angeles plain, to make yet another pattern of overlay and to give dramatic advantages of location, for instance, to Pasadena, just northeast of Los Angeles at the very foot of the San Gabriel Mountains. From a rose-covered cottage in Pasadena, it was a simple but dazzling experience of a winter morning to take the scenic railway to the top of snowy Mount Lowe, return to a picnic lunch in an orange grove, then travel on the interurban Red Cars to the Santa Monica beach and be back home for supper in Pasadena—all in the same sunny day!

The Red Cars formed a network that cities are spending millions to reproduce today. The whole system was bought after World War II by a large automobile company to remove competition with the motorcar. By that time yet another layer had appeared: major automobile streets (Figure 3) had spread across the plain in an irregular net with interstices roughly a mile across. In these spaces the smaller grids of residential streets emerged, establishing a characteristic pattern: strip commercial shops and offices face the main streets, parking lies just behind, and individual houses line the streets behind that. Over the century since the Yankee waves began, the interstices have mostly been filled with little houses, stretching forever across the plain. But the sunshine is dimmed on their porches, and their rosebushes are stunted by fumes from the very gasoline that now brings their inhabitants from distant places of work and play. The clear sense of memorable place has clouded, the prideful distinctions between Pasadena and Monrovia and Riverside supplanted by the confusions and indistinctions of places even most natives have never heard of: Lakewood, Brea, Carson, Montebello, and a host of others.

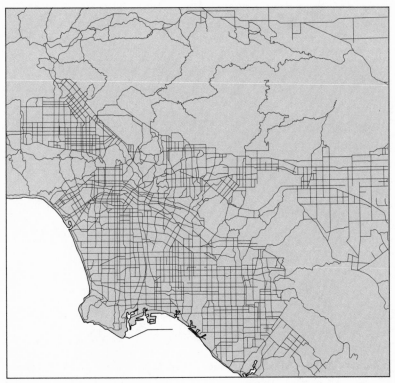

FIGURE 3 · MAJOR STREETS

There are more layers to go: we still must superimpose the patterns of impurity pouring out of cars and the Fontana steel mills (Figure 4) and overlay temperature maps (Figure 5) describing a coast tempered by ocean breezes while inland valleys swelter or freeze with the seasons. On top of all these layers we can finally place Los Angeles' horizontal monuments, the freeways (Figure 6), sometimes thrillingly choreographed at the interchanges, and almost always high, with sweeping views of the cities, the plain, and the mountains behind. The freeways afford the best chance to make physical sense of the place, but they remain apart: they do not determine the shape and location of buildings as the street grid of Manhattan does. Here in Los Angeles the shape of the city is soft at the edges, piled layer on layer, cloud on cloud, composing a hazy pattern of amenity that leaves only a few special places unengulfed, survivors in a paradise awash.

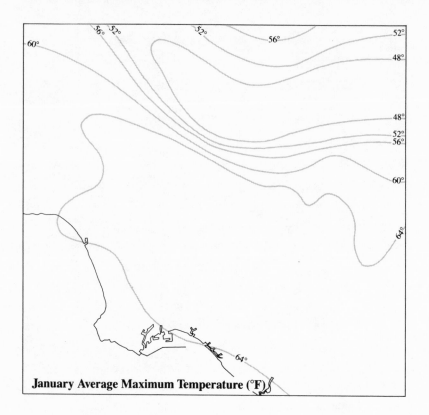

January Average Maximum Temperature (°F)

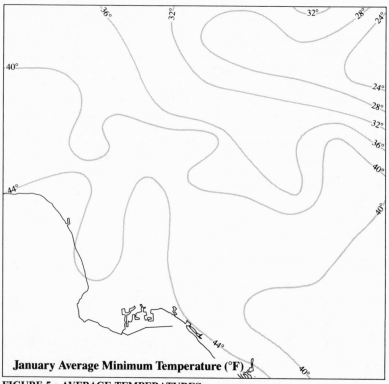

January Average Minimum Temperature (°F)

FIGURE 5 · AVERAGE TEMPERATURES

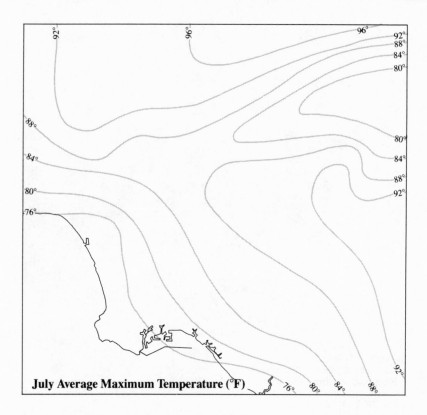

July Average Maximum Temperature (°F)

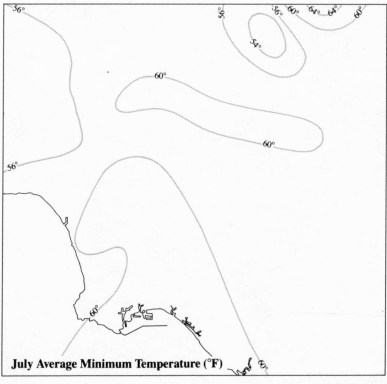

July Average Minimum Temperature (°F)

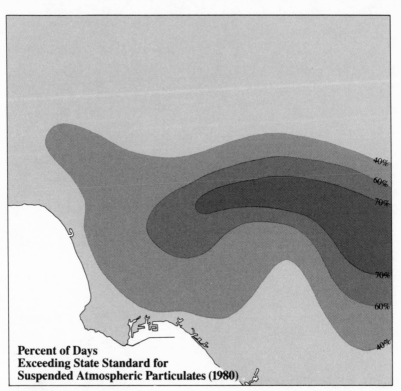

Percent of Days
Exceeding State Standard for
Suspended Atmospheric Particulates (1980)

FIGURE 4 · IMPURITIES

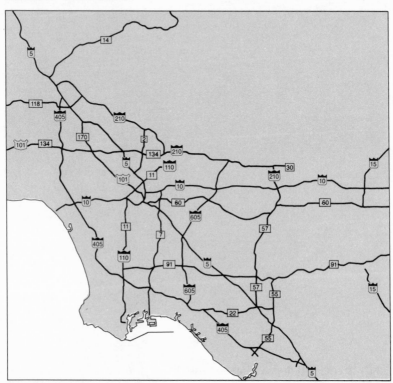

FIGURE 6 · FREEWAYS

NOTE: This book was written by Charles Moore, who is in his fifties, and by Peter Becker and Regula Campbell, who are in their thirties. We would have liked to stick to the royal and editorial "we," since we have worked together closely, but vivid personal recollections of the 1930s, for instance, by the younger authors just won't wash. Therefore, we have adopted the following code: on the few occasions where an "I" is used instead of a "we," the "I" is Charles Moore.

ADDITIONAL NOTE: Because Los Angeles is so big and has so many streets, the serious explorer would be well advised to buy the spiral bound and exhaustively indexed maps for the area produced by Thomas Bros. Maps, California's unerringly masterful cartographers.

I/DOWNTOWN

Oviatt Building

Many descriptions of Los Angeles would leave you believing that it doesn't have a downtown but is a cluster of suburbs engaged in a forlorn search for a center. There are people who have been residents in corporate Los Angeles for years who claim they have never been downtown, though they will generally admit to having soared by it on the freeway. It is, therefore, somewhere between an act of faith and an act of defiance to start this book with a description of that frequent phoenix. Los Angeles *does* have a downtown, almost two hundred years old in spots, with a regular grid of streets and some very tall buildings. The grid collided with the nearby foothills, especially a steep knob named Bunker Hill; and the most colorful early lore describes the private dooms of entrepreneurs struggling to get goods and water and people up its steep slopes. After a radiant middle period graced by gingerbread mansions, the Urban Renewal bulldozers of the 1960s initiated a new phase by removing everything, including the hill.

The first several decades of European occupation (after 1781) in this muddy and dusty proto-paradise were hardest on the Indians, who were suffering genocide. The next decades (after Mexican independence in 1821) were uncomfortable for the Mexicans who succeeded them, as they in turn were pushed out of their patrimonies by hordes of Yankee settlers. The Chinese and Japanese came

I 1 A · *Old Plaza with Pico House*

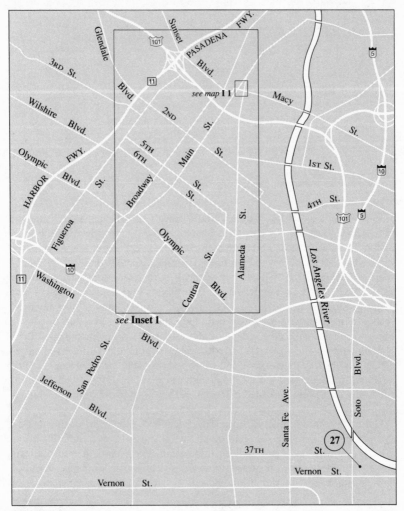

I/DOWNTOWN

too and were pushed into corners, then into picturesque ethnic downtown villages. The most recent turn of the Wheel of Just Retribution has brought the Hispanic people back downtown, millions of them: Chicanos (born north of the border, of Mexican ancestry), Mexicans and Central Americans—some U.S. citizens, some legal immigrants, and some more (perhaps a million) illegal, many of them too frightened of deportation to claim any of their rights. But their presence is felt: Broadway, downtown's old main artery, now resembles a giant Mexican village in perpetual full fiesta.

Away from Broadway, downtown is not compact. Perhaps the best way to visualize it is by starting from the slight rise where Bunker Hill used to be. On the west side of the hill runs the Harbor Freeway; on the south side is the startlingly unprepossessing business and financial center of the western United States, fashioned of straight-up-and-down new buildings, rising without any ceremony at bottom or top to arbitrary and unpredictable heights, like so many random extrusions. The closest parallel is perhaps an asparagus patch, where

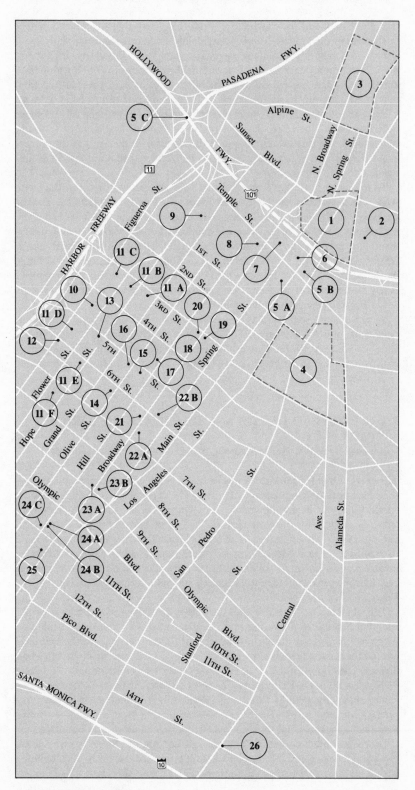

I/DOWNTOWN (INSET 1)

the tallest stalk and the shortest are just alike, except that the tallest has shot farther out of the ground. The L.A. asparagus patch is particularly shiny.

East of Bunker Hill and the asparagus patch runs Broadway, in nonstop noisy celebration, marking the eastern boundary of downtown. North of Bunker Hill lies what is supposed to be the biggest collection of government buildings in the country, outside Washington. Its westerly part bumps into the Music Center, an attempt similarly to concentrate culture. On the map all this looks orderly enough, unified by the grid: twelve or fourteen blocks north to south, only about seven east to west. The order is deceptive: in the heart of this motorage downtown are places (like the Bonaventure Hotel) that are just about impossible to reach on foot.

To the north of the government center runs an east-west freeway, the Santa Ana, which becomes the Hollywood Freeway where it intersects the Harbor Freeway, which becomes the Pasadena Freeway at a celebrated four-level intersection now overhung with vines, the quintessential Angeleno romantic monument. Just north of the Santa Ana is the plaza where it all began, with Union Station, Olvera Street and El Pueblo de Los Angeles State Historic Park. Three blocks north of that is a made-up ethnic theme park called simply Chinatown. A few blocks south of the Santa Ana Freeway, three blocks east of Broadway, is Little Tokyo, bigger, newer and more urban.

Since there are some bleak no-man's-lands between and around these wonders, walking is for the hardy. You'll pick up the city's rhythms better at the wheel of your car, as the natives do. But from the car you'll also miss many gratifying details, so it's best to brave it and walk as much as you can bear.

I 1 · EL PUEBLO DE LOS ANGELES STATE HISTORIC PARK
Bounded by Macy, North Alameda, Arcadia, and North Spring streets

The heart of this Hispanic town was its plaza, and it seems appropriate, though it is some distance in space and spirit from the skyscrapers of the financial district, to start our look at downtown here. One of the few major historical sites left in Los Angeles is the State Historic Park. It comprises the Old Plaza itself, laid out in 1815; Olvera Street, lined with nineteenth-century buildings (redone in 1929 as a "typical Mexican marketplace"); and another block of venerable nineteenth-century brick buildings. Despite encroaching development and recent blockbuster restoration, a visitor can still get a feeling of old Los Angeles here.

The Old Plaza (1 A) is a restful, shady spot. Its tiled benches under huge old Moreton Bay fig trees offer pleasant places to sit; street vendors sell fresh fruit with cool drinks and snacks; and between the other visitors and the buildings around the square, there is always plenty to see. To the west, at 535 North Main Street, is the Plaza Church (1 B) (1822, 1861 and after), more formally La Iglesia de Nuestra Señora la Reina de Los Angeles de Porciúncula, the oldest religious edifice in the city, built by Franciscan fathers and local Indians. It looks appropriately Mexican rustic. The beige plaza façade of gabled end and bell tower resembles a location shot from a spaghetti Western: almost right but not quite.

On the southeast corner of the plaza and Los Angeles Street is Fire Station No. 1 (1 C) (1884), the city's first. It's a straightforward two-story brick building with a machicolated parapet and a few Eastlake flourishes, now a little muse-

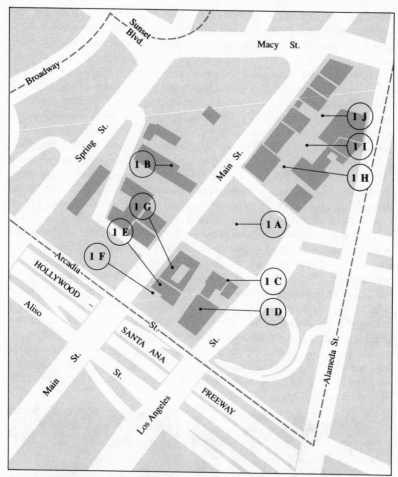

I 1 · EL PUEBLO DE LOS ANGELES STATE HISTORIC PARK

um. South of it, at 415 North Los Angeles Street, is the carefully restored Garnier Block (1 D) (Philippe Garnier, 1890). This solid brick-and-sandstone structure, derivative of the Richardsonian Romanesque, which had been in vogue farther east, was built after downtown had shifted southwest and the Chinese had moved in. The south end of the building was lopped off when the Santa Ana Freeway breezed through in the early 1950s. Across the alley, at 420 North Main Street, is the city's first theater, the Theater Mercedes (1 E) (Ezra F. Kysor, 1870). This three-story building, with its 400-seat theater on the second floor, was elaborated in an up-to-date Italianate style. But by 1878 performances had stopped, for this first downtown was already in decline. Next door, at 416 Main, is the two-story, earlier and simpler Italianate Masonic Temple (1 F) (1858), one of the oldest commercial buildings in Southern California still standing.

Nearby, facing onto the plaza at 430 North Main Street, is the Pico House (1 G) (Ezra F. Kysor, 1869), the city's first three-story masonry structure and its handsomest example of the Italianate commercial style. It was built as a hotel by Pio Pico, the last Mexican governor of California, and was long known as "the finest building south of San Jose." The elegant façade (now beautifully restored) of elaborate and deeply incised arched openings relied on a combination of restrained Classical elements and ample money, but the great acclaim of the hotel was based on its widely advertised gas lighting fixtures and two zinc bathtubs.

At the north end of the plaza is the entrance to Olvera Street (1 H), the city's oldest theme shopping mall. Unlike Chinatown or Little Tokyo, Olvera Street is an entertainment center more than an ethnic neighborhood. This tiny pedestrian way, paved with Spanish tiles and brick, has over seventy businesses lining it. Rustic brick-and-adobe buildings are packed together, with porches and outdoor cafés arranged in festal emulation of a Mexican border town. Often their floor levels are not the same as the street's, so special flights of stairs and diagonal views lead up and down into colorful shops. Open-air stands selling Mexican candy, taquitos, ceramics, postcards and huaraches fill the center of the street, in the dappled shade of canvas awnings, palms and ancient olive trees.

At 14 Olvera Street is the Avila Adobe (1 I) (ca. 1818), the oldest house in Los Angeles, now a museum. It meets the street with a heavy beamed porch covered in grapevines. In back, the house wraps around a dusty Early California courtyard with a few fruit trees and cactus along the edges. A little farther down Olvera Street is a fountain and a triple row of bricks, which is all that remains of the Zanja Madre (the Mother Ditch) (1 J), the water course that brought water from the Los Angeles River to the pueblo between 1781 and 1863.

Like the rest of the public realm in Los Angeles, the Old Plaza is exotic, charming and hopelessly inadequate. It is odd that the center of one of the world's great cities should be occupied by a South of the Border tourist trap, but it's a charming little tourist trap and a useful reminder that the tiny pueblo once served by a single ditch lies not much more than a century behind the bumptious metropolis.

I 1 H · *Olvera Street*

I 1 I · *Avila Adobe*

I 2 · UNION STATION
800 North Alameda Street
John and Donald B. Parkinson; J. H. Christie, H. L. Gilman, R. J. Wirth, architects; Herman Sachs, color consultant; Tommy Tomson, landscape architect, 1934–1939

Union Station, in its heyday, was the western end of the line for rail passengers from all over the North American continent. Its architectural style, restrained

I 2 · *Union Station* I 3 · *New Chinatown*

Spanish Colonial Revival with Streamline Moderne touches, has soaked up the romance of the ranchos and beamed back a vigorous assertion of the city's modernity. In true California style, indoors and outdoors are artfully interwoven in the design. The shadows of slender Mexican fan palms caress the huge white walls, while tall and glassy arched openings allow shafts of sunlight to slip through the lofty interiors. A giant-size freestanding arcade connects the main concourse to the restaurant, encouraging travelers to enjoy the California climate en route. Behind the main concourse the high-ceilinged waiting room is filled with light from flanking courtyards. The northern court contains California live oaks and jacarandas, the remains of a fountain, and beautiful tiled benches. Over the north wall loom the domes of the post office next door. The southern courtyard was originally planted to be the quintessence of Southern Californian garden design. Landscaped with now-enormous fig trees and Mexican fan palms, birds-of-paradise, ginger and orchid trumpet vines, the garden was meant to provide a fragrant haven for travelers already intoxicated with the thrill of having arrived in Eden, or despondent over oncoming exile.

The detail is as sophisticated and sure as the spaces. Interior colors are muted earth tones; the walls are warm gray concrete block. Small openings are accented by white shell-like moldings that slither around the edges. At the east end of the waiting room, thick columns sport a wainscoting of colorful ceramic tiles patterned like Navajo rugs; the pattern changes its scale as it slips down onto the ceramic tiled floor. The presence of most of the original furnishings keeps alive the building's exuberance. Heavy wood chairs in the waiting room offer comfort and privacy from the crowds that are no longer there. Glass-backed Art Deco signs still provide elegant directions. An original drinking fountain in the main concourse sums up the verve and careful opulence of the whole place: its basin is Z-shaped, cut into a single block of dark marble with a font at each end of the Z, the drain in the middle. The near-desertion of the station now puts a nostalgic golden patina of time and shifting fortunes over a still modern masterpiece.

In the 1930s, Streamline Moderne, the "smart" style, swept the nation; everything from toasters to department stores was streamlined. Among the most felicitous uses of the style were the aerodynamic trains of Norman Bel Geddes and Raymond Loewy. These sleek, powerful vehicles streaking across the American landscape captured the imagination of the nation. Architects, engaged to design new train stations, were quick to employ Streamline Moderne, echoing the lines of the trains, though the traditional railroad station in Southern California was still designed in Mission, Spanish, Pueblo or Churrigueresque style.

The Streamline Moderne, like its Hispanic predecessors, did not eschew ornament, unlike the International Style that began in the same era: witness the dazzling semi-Navajo chromed interior of the Super Chief club car, or the parallel Navajoid manifestations on the walls of Union Station. This is a remarkable building, at once chic Moderne, regional southwestern (as befitted arrival at the end of the line) and radiant Spanish Colonial Revival; it is a triumph that transcends but never avoids style.

I 3 · NEW CHINATOWN
Bounded approximately by North Alameda, Ord, Yale and Bernard streets; main activity is between the 700 and 1000 of North Broadway, ca. 1930 and after

New Chinatown, moved when Union Station was constructed, is both a tourist spot and a working community. Its center covers two blocks of picturesquely disposed pedestrian streets that run between two-story buildings with suitably Oriental motifs grafted onto surfaces of beige, green or salmon stucco trimmed in red, aqua or gold wood and tiles. Roof lines are accented with tiny lights, neon strips or scampering dragons. Octagonal windows, moongates, curved roof lines and continuous balconies spice up the shops and restaurants.

The highest concentration of Chinese ornament appears along Gin Ling Way, a pedestrian street between Broadway and Hill Street, about halfway between College and Bernard streets. Behind elaborate gateways, tiny streets amble past buildings that seem almost to founder beneath intricate masses of brightly colored tiles and carved wood and overhanging upturned roofs—even the phone booths have become vermilion pagodas. Near the middle, across from Sincere Imports, is a wishing-well fountain made up of a six-foot-high mountain with small plants and smaller statues within a fish pond. Tiny paths and bridges lead up to figures of the eight Chinese Immortals, with, at the top, the inevitable goddess Kwan Yin protected by blue lions and a shrine. The plaza continues across Hill Street into Chung King Court, where there's another fishpond and a miniature mountain with a Kwan Yin on top, though it's all considerably smaller and tamer than the first.

Most of the newer buildings have joined in the excitement as well: tiled roofs with upturned corners cover an Oriental Union 76 gas station (900 North Hill Street); super-torii Japanicisms envelop a Bank of America (850 North Broadway); Foo dogs and ginkgo trees flank the front door of an East-West Federal Savings (935 North Broadway). The Mandarin plaza (970 North Broadway) contains a particularly traffic-stopping yellow-and-orange pagoda roof at the entrance to its ordinary stucco shops. The cunning fake chinoiserie of it all is in danger of being attacked as blatant racism these days, but its innocence should serve it as a shield.

I 4 · LITTLE TOKYO
**Bounded approximately by First, Third, South Los Angeles and Alameda
streets**

California's dismal history of racial oppression didn't stop when the Indians
were wiped out. One of its most recent manifestations was after Pearl Harbor,
in 1941, when U.S. citizens of Japanese descent were thrown out of their homes
(to the enormous profit of real estate speculators) and sent to internment camps
inland. Ever since their return at the end of World War II, Little Tokyo has
been the cultural center of Los Angeles' Japanese community, one thousand
strong. Located in just a few blocks bordering First Street on the eastern edge of
the civic center, the area contains over a hundred Japanese American businesses.

First Street is the attractive major commercial strip. Although the two-story
buildings have not been flamboyantly Orientalized, the tiny scale of the shops
and the delicate merchandise and plastic-food displays in the windows speak of
Japan. The area remained unchanged until the recent completion of the New
Otani Hotel and Japanese Village Plaza, which have brought in waves of tourists.

The Japanese Village Plaza (between First and Second streets, near Central
Avenue) might be seen as just another in an overabundance of theme shopping
centers, but in this case the exotic atmosphere is a delight and a success. An
open-air, village-scaled pedestrian mall winds through an entire block; on each
side are one- and two-story shops with white stucco walls, blue-tiled roofs and
exotic details such as round-timber porch columns and wood slat screens recollective of bamboo, all used with just enough restraint. The narrowing and opening out of the walkway provides a rich sequence of spaces and views: a splashing
fountain enlivens one jog; a careful composition of natural rocks and ginkgo
trees bedecks another; the north end is marked by a tall, heavy-timbered tower
with another blue-tiled roof. Village Plaza is a masterly addition to Little Tokyo, very much in the spirit of the place and far more interesting than the New
Otani Hotel (120 South Los Angeles Street), which is just another high-rise with
a standard collection of pastel-awninged boutiques at its base. But the New
Otani does have a pleasant and startlingly sited Japenese garden, complete with
rocks and trees and waterfalls, on a third-floor roof terrace.

I 5 · LOS ANGELES CITY HALL
200 North Spring Street
*John C. Austin, John and Donald Parkinson and Albert C. Martin, Sr.;
Austin Whittlesey, interior, 1926–1928*

Every world city is represented to us by an image or landmark, but Los Angeles
has been hard pressed to provide just the right one. Some images have blossomed out of almost nothing, like the huge white HOLLYWOOD sign on the side
of Mt. Lee in the Hollywood Hills, and some have fallen into neglect, like the
Venice canals. Some are ambitious but slightly too silly to succeed, like the
theme building at the airport. If there has come to us a single image of L.A., it
is doubtless the tower of City Hall, with the world's first four-level freeway interchange nearby, dripping vines like a Piranesi view of ancient Rome.

Since its completion, City Hall (5 A) has been the enthusiastically received

I 5 · *Los Angeles City Hall*

symbol of the city. While it is displayed on police badges and official documents, it gained its widest recognition as the frontispiece for the popular 1950s
television series *Dragnet.* Until 1957 the Los Angeles building code allowed no
buildings to be over 150 feet high—except City Hall, at 28 stories, towering
above the rest. Since then, despite the fear of earthquakes, other higher buildings have appeared, but the readily identifiable shape of City Hall still pinpoints
the civic center for motorists on the Santa Ana, Hollywood and Harbor freeways.

It was decided that the architecture of City Hall, though it might seem to be a
direct copy of the glorious Public Library of the years just preceding it, would
not owe allegiance to any one style, but like the city at large, should draw from
a mélange of loosely re-created styles. With new-found local pride extended
statewide, special care was taken to incorporate materials produced in California. The exterior cladding up to the fourth floor is California granite; the cere-
monial doors of the Romanesque forecourt are cast from bronze amalgamated
from California ores. The list goes on, though perhaps the most enthusiastic use
of native materials is in the cornerstone, laid by the Native Sons of the Golden
West. It contains such telling documents as a Los Angeles telephone directory,
signatures by the personnel at the mayor's office, and a list of employees at the
Raymond Granite Company, carvers of the stone. The mortar used consists of
sand from each county in the state, cement from each California cement mill,
and water from each of the twenty-one missions—producing a geological, technological and historical coup of dazzlingly restricted dimensions.

The landscaping, too, reinforces this rampant eclecticism, combining the ex-
oticism of Mexican fan palms with more traditional public-building landscaping, formal sweeping lawns, clipped shrubs and shade trees, with a generous
sprinkling of the city's official flower—you guessed it—the bird-of-paradise.

There are very few monumental spaces in the building's workaday interior.
The four-story rotunda described in the folders as Romanesque and Byzantine

is actually straight from Hollywood, innocently splendid in its colored marble mosaics and columns. It looks very large in photos, quite small in real life. The balcony ringing this room affords a good view of the elaborate floor, which resembles an overhead shot of Busby Berkeley pattern dancers. From an observation deck are excellent views of downtown architecture complete with helpful identifying diagrams. On a clear day you can get an idea of the enormous size of the city as it stretches to the horizon; if it's smoggy, you'll doubtless see as much as you can stand.

There are two other man-made L.A. symbols nearby: at the southeast corner of Temple and Main streets is the Triforium (5 B) (Joseph Young, 1975); northwest of City Hall is the four-level interchange (1949) of the Santa Ana, Harbor, Hollywood and Pasadena freeways. The Triforium is a stupefyingly unsophisticated attempt to bring art and science together for public benefit. Interspersed with oval speakers, 1,494 colored glass prisms are hung in beehivelike groupings from a triangular concrete base. Although it was designed in the 1970s, the Triforium is a quintessentially mid-sixties piece featuring sound piped through the speakers and translated by computer into a flickering light show of the electrified prisms. Touted by its creator as "a technological and artistic joining of artist and scientist," and "a fitting structure for a great metropolis," it turned out to be a very expensive joining, which elicited great public outcry. The artist wouldn't even allow postcards.

The freeway interchange (5 C) on the other hand, is as astonishingly beautiful as the Triforium is presumptuously grotesque. It is said to be the world's second most heavily traveled intersection (leading to endless wonder about where number one can be), servicing about four hundred thousand vehicles daily and appearing on postcards with captions like "Dig These Freeways!" and "L.A.'s Fabulous Freeways." Though there are other freeways now with bigger interchanges, as many curves, more sweeping off-ramps, and even more expansive landscaping, here is the tender progenitor of them all, hovering by now on the edge of the poignant. Its semitropical garlands festoon a heritage that seems much older than that magic moment thirty years ago when the freeways were forerunners of a brave new world.

I 6 · UNITED STATES COURT HOUSE
312 North Spring Street
G. Stanley Underwood, 1938–1940

This is the stripped-down PWA Moderne of the Great Depression at its L.A. finest. Despite the grit of forty years, the exterior gleams with Faith in the Future—light-colored masonry, perched on a slick base of pink-veined black marble. The composed dignity of the massive rectangular blocks may have projected a hope that the government's presence would provide stability in the face of national economic disaster.

The interior is streamlined, rich and machine-age elegant. The Main Street lobby is capsule-shaped in plan, with larger-than-life statues in the PWA style at the niched ends: on the south is an eight-foot stone sculpture, "Law," by Archibald Garner; on the north is "Young Lincoln," by James L. Hausers. Most surfaces are stylish rose marble and sienna travertine with fittings that include light fixtures of the flying-saucer persuasion and twin airstream escalators of shiny aluminum. The escalator ride to the third-floor courtrooms is an homage to the machine. It carries lawyers, defendants, judges, witnesses and visitors alike with beauty, grace and unflinching inevitability.

Upstairs hallways are paved with diamond-patterned terrazzo in yellow and dark gray between thin aluminum strips; the walls have dark marble wainscoting. Most of the doors are made of ribbed aluminum, though the ones to the courtrooms, as in Captain Nemo's *Nautilus,* are covered in maroon leather with aluminum studs and ship-door handles. Even the restrooms are De Stijl compositions of gray-and-black glass tile. Not even half a century has passed, but this building has already become a voice from the past, thrillingly close but irretrievably gone.

I 7 · HALL OF JUSTICE
210 West Temple Street
Allied Architects of Los Angeles, 1925

The oldest structure left in the civic center, the Hall of Justice was designed when Classical detailing was a requirement for all public buildings, even in Eden. The Allied Architects apparently enjoyed the constraints. They faced the building in California granite, with highly rusticated walls pierced by single windows all the way to the ninth story. Then comes a one-story entablature, which serves as base for a giant three-story temple front (where the jail cells are) with tall polished-granite columns. Above this is another story of entablature, whose cornice conceals one last story with a sloping roof. The barrel-vaulted entrance foyer, which runs completely through the building, is a Classical extravaganza of gold marble walls, enormous Ionic columns and a gilt-edged coffered ceiling. Set squarely on its hilly site, the Hall of Justice is imposingly solid and dignified, just the sort of building to inspire confidence in governmental proceedings, though visions of ephemeral airborne temples seem clearly to have been dancing through the architects' heads.

I 8 · HALL OF RECORDS
320 West Temple Street
Richard J. Neutra and Robert E. Alexander; Douglas Honnold and John Rex; Herman Charles Light and James R. Friend, 1962

The Los Angeles County Hall of Records was designed by one of the city's best-known architects, Richard Neutra. His careful composition of blank rectangular volumes juxtaposes finely inscribed window walls in an idom he had pioneered thirty years earlier. Various solid blocks, particularly the ones in the middle, are sheathed simply in small tiles of coral, brown or light gray. Glassy wings that face south are protected by vertical aluminum sunshades, as are the ones on the north. Though the landscaping is 1950s exotic, including liberal use of banana trees and birds-of-paradise, the building itself, which provided a rare opportunity for a significant Los Angeles architect to work on a grand scale, expresses surprisingly little about Southern California, the civic center or the people who use it. Mr. Neutra, for all his prowess, seems to have had little to say about a hall of records.

I 9 · MUSIC CENTER
North of First Street between Hope Street and Grand Avenue
Welton Becket and Associates, 1964–1969

Ah, the sixties! It is of course much too soon to attempt to discern parallels between the windy grandiosity of official Late Modern Architecture and the vast monuments that loaded down imperial Rome on its extensive skid. Actually, though there are many pleasures lurking in Pure Classical Forms Gone Wrong, it is much more difficult to locate the Redemption Factor in the Depression-born (later precast) stripped-down arcades of our own time. And the Music Center takes the Late Imperial Depression Style cake.

Two enormous rectangular solids flank a cylindrical peg in a square watery hole, all of it flanked and outflanked with a colonnade of spindly, enormous and altogether scaleless columns. This colonnade sometimes decorates the buildings and sometimes marches around to take you under inadequate cover *almost* to where you'd like to go. To preserve the purity of the whole, the central cylinder, which is called the Mark Taper Forum, can only be reached through the rain across a bridge because the colonnade, which clomps around the outside edge of the pool, is either too important or too clumsy to make any gesture toward the entrance door. The larger of two flanking theaters is called the Dorothy Chandler Pavilion; the other, almost as large, is the Ahmanson. They are both dazzlingly opulent.

It's all very L.A. and many people love it. But think what a wonderful acropolis might have ensued if this had happened thirty years sooner; it might have had the radiance of Union Station, with all the decorative pleasures of the Streamline Moderne *and* the Spanish Colonial Revival instead of the harshness of this cruel stepmother of a style that eschews ornament and haughtily rejects delight. Also, at an earlier date, the designers might have remembered that you have to *get* to an acropolis. (The Athenians managed it with some splendor through their Propylaea.) The main access to the Music Center is up from basement parking. Otherwise you crawl up some emergency stairs that allow you to feel you've arrived at the service entrance. You feel really silly if you've gotten all dressed up.

I 10 · BONAVENTURE HOTEL
404 South Figueroa Street
John Portman and Associates, 1975

Two of the most damaging criticisms leveled against architects are that 1) they treat their buildings as though the world around their sites were nonexistent, and 2) they make uninhabitable objects. Both these criticisms apply, with a vengeance, to the shiny new hotel John Portman's office designed along the freeway edge of downtown. They are leveled, however, with some rue, since that same office was responsible for the first decent, even noble spaces anyone had put into American commercial buildings for a long, long time. The very special attribute of the Hyatt Regency in Atlanta, their first success, lets you glory in your own importance by making you feel "centered," a term used by dancers to describe a state of physical presence, balance and well-being. The Atlanta hotel has a soaring central space surrounded by individual rooms. Clearly understandable elevators soar up, as in the splendid Bradbury Building (page 24) in Los Angeles. The visitor, himself, is the centerpiece.

This Los Angeles version of a Portman hotel, on the contrary, has a solid cylindrical core in the middle with four smaller cylinders around it; human circulation squeezes into a skylit bagel of space between the central core and the perimeter cylinders. You are likely to move around and around that bagel with increasing frenzy, since you can't help feeling that you're lost. The place is as frustrating as a Piranesi prison drawing—it's all alike, and you never know when you've arrived. If you look up, you see dirty skylights; if you look down, you see pools with bottoms apparently coated with tar; and if you look sideways, you see through glass to the unfinished insides of elevator shafts.

From a distance, the Bonaventure is pretty wonderful, certainly the flashiest, brightest and most romantically futuristic bauble on the Los Angeles skyline. It lifts itself with flashing arrogance high above the surrounding streets on a solid concrete base. Close up, though, you see how the base affronts the sidewalk; access into it is hard to find, and assertively demeaning.

I 11 · HIGH-RISE OFFICE BUILDINGS

A · CROCKER CENTER
333 South Grand Avenue, bounded by Grand Avenue and Third, Fourth and Hope streets
Skidmore, Owings and Merrill, 1982–1983

B · SECURITY PACIFIC NATIONAL BANK
333 South Hope Street, bounded by Hope, Flower, Third and Fourth streets
William L. Pereira Associates, 1975

C · LOS ANGELES WORLD TRADE CENTER
350 South Figueroa Street, bounded by Third, Fourth, Figueroa and Flower streets
Conrad Associates, 1974

D · ARCO PLAZA
505–555 Flower Street, bounded by Flower, Figueroa, Fifth and Sixth streets
Albert C. Martin and Associates, 1971

E · FIRST INTERSTATE TOWER
707 Wilshire Boulevard, bounded by Wilshire Boulevard and Sixth and Hope streets
Charles Luckman and Associates, 1973

F · BROADWAY PLAZA
Between Flower, Hope, Seventh and Eighth streets
Charles Luckman and Associates, 1973

All products of the corporate 1970s, these monoliths are in the mode that has come to signify a prosperous, serious and modern city center. They stand, just east of the Harbor Freeway, like a multistoried theatrical backdrop. Their slick, spare façades act as an uneasy foil for pedestrians and such smaller buildings as the Public Library and the Biltmore Hotel. Like the large-scale brush strokes on the last layer of a scenic scrim, these buildings look best from a distance—from Bunker Hill or the freeways, where they look like the small-scale models that

I 10 · *Bonaventure Hotel*   I 12 · *Linder Plaza*

must have been used to design them, where the human body is too tiny to have entered into consideration. Each one of these office buildings is loaded with extras, including fountains, sculpture, banners, landscaping and expensive surfaces, but the amenities don't seem to go well with one another or combine to produce any overall effect; each seems to be the work of a separate department in the architect's large office. The divisions leave little room to escape the predictable and nowhere to sit down even if you do.

The newest insertion, Crocker Center, is a pair of shiny red granite polygonal towers, fifty-two stories high, with a collection of smaller granite blocks around the bottom. In an atrium between the blocks, landscape architect Lawrence Halprin will soon install a water garden, which is almost guaranteed to be spectacular. Across the street, the Security Pacific National Bank Building is another fifty-two-story extrusion, this time with uninterrupted white vertical ribs that separate slots of black glass. A three-story vermilion sculpture by Alexander Calder fits right in. Nearby are a small number of hard-edged but almost human-scale gardens that feature pools and waterfalls, willow trees and bright flowers, and a few places to sit. The dreary World Trade Center can be reached, should you are to reach it, by a pedestrian bridge over Flower Street; another bridge goes from there to the Bonaventure Hotel (page 15). The smooth and handsomely detailed twin monoliths of Atlantic Richfield Company's ARCO Plaza create a curious tension in the air between them and serve as a surreal background to the Public Library (page 18). At the street level is the inevitable uninhabitable windy plaza with Art, and below that an underground shopping plaza, recalling the ones that appeared first in Montreal in the late sixties. The type is more appropriate to the climate of Montreal than to what had previously been billed around here as an earthly paradise.

In this asparagus patch the First Interstate Tower, the tallest stalk of them all, is amazingly high for its tiny site. Just slightly set back from the street, it thrusts up sixty-two undifferentiated floors. The Broadway Plaza, unlike ARCO, pulls up the shopping mall aboveground to reveal a high space with escalators. A glassy roof above the main gallery makes the dark brick walls seem almost cheerful, and a relatively festive air is achieved with banners, sparkling lights and human movement. All this, alas, from the outside, is only visible through a glass face on the north; otherwise, the city streets are resolutely walled out. Two glass towers stick up from the north end of this city block of red brick; one of them is a hotel, capped by a flying saucer restaurant.

While these buildings are not particularly fascinating one by one, they are the highest and thickest asparagus patch on the Los Angeles plain, or indeed anywhere west of Chicago, and they constitute a vividly visible downtown, called by the locals, not surprisingly, "downtown."

I 12 · LINDER PLAZA
888 Sixth Street, at the south corner of Figueroa Street
Honnold, Reibsamen and Rex, 1973–1974

From any distance, this little (fifteen-story) high-rise looks like William Powell at a convention of pro football players. Shining with understated but obvious charm among its larger, heavier neighbors, it feels much friendlier than the behemoths around it. The building is triangular in plan; its western and southern façades are thin flat skins of pale gray steel and bluish mirrored glass. The steel panels are cut with grooves about two inches thick in a sort of tartan pattern that creates the appearance of cut blocks and calls attention to each floor. The panels wrap around the curved corner, then are sharply cut back at a tier of balconies on Sixth Street. Glass covers the rest of this eastern façade, shaded from the morning sun by the ARCO towers across the street, and reveals the building's activities to passersby. Carefully designed, stylish and delightful, this building is magnified by the presence of the bland giants all around it. There is some of the panache of David facing Goliath or Jack taking on the Giant in all this, though Linder Plaza clearly means the ARCO towers no harm.

I 13 · *Los Angeles Public Library*

I 13 · LOS ANGELES PUBLIC LIBRARY
630 West Fifth Street, between Flower and Grand streets
Bertram Grosvenor Goodhue with Carleton M. Winslow, architects; Lee
*   Laurie, sculptor; Hartley Alexander, creator of the literary program, 1925*
Open Monday, Wednesday, Friday and Saturday, 10–5:30; Tuesday and
*   Thursday, 12–8; closed Sundays and holidays*

Los Angeles is a city full of environmental, even architectural, experiences and some of the best rides in the world. But it has very few great buildings, or maybe just one. The one would be the Los Angeles Public Library, for which the city had the extraordinary good sense in 1922 to commission Bertram Goodhue, of New York and Santa Barbara. Goodhue had designed by then, among other works, Saint Thomas' Episcopal Church on Fifth Avenue in New York, in the

Gothic style, and buildings for the 1915 Panama-California Exposition in San Diego, in flamboyant Churrigueresque. For Los Angeles, he would invent a new style: proto-Modern, in that it is a style of clean, sharp and powerful planes; anti-Modern, in that it delights in the rich associations of literature and memory that the Modern Movement in architecture was soon to declare invalid.

The library doesn't have visible predecessors, but it does have an important sibling, and local successors. The same trio who created the library (Goodhue as architect, Lee Laurie as sculptor, and Hartley Alexander as developer of the subject matter of the art and the inscriptions) also collaborated on an even more magnificent building, the Nebraska capitol in Lincoln. Closer to home, the Los Angeles City Hall would not have risen as it did without the initiative of Goodhue's library.

Delight in the masterwork has sometimes faded through the years; librarians have taken up new mechanized methods of book retrieval and of air conditioning, architects have lost confidence in the efficacy of architecture itself, and by now the ideal metropolitan library is more a suburban warehouse than a downtown masterpiece. This one, therefore, is in continuous jeopardy.

The library makes its site seem generous, though lesser architects might have complained that the half-block parcel was too small for a civic monument. Goodhue magnified the parcel with a central fat tower (with books inside) surmounted by a tiled pyramid, around which each face is composed. The south face terminates Hope Street, with transverse terraces planted like a Mayan dream; the east face, opposite the Biltmore Hotel (p. 21), is rendered much more informal by a small-scale children's wing, which leaves room beside it for an intimate garden filled with jacaranda trees, blossoming vivid blue in June; the north side faces Fifth Street, symmetrical and urban; and the west side, the noblest of all until the vandalous insertion of a parking lot, was entered on axis at the end of a long reflecting pool flanked by cypress in an Arabian Nights vision out of Samarkand. Across the street by now loom the twin towers of ARCO, straight out of Tolkien/Mordor.

One of the chief glories of the library is Lee Laurie's crisp and powerful sculpture, which seems an integral part of the whole. Tall, clear plinths rising out of the ground have their crystalline structure revealed by a single chamfer and then another. Suddenly they break into prisms at the top and become the heads or sometimes the torsos of personifications of Science, the Arts, Statecraft, Philosophy, Letters and History. Some hold staffs, which are also the last unshattered fragments of the crystalline structure. On the south terraces below them, rows of cypress and olives vividly recall the classical past.

The first few moments inside are a letdown. Ahead stretches a long, wide corridor, with a vaulted crossing in the distance, a handsome tiled floor, some tiled wall panels, and openings into unexpectedly plain reading rooms. Other openings lead into a stairway with a coffered blue stenciled ceiling. At the top of these stairs is a pair of black marble sphinxes, symbols of the mysteries of knowledge, with heads that suggest torchères; on the landing is the extraordinary "Statue of Civilization," a very serious lady with the ring of the Valkyries; she lies behind us as we ascend into the breathtaking vaulted central rotunda. Its murals, 9,000 square feet of them, were painted by Dean Cornwell in 1933. They depict the history of California, jam-packed with padres, Indians, Indian babies, sheep, a mule, dancing señoritas, people building a mission, conquistadores, marvelous ships and flags, and lots of Spanish navigators and American gold miners. In the middle of a light fixture is a beautiful translucent globe with the signs of the zodiac.

The History department on the south side is Spanish Colonial. It features another magnificent stenciled ceiling with heavy beams and coffers, all made of concrete that looks like wood because of the boards that formed it. Here are more California scenes all around; a set of big south-facing windows is surrounded by murals of the building of a mission and a relief ship arriving at San Diego. The southwest corner room has still another luscious concrete ceiling that looks like stenciled wood. Just past the southeast corner of the library is an extraordinarily pleasant little courtyard, very simple with a column in the middle, an arcade along one side, four jacaranda trees in tiled planters, and bas-reliefs on the walls of scenes from fairy tales.

The Children's Literature department, just past this courtyard, is appropriately lower and even more completely muraled, this time by Julian E. Garnsey and A. W. Parsons, with vivid storybook paintings taken from Ivanhoe, including Robin Hood and Richard the Lion-Hearted and jousting knights in armor. Stenciled patterns in the faux-bois ceiling echo the colors on the walls.

The much simpler rooms like Popular Reading, undefended by art, have gone to grunge in the last decades, but where there is painting or sculpture or tile, the library gleams still, all the way up to the tiled sunburst on its pyramidal top.

I 14 · OVIATT BUILDING
617 South Olive Street
Walker and Eisen, 1927–1928; restored in 1976

In 1925 James Oviatt attended the Paris Exposition Internationale des Arts Décoratifs, which boosted Art Deco, and fell in love with the new style. Like many other Californians, he gave substance to this passion by commissioning a building. He engaged a local firm of architects to design the Oviatt and Alexander men's store and office building, but he incorporated French expertise wherever possible. Remarkably enough, the resultant structure comes off understated, elegant and French. Oviatt sent one designer to do fieldwork in Paris, and had all the fixtures, carpets, draperies and stairways made in France and shipped to Los Angeles. René Lalique was retained to design and fabricate all the decorative glass. This became his largest commercial commission in Art Deco, so the work was exhibited in Paris before it was sent over. While most of the glass is in popular Art Deco patterns, some was especially designed with Los Angeles in mind; the elevator doors, for instance, are covered in oranges. A new white metal, "mallechort," named for its French inventors, Malliot and Chorier, was used for mailboxes, light fixtures and doors.

The marquee is a stunning three-dimensional interplay of deep red, maroon and dark blue panes of frosted glass (most are now replicas) connected by thin strips of silvery mallechort. Above the marquee are three showcase windows that rise up the simple Romanesque façade, which is ornamented with a graceful neon sign. At the top was Oviatt's ten-room penthouse behind a delicate zigzag clock. The apartment was furnished in Deco high style but looked out onto a garden roofscape that was thought to be Italian Romanesque but managed to include a swimming pool, tennis court, fountain, sundeck and barbecue. A miniature tower and the bell tower back of the clock provided a foreground for the then unobstructed view of Los Angeles.

Recently the Oviatt Building has been handsomely restored as an office building, with a restaurant in place of the men's store. Dinner is served in the midst of hand-carved cabinets, which now hold bottles of wine instead of shirts.

I 15 · PERSHING SQUARE
Bounded by Fifth, Sixth, Hill and Olive streets
Stiles O. Clements, parking garage, 1950–1951

Apart from the lawn at the Public Library, the only park in downtown Los Angeles is Pershing Square, which has been transmogrified once too often. At one time, giant banana trees, birds-of-paradise and palms grew in vigorous profusion beside brick-paved walks and wooden benches to provide relief from the hard surfaces of the surrounding city; free-lance evangelists and political reformers gathered here to spread their messages to less hurried Angelenos. Since this last piece of vacant public property was declared a park in 1866, it has collected the usual rich mementos of such places: a bronze cannon from Old Ironsides, a Spanish-American War memorial; a statue of Beethoven; and a plaque dedicated "In Memory of Benny, A Squirrel."

But in 1950 this all changed. The specimen trees were boxed up and replanted along freeways and in other parks—some even made it to the Jungle Cruise at Disneyland. The entire block was excavated for a multilevel underground parking garage with a new, safer and saner park on its street-level roof. Trees now grow in planters, so they are small and provide little shade. Lawns and a few flowers make up the rest of the characterless landscaping, bleak presumably to discourage crime, which is known to flourish in the shade. A standard fountain squirts forlornly in the center; concrete planters and benches begrudgingly provide seating, and KEEP OFF THE GRASS signs are everywhere. The haranguing eccentrics have been replaced by varieties of Skid Row residents who ignore the signs and bring their own plumage. Once a cool jungle paradise in the heart of downtown, Pershing Square has been modernized into a hot five-acre rooftop.

I 16 · BILTMORE HOTEL
515 Olive Street, at the west corner of Fifth Street, across from Pershing Square
Schultze and Weaver, 1922–1923, 1928; restored by Phyllis Lambert and Gene Summers, 1976–1979

The new Bonaventure Hotel aggressively repels its corner of downtown Los Angeles, but its earlier equivalent, the Biltmore, opens up to the city and casts a glow over the whole part of town just west of Pershing Square. Civilized sorts of places like airline offices face the sidewalk; beautiful surfaces and evocative spaces lie just inside every door. The great old hotel had slid into a kind of disreputable senility when Phyllis Lambert and Gene Summers came to its rescue; they have unstintingly restored it to a splendor even more opulent than the original.

The interiors slide with sybaritic abandon from Pompeiian to Churrigueresque, with acres of marble, elaborately painted and gilded ceilings, and walls paneled in dark green and gold. A grand two-story cross-gallery, usually approached from the side, cuts through the main floor. The lobby, reached off Pershing Square and perpendicular to this gallery, is one floor below, allowing someone above to view the lobby from a Churrigueresque balcony and then to enter it in an impressive sweep down a sumptuous stair. A traditional Spanish ceiling with deep reveals is richly painted, new gold against soft green and black, with indirect lighting and grand chandeliers. The stairs to the cross-gallery are flanked by Solomonic twisted columns entwined with grapes and leaves.

The grand ballroom, lavishly restored as well, has crystal-and-gold chandeliers between composite columns, and a concave ceiling with a resplendent Pompeiian motif. More rooms, almost as dazzling, open along the half-block length of the grand hallway. In contrast to all this are the spare new furnishings—the very best Mies van der Rohe, Barcelona chairs and all—but the vigor of the new seems hardly a patch on the lovingly resurrected old glories.

I 16 · *Biltmore Hotel*

I 17 · NATIONAL BANK OF COMMERCE BUILDING
439 South Hill Street
Walker and Eisen, 1929–1930
Now occupied by Mission Floors

The narrow façade of this winsomely slender little skyscraper is one of the marvels of downtown Los Angeles for the way the four simple limestone shafts ascend and melt miraculously into human heads and shoulders and arms in a miniature reprise of Goodhue's library. On an entablature above the arched entry, from the outside edges of the building toward the center, are more figures representing the history of mankind: Stone Age man wielding primitive tools; Egyptian, Roman, Greek, Medieval and Renaissance man—all are featured, culminating in Modern (American) man in the center, the very image of Charles A. Lindbergh. Two inscriptions, which pretty much sum up one aspect of the California Dream, are engraved below this assemblage: "Opportunity is more powerful even than conquerors and prophets" (Beaconsfield), and "Wealth means power, it means leisure, it means liberty" (Lowell). Imagine all this on a tiny façade. The Elks Club (page 144) picks up this head-and-shoulders development on a far grander scale, but with no more earnestness.

I 17 · *National Bank of Commerce Building*   I 18 · *Broadway, Arcade Building*

I 18 · BROADWAY

The northern part of Broadway has, since the early days of Los Angeles, been one of downtown's focal streets, a street for pleasure and for the thronging of people. When the Yankees came, it was their main street, the chief site for the burgeoning businesses that catered to the growing city. During the early part of the twentieth century, it was a predecessor to Hollywood Boulevard, lined with first-run motion picture palaces. During the 1930s and '40s the movies drew large crowds, and pleasure-oriented establishments flourished. Then in the late fifties and sixties downtown declined as the affluent and mobile sought excitement in newer places. Broadway served downtown workers by day and was largely deserted at night. Today it is once again teeming with eager crowds, reclaimed by L.A.'s exploding Latin-American population.

Modern usage owes a great deal still to the Latin paseo, where boys walk one way around the plaza, girls the other, to see and be seen. Broadway is tumultuous, the paseo partly giddily motorized, but it is still a place to see and be seen. On any day, but especially on Sunday, the commodious sidewalks are jammed with people shopping and eating, or just hanging out. The street is filled with cruising cars, which are sometimes gaily decorated with paper flowers. It is four lanes wide, allowing faster inner lanes, slower outer ones, with a buffer zone of parking. The parked cars help to separate the pedestrian zone; drivers can sit in them, lean on them or just show them off to passersby.

The façades of the old (late 1830s to 1930s) multistoried office buildings line the sidewalk edge, providing inexpensive quarters for businesses sufficiently small-scale, neophyte or fly-by-night. Their shop fronts often greet the street with display vestibules, drawing potential customers out of the main sidewalk flow and into their forecourts. Here, in Mexican fashion, goods are set out on tables while salesmen stand ready to bargain to the musical accompaniment of *discos latinos*. Gaps between buildings are filled (as usual in Los Angeles) with parking lots, but they also house street vendors. Some of their stands are elaborately roofed but without walls during open hours; metal grates roll down to close. Others are simply tables displaying bright mechanical toys, or wig racks, or exotic fruits, ice cream, *carnitas* and *burritos*. The carnival foods add to the pleasure of the strollers, encouraging them to inhabit the street just for fun. The sumptuous old movie houses, now offering Mexican cinema, are open day and night.

Today, in this richly peopled hoopla, it is hard even to find the buildings along Broadway that now serve as backdrop to a movable fiesta. But there are a number of opulently compelling façades, and one genuine masterpiece, the Bradbury Building.

I **19** · *Bradbury Building*

I 19 · BRADBURY BUILDING
304 South Broadway, on the south corner of Third Street
George H. Wyman, 1893
Open to the public Monday through Saturday; admission fee

As you walk along the particularly unprepossessing block of Broadway toward Third Street, there are very few clues that just inside the building on the corner lies one of the most thrilling spaces on the North American continent. It is not undiscovered, as you will note when they ask you for two dollars for sightseeing purposes. But the thrill of discovery is there each time: it's always far more wonderful, more ineffable, more magic than memory allows.

The Bradbury Building is brick on the outside, five stories high, not very large. Entrance is through an arch, nicely detailed but unremarkable. Then it happens: very close ahead to the right is a grand little stair that sweeps up, and your eyes with it. A great skylit space lies directly beyond this stair; halfway back, two elevators rise in open cages, one to the right, one to the left. Then in the distance is another stair, whose last flight sweeps down diagonally opposite the first. The elevators establish bilateral symmetry that is wrenched into an asymmetrical double spiral by the two staircases.

The first floor is smallest, with yellow glazed-brick walls, which are largely solid except for some windows opening into a restaurant, and wrought-iron grilles that give entry to the elevators. Above the first floor is a wrought-iron railing, and the space becomes wider for three more floors. It widens again on the top floor, under a full-width skylight, which is raised on a clerestory. It brings to mind the dome at Hagia Sophia in Istanbul, whose clerestory lantern caused the ancients to think the dome above was hung "on a golden chain from heaven," so weightless did it appear. Here the clerestory also helps ventilation.

But the place is not magical because of its size. The first-floor space can't be more than sixteen feet wide; the whole court is not much more than a hundred feet deep. The light is exquisite, at once bathing everything and recording changes as it penetrates farther and farther down into narrower spaces. And the space is eminently inhabitable, offering surprising and delightful resting places on every level. But it is more than all this; you can do no less than see it, and walk in it, and deduce what makes it so.

I 20 · MILLION DOLLAR THEATER
307 Broadway, at the west corner of Third Street
Albert C. Martin, Sr.; William L. Woolett, theater, 1917

Built when films were soundless and South Broadway was awash with eager moviegoers, the Million Dollar Theater is the grande dame of motion picture palaces, one of the first in the United States. Since movies and movie houses were completely new then, their architects were not bound by previous models. In this case they chose to emulate many filmmakers of the day who, instead of making sets in any one historic style, allowed themselves the pleasure of making up their own. Borrowing from numerous sources—some real, some fantastic—they achieved memorable images to meet and extend the audience's desire for the exotic.

I 20 · *Million Dollar Theater*

I 20 · *Million Dollar Theater (side entrance)*

The Million Dollar was Sid Grauman's first venture into cinematic fantasy, built four and nine years, respectively, before his vision grew more specific with the Egyptian and Chinese theaters. It could be said to lack some of the sophisticated restraint of the later works: the Million Dollar's exterior drips with outsize Churrigueresque ornament, some traditionally Spanish, some brazenly Western. Resembling an aging Miz Kitty in her dated dance-hall finery, it oozes populist character. Longhorn cattle skulls resplendent with life-size bronze horns nuzzle volutes and Spanish moldings; bison head corbels support a silent-screen parade of statues representing the Fine Arts, including an exotic Balinese maiden symbolizing Dance, a gentleman with a smock and palette for Painting, and, of course, a cinematographer behind his Camera.

The lobby has been brutally remodeled with discordant new carpeting and a centrally located sixties snack shack. The theater itself, perhaps because it is mostly in the dark, has been spared. It is Baroque and Spanish, but not Spanish Baroque. Two huge white Corinthian columns flank the stage, supporting nothing. An intricately carved organ screen, possibly Moorish in its inspiration, wraps back from the stage. Beautifully soft backlighting in peachy tones plays up the contrast between delicate openings on the massive dark-colored screens and the enormous columns to make a good beginning for what turned out to be the epochal adventure of the movie palace.

I 21 · LOS ANGELES THEATER
615 South Broadway
S. Charles Lee, 1931

The Los Angeles Theater is still another pleasure palace, the last great one on Broadway and the most lavish. Its narrow façade is dominated by two huge elaborately decorated Corinthian columns, like a pair of Baroque candlesticks, which hint at an incredibly rich interior. The two-story lobby is poignant in its state of almost terminal decay, but it still gleams faintly in rose, pale green, gold and crystal Rococo elegance. Corinthian pilasters, graceful chandeliers and great mirrors divided by curved mullions are cushioned in profuse plaster ornament. On the stair landing to the mezzanine, a four-tiered faux-fountain drips strings of crystal water into a mosaic basin guarded by white marble sea serpents. The auditorium is equally lavish, with two balconies and opera boxes flanking the stage. A flamboyantly gilded molding sets off an ornately coffered ceiling.

Downstairs are the lounges: ladies', men's and smoking, the latter a thirty-five-by-sixty-five-foot oval. Dark wood paneling covers the walls, and green marble slides around the perimeter alongside the original floral-patterned carpet. The ceiling is backlit Steuben glass. Gorgeous arched doorways lead to the refreshment room, now a small theater, and to the ladies' lounge, which is a bathroom of many marbles; each of the sixteen toilets occupies its own little room; each toilet is a different-color porcelain, each room a different-color marble. The ladies' makeup/lounging room is an oval with little marble vanities placed along mirrored niches in the wall. Plaster garlands and leaves and swags of flowers are repeated between slender brass columns that conceal the makeup lights. The men's room has colored marbles too, with pale green fixtures and ornate terrazzo floors.

Unstintingly sumptuous, the Los Angeles Theater was planned in careful contrast to the Depression that lurked just beyond the doors. Like the movies they showed, all these theaters acted like magic carpets to carry you for a few special hours away from the tawdry and the pinched.

I 21 · *Los Angeles Theater*

I 23 · *Eastern Columbia Building*

I 22 · CLIFTON'S BROOKDALE CAFETERIA
648 South Broadway
Plummer, Wardeman and Becket, 1935
Open daily, 6 A.M.–9 P.M.

The Clifton's Cafeteria on Broadway (22 A), one of two originals, was built in the early 1930s by Clifford E. Clinton, a Christian philanthropist who never turned anyone away hungry. The two were once famous as "The Golden Rule Cafeterias," for customers who didn't have the price of a meal were allowed to pay whatever they could afford. But Mr. Clinton provided more than good food for his patrons; he created oases. The Olive Street branch was tropical, with a fountain, artificial palms, flowers and real canaries. Unfortunately it has been remodeled, but the Brookdale on Broadway survives almost intact.

For the local workers and residents, the few tourists and the many down-and-outers who took their meals here during the Great Depression, the views paved in terrazzo on the sidewalk in front must have summed up the dream of Southern California: oil fields, Catalina, La Brea Tar Pits, movie studios, Griffith Park Observatory, Hollywood, Hollywood Bowl, the desert, City Hall, the stadium in Exposition Park, orange groves, missions and beaches.

Entry is through a forest grotto, where the clatter of dishes is masked by a mountain stream. The warmly lit, low-ceilinged serving area is cheerful and cozy and filled with aromas of food, which is just about the same as always—carrot-and-raisin salad, chipped beef on white bread, macaroni and cheese, and rice pudding. The quality has been maintained, and the strawberry pie is terrific. The cashiers are housed in little forest booths at the edge of the main dining room, a two-story sylvan fantasy. The major wall is richly painted as a California redwood forest at sundown; a surprisingly realistic setting sun is a circle of canvas with a light shining behind. In front of the mural are redwood tree trunks.

A waterfall freshens the room as it splashes cheerfully alongside tiers that descend from a second-floor dining room. Seats beside these tiers or on balconies at the edge of the upper room are certainly the best in the house. From them you can look between the trees at backlit color blowups of California scenes, a miniature Hansel and Gretel church with a blue neon cross, a giant fireplace with an effective fake fire, or, just as interesting, the interplay of diners. Still a haven from the streets, Clifton's functions as a sort of inexpensive downtown ski lodge, offering to anyone a part of the California good life.

Not far from Clifton's is Finney's Cafeteria (22 B), formerly the Chocolate Shoppe (217 West Sixth Street, Plummer and Feil, 1913), which centers on a Dutch theme. Beautifully crafted tiles by Ernest Batchelder cover the walls in earth tones. The interior is almost untouched; richly shaded tiles and murals provide a happy contrast to the daytime glare.

I 23 · EASTERN COLUMBIA BUILDING
849 South Broadway, at the north corner of Ninth Street
Claude Beelman, 1930

An outstanding example of 1920s Moderne, the thirteen-story Eastern Columbia Building (23 A) resembles a beautifully detailed cloisonné music box more than a building. All its exposed surfaces are covered with terra-cotta tiles, mostly a delicate shade of mint green; in their midst a series of deep steel-blue vertical stripes with gilded zigzag inserts travels up the buildings. The upper reaches step back and up to a two-story clock tower, whose chimes still sound the time. Vertical bands of windows and alternating piers that fly free at the top justify the romantic notion of "skyscraper," quite different from the concept "highrise," whose floors multiply in response to the speculator's balance sheet. The ground floor has been remodeled, but the terrazzo zigzag patterns in the sidewalk still echo the vanished designs.

Across the street, at 850 South Broadway, is another of Claude Beelman's multistoried extravaganzas, the Ninth and Broadway Building (23 B) (1929). As with the Eastern Building, narrow piers separate the windows and their terra-cotta spandrels, this time swarming with stylized floral motifs. Together these structures recall the elegance and sophistication of the last days before the Great Depression.

I 24 · MAYAN THEATER
1040 South Hill Street, near the east corner of Eleventh Street
Morgan, Walls and Clements, 1927

The Mayan Theater (24 A), which fairly explodes with enthusiastic pre-Columbian exaggerations, was designed during the feverish twenties, when architects were forced to look beyond the styles of Europe for sufficiently exotic motifs. Cast-concrete decorations, vaguely reminiscent of Monte Albán or Teotihuacán or other places far from Mayaland, flow in bands across the façade, punctuated by patterns of stylized human and animal heads. Above the marquee rises a gallery of priest kings, strangely adorned in Plains Indian feathered headdresses. The less decorated wall areas are rendered to resemble massive cut stones. The final bravado comes not from the original sculptor, Francisco Comeja, but from a recent remodeler, who painted the neutral concrete in bright folk-art colors, to the horror of such few purists as exist around here.

The interior is in nearly mint condition. The lobby, small and dark like the interior of an ancient temple, has a ceiling coffered and delicately painted with pre-Columbian motifs, which seem to carry the patina of centuries. Giant serpent's heads with grinning teeth flank the stairways. On the mezzanine, huge spooky corbels support heavy beams with more ancient painting on the ceiling between them. The auditorium is overwhelming: flanking the stage are enormous fragments of primitive walls that are made, apparently, of tremendous cut stones like the giant but precise building blocks of Machu Picchu. The central light fixture is a multilayered, many-faceted sun symbol. This may be the only fully pre-Columbian movie theater extant and should be seen before it, too, joins the dust of the ages.

Next door, at 1050 South Hill Street, is another flamboyant theater, the Belasco, now the Metropolitan Community Church (24 B). This Pineapple Gothic Churrigueresque eruption, designed a year earlier by the same architects as the Mayan, sports a richly squirted pastry-tube cornice, arches outlined by voluptuous moldings, outspread eagles and spiky tropical foliage sprouting above the niches of life-size saints. Even so, the Belasco has been put in the stylistic shade by its Mayan neighbor.

Across the street, at 1061 South Hill Street, on the north corner of Eleventh Street, is Tony's Burgers (24 C) (ca. 1939), the only log cabin in downtown L.A. Now painted bright red with red mortar between the stones of its false chimneys, this little diner is an especially vivid example of the city's multitude of parking-lot fast-food stands. The door handles are small skillets; a clock on the sign is another, much bigger skillet. Tony's physical scale is tiny, but its visual impact boggles the mind.

I 24 · *Mayan Theater*

I 25 · LOS ANGELES EXAMINER BUILDING
IIII South Broadway, between Eleventh and Twelfth streets
Julia Morgan, 1915

William Randolph Hearst went to the San Francisco Bay area to find an architect for his Los Angeles newspaper offices. He found the remarkable Julia Morgan, who worked closely with him for decades, especially on his own fantasy castle at San Simeon. This first woman graduate of the École des Beaux-Arts in Paris maintained a no-nonsense practice, imaginative enough but altogether without the exaggerated delicacy of the Edwardian female stereotype.

Miss Morgan came to Los Angeles when the Mission Revival was in full swing. In that manner, therefore, the massive block-long Examiner Building sports a tower with a colorfully tiled dome on every corner and a small thin bell tower on each side of an elaborate central entry. Between the bell towers is a curving parapet wall edged in sinuous moldings and pierced by a quatrefoil window in the middle, a sort of cleaned-up version of the window at the Carmel mission. Behind the façade rises another, much larger tower with an arcaded loggia, an overhanging red-tiled roof, and then a domed rotunda with a high lantern. Above blind arcades along the streets, Spanish grillwork helps generous second-floor windows to look like balconies. For all its businesslike restraint, this building is worth a pilgrimage; there are, after all, not many Julia Morgan works in Southern California.

I 26 · *Coca-Cola Bottling Plant*

I 25 · *Los Angeles Examiner Building*

I 26 · COCA-COLA BOTTLING PLANT
1334 South Central Avenue, at the east corner of Fourteenth Street, Los Angeles
Robert V. Derrah, 1936–1937

The Coca-Cola Bottling Plant is no simple manufacturing plant; it has been remodeled to look like an ocean liner. The transformation is complete: the initial buildings have been artfully smoothed and rounded and joined together, portholes replace windows, and pipe railings line second-story decks; arched metal doors and plaster rivets line the steel-smooth white plaster walls, a black wainscoting with a red stripe marks the waterline, and a flying bridge commands the entire assemblage. All the while, this building manages to adhere to most of the tenets of the Modern Movement—simplicity, pure colors, flowing lines, and contrasts of light and shadow. But it vehemently denies two overriding constraints: that materials should be used honestly, and that form follows function.

Therefore, it has succeeded in becoming not a building but an ocean liner, mysteriously beached near downtown L.A., far from the harbor, a container for containers.

The original contained item was the classic Coke bottle, inaugurated in 1916, which was itself a remarkably sophisticated piece of design. Coke represented the good life, available to all by mechanization. While Coca-Cola was a pleasure almost anyone could afford, the 1930s ocean liner represented the quintessential luxury, a new setting for the pleasures of the eternal bon vivant. In movie houses across the nation, Fred Astaire, Ginger Rogers—even the Marx Brothers—danced their way across the Atlantic (vast decks safely underfoot) in stylish, ultramodern surrounds. Here Robert Derrah lets the very bottles of Coke, and presumably their drinkers, join the party.

I 27 · FARMER JOHN'S PACKING COMPANY MURALS
3049 East Vernon Avenue, bounded by Vernon, Soto and Thirty-Seventh streets, Vernon
Painted by Leslie A. Grimes; after 1968, by the Arco Sign Co., 1953 to present

The Farmer John's meat-packing company is a standard conglomeration of industrial buildings, with one exception: the group has been transformed into a *trompe l'oeil* Hog Heaven. All the public façades have been painted with precision and barnyard brio into cheerful farmyard scenes. Piglets, sows and hogs romp in gay abandon across the sunny countryside, wallowing in mud baths, raiding cornfields and even detaching themselves from the buildings' planar surfaces to climb into the office windows. Cows, pheasants and farm kids all join in under the benevolent gaze of Farmer John himself. The mural even stretches along the wall that borders the empty Los Angeles River. The painters sometimes incorporated building elements into the picture: a real door becomes a barnyard gate, a warehouse window is an opening in a barn; or sometimes elements are painted out—a maze of pipes disappears into blue sky and fluffy clouds, or a wall vent becomes barn siding.

Despite the happy-go-lucky character of the painting and the unexpected delight in finding it here, there remains a pervasive sense of the surreal, if not the sinister, even beyond the fact that Leslie A. Grimes, the original artist, fell to his death from a scaffold here in 1968. Inside these walls, pigs are mechanically butchered, cured and packed, transformed from pig into sausage, while outside, their images frolic in a sunny vision of piggish afterlife.

I 27 · *Farmer John's Packing Company Murals*

II / DISNEYLAND

Main Entrance

Take the Harbor Boulevard exit from the Santa Ana Freeway, Anaheim
Walter Elias Disney, 1955 to present
Open daily, 9–midnight in summer; Wednesday through Friday, 10–6,
  Saturday and Sunday, 10–7, fall, winter and spring; admission fee; call
  (213) 626-8605

The downtown of the City of the Angels lies very close to its birthplace, and as we've seen, sports high buildings, enthusiastic decorations and an occasional architectural masterpiece. Despite its venerable background it is not the heart of Southern California. That title belongs, if anywhere, to an altogether synthetic and recent place that lies in Anaheim, some thirty miles away. There, at Disneyland, Walter Elias Disney's fantasy of model railroads and Mickey Mouse has materialized. It should surely come as no surprise that this place, the real public realm of Southern California, is made-up theater; Noël Coward prepared us for that. What may come as a surprise is how richly Disneyland offers us insight into many layers of reality. People often use Disneyland as a synonym for the facile, shallow and fake, just as they use the term "Mickey Mouse" to signify the egregiously trivial. It just doesn't wash: this incredibly energetic collection of environmental experiences offers enough lessons for a whole architectural education in all the things that matter—community and reality, private memory and inhabitation, as well as some technical lessons in propinquity and choreography.

But it isn't perfect, and that's a good place to start. A key to Disneyland's imperfection comes from Bruno Bettelheim's book about fairy tales, *The Uses of Enchantment.* Mr. Bettelheim points out that fairy tales are important, perhaps even necessary aids in growing up: they introduce Evil (like toxins/antitoxin that contain a controlled amount of the disease they fight) so children will not be altogether flummoxed when they meet the real thing. Disney's tales reduce Evil to buffoonery, which renders Good more like goody-goody. There is, anyhow, little content in the Disney narrations: at the ride called Pirates of the Caribbean you won't get any insight at all into real pirates or their terrified victims. But, such imperfection aside, you will have a series of environmental experiences of great power; and if you have a store of memories already collected (adults have an advantage over children here), you'll find these memories stimulated as you might in few other places on earth.

Disneyland is a great collection of places. There have been such collections before, like Hadrian's villa outside Rome, where the emperor assembled images of wonders from all over his realm. But such earlier examples were mostly per-

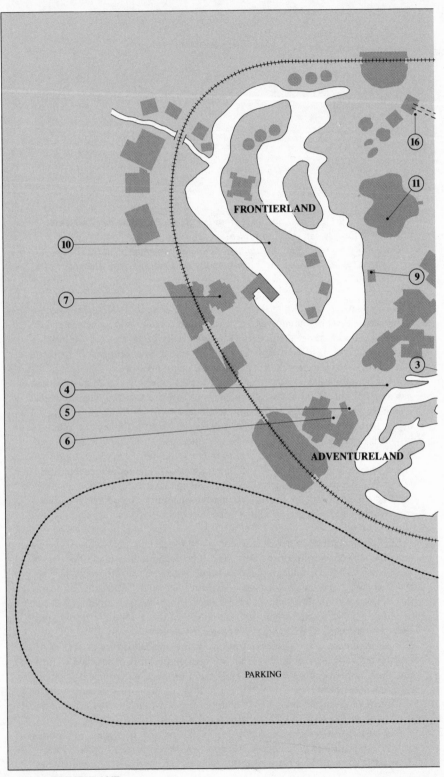

FRONTIERLAND

ADVENTURELAND

PARKING

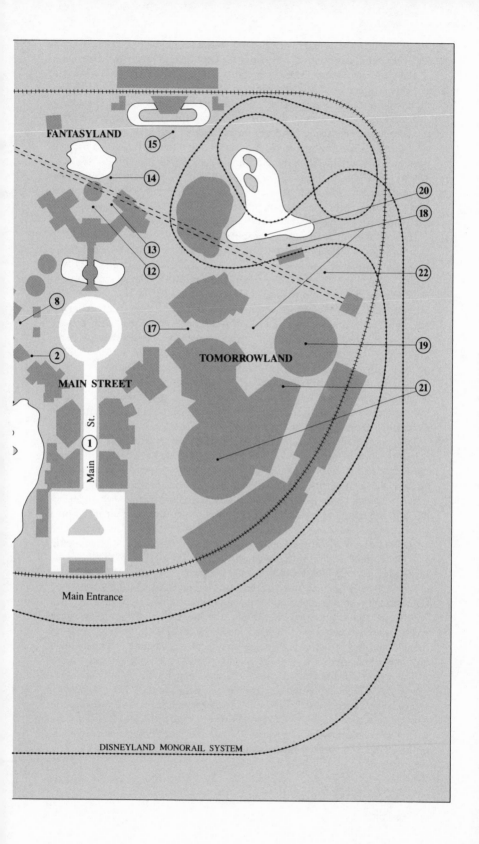

FANTASYLAND

⑮

⑭

⑬

⑫

⑳

⑱

⑧

②

⑰

MAIN STREET

⑲

TOMORROWLAND

㉒

㉑

Main St.

①

Main Entrance

DISNEYLAND MONORAIL SYSTEM

sonal, keyed to the singular vision of one powerful individual. Disneyland, on the other hand, has been populist from the start, meant to stir the imagination of many different people who bring widely varying sets of personal memories. The generally accepted way of coping with this diversity is to abstract ideas and shapes to create a "loose fit" that will accommodate everyone. At Disneyland, two other modes are favored. The first is a kinesthetic excitement that addresses the collective unconscious by engaging the human body, choreographing our walk through changing spaces and moving us gently (on carriages and boats) or thrillingly (on aerial cable cars) or with a jolt (on bobsleds and roller coasters). The second is a remarkable use of propinquity, the close juxtaposition of very disparate places. No matter how intense, how precise, how evocative, how specific the place where you are, you're just a step from a very different place. If one spot doesn't move you, go a very short distance and they'll try again.

The layout is a masterpiece of propinquity. From an enormous parking lot you can board a little tram to the main gates, which are clearly announced by a Victorian railroad station just behind. The station sits on top of a heavily landscaped railroad embankment that encircles the park and visually separates Disneyland from the rest of the world. This berm is embellished with a huge floral likeness of Mickey Mouse, which changes colors with the seasons. After you buy your ticket, you pass through one of two tunnels under the tracks and into Main Street, which takes off straight ahead toward Sleeping Beauty's Castle and the center of the park, a circular plaza that offers immediate choices around its perimeter: the main entrances to Adventureland (with New Orleans Square behind it), Frontierland, Fantasyland and Tomorrowland. Between the lands, the boundaries are not so clear: appropriate landscaping and changes in architecture ease you from one to the other, but from the central plaza no entrance to anywhere is more than a few steps away.

The juxtaposition of various levels of reality is even more astonishing. Which is more real, it is fun to ponder, this or Santa Barbara? Which did itself over "Spanish" after an earthquake in 1925? How does the reality of Disneyland in farthest Anaheim stack up against the Roman Forum, where a few significant stones lying among the acanthus leaves allow us to conjure up our own images, filling in the spaces between the stones with our own dreams of ancient Rome? How real is it that Disneyland has the ninth largest submarine fleet on the planet? Or that the water in the fountains is dyed gray to make it look authentic? Was there social reality in the replacement of Indians by bears in the section now called Bear Country? It is, for some, astoundingly real to begin the Pirates of the Caribbean ride in a synthetic boat under a fake sky, sharing a mysterious Cajun bayou with a group of diners having real lunch on a real terrace.

What all this is about is inhabitation, the human act of being somewhere where we are protected, even engaged, in a space ennobled by our own presence. Inhabitation is a powerful reality that architecture is supposed to be all about but more often isn't. It is a reality vividly present at Disneyland, whose own reality is so often dismissed. Hence the extensive inclusion of this place, these rides, in a book about architecture: people have here a sense of being somewhere and of being someone special, of being not merely celebrants at a real affair but also the objects of celebration. On top of that, you can't help feeling important when you are being greeted by Mickey Mouse and Donald Duck and Goofy, all of them large and gorgeous and very friendly.

II 1 · MAIN STREET, U.S.A.

Just as "Once upon a time and far away" is used to establish the fantasy context for the fairy tale, familiar Main Street, U.S.A. introduces the fantastic realms of Disneyland. Reassuringly, this beginning, a festive re-creation of hometown America of about 1910, is neither too long ago nor too far away. Since many Americans feel, like Disney, a comfortable nostalgia for that innocent, optimistic pre–World War I period, Main Street allows them to start their exploration of the park at home. And since the street is not an accurate reconstruction of anything but a dreamlike evocation of that era, it finds resonance in many visitors' ancestral memories.

In the manner of a family album of smiling snapshots, Main Street recalls a cheerful and altogether cleaned-up past, one that is eternally freshly painted, blooming, tidy and sunny. To enhance the sense of play, of storybook reality, and probably more significantly, to increase our individual sense of importance and control, the buildings have been miniaturized. At street level, vehicles and buildings are reduced to nine-tenths normal scale. To make the architecture more approachable still, the scale slides smaller as it climbs, becoming five-eighths at the third and fourth levels. Moreover, the colors have new-toy intensity: the buildings are gay candy pastels; the streetcars, fire engines and carriages are rich, glossy shades of maroon, forest green, cream and red. When night falls and the lights go on, the scene becomes even more magical. Old gas lamps (scavenged from Baltimore and Philadelphia) line the street, and tiny lights sparkle everywhere, twinkling in the trees and outlining each mansard roof, each broken pediment, each cornice.

Main Street starts in the Town Square, which contains a small, traditional circular park. One like it can be found in the city of Orange a few miles away (page 61). On the west is the city hall and fire station (its second floor used to house Walt Disney's apartment); on the east is the ornately gabled opera house; on the south is the clock-towered railway station on its terraced berm. To the north, Main Street begins, solidly lined with shop fronts. From the sidewalk these appear as individual structures—with separate roof lines that pop up and out, a variety of porches on different levels, and façades of clapboard or brick—but inside, the spaces all run together.

In the run-together space behind the façades, as in many other emporia in the Magic Kingdom, things are sold. Many are souvenirs, of hefty price and mini-

II 1 · *Main Street, U.S.A.*

II 1 · *Main Street, U.S.A.*

mum interest, except maybe for the Mickey and Minnie Mouse wristwatches. Elsewhere food is purveyed. Its price is hefty, too, its interest more minimal still, as if the market analysts had determined that McDonald's had set the patrons' gastronomic horizons, for good. Do not be misled by allusions to exotic regional menus; there won't be anything inside that isn't fully familiar to the littlest consumer. Also familiar but altogether remarkable are the young people selling and serving and running the rides: they are clean-cut to their clear young eyes, and though they are said to enjoy switching jobs and costumes around the park, they always seem to be the creatures of a divinely inspired Central Casting.

Two restaurants, the Plaza Inn and the Plaza Pavilion, anchor the far end of Main Street. On the right, the Plaza Inn is an Edwardian fantasy where lunch is served and recollections of a tender past are everywhere. The interior is filled with genuine beaded-board ceilings, brackets, curlicues and volutes. The outside is rich with vine-covered trellises over a pleasant terrace where you can sit and eat a few steps above an umbrella-covered patio. From the terrace you can see under the umbrellas to the central plaza where there is a grove of olives, some *Ficus benjamina* (of the sort that expensively grace New York City apartments) and gnarled old jacaranda trees, which bloom brilliantly blue in June. The trees provide reality on an immediate level that remains unshattered by the appearance of the plastic Matterhorn looming above palm trees, olive trees and umbrellas. The Plaza Inn combines Victorian Gothic tracery, a set of Corinthian columns and Tiffany-like stained-glass ceilings lighted from above to give an air of opulence that graciously accepts its casual white metal garden furniture. The architectural details outside are endlessly diverting. Dormers sport volutes that go not in the plane of the window, the way they usually do, but forward, flanking the sides like cheeks; on top of each dormer is a lunette and above that is a freestanding pyramid flanked by orbs. The details are meant to charm, and they do. Under the marquee, past a tasseled yellow awning, past beveled glass that sparkles around the door, is a sort of console with a stained-glass cabriolet top, which lends elegance to the cafeteria line you are about to enter.

Across Main Street from the Plaza Inn is the Plaza Pavilion, an even more light-hearted structure with terraces and arbors and a pair of beautiful little gazebos. A steep gable at the entrance has particularly exuberant shapes recollective of about 1875. Behind that is a mansard roof topped by a little railing. A modern octagonal vent in the middle of all this presses home a series of messages at once Victorian and strangely futuristic, like a Ray Bradbury short story about nostalgic Martians.

A river at the edge of the plaza has springs that make the water ripple and look real, especially real with its carefully mixed gray-green dye. The shores are lined with native and exotic plants, from periwinkle to birds-of-paradise, banana shrubs from China, and several kinds of bamboo. In front of us is Sleeping Beauty's Castle; flanking it, around the circular plaza, are all the other lands of Disney: Adventureland, Frontierland, Fantasyland and Tomorrowland.

II 2 · ADVENTURELAND

Adventureland, a three-dimensional counterpart to Disney's true-life adventure films, is a sampler of forms from most of the exotic parts of the planet. Entrance is across a little bridge from the plaza: Polynesia beckons just inside an elephant-tusked gateway, and tiki torches lean out across the river, which has grown suddenly dark and narrow. Bamboo groves, steep thatched roofs and Aku Aku masks adorn the entrances to the Enchanted Tiki Room (a variety show of jabbering birds and talking flowers) and the Tahitian Terrace, a luau restaurant.

On through the entrance is a building whose many parts make up the Adventureland Bazaar. The design is mostly Mexican—except that the places where awnings might be expected are thatch—with a frontier Humphrey-Bogart-in-the-Sierra-Madre quality to the carefully broken-off stucco. As we proceed, the décor becomes more African than anything else; then it slopes off into a kind of Caribbean mode with awnings sheltering a big game shoot. Next, we slip quite naturally into a building that would be at home in Timbuktu with rather Beau Geste conceits, including figures resembling African tattoos. Oddly enough, it houses Guatemalan weavers. Next come umbrellas with what must be Arabian motifs and a wonderful multiply coned and thatched gazebo. After that we soon come to false-fronted structures from the American Old West, which give way almost immediately to the final building of the group—pure Beverly Hills French. The whole dazzling stretch from Mexico to Beverly Hills is made to work by an intensely sophisticated eye toward ornament. The colors, too, are elegant and knowing. Even the simplest building, whose style is hardly perceptible, flaunts ocher, mauve and puce under a pale green trellis.

II 3 · JUNGLE CRUISE

The ticket takers for the Jungle Cruise, which lies opposite the Adventureland Bazaar, wear leopard-skin bands on their straw hats and affect an air of swagger that is meant to tell us something about White Hunters. They usher us onto boats named *Kissimmee Kate, Mekong Maid, Ganges Gal* and *African Queen*. It looks like Humphrey Bogart has been here, too. On board is a fake boiler with

II 2 · *Adventureland* II 3 · *Jungle Cruise*

chimney and what seems to be the engine, though actually the boat is dragged around on a track under the water. It travels what seems to be a long way in a tiny compass.

The voice of the White Hunter guide takes over: "Up on the left here is an ancient shrine destroyed years ago by an earthquake. Then in the archway ahead we enter the ruins of an ancient city. There is a twitching spider web . . . don't make excessive moves now; these are king cobras, a venomous snake . . . and that's no ordinary lion skin, either; that's a Bengal tiger and it can jump over twenty feet. The problem is, we are only nine feet away! Let's get out of here!"

The jungle, curiously, grows more beautiful (and more real, with banana palms intensifying the tropicality) as the patter drones on. There are pretty waterfalls, from which the viewer is likely to be distracted by gamboling plastic elephants. The dramatic pattern is to render the jungle menacing and then help the visitor overcome the menace with hearty jokes and pretty vistas. It never comes close to working, since in this resolutely clean and cheerful land a menace doesn't have a chance; but the Jungle Cruise does make a nice ride, with jungle sounds that have been carefully researched, for the most part. From the time you wait in line until you disembark, you will be assailed by not only the pulsating rhythms of jungle drums but also the cry of the kookaburra bird (familiar for echoing through nearly every jungle movie ever made) though, in fact, the kookaburra is native only to New Guinea and Australia.

II 4 · SWISS FAMILY ROBINSON TREE HOUSE

One of the pleasures of a day at Disneyland is the enormous variety of pacing, from organized tours like the Jungle Cruise to more casual, spur-of-the-moment opportunities like a visit to the Swiss Family Robinson Tree House. This latter lies high up in one of the largest banyan trees in the world, surely the only one made of reinforced concrete and, leaf by convincing leaf, of plastic. The tree house, which is just a turnstile away from the Adventureland Bazaar, reproduces, of course, the setting for the early-nineteenth-century story of David Wyss's inventive and civilized Swiss family marooned on a South Sea Island.

Visitors take a walking tour on rickety stairs that meander up through eighty feet of foliage past multileveled rooms furnished from island materials—an ingenious stream-powered water wheel, a giant clamshell sink and bamboo plumbing. There are many items salvaged from the shipwreck as well, including a water-powered organ that provides continuous musical accompaniment. The treetop offers views down on the Jungle Cruise, New Orleans Square and Frontierland, and you are amazed at how high you have climbed without much noticeable physical exertion.

II 4 · *Swiss Family Robinson Tree House*

II 5 · PIRATES OF THE CARIBBEAN

This is surely the most sophisticated ride in Disneyland. It has the largest capacity of any, and needs it, to accommodate the enormous crowds that come here for the skillfully choreographed motion, the spatial excitements and the exotic scenery. Its silly storyline and its yo-ho-ho pirate music have the power to set the teeth on edge, but its idiom, which falls somewhere between the creation of a setting and the telling of a story, is so superbly handled that the lack of narrative content seems scant bother. The participant gets into a little flat-bottomed boat that is pulled along in a channel of water, which softens the ride and adds a certain psychic distance to the proceedings. The first few moments are perhaps the best: the boat heads into an eerie backwater of the Mississippi River with a vast twilight sky painted overhead; on the left is a mechanical Cajun rocking on his porch; on the right are real diners having real lunch at a real restaurant, the Blue Bayou.

Then the boat pops into a tunnel where even the shrieks from riders in front don't prepare you for a thunderous plunge into darkness. A series of visions present themselves, first of simple spiders and creepy things, then of mysterious scenes of a shipwreck. After this come treasure troves meant to dazzle the eye, which do rather tire the mind, mostly because they bear such strong resemblance to the attic of a theatrical costume emporium. They are, however, sufficiently diverting so that the next spatial experience comes as a surprise: the boat shoots down another long incline into a huge vaulted magical space and heads out across the water under a giant Caribbean night sky. But now the boat has come between a pirate ship and a fortress on the shore; people in the two are firing noisily at each other, and cannonballs appear to splash dangerously close; the rider is spared, however, and his craft turns upriver into a town. With a maddening nautical ditty in the background, there ensue various animated acts of wanton cruelty and greed as mechanical pirates pillage and burn the place— though all of it is rendered harmless and therefore not especially interesting by that curious Disney touch that so hams up and thereby emasculates evil. It's astonishing how this pin-brained apotheosis of sloth and stupidity can be so fascinating.

II 6 · NEW ORLEANS SQUARE

Just off the waterside promenade that looks out over the ships, rafts and canoes of the Rivers of America are the sheltered, highly picturesque and softly handsome walkways and little plazas of New Orleans Square. It is meant to remind us of the French Quarter in New Orleans, and does, though it hardly resembles it. The real one, for instance, is laid out in a rigid grid plan, while this is as irregular as a medieval village. Like Main Street, this setting is not a reconstruction but an impressionistic interpretation of a piece of the American past. The considerable conviction of the New Orleans–inspired detailing in these intimate spaces creates a sensuously romatic, swashbuckling, yet gentle scene. The colors are those of New Orleans, all soft creamy ochers, pinks, salmons, peaches, delicate grays and turquoise.

Café Orleans faces Royal Street behind a lacy set of dark green iron columns that support second- and third-floor balconies framed in ironwork filigree and lined with potted plants. French doors with louvered shutters open onto the balconies, which get smaller as they go up, like the fronts on Main Street. The café, with its red- and beige-tiled floor, zinc-topped coffee bar and hissing brass espresso machine, looks out through arched French doorways to a terrace filled with red-and-white umbrellas.

Across Front Street from here is another restaurant, the French Market. Its dining patio is surrounded by a green filigree wall and covered by awnings in especially luscious shades of mauve and beige. Farther up Front Street, Mlle. Antoinette's Parfumerie sparkles with tall mirrors, crystal countertops, chandeliers and perfume bottles displayed against pale mint-green walls. At the end of the street is a tiny half-hidden courtyard wrapped around with a sweeping stair. Inviting little flowerpots line the steps, but the door at the top is locked. The rooms behind were being decorated for Walt Disney, as a private retreat in the heart of his Kingdom's prettiest and most magical corner, when he died in 1966.

Through an archway on the left is the most special restaurant in Disneyland, the Blue Bayou. Inside, against the front of a plantation house, a dining terrace overlooks the wide stretch of river that is the beginning of the Pirates of the Caribbean ride. The light is soft twilight with cloudy streaks in a vast sky, which is painted to seem altogether real. Strings of Chinese lanterns glow above the tables, and fireflies twinkle in the moss-hung trees. The sounds of crickets, frogs and a banjo far away float up from the bayou. Beyond the little boats, which slip past silently on their way to the pirates' lair, the scale diminishes into the distance, past Cajun shacks and mangrove trees and into the dark night.

The Haunted Mansion is a badly flawed ride, if only for the smug and supercilious treatment it bestows upon ghosts, just because they are dead. Even so, it is surely one of the most skillful, sophisticated and engrossing spatial sequences on the planet. It is useful to see the ride as a progression from outside the event, where the observer and the observed are at some distance, to the inside, where the observer, mind and body, has entered into the observed, so that it finally envelops him and even at the end makes an attempt to enter him. While the spatial arrangements are performing this envelopment, a series of carefully contrived odors and eerie music is closing in as well.

The waiting line takes the visitor along the front porch of a well-maintained antebellum mansion and into a normal-looking rectangular vestibule. Then comes an octagonal room, which is actually an open-topped elevator. The height of the space increases as the elevator platform goes down; then a change in light reveals an infinite extension upward, past a body hanging from a cobwebby gibbet. The first magic moment occurs when the elevator door opens and you proceed out into a long, handsome gallery where regularly spaced windows along one wall reveal a lightning storm raging outside. The effect is profoundly moving. Some rather tacky paintings on the opposite wall suffer a black light change from cheerful to dismal. At the end of this hall you find yourself regarding some intaglio busts, which make you feel curiously as if you are inside the faces rather than confronting them.

You now get into a little car (called a Doom Buggy) with one other person and head off toward far stranger places. Your car glides through a long hall with a floating chandelier, moving coffins, wiggling doors, a clock whirling backward to destroy time and finally a crystal ball on a table with a tiny head projected inside. The disembodied head (an object observed, still outside the observer) is uttering a message meant to be at once mysterious and chilling, but it's too soon drowned out by screams that issue from a vast space ahead. You are now high up, looking down into a long and elegant drawing room: at one end, waltzing couples, half transparent, seem to whirl in a dream; at the other end are the remnants of a banquet, redolent of still more ancient times, lost loves, cobwebs and death. It is all done with mirrors and is one of the really moving moments at Disneyland. Next is a graveyard with quivering statues of a terrified watchman and his dog and many too corporeal spirits pushing up out of their coffins or singing in barbershop quartets.

II 7 · *Haunted Mansion*

II 8 · *Frontierland*

Attention is at first focused on discrete objects separately displayed; even the talking head has been pulled out and placed in limbo. Then the field is expanded to cover the whole range of vision above the drawing room. The environment is now continuous, all around as you move in the little car through this graveyard at night with clouds and soft lights. It provides an enveloping bath of mystery and terror, mitigated by the silly dancing ghosts doing their cheerful little bits to dispel our fright. In the coda, as you come close to disembarkation, more mirrors do their tricks, so that one of the ghosts seems to join you in your Buggy.

II 8 · FRONTIERLAND

On the plaza, near the jungle bridge to Adventureland, stands the entrance to Frontierland: two log blockhouses flank the open gates of a cavalry fort. The visitor passes between the gates to find a classic one-street Western American town of the 1870s, with two-storied false-fronted shops along wooden sidewalks. A distant view of riverboats cruising the Mississippi around Tom Sawyer Island is framed by vignettes of the America of cowboys and Indians. Frontierland is the park's most familiar Land; hardly a visitor is unacquainted with the world's best-known Americans—Indian scouts, pioneers, inventive Yankees, irascible common men, and certainly the cowboy.

Along the street, the Frontier Trading Post and the Davy Crockett Arcade sell Western souvenirs such as fancy leather belts and decorated tepees and rock collections. The posh Pendleton Woolen Mill shop offers up the company's woolen shirts, cowboy outfits and even Stetson hats, especially appealing to fancy dressers from foreign lands. The Shooting Gallery (whose targets are repainted nightly, so elegant is this rustic frontier town) is sheltered by a narrow pergola made of remarkably realistic concrete tree trunks. Around the corner is the Golden Horseshoe Saloon, which presents a cleaned-up Wild West review, featuring Vestal Virgin dancing girls and a shoot-'em-up cowboy who serves Pepsi-Cola in place of shots of redeye. On the right comes a sudden list toward Mexico: beyond a bougainvillea-covered trellis at the Casa de Fritos you can buy an industrialized taco.

II 9 · MARK TWAIN STEAMBOAT

The *Mark Twain* turns, on its own steam, round and round the doughnut of water called the Rivers of America, which is basically the Mississippi. The scenery is natural and often beautiful, but the real focus of the ride is the boat itself. The sparkling white stern-wheeler, which is a five-eighths scale replica of the real thing, preserves much of the finely crafted elegance of its predecessors. All the ingredients are here, from the pilot's cabin above the triple decks to the working engine and the great paddle wheel.

From the jetty with its bales of cotton you can see a gentleman in a red bow tie leaning out of the pilothouse. He must be the pilot because he looks too clean-cut for a captain, more clean-cut even than the players in a nearby band in their ice cream suits. Bells ring and the band plays serenades. From the top deck there is a splendid view of the sidewalk cafés along New Orleans Square and of crowds eating their ice cream bars and dropping the wrappers, only to

II 9 · *Mark Twain Steamboat*　　　　II 10 · *Tom Sawyer Island*

have them picked up seconds later by appropriately uniformed and clean-cut persons. The triple-globed gas lamps along the river's edge sport rosettes and banners reminiscent of the platform for Abraham Lincoln's second inaugural. On the other side are keelboats, their corners all angled and cute, and Tom Sawyer's Raft.

Then comes luxuriant vegetation, which runs right over the banks onto this mighty body of water. The edge of the river is particularly beautiful near the spot where Indians appear to have shot a settler; he lies dying in front of his cabin, which is burning brightly, as evidenced by the skillfully rippled cellophane. Across from here, black-bottom deer wag their mechanical tails; behind them, numbers of plastic Plains Indians in colorful costumes tread their way among real rocks, real rapids and real ducks. Next comes an Indian village, where friendly-looking Indians (plastic) pursue their native crafts. In a nearby stream a pair of moose (not real) are eating up a lot of grass (probably real but possibly synthetic). And then you are back where you started.

II 10 · TOM SAWYER ISLAND

Disneyland is at once a major extension of Southern California's public realm and Walt Disney's personal monument to his boyhood near Hannibal, Missouri, which was Mark Twain's hometown, too. It is no surprise, then, that the one piece of Disneyland actually designed by Walt Disney himself is Tom Sawyer Island, which lies in the middle of the Mississippi with the *Mark Twain* riverboat steaming round and round.

A raft piloted by Tom Sawyer himself crosses over to this collection of touchable artifacts meant to excite the imaginations of children. Narrow, spooky passageways tunnel through molded rocklike substance to various hideouts; tiny corridors and windows penetrate the spires of a rock castle; giant boulders tip and turn in a woozy primeval playground; a wooden tree house hides in the boughs of a concrete tree; pontoon and suspension bridges rock and bob with every footstep; and soldier-uniformed security officers watch over the melee from a Hollywood Western cavalry fort.

The place remains just as Disney designed it—full of secret and private pleasures for a child. Adults almost always find everything too small and boring, preferring instead the more complex, carefully orchestrated amusements of the mainland.

II 11 · BIG THUNDER MOUNTAIN RAILROAD

This artfully disguised roller coaster has replaced one of the most pleasant places in Disneyland, Nature's Wonderland, where a little train took you from a small-scale mining town through a southwestern landscape of Disney animals, boiling paint pots, careening boulders and a beautifully mysterious grotto with colored lights. It was one of Disney's most successful mixes of real and fantastic—the naturalness of the fairy tale and the fantasy of nature, but it must have seemed too tame (and unprofitable) in this age of great roller coasters. It was swept away in favor of a newer, higher-tech, more kinesthetic experience—a ride on a runaway mine train. Much of the Western scenery is still there, but you spend so much energy avoiding having your neck snapped that there is little left for environmental observation.

One distinct improvement of the remodeling is the careful arrangement of the long waiting line so that it becomes a part of the ride itself. The sights along the way help to set the mood as the line winds down though a narrow trail in Bryce Canyon; you pass a small frontier town and a half-buried dinosaur skeleton and then shuffle under a trestle that carries the returning cars of shrieking passengers.

You finally board the train, whose chunky, top-heavy appearance belies its grip on the rails, and clatter off through a tunnel, a favorite Disney device for announcing the suspension of disbelief. The train hurtles through canyons, past cactus, coyotes, buttes and buzzards, and plunges into dark mine shafts and more tunnels. At one point it heads directly for a roaring waterfall; at another, the rock walls tremble and boulders tumble in a mock earthquake. The runaway train finally splashes into a stream and rounds a bend, and you are back, very quickly, in Frontierland.

II 12 · *Sleeping Beauty's Castle, entrance to Fantasyland*

II 11 · *Big Thunder Mountain Railroad*

II 12 · FANTASYLAND

At the end of Main Street, past the central plaza and over a swan-filled moat, lies the drawbridge to Sleeping Beauty's Castle: a delicate, tiny structure, with none of the loom of a castle about it. To the right of the bridge are flat rocks, trees, a dreadful little grotto with Snow White and the Seven Dwarfs, and a white ceramic secular crèche with Bambi, too. Brace yourself, because you will now hear an endless repetition of "When You Wish upon a Star" as you enter through the gates of the castle and come immediately out the other side into Fantasyland.

Fantasyland is a great deal thinner, less architectural, more brightly abstract and more childlike (of course) than the other lands at Disneyland and has mostly small rides for small children. Though many are just standard carnival attractions overlaid with images from Disney cartoons, a surpassingly gorgeous carousel lies directly ahead as you pass through the castle. Surrounding it are entrances to Fantasyland's interior rides. Two of them are worth an adult visit: Mr. Toad's Wild Ride and Peter Pan's Flight.

II 13 · MR. TOAD'S WILD RIDE and PETER PAN'S FLIGHT

These are both small-scale, relatively old-fashioned but powerfully engaging rides inspired by Disney's animated movies *The Wind in the Willows* and *Peter Pan.* One re-creates Toad's breakneck automobile drive through the English countryside; the other, the children's flight with Peter Pan to Never-Never-Land.

To accompany Toad, you board a miniature vintage motorcar with its useless steering wheel and hurtle off into a scenic maze of Day-Glo images painted on black backdrops. Policemen whistle at you to stop and then are whisked aside as you break through barriers of many kinds. Next comes perhaps the finest simple illusion in the park. In the midst of the general cacophony you hear the sounds of an approaching train; suddenly its great headlight appears out of the gloom directly ahead and the roar of the train thunders to a crescendo; you brace yourself but the impact never comes, for the light beam and the sound turn out to be the only physical attributes of this rampaging locomotive. Then, abruptly, you are out in Fantasyland again.

Peter Pan's Flight is a very short ride, one of the earliest in Disneyland and made for little children, but its first few moments are breathtaking. Your tiny pirate ship suddenly sweeps up above a bed, out through a window and across the night sky high above London. After London, the fantasy becomes a little thinner. The cellophane construction of tropical volcanoes is a bit too visible, and the fluorescent mannequins of Captain Hook and Smee are a little too cute. But the beginning of this ride and the end of Toad's manage to pull you all the way out of the ordinary.

II 14 · STORYBOOKLAND

Storybookland is an astonishingly beautiful and moving place. Adults might pass it up, thinking it was made only for small children. It was not. The clarity of detail and the inventiveness of the tiny models of gardens and towns and magic places is such a pleasure that it becomes great fun for grownups as well. There are two ways to see it: from the Casey Jr. Circus Train or from the canal boats. The train rattles above the little landscape at great speed accompanied by nonstop inanities. It is much better to take one of the boats: they glide silently through the canals and get you much closer to the magic miniatures of places

II 14 · *Storybookland*

you know and love, especially if you come here with childhood memories still well formed.

Your boat takes off through Monstro the Whale's mouth and comes out in a miniature landscape full of sophisticated, multilayered nostalgic pleasures for adults. You float past the cottage of the Seven Dwarfs and their diamond mine, the White Rabbit's hole, Ratty's and Mole's houses on a narrow island, and Mr. Toad's baronial English manor with its curious plastic pavilion. Up ahead are pink spires of the castle where Cinderella attended the ball, and below that, the village where Prince Charming looked for her. Then appears a hillside garden quilt, an altogether original and amazing set of forty-seven succulent beds held together with giant imitation stitches. The Swiss Alps are next, rising above the village of Geppetto and Pinocchio, and across the canal is a view of windmilled farms behind their dikes.

For all its childhood remoteness, this little land is in a central location. You can look up past tiny trees and Alps past mind-boggling leaps in scale to Big Thunder Mountain, Sleeping Beauty's Castle and the towering Matterhorn.

II 15 · IT'S A SMALL WORLD

Some people have venomous attitudes toward *all* of Disneyland. Ours extend only to something called It's a Small World. This extremely popular ride, which began life as the Pepsi Pavilion at the New York World's Fair in 1964, can, along with the Pirates of the Caribbean, accommodate more people than any other at Disneyland. It has elegant graphics and elaborate collage effects, and involves cruising on waterways through numerous chambers filled with dancing dolls. Though the dolls have all been pressed from the same mold, they describe their separate ethnicities with their native costumes and seem to sing along to a sound track that chants "It's a Small World After All" over and over and over.

The trouble with this experience, aside from the fact that it so exaggerates the goody-goody aspects of Disneyism as to make them intolerable, is that the damn song stays in your head for months. Therefore, gentle reader, consider this heartfelt proposal that you not go near the place.

II 16 · SKYWAY TO TOMORROWLAND

The brightly colored plastic cabs of the Skyway glide through the air between an alpine hut in Fantasyland and a sleekly modernistic Tomorrowland station. With swift precision and grace, they sail out over the toy-box pastels of Fantasyland (revealing more than you would like of its unadorned rooftops) and the waterways of Storybookland and through the Matterhorn; you come out over Tomorrowland's tropical blue lake, where a submarine fleet plies past the tracks and roadbeds and machinery on which this Land's various modes of futuristic transport move.

The passage through the Matterhorn is one of the most exciting, revealing and moving moments in all of Disneyland, or anywhere. The simultaneous motion of you on the Skyway and the bobsleds hurtling desperately diagonally inside (rather than outside) the mountain, the slow Peoplemover and Monorail drifting like clouds outside the peak and the water crashing down the slopes make lively sport of the reality they invert.

II 17 · TOMORROWLAND

A good case can be made on evidence collected from all over that the future came and went in about 1957. That case is considerably strengthened at Tomorrowland, Disney's now altogether passé vision of the future. From the beginning it was conceived not as a science fiction fantasy but as a "blueprint for the future" and was, therefore, the riskiest venture in the park. Disney was serious about it and hired such brilliant consultants as Willy Ley and Wernher von Braun. But all they managed to come up with was a bland arrangement that looks more like downtown Santa Monica than the twenty-fifth-century Omaha of Buck Rogers or the splendid sleek sets for the movie of H. G. Wells's *Things to Come.* The pallid, curving 1950s shapes certainly didn't adequately predict the future: the streamlined canopy on the Mission to Mars and the sleek volcano of Space Mountain have little in common, for instance, with the nonaerodynamic, insectlike vehicles NASA eventually built.

At first the attractions and exhibits of Tomorrowland really did try to showcase "Tomorrow." The Monsanto House of the Future, cross-shaped in plan with a series of "living environments" cantilevered from a central support, sought to prefigure the use of plastics in building design, though probably its most memorable innovation was the telephone and sound system in the prefab shower. By the late fifties the house could no longer meet the legislative standards designed to improve housing, so the whole thing was removed and the future went away. All that's left in Tomorrowland is the past's look into the future, which today is a slightly chilling period piece.

II 18 · PEOPLEMOVER and MONORAIL

The Peoplemover, Tomorrowland's "Highway in the Sky," opened in 1967 to a flurry of interest among the public, city planners and transportation engineers. An early ecological solution meant to please everyone, it runs on "pollution-free" all-electric energy to salve the environmentalists, offers individual modules for those accustomed to their own car, and sports just enough new technology to impress the professionals. You climb a ramp to the loading dock and step onto a circular platform that rotates at the same slow speed as the cars. These then take you on a long, slow scenic ride on a track held aloft on huge precast concrete columns that march through Tomorrowland. At the end, the ride passes through a special tunnel with fast-paced 360-degree film projections, lifted presumably from a Disney science fiction movie; this cleverly contrived special effect allows your clunky little Peoplemover to spin off through the galaxy, do battle with alien spacecraft, and for a few seconds, travel at the speed of light.

The Disneyland-Alweg Monorail was inaugurated in 1959 in ceremonies presided over by Vice President Richard M. Nixon. It was America's first passenger-carrying monorail operating on a daily schedule, connecting the hotel with the park on a two-and-a-half-mile loop. The streamlined trains look a little like sleek, scaled-down observation cars on the old Super Chief as they glide silently overhead on rubber tires along a concrete beamway. The ride, slow as it is, provides unexpected delights, especially since its destination can be "Adultland" at the Disneyland Hotel bar.

II 18 · *Peoplemover and Monorail*

II 17 · *Tomorrowland*

II 19 · AMERICA SINGS

Tomorrowland has always been the catchall for Disney's miscellaneous activities—the circle-vision theater, the Art of Animation, and the sets from *20,000 Leagues Under the Sea* all landed here, though none has any real connection with things futuristic. America Sings, which made its debut as the General Electric Pavilion at the 1964 New York World's Fair, fits more easily into Tomorrowland for two semifuturistic reasons: it is a theater in the round in which the audience moves instead of the stage; and the performers are not of flesh, but of fake fur and electronics. The stage is populated with singing animal caricatures: a wise owl and a golden eagle in Uncle Sam garb are masters of ceremonies; fat chickens and dapper foxes act as ethnic gospel singers; a flock of geese form a barbershop quartet; and an Elvis-like impersonation comes out of a droopy hound dog. The show is well-paced and visually dazzling, and it contains some perfectly decent and praiseworthy American folk songs, several cuts above the musical fare elsewhere in Disneyland.

II 20 · SUBMARINE VOYAGE

Disneyland has the ninth largest submarine fleet in the world, sailing through clear blue-green water that has not been dyed gray. The Submarine Voyage is a supercharacteristic piece of Disneyland: fascinating, beautiful and important, full of deep and sincere messages, at times hokey and in spots absurd—for instance, loudspeakers bombard the people trapped in line with exhortations to preserve the mineral and vegetable wealth of the oceans.

At last you climb down a circular stair into a submarine, a beautiful blue-gray machine, and sit looking through tiny portholes at the world beneath the waves. After the Captain calls "Dive!" masses of rising bubbles create the illusion of deep descent, even though the boat doesn't really submerge at all. As the crew chatters away on an intercom, the submarine passes intricate coral reefs and colorful marine life, including a giant clam. The craft dives deeper (more bubbles) to avoid a storm, traverses a ship graveyard with sunken treasure and dives again to clear the polar icecap. Eerie, luminescent creatures glow in the eternal darkness. The sub rises a bit and passes a giant squid, mermaids and an underwater volcano erupting over ruins of the lost continent of Atlantis.

After outmaneuvering a sea serpent, the submarine surfaces. You return to port, perhaps a little edgy that the ecological earnestness and the mermaidenly hokum have been so conflated, but pleased, withal, to have been part of a very good show.

II 21 · MISSION TO MARS and SPACE MOUNTAIN

These two rides attempt to simulate space travel. Mission to Mars, a replacement for the old Flight to the Moon, employs a 1950s serious scientific approach. In the wake of NASA's successful interplanetary travels, the ride seems rather old-fashioned and naïve, definitely pre–*Star Trek.* You sit in a circular room on steeply tiered plastic seats with the rocket's nose presumably overhead. Large screens on the floor and ceiling reveal the seat-shaking blastoff: Earth diminishes, Mars approaches; and then you turn around—no one actually disembarks on Mars. It's a soothing down-home ride for a tired part of the day.

Space Mountain, on the other hand, is a more up-to-date, heart-in-the-mouth device for jerking around in the galaxy. It is housed inside a big white concrete dome, which is set far back from the moving-ramp entry, behind buildings angled to make it look gigantic and more galactic. Buck Rogers spires bristle around the top. After waiting in line in a upper-level forecourt, you enter a tunnel that crackles with the sounds of space talk. The tunnel winds down and opens into a cavernlike room filled with blinking computer consoles, space-age machinery, and, below, loading docks for little space cars. You have just experienced the best part.

The space cars resemble slick and slightly sinister Matterhorn bobsleds. Once strapped into one, you are flung into the mountain, which becomes a dark cosmos. The car speeds through the darkness, pitching and rolling at breakneck speed, passing twinkling lights that might be stars or planets. After a couple of disorienting and terrifying minutes, you return to the station feeling like an Air Force recruit fleeing a flight simulator. Certainly not up to the scream power of Magic Mountain's roller coasters (page 391) or the complex pleasures of the Pirates of the Caribbean, Space Mountain is a flat if frightening disappointment. The Disney engineers might have left well enough alone with their earnest Mission to Mars.

II 22 · AUTOPIA

It may seem outrageous to those of us who have just fought miles of freeway traffic on the way to the Magic Kingdom to discover that this miniature freeway is one of the most popular rides in the park.

After passing a driving exam that consists of proving you are at least four feet tall, the operator takes possession of a scaled-down 1950s convertible that closely resembles the one Mickey Mouse took to driving once he had moved from short pants to Bing Crosby outfits. The gasoline-powered fiberglass car produces a satisfying roar when the pedal is depressed, and it belches real exhaust from its tailpipe. The concrete roadway curves past traditional Southern California freeway landscaping and miniature highway signs, but the illusion of actual Los Angeles travel becomes a touch too real when traffic jams develop and the cars collide.

Here must be the kind of experience that Bruno Bettelheim favors: an opportunity to organize young people into a less threatening version of a role they will assume as adults. So a stress-filled necessity becomes miniaturized, understandable, but still real—a training freeway.

III / ROUTE OF THE PADRES

Mission San Gabriel Arcángel

In the early nineteenth century, the mainland route to Los Angeles went up along the coast, from the south; it was called El Camino Real, the Royal Highway, the Main Street and lifeline of Old California. Ramona's image added deep new tones to its romantic luster, but there is plenty of actual brick and wood

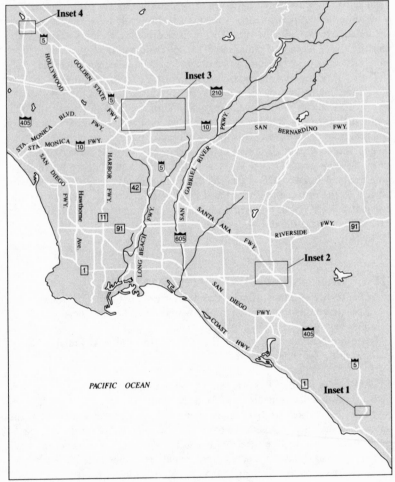

III/ROUTE OF THE PADRES

and adobe left to speak of those poignant times. This chapter will take us along the Camino Real, between the missions near Los Angeles, catching a number of places that interest us along the way. Some of these places are brand-new, so no chronological coherence can be claimed for this route, but with distances so great, chronology must give way to convenience.

El Camino Real was the footpath followed by Padre Serra and the other founding fathers as they established the twenty-one missions of California; on foot, the missions were about a day's journey apart, beginning, in 1769, with San Diego de Alcalá. (There are a number of missions below that, in Baja California, but they have never found their way into the Yankee limelight.) The string ends, six hundred miles north, with Sonoma (1823), but the missions in between were not founded in strict geographical sequence.

The three that concern us are, from south to north: San Juan Capistrano (1776), the seventh to be founded; San Gabriel (1771), the fourth; and San Fernando, Rey de España (1797), the seventeenth.

The missions were more than churches. Each was a trade school with an attached chapel, both requiring lifelong attendance. The Indians were taught fifty-four trades and occupations, including painting, sculpture and music, but the main activity was coping with the near-desert landscape. The padres at San Gabriel controlled 1½ million acres, which was theoretically being held in trust for the Indians. In fact, after Mexican independence, in 1822, the missions were secularized and pillaged by Spaniard and Yankee alike, and the Indians were driven off. But lovely, picturesque, romantic and well-gardened ruins remain.

The route of our own pilgrimage takes us through Santa Ana, the county seat of Orange County and the center of Valencia orange growing until the 1950s. Nearby is Anaheim, settled by Germans and filled out by Walt Disney and others; and then comes Whittier, named in 1887 for John Greenleaf Whittier by Quakers from the Midwest. This was an avocado center, home of Richard Nixon and, more substantially, one Frank Wiggers. Mr. Wiggers arrived in Whittier in 1888, an invalid. Two years in Eden cured him, and he became the quintessential booster. He organized "California on Wheels," a railroad car filled with the produce of California, and traveled around the country visiting every state fair. "God," it used to be said, "did much for Los Angeles, but Frank Wiggers did the rest."

III 1 · MISSION SAN JUAN CAPISTRANO
At the corner of Camino Capistrano and Ortega Highway, San Juan Capistrano; take the Ortega Highway exit from the San Diego Freeway (5)
Padre Junipero Serra, Church built, 1806; destroyed by earthquake, 1812
Open daily, 7–5; admission fee

Fifty-five miles south of Los Angeles, the freeway goes through a pretty valley between gentle hills, three miles in from the sea. Alarmingly close to the freeway exit, the Mission San Juan Capistrano still slumbers behind its walls, at the gateway to the town that bears its name. Its church was destroyed by an earthquake in 1812, just six years after it was finished; only the lower part of the walls and the vaults behind the sanctuary still stand. The ruins of this church have become ornaments in a very pretty southwestern garden with roses and trees, prickly-pear cactus and raked sand, and old wagons with solid-wood wheels.

III 1 · *Mission San Juan Capistrano*

III 1 · *Mission San Juan Capistrano, Bell Wall*

The church was huge, big enough for two thousand people. It was a Latin cross in shape, roofed over with domed vaults, and is said to have had a massive tower at the entrance, all gone now. But there is enough left in the sanctuary to imagine what it must have been like.

It seems to have been far more up to date than might be expected of such a vast construction so distant from its Spanish sources of inspiration. There is much less of the exuberant, late-eighteenth-century Mexican cake-decorator's Baroque than the date would indicate, and much more of the subsequent somber nineteenth-century Mexican architecture, cool and strict. But, luckily, it does miss some of the more dismal aspects of that cool and classical Mexican style (one of the gloomiest reform architectures the world has produced), thanks largely to the vegetation: oleander of a rare peachy-pink shade, roses, lantana and, especially, bougainvillea that climbs around the ruined walls.

The prettiest place here, behind the left transept of the ruined church, is a Sacred Garden with a little fountain and a wall of bells; but the most historic is the chapel, which remains intact. It is the oldest building in California and the only church left in the state that was used by Padre Serra, still a revered household name in California despite his unseemly interest in whipping Indians. Because long roof beams were not available, the chapel is very narrow and simple. It is handsome, too, thanks partly to a splendid three-hundred-year-old reredos from Barcelona; but a few simple, bright wall paintings and stencils on the white-painted wooden ceiling contribute, more than the fancy imported reredos does, to a sense of simple poetic piety that renders this humble chapel deeply moving.

To the west of the chapel is a large court with a particularly handsome fountain, which used to splash into a basin full of carp. Along the north side of this patio are handsome arcades with tile floors, simple wood-beam ceilings, and brick arches, including an eccentric diagonal arch in one corner. The sun streams through the bougainvillea onto ancient adobe walls, which have been stuccoed and painted in ocher, cinnamon, pink and peach. Behind the north wall are dioramas that recount the local history from the coming of the padres to the completion of the first mission building in San Juan Capistrano in 1776, very different from the 1806 building whose ruins you see. Farther along this wall you can look through a window at an exquisitely detailed seventeenth-century Neapolitan nativity. Despite its finery, it seems to fit well in this calm and humble place. Fitting less well nearby is a new wall that someone has tried to fix to look old. It looks new, and aggressively crummy.

That unpleasant sight is succeeded, fortunately, by jacaranda trees, fragrant Cape honeysuckle and a special ogival arch with an acanthus keystone. Then, in a courtyard near the entry, there is a pepper tree of astonishing dimensions; its trunk must be six feet in diameter. It is beautiful, too, and because it is alive, it links us even more closely than the stones do across two centuries to a time that seems infinitely long ago.

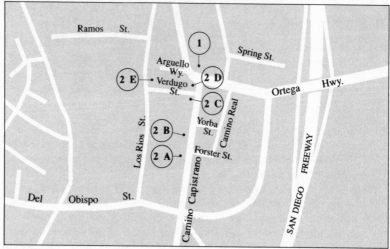

III/ROUTE OF THE PADRES (INSET 1)

III 2 · SAN JUAN CAPISTRANO
Along Camino Capistrano

San Juan Capistrano revels in its Old Spanish Days image; even the gas stations at the freeway off-ramp are done up with plastic red-tiled mansards and silent bell towers, but still, the little town manages to be convincingly picturesque. Camino Capistrano, the main street, is a pleasant place to walk.

At 31891 Camino Capistrano is the historic El Adobe de Capistrano restaurant (2 A) (ca. 1932), which has united the Miguel Yorba adobe (1778) and the Juzgado, the town's first courthouse (1812), using parts from the ruined mission. A dramatically spacious interior steps down and back between the ancient buildings to a garden courtyard with a translucent plastic roof; on the left, a stairway leads to the old jail in the basement, which was once, it is said, the last quarters of the notorious Mexican bandit Joaquín Murrieta, and is now a wine cellar. Nearby is the two-story García Adobe (2 B) (31861–31843 Camino Capistrano; ca. 1845), whose three-foot walls have housed a hotel, a general store and Capistrano's first post office; now there are little shops there. A second-story balcony, added in the 1880s, makes this the only surviving Monterey-style house in Orange County, according to the bronze plaque in front. The height of the balcony and its elaborately scrolled trim, now engulfed by bougainvillea, does make the García Adobe strongly reminiscent of adobes near the northernmost mission, in Sonoma.

At the southwest corner of Camino Capistrano and Verdugo Street is Franciscan Plaza (2 C), a new shopping center dressed in white plaster and red tile;

it looks a lot like present-day Monterey. Across the street, at the northwest corner of Camino Capistrano and Verdugo, are a number of souvenir shops (2 D) behind a simple, Irving Gill (page 121) sort of white arcade. One block west, at 26701 Verdugo Street, is the Mission Style Santa Fe passenger depot (2 E) (1895), complete with a domed tower. Like the courthouse, it has been turned into a restaurant, only this remodeling was done in 1975, so the remodelers glassed in the arcade to look like a greenhouse and stripped the walls of their stucco dress; the depot now stands in its brick underclothes, a trendy homage to the 1970s dictum that old brick plus ferns equals restaurant.

III 3 · ORANGE PLAZA
At the intersection of Chapman Avenue and Glassell Street, Orange
1886

At the center of the city of Orange is a charming plaza arranged around a traffic circle with a pretty park in the middle (3 A). The streets are small, with diagonal parking along their edges. Continuous turn-of-the-century commercial buildings enclose the space and make it seem complete. The park is planted with Edwardian favorites: heavily scented magnolias, Canary Island palms and, naturally, orange trees. During Christmas the palms are decorated as Christmas trees, and a tinsel snowman stands among the oranges. At the park's center a fountain splashes into a pretty basin of orange and red and cobalt-blue tiles. Pine trees are planted around the edges, helping to provide shade in this perennially sunny place; the silky green boughs complement the red brick of the sidewalks and the many corniced buildings. A little one-story building at 44 Plaza Square is covered in vine ficus; even its decorative urns are clothed in dense vegetation, an appealing contrast to the smooth finishes of the adjoining buildings. The northeast side of the plaza is dominated by a bank with grand Corinthian pilasters that support a frieze of Mexican señoritas dancing gaily.

Once there might have seemed nothing unusual about this little plaza, but now it stands out as an island in the sea of newness and sameness in which Orange County is awash. The contrast is heightened by the new City Shopping Center (3 B), not far to the west, which is two hundred acres of regional business and shopping, perhaps intended as a pilot model for the colonization of one of the solar system's outer planets.

III 3 · *Orange Plaza*

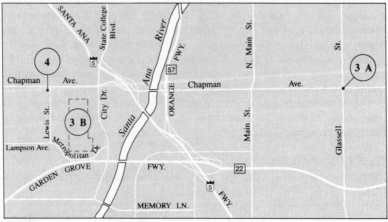

III 4 · CRYSTAL CATHEDRAL

12141 Lewis Street, on the southwest corner of Chapman Avenue, Garden Grove

Philip C. Johnson and John Burgee, 1980

Two enormous apparitions, the stuff that dreams are made of, rise up beside the freeways in Anaheim and Garden Grove. Their insubstantiality is enhanced if, as usual, the smog is shrouding them. Their beauty from the freeway seems more apparent to some than to others and seems to be based more on association than on, say, proportion or other intrinsic properties. The first apparition, which has been there since the fifties, is the Matterhorn at Disneyland (page 51). The other, brand-new in 1980, is the Reverend Robert H. Schuller's Crystal Cathedral, designed by Philip Johnson and John Burgee, and surely that renowned firm's most exciting work to date.

The Matterhorn, from the outside, is just an average-size, rather lumpy

III 4 · *Crystal Cathedral*

mountain; the excitement is inside, where bobsleds hurtle and gondola cars sail through. The Crystal Cathedral, more simply faceted, is not all that prepossessing from the outside either: at 207 feet by 415 feet in plan, 128 feet tall to its highest point, it is not really gigantic for a cathedral, and its mirrored glass skin, animated by strips of awning windows, is straightforward rather than elegant. But inside the space is a thriller.

The plan is shaped like the kind of elongated four-pointed star found often on Christmas cards. Triangular balconies fill the two end points and one of the sides; the seating in the flat, rectangular center faces toward the remaining side point, which contains a choir, an organ and a pulpit. The pulpit is off center so it can be close to a giant door that opens onto the drive-in part of the church, just outside. The roof, which sheds up to the high space directly over the pulpit, is, like the walls, all glass, mirrored to admit only about 8 percent of the light that falls on it, but that 8 percent suffuses the space with an extraterrestrial, magic glow.

It is said that Dr. Schuller (who manages most engagingly to surmount all odds and be at once optimistic and pragmatic) wanted a church embedded in nature, a bit recollective of the Garden of Eden. What he got was a church that might seem rather more at home in outer space. Not even a Southern California landscape could stand up to this place, although the structure, which is a three-dimensional frame of white-painted steel tubes just inside the glass, is sufficiently intricate to create a landscape in itself. The structure and the glass and the glow is so magnificent that the more mundane appointments, however sumptuous, end up seeming earthbound, even a bit tacky: matched panels of marble on the pulpit front appear as klutzy as the blue-lined raised pool that bisects the main floor on its way to the altar.

When Dr. Schuller starts to speak (and at other times too), the ninety-foot-high doors near the pulpit swing open (on hardware developed for Cape Canaveral), the water jets outside die down and the show goes on. Maybe the memory of that famous jet which came and went in Jacques Tati's movie *Mon Oncle* is still too strong, but it is hard for some of us, though apparently not for many others, to catch the serious religiosity in messages prefaced with dancing waters.

The new cathedral forms a courtyard with Dr. Schuller's earlier church, a handsome one designed by Richard J. Neutra in 1961, with a side that opens to include the drive-in congregants; there is also a fifteen-story tower added in 1967 by Richard Neutra's son, Dion. The Neutra church sits superbly in the midst of a maturing landscape, and comes, one would think, much closer to the Schuller Arcadian ideal. But the Crystal Cathedral, in its magnificence, makes its own standards.

III 5 · MISSION SAN GABRIEL ARCÁNGEL
537 West Mission Drive, San Gabriel
Padre Antonio Cruzado, Church founded, 1771; nave built, 1791–1805;
other structures built and remodeled, 1804 and after
Open daily, 9:30–4; admission fee

The San Gabriel Mission differs from the one at San Juan Capistrano in that it is still there. The great earthquake of 1812, which destroyed San Juan Capistrano, had only a flat roof of brick and mortar to shake down here, since an earlier quake, in 1804, had already dispatched the heavy vaulting. But at San

III 5 · *Mission San Gabriel Arcángel*

Gabriel the roof was quickly replaced. On balance, San Juan Capistrano seems to have been the more fortunate. San Gabriel, narrow and low and long and dark under its reconstructed gable roof, and reached by way of a particularly repellent gift shop, has been enthusiastically modernized over the years; undoubtedly, such a fate would have been spared it if only the roof had been left off so the place could become a decent ruin.

The building got off to a good start. It was one of just five of the California missions to be built of cut stone and brick. Its designer, Father Antonio Cruzado, came from Córdoba in southern Spain, so a Moorish influence is often imputed to the heavy construction. A handsome reredos, complete with Spanish saints, was delivered from Mexico City in the 1790s. The saints remain, but the ceiling and roof, rebuilt in 1886, are curiously awkward, gloomy and macabre.

But this is Southern California, and the luxuriant grounds are a delight. A

III 6 · *San Gabriel Civic Auditorium*

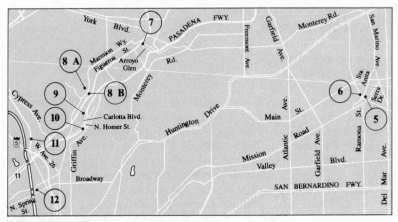

III/ROUTE OF THE PADRES (INSET 3)

splendid pergola alongside the nave holds grapevines planted in 1930; their trunks are now about a foot in diameter, with branches that spread along the beams, around the corner and into the sunshine. Nearby, enormous olive trees, planted as long ago as 1860, grow in raised circular podia. Another beautiful and much photographed object in the garden is the bell wall, which extends and enlivens the south side of the nave. There are a number of gardens (one with graves, another with cactus), the inevitable statues of Junipero Serra and a shed in which simple, rough and very appealing models of the mission are kept. There is a sundial, which says: "Every hour wounds, the last one kills." Watch out for those folks up at the gift shop.

III 6 · SAN GABRIEL CIVIC AUDITORIUM
320 South Mission Drive, San Gabriel
Arthur B. Benton, 1923–1924
Built originally as the Mission Playhouse

About a block north of Mission San Gabriel is the Mission Playhouse, now the San Gabriel Civic Auditorium, which was commissioned expressly to house productions of poet John Steven McGroarty's romantic pageant, *The Mission Play,* a dramatization of the history of the missions from riches to ruins. The play was performed 3,200 times before it closed in 1933. The building seems to be a festive stylization of the Mission San Antonio de Padua just south of Carmel, which alone among the missions has a freestanding parapet wall with a bell tower, behind which looms the gable roof of the nave.

Like *The Mission Play,* the building is a grand, carefully edited image of the past. Set at a dramatic angle to the street, it faces southwest to catch the full glow of the afternoon sun; dark shadows outline symmetrical reveals and openings in the brilliant-white walls. A triple-arched entrance, a large arch flanked by the smaller ones, is echoed by doorways behind. Sombrero-shaped urns cap the columns between the arches, and an enthusiastic three-dimensional shield tilts over the center. It all manages to be serious yet cheerful, an entertaining foil to the San Gabriel Mission around the corner. And it manages to provide the Hispanic charm that the Yankeefied mission so notoriously lacks.

III 7 · ABBEY SAN ENCINO
6211 Arroyo Glen Street, about a block east of Figueroa Street, Highland
Park
Clyde Browne, 1909–1925
Private residence

Abbey San Encino is a house built by its owner, a printer, in styles from Mission Revival to Spanish Colonial Revival, in such vivid and heartfelt homage to Old California that the city has made it a Cultural-Historical Monument. The city has grown up around it (as has a recent eight-foot-high cyclone fence), and the sycamore-filled streambed of the Arroyo Seco has been replaced by the Pasadena Freeway, but the abbey still surrounds itself in its own aura. It sits in a grove of shaggy eucalyptus, pines and palm trees at the base of a curving cliff, which is overgrown with prickly pear, ivy, geraniums and oat grass.

In the Spanish and Mexican tradition, the house wraps around a large open patio in back. The walls are blocks of hand-carved sandstone and granite and round fieldstones; the gabled roofs are covered in red tiles; and the doors are of rough-hewn timber trimmed in huge, hammered-metal hinges. To the left of an arcaded entry porch is a massive wall with a round stained-glass window that depicts an Indian neophyte setting type under the eyes of a Franciscan. On the right, beyond a bell tower, is a basilica wing with thick wedge-shaped buttresses that alternate with narrow stained-glass windows in a fieldstone wall. The roofscape is a lively conglomeration of high and low roofs and curious chimneys, building up to a chaotic fieldstone dome above the belfry. The theatricality, even the affectation, makes this rancho seem immediately familiar; it is a real part of California's make-believe past.

III 8 · SOUTHWEST MUSEUM
234 Museum Drive, north of the intersection with Marmion Way,
Highland Park
Sumner Hunt and Silas R. Burns, 1912 to present
Open Tuesday through Saturday, 11–5; Sunday, 1–5; closed Monday and
some holidays; call (213) 221-2163; free admission

On a steep hillside overlooking the Arroyo Seco looms the austere Mission Style Southwest Museum (8 A). It is just a bit reminiscent of a Spanish monastery or perhaps a fortress in the Pyrenees or a castle in Castile or a hastily built movie set. The romantic vision slides in and out of focus, between wonder and sleaze. Dense landscaping of dark green foliage obscures the foundations, so the building appears as an outcropping of the hill itself. But even the hill has something suspicious about it.

The Southwest Museum was the final product of Charles F. Lummis' archaeological pursuits (page 67) and is a fascinating showcase of American Indian artifacts. It includes an extraordinary collection of baskets, a beautiful but sinister group of very old kachina dolls, an illuminating array of assorted relics in handsome display cases and a vivid rendering of Custer's Last Stand drawn by an Indian participant. The place is an attic storehouse of native culture.

For the full treatment, enter the museum through the hill. A monumental Mayan entryway, which juts out mysteriously from the base of this luxuriant slope, leads to a long, eerily lit tunnel that ends at an ancient elevator. Set into

III 7 · *Abbey San Encino*

III 8 · *Southwest Museum*

the walls of this dim passage are little dioramas that illustrate various Indian ways of life: Anasazi in their red rock cliff dwellings, Plains Indians in their tepees, locals in their wickiups, and more. The elevator lifts the visitor high above all this and into yet other worlds, incredibly rich and wonderful and charged with magic.

At the base of the hill, across the railroad tracks at 4605 N. Figueroa Street is an unpublicized holding of the Southwest Museum, the Casa de Adobe (8 B), a replica of an Old California hacienda, built in 1918 by the Hispanic Society of California. In 1925 it was donated to the Southwest Museum, which opens it to visitors during the same hours the museum is open. The intention of the builders, who were caught up, along with Charles Lummis, in the fever for Mission Revival, was to create a composite of all known Spanish adobes in California from 1800 to 1850, using historically sanctified materials and methods of construction, for the most part; whatever the place lacked in authenticity would be made up for in a sort of distilled perfection.

III 9 · LUMMIS HOUSE
200 East Avenue 43, at the west corner of Carlota Boulevard, Los Angeles
Charles F. Lummis, 1897–1910
Now the headquarters of the Historical Society of Southern California and a museum; open Wednesday through Sunday, 1–4; free admission

Charles Fletcher Lummis was a Harvard-educated journalist who made Los Angeles his home after walking here, as a correspondent for the Los Angeles *Times,* on a three-thousand-mile trek from Cincinnati that ended on January 31, 1885. From that date, at the height of California's "Boom of the '80s" and just a few months after the publication of Helen Hunt Jackson's *Ramona,* until his death in 1928, Lummis never stopped writing and speaking about and generally boosting the Southland, a word he claimed to have coined. He was also the first person to say "See America First," although the America he had in mind was centered in Southern California. More erudite and eloquent and less self-serving than other promoters during that confident time, Lummis gathered around him a host of luminaries, mostly artists and writers, and became one of the hardest-hitting champions of Southwest culture and Mission Style architecture. He founded, near his house, the Southwest Museum (page 66), which was dedicated, like Lummis himself, to American Indians, with whom he had lived for a number of years; he was the driving force behind the Landmarks Club, which managed to save four of the missions; and he built this house with his own hands between 1897 and 1910 as an example of the style of architecture and the way of life he had spent most of his own life crusading for.

Lummis named his three-acre rancho El Alisal (The Sycamore) after the trees that grew all around, one of which still shades the courtyard in back of his one- and two-story, L-shaped house. The rustic and relaxed, determinedly added-onto demeanor of the house belies the stalwart construction, of giant boulders, brought up from the arroyo, and of yards of concrete. Walls are one to two feet thick, with buttresses often three times that. Hand-hewn timber ceilings, as well as the telephone pole beams of the living room, are drenched in fireproofing chemicals. The roofs are asbestos shingles; the floors are concrete. This all-out elegy to the memory of Ramona was meant, said its builder, to "last for a thousand years."

III 9 · *Lummis House*

The sunny façade, a ninety-one-foot-wide stone fortress of a wall, is softened by climbing vines and livened by an array of arched windows and doors, no two alike, in dark wood frames. Near the middle is a pair of giant front doors, thick slabs of iron-studded wood that weigh half a ton each. On the left, a two-story medieval turret, unlike anything left from the padres, mixes fierce crenellations on top with welcoming windows in the base. Next to it, stepped back a few feet, a Mission end wall, with bell, curves between two high chimneys.

The interior, of light plaster, colorful tile and rustic though carefully textured wood, is a comfortable blend of Old California and anything else that caught Lummis' eye. The rooms are filled with fragments of ancient Latin-American structures that Lummis collected on his travels. They are filled, too, with fragments of the builder's personality, particularly heartfelt in the striking Indian patterns he carved on the cabinets and window seats, and in the photographic images he tinted onto the living-room windows. Oddly, the most thoroughly Mission-looking part of the house is the kitchen, where the ceiling slopes up to a central chimney, as if the whole room were an oven.

III 10 · HERITAGE SQUARE
3800 North Homes Street, near Avenue 43, Los Angeles
Grounds are open the second Sunday and third Wednesday of each month, but the houses can be seen from the gate; admission fee

Heritage Square is an open-air museum of Victorian architecture made up of ebullient old piles from other parts of Los Angeles that had found themselves in the paths of the bulldozers. The ten-acre site, not far from downtown Los Angeles, is highly visible from the Pasadena Freeway. The houses, newly painted and surrounded by almost bare ground, resemble nothing so much as a stylistically anachronistic used-car lot. So far there are five structures here, and many others seem to be on the way.

The Hale House (ca. 1888), the most fully restored, is a daring celebration of Queen Anne with exuberant Eastlake ornament. It is encrusted with intricate woodwork and painted an authentic rosy red and mint green. Two tall chimneys with eccentric three-dimensional brick patterns vie with the fleur-de-lis finial of a high corner turret to establish the house's enthusiastic verticality. The front and rear parlors and the dining room have been accurately refurbished, down to the wallpaper and fireplace tiles.

The Valley Knudsen Garden Residence (ca. 1897), is a resplendent mansarded structure replete with thin rectangular dormer windows framed in spit-curl moldings. Next comes the Mount Pleasant House (ca. 1876), whose centerpiece is its two-story bay punctuated with flat arched windows. The Beaudry Street House (ca. 1889) has Italianate tracery that overlays a rich assortment of fat Queen Anne and skinny Victorian embellishments. The Palms Railroad Depot (ca. 1888), the last remaining Victorian station in Los Angeles (outside of Universal Studios), is covered in chaste board-and-batten on the first story with more lascivious fish-scale shingles above.

The Cultural Heritage Board, the body responsible for this collection, has decided, for what appear to be both compositional and narrative reasons, to concentrate on the flamboyant structures built in Los Angeles between 1860 and 1910. Anything older would likely be adobe and crumble on the mover's rig.

III 10 · *Heritage Square*

Things newer haven't yet acquired the patina that qualifies them for admission to this select company. But patina accumulates fast in Southern California, and the 1930s may arrive soon at Heritage Square.

III 11 · LAWRY'S CALIFORNIA CENTER

570 West Avenue 26, near the intersection of San Fernando Road, Los Angeles
Willis Hutchason and Calvin Straub, manufacturing plant, 1953 and after; front buildings, 1979
Open daily, 10–5; tours of plant, Monday through Friday, 11:30, 1:30, 2:30; free admission; restaurants open for lunch and dinner; call (213) 225-2491

Lawry's California Center, where Lawry's food seasonings are manufactured, is a very pretty place in the San Fernando Valley; the public is invited to try lunch with sangría or margaritas, stroll around or sit around, and soak up Ramona's heritage. There are several Hispanic patios, through which mariachis stroll past white walls on which play the shadows of broad-leaved plants and striped canvas canopies. There are arches in the thick walls, the roofs are of red tile, fountains play, the wood is dark, the flowers bloom profusely. And there are gifts to buy. It is charming, but it is all as surrealistically clean, like a setting for a Hollywood musical, which renders it just a shade sinister, like the blank and empty eyes in the gorgeous open face of the prototypical California cheerleader —happy-spirited, beautiful and dumb. It surely seems unfair to allege that the absence of dirt signals the absence of thought, yet it just may be that a little bit of mess is required to germinate seriousness.

Serious or not, the center has two outdoor restaurants, three bars, a wine and cooking shop, and a gourmet gift shop with cooking classes. The nearest thing to it in mood is the handsome headquarters of *Sunset* magazine on the San Francisco Peninsula; there, as here, everything is green: not only the plants but the cuisine as well, the lettuce and the spinach and the avocados and the ensuing guacamole. Behind the shrubbery lie the company's corporate offices and the manufacturing plant, open for tours.

III 12 · YANG-NA

In Downey Park, between North Broadway, North Spring Street, and the Los Angeles River, Los Angeles
1769

Spain's headlong rush to colonize great stretches of the New World in the 1520s and '30s slowed almost to a halt during the next two hundred and fifty years; by the mid-eighteenth century, Spain was facing fierce competition for North American territory from France, Russia and Great Britain. To strengthen Spanish claims on the continent's western coastline, an expedition headed by Capitán Gaspár de Portolá and Padre Junipero Serra was sent north in 1769 from Baja California to the fort at Monterey in order to select sites for garrisons and missions.

The account of the journey's official diarist, Padre Crespí, has preserved the reactions of the first Europeans to the California landscape. About the future site of Los Angeles, he wrote, in the last days of July 1769:

> *After travelling about a league and a half through a pass between low hills, we entered a very spacious valley, well-grown with cottonwoods and alders, among which ran a beautiful river from north-northwest, and then doubling the point of a steep hill, it went on afterward to the south . . . . As soon as we arrived, about eight heathens from a good village (Yang-Na) came to visit us; they live in this delightful place among the trees on the river.*

Today a bronze plaque mounted on a boulder in a little triangular park commemorates this auspicious beginning. The spacious valley is now crowded with millions of people and their buildings and cars; the river is now confined within concrete channels; and this park, the site of Yang-Na, has only a few of its sycamores left. We have only this much diminished site and Father Crespí's account to help us recall that legendary Arcadian place.

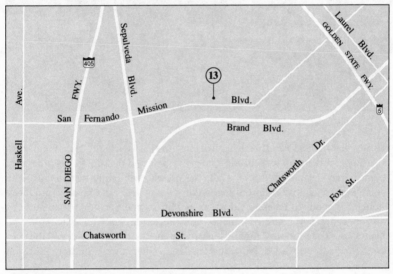

III/ROUTE OF THE PADRES (INSET 4)

III 13 · MISSION SAN FERNANDO, REY DE ESPAÑA
15151 San Fernando Mission Boulevard, Mission Hills
Church built, 1804–1806; restored, 1941; rebuilt, 1974
Convento built, 1810–1822
Open Monday through Saturday, 9–5; Sunday, 10–5; admission fee

After over a hundred years of slow deterioration, vandalism, earthquakes and arrogant restoration, the Mission of Saint Ferdinand, King of Spain, was fully rebuilt in 1974 after the 1971 earthquake. Unlike the showcase ruins of Mission San Juan Capistrano and the much propped-up San Gabriel, both of which fairly reek of the day-to-day histories of their Spanish and Indian inhabitants, the reconstructed San Fernando Mission, like pre–Clint Eastwood Westerns, evokes a precise but implausibly well-scrubbed version of the past. Like those old movies, this new mission provides many pleasing and poignant passages, for the restorers lavished great care on their re-creation.

The mission, located on the northern edge of the San Fernando Valley, came late in the series, (the seventeenth of twenty-one). It was to fill the gap between

III 13 · *Mission San Fernando, Rey de España*

the San Gabriel and San Buenaventura missions but is actually located far closer to San Gabriel than to Ventura. The padres selected this site for its proximity to water, good land and, best of all, the presence of Indian farmhands. The founders made a wise decision, for within twenty years the mission produced enough for goods to be exported as far as Mexico and Spain. At that time the mission and a few scattered ranches had the fertile San Fernando Valley to themselves. Today a busy highway narrowly misses the front wall of the *convento,* the padres' arcaded living quarters, and trailers nuzzle up to the mission grounds.

Succulents and cactus flank the entrance to the inevitable gift shop. Past this is a grand yet intimate courtyard with olive trees, more cactus and succulents, and a central fountain made of red tile. The south and west edges of the courtyard are bordered by one-story, one-room-deep structures with red-tiled roofs. The mission church, which is about twice as high as its neighbors, sits on a raised platform at the north end, behind the magic shadows of tall palm trees. The eastern edge is enclosed by a recent group of red-tiled school buildings, partially hidden behind a thickly planted fence. Although a false suburban note is set by a newly planted lawn where raked earth ought to be, the thick walls around the courtyard are beautiful, painted sandy beige and pierced by deep-set windows with dark wood lintels.

A door in the west wall leads through a small museum to an even smaller courtyard; here, a little freestanding archway leads to the *convento.* Its two-story, 243-foot-long plastered wall is enlivened by small windows and doors of widely varying shapes and sizes and by specimen cactus and palm trees, pale gray and green, along the base. Inside is a series of plain, high-ceilinged rooms that receive only a glimmer of light through tiny openings in the four-foot-thick walls. La Sala, the largest and most elegant reception room in any of the missions, used to be entered from the south, through double doors topped by a shell arch and flanked by windows set in pointed Moorish arches. The room of the first bishop of California is nearby, with his few but very rich effects, including hand-embroidered hair shirts. The *convento's* southern façade, which once fronted on El Camino Real, has a much photographed arcade of nineteen semi-circular arches supported by heavy square columns.

To the north is the church, reached through a courtyard garden bordered by a little water course and by bamboo and banana trees and other tropical plants. Its western entry façade is powerfully plain: an arched doorway with a single window above and a little belfry on the right are the only elaborations on the smooth wall, except in the afternoon, when a queen palm casts delicate flickering shadows. The 1974 reconstruction is lovingly if spuriously authentic, a meticulous reproduction of a flamboyant earlier restoration completed in 1941. The white plaster walls are richly painted with Indian patterns and with *trompe l'oeil* niches, pilasters, moldings and wainscoting, all in soft shades of aqua, rose and brown.

Across the boulevard lies the Memory Garden, inspired by the gardens of the Santa Barbara Mission. The main courtyard's original fountain, a replica of one in Córdoba, Spain, was moved here in 1921. The obligatory statue of Fra Junipero Serra, olive trees, two beautiful grape arbors and one more fountain help complete the set. Chalk up one more for Ramona.

IV / ROUTE 66

Riverside Mission Inn

The visions of any city we remember and cherish are often the ones that have to do with getting there. New York and San Francisco are generally first spotted across water, and the image that impresses us is that of an island. Los Angeles is the opposite: for Americans, since someone named William Wolfskill first blazed the trail in 1831, access to Los Angeles has been overland, and celebrated that way, from the Mormons to the health seekers of the 1880s to John Steinbeck's refugees from the Dust Bowl in the 1930s, to the bigger floods of mobile Americans in the years since World War II. By now, of course, many visitors come via L.A. International Airport and the car rental counters there. Still, the controlling image of Los Angeles surely is that of an Eden at the end of a long, dusty overland trail.

It seems appropriate, therefore, in this chapter to propose a ride over the last sixty miles of the road from the East, following for the most part that same Route 66 which John Steinbeck's displaced persons traveled in *The Grapes of Wrath.* U.S. Highway 66 is no longer the main route from the East, or even a main route at all, but it still stirs up powerful images. The highway arrives out of the high desert, south through Cajon Pass to San Bernardino. The air has always grown misty there, after thousands of miles of clear desert, and is by now likely to be egregiously and dismally smoggy as well, but it improves gradually on the trip west toward the ocean; so take heart, if not breath.

San Bernardino, still about sixty miles from downtown L.A., is a blue-collar town. Mormons from Utah came here in 1851 and laid out a spacious gridiron in the manner of Salt Lake City (which their colleagues had founded three years before), but they were recalled by Brigham Young in 1857. The railroads came in 1883; an annual Orange Show arrived in 1910; and now Joan Didion writes movingly about what it's like here when the wrong winds blow.

Other cities are very near: Redlands, named for the color of its soil, is a university town with a tradition of fine houses; and Riverside (*né* Glenwood) boasts one of the few three-star buildings in this book, the Mission Inn. Farther west lies Fontana, whose steel mills qualify as the producers of the most dangerous smog in the Los Angeles Basin. This city's other cultural claim to fame is as the birthplace of the Hell's Angels.

Other towns along the route have an especially generous whiff of Old Southern California about them; even their names have a certain feverish quaintness. Azusa, for instance, is reputed to be a version of "from A to Z in the USA," though a more plausible tale has it deriving from an Indian place name, Asuksagua or Houkesagua. Cucamonga means "place of many springs" or maybe "lewd woman" in Shoshone; grapes have been grown there since 1839. Upland

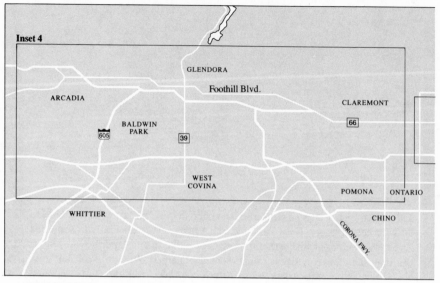

Inset 4

GLENDORA

Foothill Blvd.

ARCADIA

CLAREMONT

66

BALDWIN
PARK

605   39

WEST
COVINA

POMONA   ONTARIO

WHITTIER

CHINO

CORONA FWY

IV/ROUTE 66

and Ontario were founded during the influx of 1882 and were given names with more modest back-home recollections; Pomona was a contest winner, with a nod to the classical goddess of fruit. La Verne was renamed in 1917 from Lordsburg, to which in 1890 the Santa Fe Railroad offered "a free ride from anywhere east of the Rocky Mountains. . . . Anyone purchasing $500 worth of lots in Lordsburg will have his fare paid, and for $750, the fare of two persons." The Dunkers, members of the German Baptist Brethren Church, took them up on the offer. Monrovia, of course, was named after someone named Monroe, who bought it in 1886. Arcadia, the quintessential California name, was the dream town of Lucky Baldwin, the quintessential California success story. The young entrepreneur arrived in California from Ohio with just his wits, built a fortune

IV I A · *Wigwam Motel*

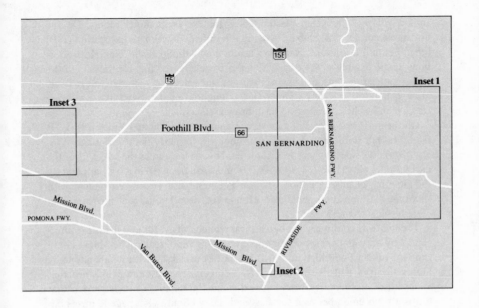

in San Francisco, and retired south to relive the romance of the ranchos in an only slightly modernized adobe.

The most stirringly nostalgic stretch of Route 66, reminiscent of scenes from an old movie about coming to California, lies between Fontana and Rancho Cucamonga, bypassed now by freeways, a movingly seedy reminder of how small almost everything man-made in Southern California used to be and how large almost all of it is now. It seems really to have been an Arcadian life, not only for the Lucky Baldwins, but for the small-time entrepreneur as well, who might build his personal fantasy to catch the passing eye. One of the most startling of these fantasies, near the border of San Bernardino and Rialto, is the Wigwam Motel (I A) (2728 West Foothill Boulevard, Rialto; F.A. Radford, ca. 1948), an

IV 5 · *Riverside Mission Inn*

Indian village of nineteen plaster tepees that serve as motel rooms. On the northwest corner of Archibald Avenue is a little defunct 1920s gas station (I B) (9670 Foothill Boulevard, Rancho Cucamonga) with Spanish Colonial recollections; it still extends a welcome with a porte cochere, too tiny for the cars of the fifties and sixties, but once again just right since the 1973 embargo. Next door, at 9656 Foothill, is Dolly's Diner (I C), long and miniaturized like a railroad car, which has been serving up hash browns since 1944.

On the northeast corner of Vineyard Avenue are the Thomas Vineyards (I D) (8916 Foothill Boulevard, Rancho Cucamonga), formerly the Cucamonga Winery (1839), the oldest winery in California. Now it lies across the street from the flashy Roller City (I E) (8874 Foothill Boulevard), designed in a style apparently the offspring of miscegenation between Polynesia and Texas, resplendent with shooting A-frame roofs, gold and salmon-red decorations, and intricate concrete-block screens.

The highway continues through a rural stretch; vineyards and fields are interrupted by great dark lines of fragrant eucalyptus windbreaks. The Magic Lamp Inn (I F) (8189 Foothill Boulevard) astonishes passersby with its abandonedly lumpy tile roof laid like the scales of a dragon. The restaurant is a heartfelt amalgam of multicolored brick, leaded stained glass and a cactus garden that forms a vivid union between the East and the old Southwest: pagoda meets hacienda, and it's true love.

The last part of this chapter's ride along Route 66 passes through towns that were once part of Lucky Baldwin's 54,000-acre rancho. The highway continues past them, to Los Angeles and the ocean, but our Route 66 for now starts at Redlands and ends in Arcadia, at Baldwin's house, where the Los Angeles Arboretum keeps alive 127 acres of the grandest personal fantasy of them all.

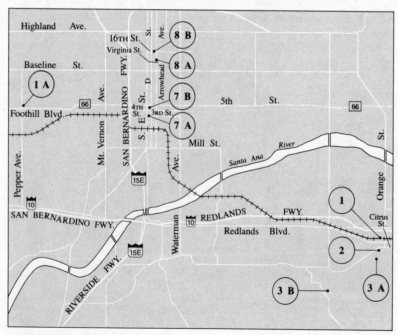

IV/ROUTE 66 (INSET 1)

IV 1 · SANTA FE RAILROAD STATION
West side of Orange Street, between Stuart Avenue and Redlands
Boulevard, Redlands
John Bakewell and Arthur Brown, Jr., 1909–1910

In Redlands, the Santa Fe Super Chief used to unload its passengers at a turn-of-the-century Tuscan temple. This monumental little railroad station, abandoned now but still in good condition, consists entirely of a long open-air gallery that runs parallel to the tracks. Paired Tuscan columns and a Classically detailed entablature, gleaming in cream-colored plaster, support a red-tiled roof with a pediment and a belvedere on each end. In between some of the columns, serving to relieve their relentless march, are pier-like walls that frame rectangular entryways and transoms garlanded with fruit and flowers. A small ticket office, the only required enclosure in this Arcadian climate, nestles up against the center. Nearby, a row of Italian cypresses echoes the row of columns. Warm breezes drift through the dark green boughs, and soft afternoon sunlight makes the white sufaces glow, conjuring up visions of Pliny the Elder waiting for the last train to Pompeii.

IV 1 · *Santa Fe Railroad Station*

IV 2 · *A. K. Smiley Public Library*

IV 2 · A. K. SMILEY PUBLIC LIBRARY
125 West Vine Street, on the south side of the street between Fourth and
Eureka streets, Redlands
T. R. Griffith, 1898; wings added in 1920, 1926, 1930
Open Monday through Friday, 9–9; Saturday, 9–5; closed Sundays and
holidays

So sweetly ingenuous in its details and its mostly one-story massing, the A. K. Smiley Public Library makes a number of Mission Style gestures, though its heart is clearly Romanesque. There is red tile on the roofs and white plaster on the walls; there's a rectangular tower in the center, echoed by four little lanterns; and there are four sinuously curved Mission end walls. But underneath the plaster is red brick, not adobe, on chunky granite foundations; and almost every edge is trimmed in richly carved Richardsonian sandstone, most enthusiastically in the double-arched entrance porch with its ribbonlike stone sign. The porch continues on each side as a covered arcade, proportioned like those on any California mission, except that the bases and capitals are made of precisely detailed sandstone and the voussoirs are alternately indented to reveal that the structure is brick.

Numerous wings have been added over the years, so the building seems to wander a little, especially since the top story of the tower—its dominant Mission Style feature—was lopped off. But the long wings allow lots of natural light into a solidly nineteenth-century interior of cream-colored plaster walls, tray ceilings, and intricately carved golden oak—in the bookshelves, the wainscoting and the exposed trusses, which rest on little stone gargoyles, no two alike.

IV 3 · TWO PERIOD FANTASIES
Along West Olive Avenue, Redlands

Redlands quickly became a citrus boom town after water was brought from the Santa Ana River in 1881. Lured by the mild climate and the prospect of easy profits in agriculture, wealthy Easterners poured in, stayed and constructed elaborate houses. A drive through the southern part of town reveals boisterously lavish, beautifully landscaped turn-of-the century estates. Most were designed in the fashionable styles of the day: Mission Revival, Queen Anne or Spanish Colonial Revival—persuasions that encouraged experimentation and elaboration. Two of these, the Mission Revival Holt House and the Queen Anne Morey House, are among Los Angeles' most grandiloquent statements about the California good life.

A · HOLT HOUSE
405 West Olive Avenue, on the south corner of Alvarado Street, Redlands
F. T. Harris, 1903; remodeled, 1905
Group tours can be arranged; call (714) 792-1447

This robust example of Mission Revival, something like the fancy-dress outfits of Mexican charros, contrasts a basically simple form with generous doses of intricate ornament. The main distractions on the two-story retangular block are the sinuously scalloped edges, outlined in maroon-painted sheet-metal moldings, along the many false-fronted Mission pediment walls and along the sec-

IV 3 A · *Holt House*

IV 3 B · *Morey House*

ond-story railing of a wraparound porch. The rosy beige stucco walls beneath this piping are made to seem three-dimensional with thick plaster cartouches, reveals and moldings of some unidentifiable exotic persuasion, perhaps Mayan; intricate Spanish Baroque motifs have been embroidered at every opportunity. The porch, which becomes a porte cochere on the east, is made up of Romanesque arches, so heavy that they seem to have squashed the acanthus-leaf capitals of their stout Richardsonian columns. Nonetheless, the braidlike edges and the rows of dots around the arches bring us back to the charro costume, with its multiple silver buttons. There is something Spanish, too, in a short tower that adds some vertical panache. The interior, on the other hand, is solidly Victorian, overflowing with exquisitely carved golden oak.

B · MOREY HOUSE
140 Terracina Boulevard, on the west side of the intersection with West Olive Avenue, Redlands
David Morey, 1890
Tours given on the first Sunday of every month, 1–5; admission fee

Beautifully restored and maintained (though recently given an overly enthusiastic paint job), the elegant but saucy Morey House, with its voluptuous curves and decoration, is an endearing, intricately joined piece of Victoriana that was built by a cabinetmaker for his wife. Although it is basically a simple block, its mass is broken up by several towers and bays. On the south a grand, indeed stupefying melon dome caps a cylindrical tower that rises above a wraparound porch. Except for the fish-scale shingles, this dome, with its enormous fins that swirl up to a pointed finial, would not seem out of place on St. Basil's Cathedral in Moscow. A northern tower, a rectangle set on the diagonal, marks a Classical entry below. At the second story, tall arched windows are surrounded by intricately carved wood: basket-weave patterns, acanthus leaves and Classical moldings—so sharply cut they seem cast in iron. One of the most bombastic Victorian structures ever, the Morey House was clearly confected by a man who anticipated a future of unprecedented good times.

IV 4 · RIVERSIDE COUNTY COURTHOUSE
East side of Main Street between Tenth and Eleventh streets, Riverside
Franklin Pierce Burnham, 1904

The Riverside County Courthouse, an amazingly exuberant Beaux-Arts fantasy, is particularly astonishing in the context of its romantic Spanish Style neighbors. It is said to have been inspired by the Fine Arts Building of the Paris Exposition in 1900, but it looks more like an extravagant wedding cake, crisp and sharp-edged, colored in cream-to-beige with elaborate white decoration. Its single-story mass and simple brick and stucco construction contrast with the façade of long Ionic colonnades, life-size human figures in heroic poses, plinths dotted with lions' heads, broken pedimented moldings around tall double-hung windows, balustrades capped with urns, writhing friezes, dripping grapes, and much, much more. Endearingly pompous and optimistic, the courthouse was surely designed to bolster local pride and to impress newcomers with the degree of civilization achieved in this county, which had been formed only six years before. Local pride has suffered serious setbacks in the smoggy decades since, but the building is a hardly tarnished reminder of sunnier days.

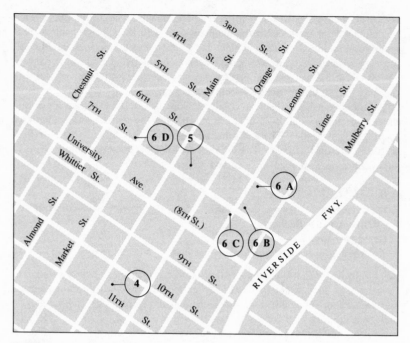

IV/ROUTE 66 (INSET 2)

IV 5 · RIVERSIDE MISSION INN
3649 Seventh Street, bounded by Main, Orange, Sixth, and Seventh streets, Riverside
Arthur B. Benton, Myron E. Hunt, Elmer Grey; later, G. Stanley Wilson,
*   with Albert Haight and Peter Weber; since 1971, Bruce W. Beebe*
Built from 1902–1935, and to the present
Originally called Glenwood Cottage
Tours given daily, 11:30 and 2:30

Descriptions of the Mission Inn (and there are many) are almost always replete with quotes. Gebhard and Winter quote Gustav Stickley, the publisher of *Craftsman* magazine and the de facto inventor of the Mission Style, who wrote blandly enough in 1904 that this was "a successful example" of same; they also quote George Wharton James, who, waxing eloquent, noted in 1914 that it was "full of charm and delight to the eye, enhanced by the wealth of romance, sentiments and history about it in every part." A folder in the hotel quotes "somebody" as having said, "The Mission Inn is not just something to look at. It is a place to feel and touch. It has a very special spirit." "It is," someone else has said, "the past, the present and the future."

This place is indeed so richly, stupefyingly full of wonders as almost to defy description. So it might be best to start with what it isn't. It isn't the greatest single architectural composition in Southern California; the Los Angeles Public Library ought to have that award. It doesn't include the most moving single space in Southern California; that must be in the Bradbury Building. It isn't even the most wonderful garden hotel; surely that is the Bel-Air. But it has the power to amaze and stagger the mind with more and more and more wonders than all the other three put together. If you could see just one building in Southern California, this would be the one. It's tacky, run-down and in spots even fallen into ruin; it lies in the basin where the most noxious air of Southern California goes to die; but it is full of care and love and imagination and desire and devotion and as full of panache as any building around. It was the lifework of one Frank Miller, who bought the twelve-room Glenwood Cottage, a small hotel that grew out of the family home, from his father in 1880 and was off on a Wincastrian building adventure that only stopped—dozens of world-famous guests and many medals later—with his death in 1935.

The place has to be fully described, because its fullness is its point. The wonders start outside, on all four sides, where the building meets the bordering streets in a variety of ways. The western side of the block, on Main Street, features an exposed concrete arcade and a row of tiny shops. The street, though, has been turned into a pedestrian mall, with care, sensitivity and no apparent success. Most of the stores have moved away, and the clatter of commerce has been replaced with the kind of sylvan peace that makes merchants' blood run cold. The north side, Sixth Street, has another concrete arcade above the sidewalk. Near the middle, the building leaps the street with a bridge to an annex where employees used to live, a forthright structure of exposed concrete and brick that glories in a candid revelation of ordinary building materials while it alludes enthusiastically to a misty Spanish heritage. Around the corner, on Orange Street, concrete buttresses fly across the sidewalk to the curb, setting up a regular rhythm and a syncopated procession of large and small elements that accompany you along the whole block, from chains made for giants to tiny gardens made for dolls. On the south, or Seventh Street side, is the main entrance. Between the sidewalk and the curb is a block-long, unroofed arcade, shaded by pepper trees; behind the arcade is a large, thickly planted garden, a sumptuous place for garden club receptions. Some remodeling here to accommodate a newer swimming pool is less wonderful, but most of the vast garden is intact, with huge arbors made of realistic concrete logs and a freestanding, ivy-covered Mission bell tower, in counterpoint to delicate rockeries of Japanese tininess.

Behind the garden is a lobby with the most gorgeous of polished wood floors, and beyond that, lunch is served in a wondrous open courtyard called the Spanish Patio, designed by Myron Hunt. The splendid fountain by Elmer Grey is also said to be Spanish, with fine polychrome tiles and four enormous creatures with water squirting out of their grins. The beasts are surrounded by asparagus ferns and overshadowed by a fat bouquet of luscious yellow and red rock roses. The views from the patio, sideways and up, are nothing less than astonishing, wonder piled dizzyingly on top of wonder. It is rumored that motifs from all twenty-one California missions are present in this cascade of Hispanicisms; but the place incorporates far more motifs than just these. The view diagonally up in one direction from the patio does go up to a massive arcade with mission bells in the openings, ending in a freestanding mission front like the fine one at the Mission San Antonio de Padua three hundred miles to the north.

The view in another direction, however, takes in a heavy log arbor with recollections of the great lodge at Old Faithful in Yellowstone; next to that is a turret, partly medieval-castellated, partly just strange, on top of which an altogether unrelated but beautiful balcony slides over to where a little piece of wall sticks out with a striking fan window over a door; on the right, the balcony wiggles past an Alhambresque row of windows. On the west wall are huge arches filled with glass and with French doors that open onto the patio; above these are Moroccan or Saudi Arabian or possibly Turkish balconies. In between everything are tiles depicting peacocks and double-headed eagles and what seem to

IV 5 · *Riverside Mission Inn*

be enormous ermine jumping upside down into a pot. On the north are more romantic balconies between della Robbia medallions and arcaded windows that lurch along in syncopated rhythms of their own. In one spot the windows are symmetrical; in another, there is a composition of two windows over three, with an unsymmetrical balcony. A giant heraldic escutcheon reads *"Está Vd. en su Casa, Amigo"* with "Glenwood" written high above that, surrounded by a padre and faithful Indians, all painted on rough concrete so that it is at once heavily Hispanic and strangely modern.

After returning to the lobby, you can walk up a stair to the second floor and come out, along the west, on the Middle Eastern balcony above the Spanish Patio. Behind it are the Lealea and Ho-O-Kan rooms, Oriental lounges that seem heartfelt—for Frank Miller had been decorated by the Japanese government. Then an opening on the northwest leads to the St. Francis atrium, a re-creation of a little European plaza with a bronze fountain in the center and a chapel on each side: one is tiny, with a low thirteenth-century ceiling; the other is huge, with a full-scale Spanish Gothic entrance and a dazzling gold reredos inside.

Back to the central stairway, you can climb up to a sunny fourth-floor pavilion with a cross-vaulted roof supported by twisted Solomonic columns; an ancient armoire stands against one wall. Big windows look down on the entrance garden, while doors on each side open onto long arbors of heavy red-stained wood that wrap around the top of the front wings. From here you can see a circle of Washingtonian palms around the pool and the Seventh Street arcade, which looks from above like an aqueduct, looping along the sidewalk and then within the garden as well.

The stair takes you up another floor to a remarkable view across the open top of the Spanish Patio to glassy upper galleries between late-Gothic crockets strangely reminiscent of the Milan Cathedral. High above the northwest corner is a clock tower with a little round railroad track on which figures slowly move around to present themselves on the hour. Looking down, the atmosphere is of some latter-day hanging gardens of Babylon: you peer through arcades in every direction to see gardens growing on roofs, inaccessible and unexpected. Nearby, groups of strange objects seem vaguely familiar. Perhaps they are chimneys or buttresses, though their function remains mysterious. Shapes that would normally be expected to be at the top of something, like the nearby San Antonio de Padua Mission front, are down at the bottom with walls climbing up past them, so that everything is jammed in, as in some dreamlike nineteenth-century vision of the past.

Then, on the northwest, there is a sudden escape to an upper-level Italian Renaissance piazza between one-story walls of ornamentally laid terra-cotta tile; in the middle is a long raised pool of waterlilies. You turn a corner and find yourself suddenly at the edge of a five-story-deep rotunda, where cantilevered stairs with thin metal railings swirl down and down and down. You turn another corner and suddenly, instead of Spanish, the style is all Chinese, and you look down over yet another set of patios. It is curious how the exposed terra-cotta block, a candid twentieth-century building material, can become, at will, Spanish or Chinese or even roughly Italian.

IV 5 · *Riverside Mission Inn*

IV 5 · *Riverside Mission Inn (detail staircase)*

A rain-cross symbol appears everywhere. It is said to have some esoteric ancient Indian meaning, but it was in fact invented by Frank Miller, who, in turning Glenwood into Riverside, was forced to invent just about everything. His city block of inventions, especially a vaulted portion designed expressly for Miller's diminutive twin sister, Alice, is full of surprises of scale and position. Things don't find themselves in ordinary circumstances; they are always special, separately and individually designed. The Mission Inn, almost uniquely, invites comparison with the Santa Barbara County Courthouse, where, also, everything is designed and the scale is dramatically bumped around, though mostly toward the grand. Here the architects were equally capable of squeezing it down toward the tiny.

This tour, lengthy as it was, missed a lot; there is always the sense here of more undiscovered wonders—if only you had taken a different turn. One intriguing possibility is to stay here, in weird palatial rooms that defy description, and to prowl the place at night. You will find, mixed with your acrophobia, high architectural adventure.

IV 6 · FOUR TOWERS

A · FIRST CHURCH OF CHRIST, SCIENTIST
South corner of Sixth and Lemon streets, Riverside
Arthur B. Benton, 1900

B · RIVERSIDE MUNICIPAL AUDITORIUM
East corner of Seventh and Lemon streets, Riverside
Arthur B. Benton; finished by G. Stanley Wilson, 1926–1929

C · FIRST CONGREGATIONAL CHURCH
West corner of Seventh and Lemon streets, Riverside
Myron Hunt and Elmer Grey, 1914

D · FOX RIVERSIDE THEATER
North corner of Seventh and Market streets, Riverside
Balch and Stanberry, 1928

This fine assortment of corner towers reinforces Riverside's magical fairy-tale atmosphere so fervently established by the Mission Inn. The white plaster tower of the Mission Style First Church of Christ, Scientist telescopes up in three stages, each one celebrated by a thick cornice of horizontal moldings and a ledge of red roof tiles; a shallow red dome on top sprouts a chimney-shaped finial. The tower of the Riverside Municipal Auditorium, though capped with a colorfully tiled dome, is as spare and serious as the rest of the building, a mixture of Mission and Spanish Colonial revivals, composed, like so many others in Riverside, of exposed concrete with large openings, sometimes arched, and plain strong detailing. On the opposite corner is the First Congregational Church, gray plaster over concrete, one of the first large buildings in Southern California to be done up in the Spanish Colonial Revival. Its tower is covered with an energetic, though geometrically precise brand of Churrigueresque ornament, designed about two years before Bertram Goodhue brought the style to feverish popularity with his buildings at the 1915 Panama-California International Exhibition in San Diego. The Fox Riverside Theater is assertively Spanish Colonial Revival with white plaster walls and red-tiled roofs and heavy arcades shading its two sidewalks. Its fat tower, built when cinema towers were meant to be grandly self-advertising, rises to a heavily buttressed octagonal belfry pierced by open archways; on top is a similarly shaped lantern with a long spike for a flagpole.

IV 7 · TWO BUILDINGS BY CESAR PELLI

A · SAN BERNARDINO CITY HALL
300 North D Street, at the west end of Third Street, San Bernardino
Gruen Associates (Cesar Pelli), 1972

The San Bernardino City Hall is probably the most endearing major building of the 1970s in Southern California, as well as the one that points most clearly to the future. On the one hand, it is a straightforward, uniformly curtain-walled block of alternately opaque spandrels and tinted-glass windows, inexpensive and, in the best sense, modest. On the other, the curtain-walled block has been shaved and sliced, mostly on its lower edges, then lifted on big, round columns with a sophistication, verve and wit that put the building in full control of a very large site and cause it to linger in the memory, as real art will.

It is not easy to define what constitutes wit in the slicing of curtain walls (or indeed in any other architectural gesture), but the quality seems to be recognizable in acts that are at once personal, surprising and special, even original, and at the same time inevitable, as if there were no other plausible way to approach the situation at hand. Cesar Pelli's San Bernardino City Hall has those concurrent qualities in full measure: it is both accomplished and easy. In Japan much is made of the art of the Zen butcher, who so perfectly slices meat where it wants to be sliced that it seems to cleave without effort and almost without the knife. The curtain-walled block of City Hall recollects this, as though it had been sliced without effort, leaving its reduced mass more spare, more alive, more expressive—and stronger, better able to command its site—than the block from which it emerged.

The surfaces over which the building hovers are handsome and pleasant, with, for instance, water sliding over pebbly ramps, but without the sense of easy inevitability that the building projects; you can still hear the designers wondering what to do next to fill up the vast space. Much of the excitement of walking around the plaza comes from the startling reflections off the chamfered surfaces at the lower corners of the building block. They leave you as forty-five-degree mirrors always do, altogether uncertain of what you are looking at, until you finally face them head-on and see yourself, peering back down from the chamfered edge, making your own decorative molding.

IV 7 B · *Security Pacific National Bank*

IV 7 A · *San Bernardino City Hall*

B · SECURITY PACIFIC NATIONAL BANK
402 North D Street, on the northwest corner of Fourth Street, San Bernardino
Gruen Associates (Cesar Pelli), 1972

A block away is Pelli's Security Pacific Bank, built at the same time as City Hall, in an alternative idiom, with skill and brio but without quite the magical ease of the other. Three sides of the bank block are gray Roman brick, slightly glazed. (A lower band of orange brick is covered by hedges.) The first story of the north side is of the same brick, but above that a glass curtain wall rises to face the San Gabriel Mountains, whose silhouette is magnificent when the smog allows it to show. Inside, a two-story bank lobby enjoys the view, as do offices on a balcony along the lobby. Here it is the landscape that turns it all into art, or at least into a satisfying Southern California experience: the drive-in tellers are reached through a closely spaced grove of queen palms, so that depositing a check becomes an activity that is both timeless and right up to date.

IV 8 · ARROWHEAD AVENUE FANTASIES
A · WITTE HOUSE
**1371 North Arrowhead Avenue, near the northeast corner of Virginia
Street, San Bernardino**
1926
Private residence

Here is one of L.A.'s witch's houses. It is appropriately minuscule, with all the
right features: a steeply sloped roof, shaggy shingles, goofy little windows with
precarious shutters, lumpy stucco walls and a rustic chimney. The features are
so right, in fact, that the architect of the much larger and more famous Spadena
house (page 215) in Beverly Hills is said to have had a hand in this one. The
present owners maintain it beautifully and have even built meticulously matching additions onto the back.

B · BUNGALOW COURT
**1550–1578 North Arrowhead Avenue, near the southwest corner of
Sixteenth Street, San Bernardino**
Jerome Armstrong, 1938
Private residences

This very pretty Spanish Colonial Revival bungalow court is a modest encapsu-
lation of a tropical paradise of the sort usually reserved for the rich only, as at
the Bel-Air Hotel (page 180). Its heart is its garden, in the center, where a lawn-
bordered driveway is shaded by overspreading white- and pink-flowering eucalyptus, maples, palms and a rare zucona tree; two Oriental magnolias bloom
pink and vivid purple from a grassy oval in the center. Along the sides, behind
flower beds and tangerine trees and mounds of shrubs and ivy, are the little
bungalows, with white plaster walls and red-tiled roofs and tiny, brick-paved
front porches. Although the walls are low, they sport big, handsomely proportioned windows, six panes over six, with large louvered shutters. At the back is
a beautiful Monterey-style apartment building, the original house here, which
was moved back to accommodate this garden of bungalows. Rural, rustic and
modest, yet sunny and urbane, this court displays many of the qualities people
migrated to California to find.

IV 9 · VIRGINIA DARE WINERY
**On the northwest corner of Foothill Boulevard and Haven Avenue, Rancho
Cucamonga**
Arthur Benton, ca. 1900

Surrounded by acres of ancient vineyards, tall eucalyptus windbreaks and the
overgrown remains of exotic turn-of-the-century landscaping, the Virginia Dare
Winery is one of the most impressive ruins in the region. It was constructed,
like the Mission Inn, in a rambling version of the Mission Revival Style, with
exposed concrete walls and a lively assortment of arched windows and doorways. But the arches are empty now, and the gray walls, covered in vines, have
crumbled into an industrial ruin, not very old, but already remote and romantic. A square tower, its roof fallen down, hangs above a hollowed-out arcade;
behind it are the high Mission end walls of the warehouses. The ancient con-

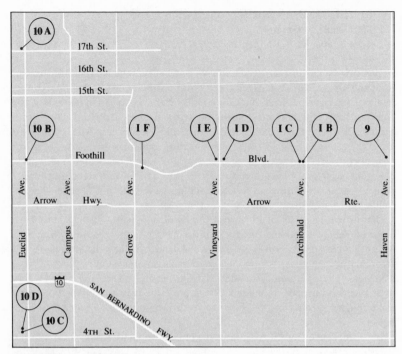

IV/ROUTE 66 (INSET 3)

crete, supported by once substantial but now decaying buttresses, has cracked and split and been mended with iron straps, now turning to rust. Only remnants of the great roofs and their timber trusses remain; the rest caved in long ago. Situated along a bleak section of Route 66 in the smoggy haze of the Fontana steel mills, the deserted winery resembles the deteriorating carcass of some huge beast; but it manages still to be impressive in its ruin. It might be unremarkable in an older landscape, but in Southern California, where hardly any buildings are going to make good ruins before they vanish, it merits at least a moment of silence.

IV 9 · *Virginia Dare Winery*

IV 10 · EUCLID AVENUE
From Upland to Ontario
George B. and W. B. Chaffey, developers, 1882

In 1891 two Canadians, George B. and W. B. Chaffey, founded the towns of Ontario and Upland, and connected them with the ambitiously scaled Euclid Avenue. For fifteen miles, from the Chino Hills on the south to the foothills of the San Gabriel Mountains on the north, this arrow-straight boulevard is lined with magnificent trees, much like a grand French allée. A fifty-foot-wide greensward down the center (where a streetcar used to run) contains a double row of palms or pepper or grevillea trees; along each side are some of the oldest and highest blue gum eucalyptus in Southern California. The dark rows of trees, much taller than any local structures, can be seen from miles away. Euclid Avenue offers, as well, a number of architectural points of interest.

One in particular seems to suggest the rustic sophistication that must have made life among the orange groves so pleasant fifty years ago. At 25 West Seventeenth Street, on the northwest corner of Euclid, is a finely detailed, two-story Georgian house (10 A) (ca. 1900), whose walls are made entirely out of local fieldstone. The round stones, collected from nearby washes and quarries, are mostly salt-and-pepper granite mixed with pieces of quartz and jasper; they create a rough yet softly colored contrast to the white-trimmed geometry of the house.

In the median of Euclid Avenue, at the intersection with Route 66, stands the imposing Madonna of the Trail Monument (10 B) (August Leimbauch, sculptor), which commemorates the 1826 expedition of Jedediah Smith and sixteen trappers, the first Americans to travel overland to Los Angeles. Erected in 1929 by the Daughters of the American Revolution, this sculpture of a pioneer woman and her children striding forward must have received many a sympathetic glance from the thousands of Depression immigrants who traveled Route 66 from the Dust Bowl to the promised land of Southern California.

Several blocks south of the monument, in Ontario, is Chaffey High School (Allison and Allison, 1935–1936), on the west side of Euclid Avenue between Fourth and Fifth streets. Though financed by the Public Works Administration in the depths of the Depression, it manages to flirt with numerous high-style idioms; its major alliance, however, is with the Churrigueresque, with special exuberance in the auditorium and the Chaffey Memorial Library. Most of the surfaces of both buildings are plain, even severe, but the façade and the major entrances are drenched in ornament whose form, scales and patterns were stylized and manipulated with abandon. In the spirit of the thirties, the architects abstracted Spanish and Mexican motifs with a number of Streamline and Zigzag Moderne flourishes. The simplification, enlargement, changes of scale, and repetition brought it up to date—and into line with a Depression budget.

The auditorium (10 C) faces the street with an eye-catching pierced false-front wall that rises up from its entry arcade the way the one does at the Mission San Antonio de Padua. A great Mission Style parapet molding with Streamline pylons at the corners emphasizes the place where the wall meets the sky. Because the higher volume of the auditorium is visible behind it, the front wall looks flat as though it had been made with a cookie cutter. While the molding could be even larger, the pylons are a fine size, with bannerlike concrete forms dripping from their bases onto the face of the wall. The library (10 D) uses many of the same volutes, niches, cartouches and moldings as does the auditorium, but its façade rises to a dominating point above the central entry.

These two buildings illustrate the extraordinary capacity of the firm of Allison and Allison to reinterpret vigrously either a historic or a current style and to whip up maximum drama within the rigid public-budgetary constraints of the Depression. The firm's designs include Royce Hall, the centerpiece of UCLA in Lombard Romanesque, downtown's California Edison Company in Classical Moderne, and MacArthur Park's First Congregational Church in English Gothic, all extremely spirited buildings.

IV 11 · CLAREMONT COLLEGES
Bounded approximately by Foothill Boulevard, First Street, Mills Avenue and College Avenue, Claremont

The six Claremont Colleges are organized on what is called in California the Oxford Plan: each school retains its individual character while the several schools share major facilities. Two of the oldest, Pomona and Scripps, have particularly romantic campuses, landscaped splendidly in a curious but comfortable amalgam of New England academic and Mediterranean monastic. The strengths of the two campuses are those that characterize Southern California: the buildings are modest, their architecture plain, but the dramatic shadows of luxuriant foliage on the sunny walls of intimate patios make for places that are poignant and powerful.

A · POMONA COLLEGE
Bounded approximately by Mills and College avenues, First and Seventh streets
Ralph Cornell, landscape and planning, 1919–1953
Founded, 1887; opened, 1888

Pomona, Claremont's first college (1887), is a liberal arts college of about 1,400 students. Its academic and administration buildings lie in an east-west band across the center of the campus; the men's dorms used to be to the north, the women's dorms to the south, though today the distinction is less clear. One inspired spatial sequence begins at a cool dark walkway, called Stover Walk (11 A–1), just south of Holmes Hall (at the southeast corner of College Avenue and Sixth Street). It runs the full east–west length of the block beneath the arching boughs and dappled shade of mature California oaks, sycamores and redwoods. From this path, others lead south into the bright openness of a sweeping garden, the Marston Quadrangle (11 A–2), framed on its long sides by huge trees and on the ends by two dignified structures: on the west is the vine-covered Carnegie Library (11 A–3) (Franklin P. Burnham, 1908) with a Classical portico, not unlike the 2,504 other library buildings that Andrew Carnegie presented to America; on the east is the massive white Classical-Moderne block of Bridges Auditorium (11 A–4) (William Templeton Johnson, 1931). Inside Bridges, the great vault of the ceiling was painted by Smeraldi in gold, silver and azure blue to depict, it is said, the constellations in the heavens on the night Mabel Shaw Bridges died.

South of this quadrangle is Myron E. Hunt's masterpiece, Bridges Hall of Music (11 A–5) (1915), of Palladian persuasion. Graceful tiers of steps lead up to an entrance loggia framed by pairs of composite columns and an arched entablature. The smooth pale gray concrete of the columns and moldings con-

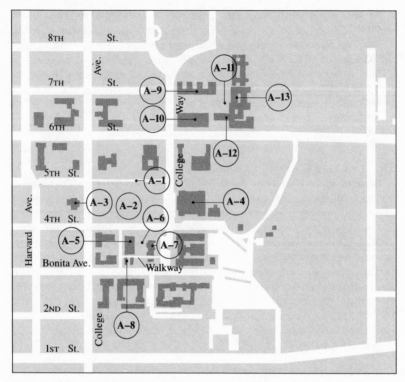

IV 11 A · POMONA COLLEGE

trasts with the vine-covered rough plaster walls and simple red-tiled roofs. Just east of Bridges, a grassy courtyard (11 A–6) lies hidden behind a plaster wall and tall plantings. The casual placement and rustic foliage of its plants soften the garden's formal composition of walls and walks. On the east side of the courtyard is Pomona's administration building, Sumner Hall (11 A–7), which had once been a Victorian resort hotel (1887), built by Claremont developers during the "Boom of the '80s"; it became the college's first building after the boom went bust. Myron Hunt moved it here in 1921 to get it out of the way and covered over the frills with gray stucco, now covered in ivy. The courtyard's south edge features a long walkway that leads through archways in Sumner and in Bridges, whose south end opens into an intimate cloistered quadrangle (11 A–8) with a little fountain in an oval of grass.

A second sequence of spaces is formed by the dormitories on the northern edge of the Pomona campus. A broad walkway, which begins on College Way, just north of Sixth Street, heads east between two dormitories: on the north is Walker Hall (11 A–9) (Sumner Spaulding and John Rex, 1953); on the south is Clark Hall V (11 A–10) (Sumner Spaulding, 1929). Both of them are styled in the austere manner of a Spanish monastery with tiled roofs and massive white walls pierced by simply framed openings. Open doorways along the south lead to small courtyards that are connected by another walkway, parallel to the first, through a lively succession of arches. The main walk ends at an austere but expansive courtyard where a circular Spanish fountain (11 A–11) splashes near a grove of gnarled gray-green olive trees. On the north, broad tiers of stairs lead up to a green playing field; the east and south edges of the courtyard are wrapped around by the handsome arcades of Clark Hall III (11 A–12) and, directly east, Frary Dining Hall (11 A–13) (both by Sumner Spaulding, 1929). Two powerful murals dramatize Frary's already dramatic entryway and dining room: "Genesis," by Rico Lebrun (1960); and "Prometheus," by José Clemente Orozco (1930).

B · SCRIPPS COLLEGE
Bounded by Mills and Columbia avenues, Ninth and Twelfth streets
Gordon B. Kaufmann, master plan and most of the buildings; 1927 and after
Edward Huntsman-Trout, landscape; 1927 and after
Founded, 1927; opened, 1928

North of Pomona College is Scripps College, a liberal arts women's college of about four hundred students, with one of the prettiest campuses in the United States. Its earliest buildings wrapped around a large open space that was given over to a great complex garden. Recent additions have intruded on this landscape, but most of the original design remains.

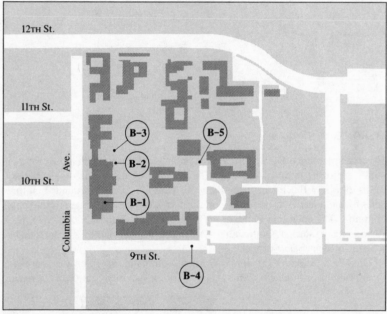

IV 11 B · SCRIPPS COLLEGE

The academic and administration buildings line the south and west sides of the campus, the dormitories line the north and east. All are in a low-key Mediterranean style with fine finishes and details: arcades, porches, ornamental screens, red-tiled roofs, stained and leaded windows and doors, tiled floors, fountains and sweeping stairs. The buildings, linked by continuous high plaster walls, form a solid wall along the street, while, on the interior, they break into individual structures separated by intimate courtyards.

One of the most pleasant examples of this courtyard format is the administration building, Balch Hall (11 B–1) (Sumner Hunt and Silas R. Burns, 1929), near the southwest corner of the campus. This many-winged building, which tiers down from three stories on the street to one story on the green, is arranged around two courts, each of similar size but different demeanor. The court on the south, filled with shaggy plants, is shaded by a long, covered colonnade and

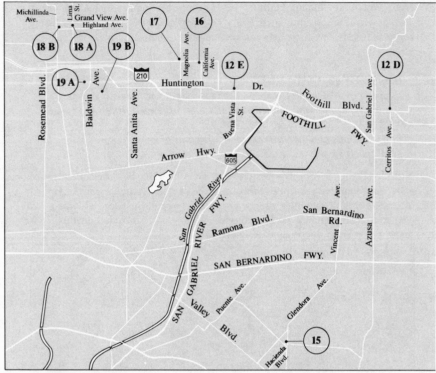

IV/ROUTE 66 (INSET 4)

twisting sycamores. The northern court, sunny and formal with a tiled fountain sunken into the middle, is enclosed on all sides by an arcade on slender columns. North of Balch Hall is another courtyard (11 B-2), surrounded on three sides by buildings, but with a view on the east side over low hedges to the grassy common. The enclosing building on the north is Dennison Library (11 B-3) (1930), one of Gordon Kaufmann's most accomplished, shaped and detailed like a Spanish Renaissance chapel.

The Music Building (11 B-4) (Gordon Kaufmann, 1935), on the south side of the campus, contains the finest single patio on campus, Seal Court, a rectan-

IV 11 B · *Scripps College*

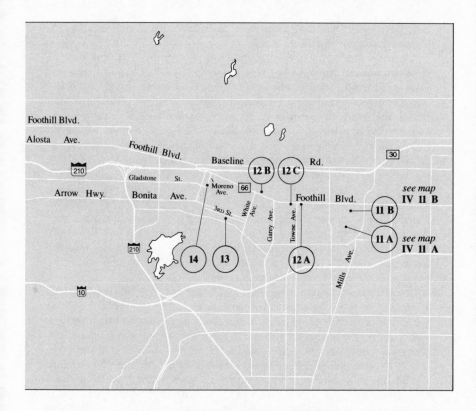

gular brick area bordered on three sides by a low colonnade and on the fourth by a one-story brick building. In the center, life-size ceramic seals squirt water from each end of a raised rectangular fountain. Chinese elms arch from planters cut into the fountain's four corners; their delicate foliage creates shimmering patterns of light on the surface of the dark pool.

The landscape includes formal rose gardens, the Elm Tree Lawn, an olive grove, allées of pollarded sycamores and ornamental oranges, picturesque greenswards planted with native oaks and sycamores, and a true secret garden, the Margaret Fowler Garden (11 B–5) (Edward Huntsman-Trout, 1924). Here lush plants cover the walls, and heavy wooden doors guard the entrances, nearly hidden in the corners. A wisteria-wrapped pergola divides the garden. The smaller sunny part, on the east, is paved in flagstones and planted with pink and white camellias and sweet-smelling dwarf orange trees; a fountain splashes against one wall. The larger part, on the west, contains formal parterres with a sunken pool in the middle, shaded by four huge olive trees. Along the south wall, a pergola of simple cylindrical columns protects a mural depicting Central American maidens. Along the north wall, an arcade with slender Corinthian columns and a red-tiled roof ends in a tiny chapel.

IV 12 · ROUTE 66 FAST FOOD
Claremont through Duarte

Route 66 offers a full panoply of commercial ventures, all designed to catch the eye of customers cruising past at fifty-five miles an hour. Somewhere along the way, the travelers will have to eat; and diners, restaurants and cafés line the highway ready to serve them.

A new restaurant row of the sort appearing all over the West runs along almost two miles of Route 66 just west of Indian Hill Boulevard in Claremont. Like multiple Athenas from the head of Zeus, these restaurants do not evolve over any decent period of time; rather, they spring full-blown from empty lots or farmland, ready for business. Along with the usual themed franchises are a large number of personal fantasies: the Shrimp House (12 A) (962 West Foothill), a life-size shrimp boat, floats in a sea of cars; the Cattleman's Wharf (12 B) (2777 Foothill) is a Western ranch house surrounded by tropical plants, old barrels and sawn-off telephone poles wrapped with rope to suggest that it has somehow made its way to the South Pacific. Since the restaurant business is statistically such a risky venture, the construction of such elaborate concoctions seems defiantly, almost grotesquely optimistic: clearly, remodeling is not easy. The Kyoto Garden Japanese Restaurant (12 C) (540 East Foothill Boulevard) has decided to play it as it lies, moving into a turreted and crenellated medieval castle, adding only a new sign and Japanese lanterns. The result is surprising, but further surprises surely await your arrival.

One of the very first golden-arched McDonald's (12 D) (563 East Foothill Boulevard, ca. 1955) continues to serve hamburgers in Azusa. The little building is all glass on the front, shaded by a wide overhang by day and brightly lit at night, so that it is always fully visible to passersby. The mullions, interior columns and counters are all stainless steel and look shiny, clean and modern. The rear of the structure is covered in gay stripes of bright red and white ceramic tile. Soaring yellow arches, streaked with neon bands, spring from the roof. On the highway side, beneath a big red sign, thick shrubbery protects a small patio, which becomes a particularly pleasant place to sit. With any luck, this little stand might escape the scrutiny of those McDonald's officials who seem bent on pulling everything indoors, into a limbo of characterless gentility.

Perhaps the oldest diner still operating along this part of the route is the Boulevard Café in Duarte (12 E) (1235 East Huntington Drive, 1936). This tiny green-stuccoed restaurant is a remnant of simpler, more frugal times. On warm days a long, breezy counter, barely enclosed by screens, opens up along the front.

IV 13 · STUDENT CENTER and DRAMA LABORATORY
UNIVERSITY OF LA VERNE
1950 Third Street, between B and D streets, La Verne
Shaver Partnership, 1973

The surrounding area offers scant preparation for the sight of these two buildings, but it is difficult to imagine what would. They are permanent tents, constructed of Teflon-covered fabric supported by center poles and mounted on concrete-block rims. The single-peaked Drama Laboratory stands upright with its white sides flowing down to a circular foundation. But the four peaks of the Student Center, like immense whirling dervishes, are raked at approximately sixty-degree angles from the center. Their swirling skirts are of uniform length, so the concrete-block bases flow up and down to accommodate the pitch. Squat concrete-block towers at the outside intersections of the cloverleaf plan contain stairways, toilets and barely noticeable entries.

IV 13 · *Student Center and Drama Laboratory*   **IV 14** · *Water Filtration Plant*

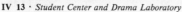

The interior is as remarkable as you might expect. The tent dances to its own rhythms, altogether independent of the dreary state-college furnishings below. Like the sides of a Big Top, the rumpled fabric is supported by huge steel rings around the columns. Giant cylindrical lights that are fastened onto these rings help a number of translucent plastic skylights along the bottom to illuminate the lofty spaces. Offices and locker rooms form a square on the lower level with a wooden sports court above them. Lounges and activity rooms fill in the curved edges. One of these spaces, the Student Health Center, is surreally inhabited by brightly colored plastic rooms, shaped like giant pharmaceutical capsules, in the best tradition of British pop architecture.

IV 14 · WATER FILTRATION PLANT
700 North Moreno Avenue, at the intersection with Gladstone Street, La Verne
Daniel A. Elliot, 1940

Once again Southern California pays tribute to one of her favorite subjects—rare imported water. The Water Softening and Filtration Plant of the Metropolitan Water District of Southern California is an imposing monument to this city's lifeblood and clearly states that the presoftening and filtering of water is an extremely important and serious undertaking. It is, as well, a splendid example of public-scale Spanish Colonial Revival architecture, constructed of unpainted poured concrete with its form marks showing, rust-colored metal sash windows and a roof of particularly luscious red tiles. The building is symmetrical in plan, two stories high, with one-story arcades that flank an entry court. Above the entry a parapet wall ends in a giant molding; behind it soars an exclamation-point tower capped with a tiled pyramid and then a red airplane-beacon finial. The official seal of the Metropolitan Water District of Southern California, mounted over the main door, illustrates that magic instant when William Mulholland, the city's power-brokering chief engineer, brought the water to Los Angeles 392 miles from the Colorado River, through his Los Angeles Aqueduct. A golden eagle and a California grizzly—both near extinction today—look on with amazement. Forty years in the smog has lent the building a certain patina, which it carries well. And the olive trees have aged enough by now to look reassuringly timeless.

IV 15 · DONUT HOLE

15300 Amar Road, on the east corner of Elliot Avenue, just west of
Hacienda Boulevard, La Puente
1968

This is drive-in drama at its best. "Donut Lane" actually leads through the
holes of giant fiberglass doughnuts that form each end of this little shed-roofed
stand. Inside the drive-through tunnel, hundreds of doughnuts of every shape
and color are displayed on cooling easels behind glass walls, with bakers working behind. The customer, then, is fully apprised of the day's selection before he
gives his order at the window. Placed in an expansive suburban setting of green
lawns and shrubs, this building is a casual but complete pop gesture, a rare
combination of drive-in and self-descriptive object. Earlier philosophers called
this sort of thing a *"Ding an Sich,"* and Robert Venturi, in *Learning from Las
Vegas,* one of our era's most influential books on architecture, defines the type
as "duck," after a stand on Long Island, shaped like a duck, where ducks were
sold. He may have missed the paradigmatic example: surely a self-descriptive
doughnut has more power over the human mind than a simple duck.

IV 15 · *Donut Hole*

IV 17 · *Aztec Hotel (detail of window molding)*

IV 16 · CRAFTSMAN BUNGALOWS

322, 328, 332 and 336 East Foothill Boulevard, on the southwest corner of
California Avenue, Monrovia
1913

This row of four well-preserved bungalows, nearly engulfed by mature foliage,
illustrates the flexibility of the Craftsman persuasion, which lay at the most
modest end of the Mission Style, very popular early in this century (page 331).
Each of these houses expresses the Craftsman ideals of simplicity, honesty and
close relationship to the outdoors, but each of them does it in a slightly different
way.

The corner house, No. 336, is made of wood with a graciously wide front
porch made of water-smoothed gray boulders gathered from local streambeds
and washes. The rough mottled-gray stones and the white-trimmed windows
contrast handsomely with the dark green shingles and exposed timbers. The
second house, No. 332, has a concrete-and-brick porch, covered this time by a
shed roof, with two big chimneys behind. The third house, No. 328, has an Oriental flavor. The rust-colored brick of its front porch complements the rich
green of its wood walls, gable latticework and thick vegetation. The fourth

house, No. 322, combines dark red shingles and white wood trim with the field-stone and brick of its porch.

IV 17 · AZTEC HOTEL
311 West Foothill Boulevard, at the northwest corner of Magnolia Avenue, Monrovia
Robert B. Stacy-Judd, 1927

Over the years, fantasies in every shade of excess have taken root along Route 66 as the hotels and motels beside the highway have engaged in every kind of theatrical display to lure patrons in off the highway. The Aztec Hotel, though it is only two stories tall, is probably the high point of this parade. Robert Stacy-Judd designed this resort hotel according to his own interpretation of pre-Columbian architecture, which he considered to be an eminently suitable basis for a true style for the Southland. He began with a straightforward structure, just one story high at the street, with balconied setbacks rising to the second floors. But this was merely the cake to the architect's icing; he then engulfed the plain walls with his own complex interpretation of Aztec ornament.

As in the Mayan Theater in downtown L.A. (page 28), the decorative elements *were* the style, so they were applied lavishly: every edge is framed with ornament, walls are covered with pre-Columbian murals, and even the glass in the French doors is angled to suggest the battered entrances to Aztec temples. The many-scaled moldings, the deep-to-shallow reveals, the various Indian heads, and more, have been coaxed out of free-form plaster with the sure hand of a master craftsman. The entry is flanked by heavily rusticated pieces whose shapes suggest at once rocks and snakes' tails; this leads through a foyer lined with tropical plants to an elaborate archway that opens into the lobby. Here wild ornament in its original paint erupts from smooth plaster walls. An enormous molding on the west wall flows down to protect a fireplace and the entrance to the Aztec Room bar. The result is so flamboyantly asymmetrical that this end of the room appears to be only a small part of some colossal Aztec pyramid that might be rising up through the building.

The Aztec Hotel has been sorely neglected, but there is still a palpable presence to this heartfelt landmark, which continues to stand out among the more up-to-date wonders along this strip. Although Mr. Stacy-Judd's pre-Columbian manifesto resulted in only a small number of buildings, this one still retains a throbbing fecundity. Offspring are surely coming soon.

IV 18 · TWO MORE PERIOD FANTASIES

These two buildings, both houses of successful immigrants, contrast the architectural longings of their two historical periods.

A · PINNEY HOUSE
225 North Lima, Sierra Madre
Samuel and Joseph Cather Newsom, 1886

The Pinney House, once a hotel, is grandiloquently Queen Anne, designed by California's most accomplished and enthusiastic period revival architects, Samuel and Joseph Cather Newsom. The Pinney house went up in the midst of the

IV 18 A · *Pinney House*

IV 18 B · *Mt. Alverno Convent*

state's optimistic "Boom of the '8os," in 1886, the same year that the Newsom brothers completed their unparalleled Victorian fantasy, the Carson mansion in Eureka, California. Here, in Sierra Madre, they began with a near-rectangular block, but transformed it into an image of opulent good cheer, thanks to their extensive repertoire of unbridled ornament. The most powerful element is a swan's-neck pediment that deeply and urgently overhangs an arched off-center entrance. Giant spools in narrow screens agitate the arch and the top edge of the porches on each side, but they go almost unnoticed next to the array of elaborate moldings, dripping brackets and sensuously turned columns. The south end is anchored by the required Queen Anne tower, but it is narrow and hexagonal and sports a surprising peaked roof. Every inch of the exterior is part of the highly volatile composition, which is thoroughly asymmetrical and amusing and yet somehow balanced and dignified. The house still faces the street from behind its white picket fence, and remains today a remarkable combination of civilized convention and mad Victorian effulgence.

B · MT. ALVERNO CONVENT
On the northeast corner of Michillinda and Highland avenues, Sierra Madre; entrance on Wilson Street
Wallace Neff, 1925

Not far from the Pinney house, the Mt. Alverno Convent, originally a private house, is one of the glorious 1920s fantasies by Wallace Neff. This grand master of the Spanish Colonial Revival was skilled at putting architectural elements from a make-believe past into gracious, flowing houses for clients who were not content with mere buildings, but wanted to evoke a whole private world. The Mt. Alverno Convent is a departure for Neff, since its correct Italian design (unlike the winsome Spanish that had never seen Spain) has a researched and serious past.

The house is a dazzling Italian villa, Michelangelesque. Its U-shaped block, a tall two stories high, wraps around a raised courtyard, which is enclosed on its open southern end by a Classical balustrade with a double stairway; two levels of graceful arcades provide shady outdoor areas on the northern end. Another tier of colonnaded porches is cut into the outside western wall, next to a quietly ebullient main entrance. The rust-colored stucco walls of the house are elegantly proportioned and robustly executed: handsomely carved sandstone embellishes every window and door and open archway; the tops of the walls are framed by shadowy wood eaves and the scalloped edges of the low red-tiled roofs. The courtyard now looks down over the remains of a long rectangular pool bordered by traditional tall Italian cypresses. The grounds, clearly distinct from the architecture, are well shaded, restful and inviting, with Italian stone pines, fruit trees, and grape vines. The landscape provides even more evidence of the strong connections, here, to the languorous mood and sunny climes of Italian fantasy.

IV 19 · LUCKY BALDWIN'S RANCHO
301 North Baldwin Avenue, Arcadia
Now the Los Angeles County Arboretum.
Open daily except Christmas Day, 9–4:30; admission fee

The romantic and at times bizarre atmosphere of the Los Angeles County Arboretum (19 A) is attributable largely to one man, Elias Jackson "Lucky" Baldwin. He arrived in San Francisco in 1853 at the age of twenty-five and quickly struck it rich in the legendary Ophir Mines of Nevada, acquiring nearly eight million dollars and a permanent nickname. After making even more money in the stock market, he decided to put his fortune into more tangible and enjoyable assets.

While riding through the San Gabriel Valley, Baldwin came upon Rancho Santa Anita and decided that it must be his. In 1875 he purchased the 8,500 acres and began to construct suitable backdrops for his true passions—horticulture, horse racing and women. Baldwin remodeled the original ranch house for himself, built a Queen Anne fantasy for his wife, and transformed the bulk of the acreage from dry chaparral to flourishing farmland and gardens. By expanding the old irrigation system, he extended plantings to the hillsides, cultivated exotic fruits and lined all the roads with ornamental trees. At the same

IV 19 A–3 · *Lucky Baldwin's Rancho, Hugo Reid Adobe*

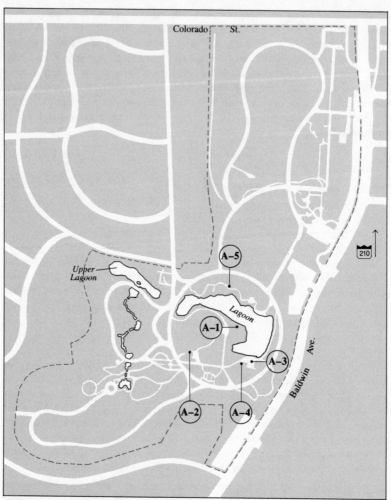

IV 19 · LUCKY BALDWIN'S RANCHO

time, he imported the finest Kentucky Thoroughbreds for breeding and horse racing; he then built the largest race track in California, which later became the Santa Anita Raceway.

A visit to the Centennial Exposition in Philadelphia in 1876 inspired Baldwin to construct his own Victorian folly, the Queen Anne Cottage (19 A–1) (Albert A. Bennett, 1881), a magnificent overgrown dollhouse that was designed originally as a palatial apartment for his diminutive third wife. After her sudden death, it was used instead as guest quarters for his business associates and lady friends. In more-recent years it has served as the backdrop for numerous movies and television shows. The dainty cottage sits on the end of a little peninsula, almost encircled by a lagoon and almost engulfed by tall palms and an overgrown jungle of rare specimen plants.

Its white-painted wood walls, under steep red-shingled roofs, are covered everywhere in delirious ornament with bright red accents. Near the middle rises an octagonal observation tower, allowing views through the trees of the surrounding estate and the lake below. A deep porch, framed in lacy wood screens, runs completely around the house, shading tall double-hung windows with stained glass in their upper sections. Visitors can peek through the windows to the tiny rooms—a bedroom, a bath, a study, a parlor, and a music and game room (there isn't a kitchen, for cooking was done nearby at the Hugo Reid Adobe, built by a previous owner of the property in 1839). Period furnishings are displayed against marble fireplaces, glittery mirrors and the finest woods in the world. An accompanying coach barn (19 A–2) (1879) is of the same Queen Anne persuasion as the cottage, lavishly ornamented and finely finished inside and out.

IV 19 A–1 · *Lucky Baldwin's Rancho, Queen Anne Cottage*

Not far from the cottage stands one of Rancho Santa Anita's earliest structures, the Hugo Reid Adobe (19 A–3) (1839). Although the Queen Anne cottage was more comfortable, Baldwin preferred to reside here and live the life of a ranchero. Like other traditional adobes, this one is a simple one-story building with thick walls, rough floors and a long wooden porch. The west side opens onto a walled, raked-dirt courtyard with a well, an outdoor kitchen and isolated plantings. Here is another rustic recollection of Old California, which is even more heartwarming now, after an extensive 1961 remodeling.

At his most prosperous, Lucky Baldwin owned one of the finest ranches in the West. Even when the bottom dropped out of his financial ventures, Baldwin's luck held and he was able to survive his last years by living off his land, California style, by combining agriculture and subdivision. His rare trees lined many of the streets in his new town, Arcadia, and at first helped the community live up to its name, though most of the trees were later cut down to make the streets wider.

In 1947 the State of California and the County of Los Angeles purchased the remaining 127 acres of the rancho and leased them to the county's Department of Arboreta and Botanic Gardens. The department restored the existing buildings and grounds, added greenhouses and displays helpful to local gardeners, and established sections for the display of plants from North and South America, Asia and Australia. They transformed the lagoon into a bird sanctuary,

IV 19 A–3 · *Lucky Baldwin's Rancho, Hugo Reid Adobe*

which lures migratory flocks, and brought back Baldwin's fancy peacocks. Since the prehistoric Gabrieliño Indians had once camped nearby, a tiny Indian village (19 A–4) with wickiup dwellings (tule reeds over rebars) was replicated next to the Hugo Reid Adobe. Nearby is an old rancho corral sharply defined by a thick hedge of prickly-pear cactus.

The county's greatest contribution, though, was the creation of a prehistoric garden (19 A–5). This was an expansion of Lucky Baldwin's original exotic plantings around the lagoon, an area that was already so thick with tropical plants that it had served as a set for the Johnny Weismuller Tarzan movies. Little paths wind through thick growths of cycads, redwoods and sago palms, some of the most primitive plants on earth; vines and bamboo create dark passageways; and a little treehouse pavilion offers displays that evoke thoughts of dinosaurs and murky primeval mists—if racing announcements aren't echoing across the street from Santa Anita Raceway (19 B), the descendant of Baldwin's race track.

Santa Anita's main building, which was designed in 1934 by Gordon Kaufmann, one of the local gentry's favorite architects, has been greatly remodeled and expanded over the years, but its 1930s high-style Georgian Modern still shines through. Its mint-green walls gleam with pale yellow accents while, along the front façade, bands of metal screens depict nearly life-size figures of a horse race in progress—all rendered in a lively perspective. Projecting wings along the front are made to look like tent pavilions with ornate iron columns, striped awnings and urns along the top. Such stylish details as streamlined reveals, hexagonal windows and metal-capped towers with exuberant finials recall the elegance and fine breeding of Baldwin's horses and provide a sophisticated setting for the enjoyment of this ancient sport.

V / PACIFIC COAST HIGHWAY

Palisades Park, Santa Monica

The Los Angeles plain is large and squarish, with impressive mountains at its north and east edges, the Pacific Ocean along the west and south. In the past decades that long Pacific shoreline and the people on it have come to be, for many, synonymous with what life in Southern California is all about. The people, especially the young surfers, are romantic figures, obsessively individualistic, courageous, rebellious, rugged, tanned, blond ("only their hairdressers . . ."), relentlessly young, their surfboards close at hand, unless you happen to see them as oafish, vacant-eyed "fun hogs." Fun, in either case, is the key ingredient, desperately sought after and sung about before and since the Beach Boys.

There are huge beaches (Venice is the largest, with 238 acres of sand and 1,260 parking spaces) and tiny ones (four acres at Corral, with parking along the highway), secluded ones and full ones. Few are empty, as attendance continues to climb from the sixty million who went to L.A. County beaches in 1977.

Our ride follows the surf most of the way, from Malibu in the northwest to Laguna Beach in the southeast, past the Getty Museum and Santa Monica and strange, bohemian Venice with its artists and filled-in canals, past Marina del Rey with its swingers, and then a string of comfortable, ordinary beach towns, Hermosa, Manhattan and Redondo, to hilly, pretty Palos Verdes, where the nostalgia for Ramona picks up. Then there is the huge port of San Pedro, and Long Beach, a midwestern outpost become big city where the Iowa State picnic once drew 150,000 and now oil wells in the harbor out past the *Queen Mary* are disguised as sleek Latin skyscrapers.

After that is another, more wonderful Venice where they've kept the canals and called it Naples, and then more beach cities, past the resort chic and sleaze of Newport to picturesque Laguna, where an art festival includes actors posing motionlessly in living representations of famous paintings. There, quite arbitrarily, we terminate our tour. The sun and the beach and the blond hair and the dazzle extend well over 250 miles from Santa Barbara to the Mexican border, so there's more for a return trip—with or without your surfboard.

V 1 · MALIBU
On the Pacific Coast Highway, approximately 18 miles north of Los Angeles

---

The very word Malibu conjures up visions of sparkling surf, sun-drenched sand, bronzed surfers, and glamorous movie stars at play. Unlike most armchair images of romantic places, this one is absolutely correct.

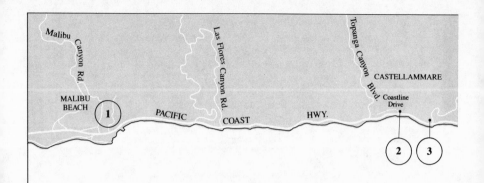

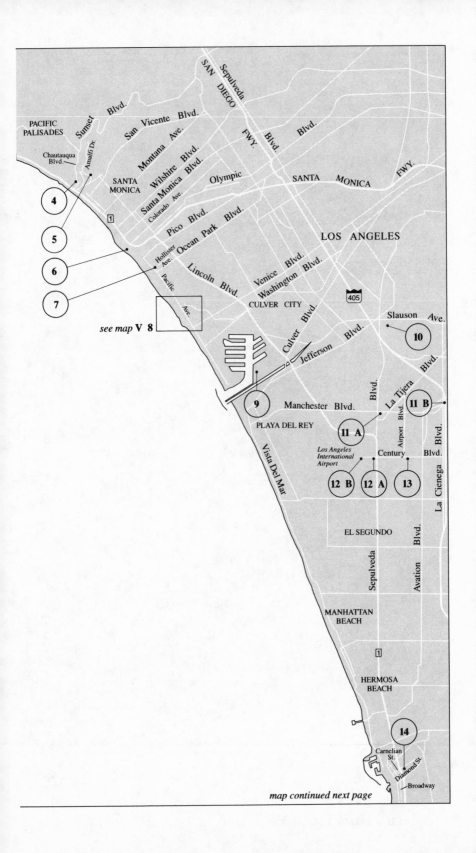

PACIFIC
PALISADES

Chautauqua
Blvd.

Sunset Blvd.

Amalfi Dr.

San Vicente Blvd.

Montana Ave.

Wilshire Blvd.

Santa Monica Blvd.

SANTA
MONICA

Colorado Ave.

Olympic

SAN DIEGO

Sepulveda

FWY.

Blvd.

Blvd.

SANTA MONICA FWY.

LOS ANGELES

Pico Blvd.

Ocean Park Blvd.

Hollister Ave.

Lincoln Blvd.

Pacific Ave.

Venice Blvd.

Washington Blvd.

CULVER CITY

405

Slauson Ave.

4

5

6

7

see map **V 8**

Culver Blvd.

Jefferson Blvd.

10

9

Manchester Blvd.

PLAYA DEL REY

Blvd.

La Tijera

11 A

11 B

Los Angeles
International
Airport

Century Blvd.

Airport Blvd.

La Cienega Blvd.

Vista Del Mar

12 B

12 A

13

EL SEGUNDO

Blvd.

Sepulveda

Aviation Blvd.

MANHATTAN
BEACH

1

HERMOSA
BEACH

14

Carnelian St.

Diamond St.

Broadway

map continued next page

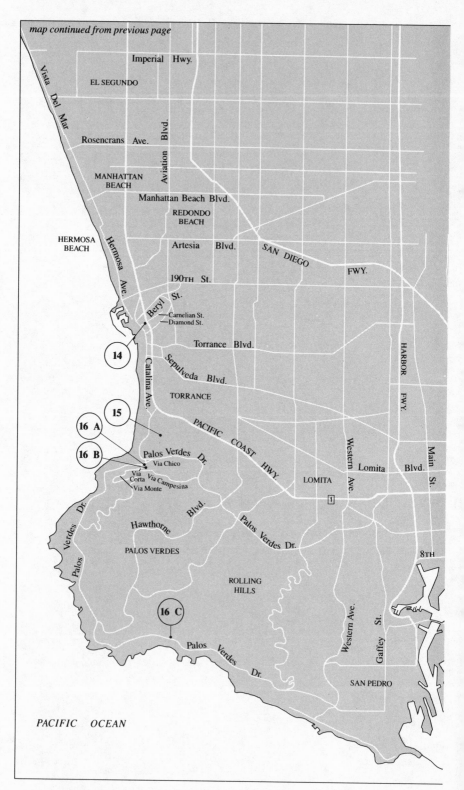

PACIFIC OCEAN

V/PACIFIC COAST HIGHWAY

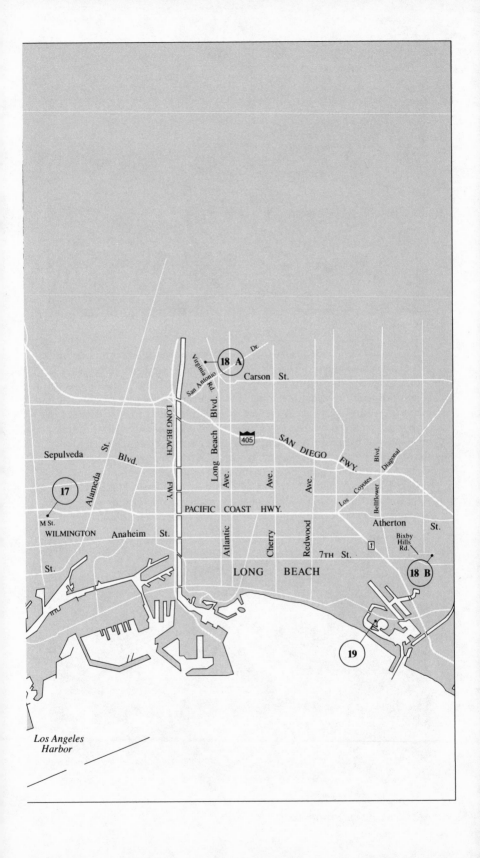

V 1 · *Malibu*

The melodic name Malibu, of Chumash Indian origin, is taken from the title of a Spanish land grant. In 1892 Frederick H. Rindge purchased 16,350 acres of this seaside land, hoping to develop a "California Riviera." Upon his death eight years later, his widow determined to maintain the property as a secluded estate. For thirty years she prevented all public encroachment with miles of wire fences patrolled by armed guards, civil and criminal suits against trespassers, and even by dynamiting of her own roads when people repeatedly broke through. Eventually the public had its way, when the Supreme Court allowed a right of way for the Pacific Coast Highway along her seashore.

In the 1920s Malibu Colony was developed at the foot of Malibu Canyon. Here, sequestered behind security gates, a number of movie stars made their homes, so Malibu became well-known to cinema fans. Just a little south, curv-

V 2 · *J. Paul Getty Museum*

ing gracefully from the simple blue and white towers of the Malibu Pier, is one of the most beautiful crescents of public beach in the Southland. With one of the best summer wave breaks in California, this shoreline has been savored by surfers and their retinue since surfing's resurgent popularity after World War II. Many surfing movies and competitions of the 1950s and early '60s took place here, reaffirming Malibu's paradisiacal image among the nation's youth.

Malibu has recently been infiltrated by some grotesquely ostentatious developments, from the new campus of Pepperdine College, like an overscaled motel set in obscenely vivid emerald lawns, to a movie star's crenellated castle made with multicolored rocks right out of the toy box. But it remains home to many other stars, still in seclusion, and to the surfers, still riding endless perfect waves; and it's still just as you might imagine.

V 2 · J. PAUL GETTY MUSEUM
17985 Pacific Coast Highway, Malibu
Langdon and Wilson, Stephen Garett, architects; Norman Neuerberg,
*   historical consultant; Emmet Wemple and Associates, landscape*
*   architects, 1972–1973*
Call (213) 454-6541 for an appointment

Though it is Disneyland that serves as the chief lightning rod for the world's attacks on Los Angeles' peculiar reconstitutions of the real and the phony, the J. Paul Getty Museum in Malibu presents a far more complex and perplexing instance of the area's inversions. The reality is meant to be a villa in Herculaneum, the Villa dei Papyri, which was buried under sixty feet of Vesuvian volcanic mud (not ash) in A.D. 79. In the eighteenth century it was accidentally discovered, and ruined, by treasure hunters hacking out underground tunnels. The miners took notes and made a floor plan with, we have to suppose, delicate, painterly eighteenth-century sensibilities. Subsequently the tunnels caved in, leaving the world with some filtered memories. Of these, an extraordinarly rich oilman, J. Paul Getty, ordered a concrete vision made.

And it came to pass that it was made near his house, in a canyon along the Malibu coast, which had been planted to appear highly Mediterranean. The canyon sloped sharply up from the sea, so the architects caused the sprawling Roman villa-of-the-memory to be propped up on a lofty concrete parking garage, at least as authentic as the vast parking lot at Disneyland. In the villa are housed three important collections: Greek and Roman antiquities, on the main level; paintings, mostly fifteenth- to eighteenth-century, on the level above that; and decorative arts, especially French furniture, 1670–1790, in a series of rooms also on the upper level. More is coming: the staggering sum that J. Paul Getty bequeathed his relatively small museum will make it one of the wealthiest in the world; it is put, therefore, in the position of trying to devise ways to do more for the world of art than just driving up the cost of Old Masters past what others can afford.

The limited parking below restricts the number of visitors that can be accommodated above and requires that you make a phone call to reserve a place, which is free. The system, for all its bother, seems altogether felicitous: it makes a trip to the Getty a special outing, something like a free pass to Disneyland.

But for all the pleasures in this sybaritic canyon, something is not right: the grasp on make-believe is unsteady. The Getty has somehow been caught halfway in the local reversal of the real and the phony, and it comes off more Beverly Hills than Roman, more 1970s than 0070s. Many knowledgeable people love it; others loathe it. Some of us figure that if we could just put a finger on exactly what is the matter, half the problems of our time might suddenly come clear. Many architects, of course, hate it because it is historicizing, because it has a specific model in the past. I can't see anything wrong there: that has been a useful basis for design in the five centuries since Leon Battista Alberti, with excellent effect, and it is hard to believe that a Classical villa wouldn't make a better setting for Classical sculpture than the standard 1950s Savings-and-Loan Style affected by many recent museums. Some architects have offered up the premise that there is good and bad Roman, just as there is good and bad everything, and that they believe this to be the latter. Too easy. Still others opine that the charge to copy a no longer visible villa, not fully described, was too narrow, that it did not engage the passions of the architects who, unconvinced, are unconvincing. That seems closer.

My own version worries about the extraordinarily bloodless, attenuated thinness of it all, which doesn't come off quite ethereal, but certainly has none of the robust touchable three-dimensionality that original Greek and Roman work seems to have. It is as though the attenuation of shapes from Baroque to Rococo (from Bernini, say, to the Adam brothers) continued without stop to our own day. Reconstructions of the past always have a great deal of the present in them, as we can see in any Victorian recall of Classical works; and at the Getty, the flattering glance of those Rococo diggers in Herculaneum is extended into the rather flimsy palette of the modern builder, dependent on slim light tracks and acoustical tile ceilings. Alas, the paintings that are counted on to fool the eye do not, and the place seems hardly ever really Roman or convincingly anything else, though some remarkable places are discernible through that wet blanket.

Access is up from the Pacific Coast Highway on a driveway made of giant concrete boulders, with a pretty little classical-romantic streamlet babbling down the middle. From the altogether unprepossessing parking garage, you walk along the front of the structure, past one handsome little fountain to an elevator, which takes you up to what is meant to be another world. Maybe the mistake is slipping the visitor into a corner of the long, symmetrical peristyle garden via what seems to be the gardener's entrance, instead of on axis, where the quality folks would have come. The long garden is a puzzle: most of its plants are overwhelmed by vast stretches of real marble underfoot that seem fake; on the walls are *trompe l'oeil* paintings that don't quite *trompe*. A real pomegranate tree, which you might not notice at Disneyland, seems a miracle of life.

The real miracles start just inside the door, past a thrillingly lavish marble lobby: wide doors at the back of the lobby open onto a peristyle with a rectangle of waterlilies down the middle, perpendicular to our approach; rooms on the left contain beautiful marble statues, like figures arrested in a dream that promise at any moment to awaken. The Getty Bronze, which appears soon after, has come alive already. This one might have been given life by the great Lysippus 2,500 years ago; it has never lost it.

On the other hand, the spaces where this bronze and other masterworks stand seem to have been denied life. Real Roman spaces of any period (I am certain of this) share one quality: power. Sometimes they are ugly, sometimes they are dull, but they are, so far as I know, never puny. It's as if McDonald's had decided to insert a Roman villa motif into one of its theme restaurants.

Past the west porch of the villa, the scene undergoes a great improvement; one wonders if those eighteenth-century miners with their flat eyeballs had missed the west garden, for it is fresh and lively and altogether three-dimensional, focused on a delightful fountain with a tiny central pyramid and little steps and Classical statues spouting water. The view from here is the best of all, through the building toward the east, past water in an atrium and the panel of water in the peristyle to another fountain playing in the east garden.

I have a feeling in these galleries much like the one I sometimes get in the houses of very rich and tasteful people—that they like their really fancy possessions better than I do, but oh how I covet the wonderful little things in the vestibules. My favorite is a box of lead fish from classical times, which were made for asking or thanking the gods for a successful catch. After those fish, it is easy to take the famous Lansdowne Hercules for granted, its dignity helped not at all by the presence overhead of beams whose phoniness is highlighted by the light slots in them.

V 2 · *J. Paul Getty Museum*

Upstairs the first item of business is a series of period rooms, which must have given Mr. Getty much pleasure. My own pleasures focus on just one of them, of carved oak painted gray and gilded, made for a house in Paris in 1755. There are, as well, partial room settings that manage to give offense with, for instance, ceiling paintings in aluminum frames just a few inches below acoustical tile with strip light fixtures all around.

The painting collections are meant to focus on Renaissance and Baroque, but again the thrill is in the ringers. My favorite of them all, not large, though it seems enormous, is the dazzlingly pretty "Spring," Opus 326 (1894), the Roman festival of Cerealia painted by Lawrence Alma-Tadema.

A museum far away that revels, like the Getty, in elements of make-believe is the Galleria Borghese in Rome, which for a long time was regarded as the finest private art collection in the world. The Getty, with all its money, will soon have to aspire to this title. Both have rich marbles and lush gardens; both fake Classical background for Classical, Renaissance and Baroque works of art. But the Borghese is convinced, and convincing, real make-believe, lavish and proud. The Getty is playing its *trompe* card too, but never quite with authority—with too much guilt and not enough gilt. Noël Coward could have warned these earnest architects about the perils of the real in Southern California.

V 3 · SPANISH COLONIAL REVIVAL GAS STATION
17301 Pacific Coast Highway, at the northwest corner of Pacific Coast Highway and Sunset Boulevard, Castellammare
ca. 1925

The only thing remarkable about the Chevron gas station at the end of Sunset Boulevard is how it is brightened by its designer's enthusiasm for the Spanish Colonial Revival. Rough-cut, hand-hewn timbers support canopies over the gas pumps. These roofs and that of the little station office are covered in red tiles, the apparently hand-formed, old-fashioned kind that are laid on with thick glops of mortar. The walls of the office are covered in lumpy white stucco, as if smeared over adobe bricks. Red-tile vents and geranium planters complete the picture. Here you can see how well the area's favorite idiom is prepared to clothe functions quite new to it. Who could have predicted that Spanish Colonial Revival gas stations would be an idea whose time had come?

V 4 · EAMES HOUSE
203 Chautauqua Boulevard, Pacific Palisades
Charles Eames, 1947–1949

We have made a point in this volume not to brag about wonderful houses that we've been allowed to visit but which the reader can't enter without an introduction, unless there is enough to see from the street to make a pilgrimage to the outside worthwhile. There are two houses, however, that force us to break our rules: La Miniatura, Frank Lloyd Wright's Millard house in Pasadena (page 318), which involves peering rudely through gaps in a hedge; and Charles and Ray Eames' house of 1947 in Pacific Palisades, which is barely visible even if you drive up a long distance past the NO TRESPASSING signs. The latter structure, in its hard-earned simplicity, says more about what's good about Southern California, about abstraction and perfection, the monumental and the miniature, than perhaps any other buildings in Los Angeles. Besides, though it is Ray Eames' very private home now, occasional groups do get a chance to visit, and the future may hold more chances.

The signals that the place gives out are deliciously conflicting: two little box-shaped buildings sit in a eucalyptus grove at the head of a meadow that drifts down to the top of a cliff and a view of the sea. The grass is the kind that used to cover California, golden in the summer, brown in the fall, bright green in the winter and spring. Here, in sight of the ocean in Los Angeles, where ground prices approach that of platinum, the sheer sybaritic crazy luxury of this low-key meadow dazzles the imagination. The house and its studio were demonstrations of the delicate and difficult act of raising to a high art the straightforward juxtaposition of standard industrial building materials, four-inch H columns and twelve-inch open-web joists, with all the connections visible. Sheet materials fill the openings. Many of the surfaces are translucent or transparent, so the shadows of the eucalyptus make luxuriously rich, endless patterns on the inside walls, which also display a wondrously grand and tiny and bright collection of folk art. There is a great story about the steel being delivered to the site for a house that was designed to look like a bridge—very popular in 1947—and being instantly reorganized by the Eameses into the two little boxes that were built.

It's a sustaining pleasure to realize that something so perfect could be so spontaneous, so undoctrinaire.

But all the organizational feats and the structural chutzpah and the wonderful collection of little objects and even the magic meadow don't themselves account for the sense of peace and satisfaction that the house induces in the visitor. It may be the only place in Southern California where the real and the romantic are both operating full tilt.

V 5 · *Burns House*

V 5 · BURNS HOUSE
230 Amalfi Drive, Pacific Palisades
*Charles W. Moore, architect; Richard Chylinski, associated architect; Tina
 Beebe, color consultant, 1974*
Private residence

There is surely some impropriety in pushing, or even describing, one's own work in a volume such as this; and in the Burns house the test of public visibility is only barely passed—the house is on an alley, invisible from its entrance side, and only partly visible from Amalfi Drive where 230 ought to be. But there is a clear view of it from Adelaide Street, across Santa Monica Canyon in Santa Monica, just east of Fourth Street. And the house exhibits, even from that distance, a set of characteristics we thought broke new ground. It is meant to be a private world, spacious on its seventy-five-foot-wide lot, and redolent of Southern California's past, distant and recent, Hispanic and Hollywooded.

Inside there is a carefully orchestrated three-way schizophrenia among: a room (the middle-height mass on the right, looking across the canyon) devoted to serious music, with a fine pipe organ; a tower room (the highest mass, in the middle) for serious writing, with a high and dark Edgar Allan Poetic stairway leading up to it, lined with books; and a pool (in front of the house, from this vantage, and behind the diagonal flat arch that frames the owner's view of the canyon) which serves as the center for a partly open-air, but private, easy and open, sybaritic Southern California style of life.

Color took on unusual importance in order to accomplish the orchestration of these three worlds—the recollection of Southern California from Ramona to Deanna Durbin—and the easy insertion into its setting of this hillside house that rises to three stories in a neighborhood mostly of one-story houses. Every surface, inside and out (there are some fifty-five altogether), is painted a different color, from mauve through gray to ochre on the outside, and from beige and gray to white inside to make ambiguous the passage of the sun across the walls, to increase the apparent size inside, and to summon up as full a set of Movieland memories as our recollection of colors might allow.

V 6 · SANTA MONICA PIER
End of Colorado Boulevard, Santa Monica
City of Santa Monica Engineers, 1909–1921

The Pacific Ocean is Los Angeles' greatest open space. Some enjoy this expanse from boats and surfboards, or with scuba gear; others enjoy it from the beach, and others still can get out on the water on an amusement pier. The Santa Monica Pier is the last one remaining of several that were constructed around the turn of the century. Gone now are its most fanciful attractions: the Byzantine La Monica Ballroom, the world's largest; the Ocean Park Bathhouse, a huge Moorish fantasy; and a lineage of thrilling roller coasters. They have all either burned or been torn down, but there are still a few enticements left, along with the Pier itself (even though much of it was washed away in a 1983 storm), to delight visitors.

A rainbow arch of neon strips punctuated with backlit lettering announces the pier along Ocean Avenue. Beyond this a steep concrete bridge leads down the palisades to a wooden deck. The walk over the bridge is tantalizing: everything is laid out before you, while the scents of popcorn, hot dogs and fish-'n-chips drift up from below, along with the sounds of seagulls, the surf and a merry-go-round's calliope.

V 6 · *Santa Monica Pier*

The first section houses a honky-tonk collection of snack-shacks, souvenir stands and games of chance. But the pointed arches and round corner turrets of the merry-go-round building and the domed towers of Sinbad's recall magical Moorish splendors. The last length of the pier, only a roadway wide, is reserved for more serious oceanic pursuits—fishing, boating and simple observation of the water. Here the wooden deck becomes a reverse fountain, a festive meeting of architecture and water, with people in the middle and the waves all around.

Along Ocean Avenue to the north stretches Palisades Park, a slender, long grassy strip squeezed between the street and the eroding bluffs. The park has some high points: at the end of Idaho Avenue is a rustic gateway of stone, red-wood and Batchedler tiles, designed by the Greene brothers in 1912; there's an intriguing antique camera obscura in the senior citizens' center; and, best of all, are glorious views of the sunset over the Pacific, framed by obligatory groups of gently swaying palms.

V 7 · HORATIO WEST COURT
140 Hollister Avenue, Santa Monica
Irving Gill, 1919
Private Residences

This modest apartment court is probably the most accessible, both geographically and intellectually, of the works of Irving Gill, a fascinating—if a bit enigmatic—Southern California figure of the early twentieth century. He died almost forgotten in 1938, but has become a regional hero since Esther McCoy's important *Five California Architects* (of which he was one) appeared in 1960. Not many of his buildings are left, and visiting most of the ones that are has to be classified as an accomplishment rather than a thrill. The excitement, in visiting his work, of collecting shreds of evidence of a fine mind at work is countered by the relentless puritanical self-denial of the architecture itself. It is a self-denial that hovers somewhere between high art and straight masochism. But it is undoubtedly this aspect of Gill's work that ensured his fame: he refined the plain white walls of the Mission Style into the even plainer white walls of the International Style with an ardent conviction closely parallel to the lifelong architectural refinements of Ludwig Mies van der Rohe. Chapter 10 will describe Gill's work in the city of Torrance, which is, to put it in its best light, astringent in its purity; but the Horatio West Court, very close to the beach, has a sun-bleached air of leisure about it that can be altogether seductive.

The format is modest, even tiny: a driveway bisects a sixty-foot-wide lot; on each side are two little two-story connected houses. The houses differ slightly from each other, with a careful juxtaposition of plain walls recollective of cubism or perhaps De Stijl, except that Gill allows the penetration of arched openings. Strip windows around the top of some volumes light porchlike rooms, each with a view of the sea. At the back, where there are tiny garages with rooms above, the cubist composition grows even more miniature. The group of dwellings has been lovingly restored, and for all its modesty, and its tininess verging on the quaint, it is, thanks to the care that animates every corner, a masterpiece.

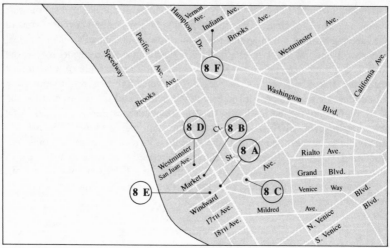

V 8 · VENICE

V 8 · VENICE
South of Santa Monica

Abbot Kinney, a midwesterner who made his fortune in Sweet Caporal ciga-
rettes, arrived in Los Angeles in 1880 after extensive world travels. After years
of boosting culture and education in this new frontier, he decided in 1904 to
shift his attention to the transformation of 160 acres of marshy tidal flats, which
reminded him of Venice, Italy, into a Venice of America. This would be the center for a cultural renaissance that would sweep the West Coast and then the
nation. He hired Norman J. Marsh to make a city plan that would connect Pacific Electric rail lines with his new streets, his sixteen miles of canals and an
Italianate central business district. He imported gondolas and singing gondoliers, and built arched Venetian bridges over the canals, a first-class hotel on a
new pier and a chautauqua hall. Here he presented prestigious performers including Sarah Bernhardt, Madame Modjeska and the Chicago Symphony, but
the public's response was cool. People took advantage of the free trolley rides
into Venice, but their interests lay in the simpler pleasures of the surf, the sand
and the curious community itself.

So, just two years later, Kinney expanded his concept of culture and recast
his high-toned community into a fun zone. Starting with a midway like the one
at the Portland World's Fair, he developed Venice over the next four years into
the largest and most elaborate amusement park in the world, precursor to the
modern theme park. The 1915 Venice Grand Prix, beauty contests and air shows
were staged to keep the crowds coming. For a decade Venice was Los Angeles'
favorite playground and resort, and Hollywood movie stars built fashionable
homes along the canals.

Then a series of fires and other natural catastrophes, engineering blunders,
civic corruption and general neglect helped to turn this once glamorous city
into a seedy backwater. The worst blow was the coming of the automobile,
which made many other resort areas equally reachable. Venice languished, and
its picturesque canals became a nuisance; in 1928, after residents voted for annexation with Los Angeles, most of the waterways were filled in.

Small pieces of Mr. Kinney's elaborate commercial center are still standing around the intersection of Windward and Pacific avenues (8 A), where only the sidewalk arcades of the old St. Marks Hotel and a few other buildings are left. The colonnades of heavy Corinthian columns that once shaded many of the sidewalks are no longer continuous, but they manage to hint at a glorious past. An eerie mural printed on a blank party wall of one of the buildings, the St. Charles Hotel (8 B) (25 Windward Avenue), extends the arcades by *trompe l'oeil* into some catastrophic future after all the inhabitants have fled. At Windward and Main Street, the outline of Kinney's Grand Lagoon (8 C) can still be seen, filled in now by a traffic circle. And there are still a few canals, within the area bounded by Pacific and Ocean avenues, Virginia and Sherman Canal courts, but the gondoliers are gone.

The real estate boom of the late 1970s and early '80s, especially for land washed by smog-clearing coastal breezes, has inspired a new wave of building in old Venice. Here are a few of the most inspired, or at least the new places most recollective of Abbot Kinney's unbounded high spirits.

Your tour of Venice should also include a stroll along the boardwalks to view the enduring oceanside carnival that has been the main draw since the town was founded. The chief attraction these days is the dazzling choreography of the roller skaters, but the enticements are annuals, not perennials; perhaps by the time you read this the astonishingly well-coordinated locals will be propelling themselves on their noses, or their ears.

D · SPILLER RESIDENCE
39 Horizon Avenue, between Pacific Avenue and Speedway
Frank Gehry Associates, 1980

By design and choice of materials, the towering Spiller duplex works hard to achieve a cheap, unfinished look. Unpainted corrugated metal siding sheaths the walls, whose studs continue on behind the aluminum-frame windows; the roofscape is littered with pieces of exposed structural wood framing, crystalline skylights and steeply angled solar collectors. As in Italy, the walls of this city palace's ground floor are blank to the street, but they open up high above.

E · GAGOSIAN GALLERY AND RESIDENCE
51 Market Street, between Pacific Avenue and Speedway
Studio Works (Craig Hodgetts and Robert Mangurian), 1980

This building recognizes the Italian theme by looking something like a tiny, modern Palladian villa crammed into a narrow urban lot. It presents an unobtrusive, almost aloof appearance to the public, focusing instead on a cylindrical courtyard within. The windowless front elevation is a taut symmetrical arrangement of huge plum-colored metal doors, lavender stucco and two bands of skidproof metal decking that serve as an inset baseboard and as a decorative representation of a balancing beam. A bowed stucco wall rising behind the streetside wall hints of the interior court. The backside (facing an alley, Horizon Court) is decorated by a more casual collage of radical chic elements—glass block, steel casement windows, an extremely thin diagonal brace supporting a bay window, light green wood frames bolted around square windows, and, of course, chain-link fence. The idiom is considerably more astringent than Kinney's Venetian, but the sure hands that put the tight cork on the brio of this little villa make it maybe the most distinguished of the new Venetian works.

F · THREE ARTISTS' STUDIOS
326 Indiana Avenue, between Hampton Drive and Fourth Avenue
Frank Gehry Associates, 1981

These three tiny studios are set in a row, perpendicular to the street, on a standard lot in a small-scale residential and commercial neighborhood. They are toylike versions of the houses of the Three Little Pigs, as if the pigs had gone to architecture school and produced these three solutions to the classic cube house problem. The first house is clad in green asphalt shingles, the second in unpainted plywood, and the third in light blue stucco. The volumes are transfigured by outsize architectural elements: stairs and chimneys are used as form-giving devices; windows are applied at surprising angles.

V 9 · MARINA DEL REY
South of Venice

Just south of Venice, Ballona Creek (bigger than it sounds) empties into the ocean through lowland that was a slough until 1968, when the city of Los Angeles completed the largest man-made small-craft harbor in the world and named it Marina del Rey. The planners then convinced a handful of developers to build a lease-held community along its edges that would be focused on a special area of human agreement: the ardent desire for fun in the sun.

The luxury-laden apartments, themed restaurants and support buildings are wrapped around the fingers of the marina. The street names—Bora Bora, Mindanao, Marquesas and Palawan—are as exotic as the foliage springing from every setback, center divider and parking-lot edge. Fisherman's Village, near the south end of Fiji Way, is a Cape Cod–themed shopping mall engulfed by banana trees, birds-of-paradise and boats so as successfully to resemble a tacky New England outpost in the South Pacific.

The places to live (somehow you want to call them complexes or facilities rather than houses or apartments, so heavy does the hand of the planner lie) are casual, low-key structures that function mostly as backdrops for the boat slips and the numerous hot tubs, swimming pools, tennis courts, saunas, gymnasiums and party rooms. The residents are given every opportunity to maintain and display their physiques in conducive environments.

V 10 · FOX HILLS MALL
On the southeast corner of Slausen Avenue and Sepulveda Boulevard, just east of the San Diego Freeway (405)
Cesar Pelli, Victor Gruen Associates, mall architects, 1973–1976

Soon after its grand opening, the Fox Hills Mall became more than just another shopping center. Tenanted by popular chain stores catering to young adults and accessible by bus as well as automobiles, the mall quickly gained the status of a hangout for teenagers. Even those without their own wheels could gather here to cruise the multilayered walkways and congregate outside the busy fast-food stands.

From outside, the mall has little shape, except at the Broadway department store (William Pereira, 1975), where bands of brick in slightly varying shades of rust and terra cotta wrap continuously around the soft-shouldered building. Inside, the covered mall takes the form of a pedestrian "street," three tiers on one side, two on the other. Ramps sweep across the space, a trendy red scaffolding stair climbs up the center, and several pairs of escalators in the major department stores dramatize ascents and descents. The stores, as in Middle Eastern souks, are open to the mall, protected at night by roll-down metal grates.

The big excitement is the ceiling, a terrible disappointment to formal purists, but an intriguing exercise in spatial legerdemain for those who enjoy seeing vast volumes slither around the corner and out of sight. For those who suppose that the space in a shopping mall must be huge but flatfooted, this slippery dream gallery will come as a revelation, though the revelation may get a little too specific when it includes all the naturally lit seams on the barrel vaults that cross the ceiling. The space invites comparison with the newer and slicker Santa Monica Place shopping mall (page 164). The teenagers seem to prefer this one, and so do some of the rest of us.

V 11 B · *Randy's Donuts*

V 11 A · *Loyola Theater*

V 11 · CALIFORNIA CRAZY

A · LOYOLA THEATER
8610 South Sepulveda Boulevard, near the southeast corner of West Manchester Avenue, Westchester
Clarence J. Smale, 1946

B · RANDY'S DONUTS
805 West Manchester Boulevard, at the northwest corner of South La Cienega Boulevard, Inglewood
ca. 1953

The giant, nearly fifty-foot-high plaster tiara above the Loyola Theater is just a little less literal than the sixty-foot plaster crumb doughnut atop Randy's Donuts down the street. As tall as they are bizarre, they were both meant to be sensational lures to the motorist.

The doughnut is placed on the roof of Randy's, as if by some giant unseen hand, but the tiara tower, a more sophisticated infusion of sign and building, grows up out of the cinema façade in a seamless series of grandiose Baroque-Deco gestures. From street level two truncated cylinders spring up to support each side of a triangular marquee, which is bordered in decorative friezes. Between the cylinders a curved parapet arcs up to a graceful, slender fillip at the center. A bouquet of fins and friezes ornaments its base, and a stylized ribbon unfurls from its apex. Long arguments are waged by architects in L.A. on the subject: What would you build to attract attention on the Strip? Clarence J. Smale knew, and the Loyola Theater deserves more attention than it gets.

V 12 · LOS ANGELES INTERNATIONAL AIRPORT
West end of Century Boulevard, Inglewood
William Pereira and Associates, 1959–1962, 1980, 1983

With the exception of a landing strip for the space shuttle in the Antelope Valley, Los Angeles International Airport (LAX) is the area's most modern port of entry. The master plan is a laudably efficient solution to the complex organizational problem of integrating airplanes, automobiles and people. A vast parking island with stacked garages is surrounded by a one-way traffic oval, recently converted with infinite tumult into a double-decked system, which is in turn surrounded by the airline terminals with the airplanes and runways beyond.

The terminals are lackluster constructions of concrete, glass and steel, devoid of any sense of place. In contrast, the hi-tech control tower and the soaring Theme Building speak garrulously of some place in our galactic future. Resembling some salvaged portion of Skylab, the control tower (12 A) is a stack of aluminum-paneled boxes that gives way at the top to a band of tinted glass; spiky antennae bristle from the roof. While the control tower resembles a man-made spacecraft, the Theme Building (12 B) is surely from another planet, more Martial than Jovial. The Martians appear to have had some trouble with earthly gravity. A great spidery four-pronged cradle was constructed, apparently, to hold a flying-saucer restaurant mysteriously up in the air. But by the time

V 12 B · *Los Angeles International Airport, Theme Building*

the services from the ground to the restaurant had been assembled, they filled a cylinder close to twenty feet in diameter, and it became evident that that could hold the saucer up more easily. So we get both, in a kind of belt-and-suspenders futurism. The flying saucer doesn't even revolve.

V 13 · *Worldway Postal Center*

V 13 · WORLDWAY POSTAL CENTER
5800 West Century Boulevard, on the south, between Airport and Postal roads, Inglewood
DMJM (Cesar Pelli), 1967

It is curious that one of Los Angeles' most urbane concrete-frame structures—and one of its most artistically expressive—is for an altogether workaday program of the U.S. Postal Service. This is the kind of job that usually falls to a giant architects-and-engineers firm for a no-nonsense answer, and so it did here, to DMJM, except that it came when Cesar Pelli was chief of design for the firm.

The stark frame, therefore, is by no means a simple one without reverberations, but strangely recalls the Byzantine (or at least the neo-Byzantine of Philip Johnson's handsome museum at Dumbarton Oaks, in Washington, D.C.) both in the shape of its column capitals and in the sense of everything being embedded in something in a kind of squashed collage. The exposed concrete post-and-beam structure, delineated by reveals, is set flush with an infill of sand-colored brick or bronze-tinted glass. The cylindrical columns merge into the capitals, which merge in turn into the floor beams. At the top of the building another reveal neatly sets off a concrete parapet as a consolidated cleaned-up entablature.

Above the long loading docks on the north and south sides, steel doors roll up to allow views completely through the block-wide structure, to make neo-Realistic sculpture of the silhouetted machines within. After the enclosed space of the building comes to an end on the southwest, the frame keeps marching along to support a bridge that connects the rooftop parking with a circular ramp—elegantly, like the rest.

V 14 · REDONDO BEACH CIVIC CENTER
415 Diamond Street, near the northwest corner of Pacific Coast Highway, Redondo Beach
Victor Gruen Associates, 1962

The Redondo Beach Civic Center manages to convey both the formality of its public role and the casual demeanor of its beach-bungalow neighborhood. This

International Style building is broken up into little single-story, flat-roofed wings and set into a luxuriantly landscaped city block. The little boxes are made up of delicate steel posts and beams, painted blue, with infill walls of glass and white-painted brick and stucco organized around a series of courtyards, walkways and covered colonnades. The elevations are lively, responding to interior demands for natural light and shade: large, glassy areas are placed on the north or where they can be protected by overhangs; strip windows on the sunny elevations are sheltered by blue-painted metal louvers. And in between everything are lawns and big trees and planters overflowing with tropical foliage, demonstrating that every once in a while, with delicate enough details and bold enough plants, the sixties could produce something Ramona could be proud of.

V 15 · VON KOERBER HOUSE
408 Via Monte de Oro, near the north corner of Via Los Miradores, Torrance
R. M. Schindler, 1931

Required by local ordinance to design in the Spanish Colonial Revival persuasion, Schindler wrapped this De Stijl composition in the red banner of the other style—curved terra-cotta roof tiles. The tiles are everywhere: they are layered over shed roofs in the usual manner, but they go up and over flat roofs, too, and sometimes sweep down stucco walls and across the tops of courtyard walls. Underneath all the gay abandon, the sophisticated interlocking volumes and voids of the design go about their own modern business.

V 16 · PALOS VERDES

The most distinctive feature on a relief map of the Los Angeles Basin is an isolated knot of hills, low but rugged, that jut into the Pacific at the southwest corner of the plain, as though they might serve as introduction to the higher hills of Santa Catalina Island, thirty miles farther to the southeast. These hills, like much of the rest of Southern California, were bare at the beginning of this century, covered, as their name suggests, by green grass in the rainy season. The land had been granted by the Mexican governor Figueroa to the Sepulveda family in 1834 and hadn't attracted much attention until 1914, when one Frank A. Vanderlip bought sixteen thousand acres of the peninsula. Vanderlip then hired landscape architects Olmsted and Olmsted and architects Howard Shaw and Myron Hunt to plan a colony for millionaires.

The development of grand estates, parks, clubs and three model villages was stopped short by World War I, but it went ahead a few years later on a much reduced scale. In 1922 and '23 the Olmsted brothers and Charles H. Cheney made a master plan for 3,200 acres with arrangements for architecture in the Spanish style. In 1934 Rolling Hills Estates was added, with a ranch motif offering an architectural choice of American Colonial or California board-and-batten, the former by Los Angeles architect Paul R. Williams, the latter by Santa Barbara architect Lutah Maria Riggs. Both of them (as they almost always did) scored.

A · MALAGA COVE PLAZA
Palos Verdes Drive West, between Via Corta and Via Chico, Palos Verdes
Estates
*Olmsted Brothers; Charles H. Cheney; Webber, Staunton and Spaulding,
1925 and after*

The most highly visible and most satisfyingly dense conflation of the Hispanicisms (with an Italian admix, which renders the whole "Mediterranean") occurs in a villagelike shopping center called Malaga Cove Plaza, which is one of
the places where the California dream floats most attractively to the surface.
Sun-bronzed shoppers jump out of their Porsches in a plaza devoted to parking;
in its center a miniature version of Giambologna's Neptune Fountain in Bolo-
gna splashes cheerfully; along the north edge are arching pepper trees.

The mode is boutique (the general store is a gift shop), but the picturesque
architecture has been composed with skill and verve and that hallmark of good
Spanish Colonial Revival, the capacity for dazzling jumps in scale. Buildings
face the parking plaza on the far long side and the two ends. At the southeast
corner is the boldest of the jumps in scale: a giant semicircular arch bounds over
Via Chico with patterned brick and grand voussoirs, the sort of thing that
might have eventuated if Ramona had run away with Giuliano de' Medici. To
the left is an elegant colonnade beneath a second story of red brick, slate-gray-
shuttered windows and a wrought-iron balcony. To the right, arcades of remarkable catholicity go all the way, on one occasion to sheer glass-walled
Modern, then lead on to picturesque pedestrian lanes and courts.

The pleasure comes, in large part, from the visible care in the details: painted
beams in the ceiling of the arcade are resplendent in green, black, white and red
stripes, then wide pink, narrow green and middle-width black stripes, and black
and red checkers. Even the brick walls, some of which seem to have been white-
washed long ago, have the look of having been cared about. And the planting—
lushly jumbled Moreton Bay fig trees, cypresses, pittosporum for fragrance,
birds-of-paradise and pepper trees, along with a large number of striped awnings—is Essence of California.

Some dense but livable apartments on the street above repay the trouble of
your peering through the gates, especially the one at 2433 Via Campesina
(16 B) (near the northwest corner of Via Chico, attributed to Pierpont Davis).
It was built in 1937 in the branch of Spanish Colonial Revival that favored minarets, in peach and light blue and creamy white, above tiny walled gardens off a
courtyard with a fountain and water channel.

V 16 A · *Malaga Cove Plaza*

V 16 C · *Wayfarers' Chapel*

C · WAYFARERS' CHAPEL

5755 Palos Verdes Drive South, Rancho Palos Verdes
Lloyd Wright, 1951 and after
Open daily, 11–4

The other high point in Palos Verdes is Lloyd Wright's Swedenborgian Memorial Chapel, called the Wayfarers' Chapel, near Portuguese Bend. Lloyd Wright, who had a long and distinguished architectural career, spent decades trying to emerge from the shadow of his famous father who, of course, is sometimes even credited with this, his son's best-known work. The Wayfarers' Chapel was built in 1951; a tower, a colonnade and a visitors' center, also designed by Wright, came later. The church started as a gabled glass box, atop a cliff high above the sea, with tiny redwood trees struggling for survival around its perimeter. After thirty-five years the redwoods have grown and the church is now a bower; the trees are so high and broad that their shape dapples and enlivens the interior and their branches make tracery even more intricate than the complex geometries of the mullions. It is reassuring that this elaborate little glass building, which seemed such a lonesome tantrum when it was new, is now sheltered—and redeemed—by the trees that were a large part of the idea from the begining.

Only people of great vision have the courage to plant slow-growing trees, though here the vision may be countered by forces greater still: on this perch along the edge of the continental plate, landslides are already carrying away the later additions. You should visit this masterpiece soon.

V 17 · BANNING HOUSE

401 East M Street, in Banning Park, Wilmington
General Phineas Banning, 1864
Grounds open to public; house tours Wednesday, Saturday and Sunday at 1,
2, 3 and 4 P.M.; free admission

Civil War general Phineas Banning, another California success story, arrived in Los Angeles in 1851 with nothing; in an amazingly short period he managed to build an extensive network of stage coach, then rail and shipping lines across the Southwest, to become known as "the father of Los Angeles transportation." In 1858 he and his partner, B. D. Wilson, founded the town of New San Pedro, which the state promptly renamed Wilmington in honor of Banning's hometown in Delaware.

The next year Banning completed his grand three-story Greek Revival house. This foursquare volume is an American child's classic portrait of a house with a gable roof, brick chimneys, white clapboard walls, and green shutters on the double-hung windows. The front door is framed by a deep double-deck porch, which supports an austerely trimmed triangular pediment. A boxy cupola on top gave Banning an observation spot to watch his ships in the harbor.

The cool order, permanence and simplicity of the front and side elevations break into a gaggle of additions around back, where three distinct volumes of various heights and shapes, each with its own ideas on doors, roofs and chimneys, clamor for preeminence. Like the add-ons themselves, the openings were placed where function dictated and space allowed to form an altogether unpredictable but certainly energetic composition.

Brick foundation walls raise the house about four feet above its flat, grassy garden; on the east a sunken, raked-earth courtyard protected by a retaining wall allows direct access between the basement and the outdoors. Out back is a barn and a fanciful arbor supporting one of the largest wisteria vines in Southern California. The rest of the grounds are, for the most part, covered in lawns and shade trees, spacious enough but apparently not a patch on the grandiose landscaping of a century ago.

V 17 · *Banning House (rear)*

V 18 B · *Rancho Los Alamitos*

V 18 · DOS RANCHOS
Two early adobes in Long Beach

In 1784 the largest Spanish land grant in California—167,000 acres—was given to Manuel Nieto for his military service to the Crown. After his death in 1804 the grant was divided among his heirs into five ranchos; Los Cerritos and Los Alamitos are two of these.

A · RANCHO LOS CERRITOS
4600 Virginia Road, Long Beach
Jonathan Temple, 1844; Llewellyn Bixby, alterations, and Ralph Cornell,
*   landscape architect, 1930–1931*
Now a museum; open Wednesday through Sunday, 1–5; closed on holidays;
*   free admission*

Rancho Los Cerritos manages to meet every tourist's expection of how an Old California adobe should appear: two-story white plastered walls and a gently sloping red-tiled roof, all surrounded by a cool oasis of mature vegetation. In front, the thick walls of this archetypal Monterey style house are punctured by rows of doors that open onto a two-storied shaded porch with slate gray wood posts and railings; well-worn bricks lead to the central entry. At the back, the shed roofs of one-story wings extend to cover porches that wrap around a sunny courtyard with a brick patio, a small pond, tropical foliage and a lawn.

Only five of the original 27,000 acres are left, and a plain front lawn has replaced an elaborate Italian garden; still, this historic rancho is considerably more romantic today than it ever was, especially compared with the early years when it was just a working ranch. Jonathan Temple bought the land from the Nieto heirs in 1843 and, with adobe bricks made on the grounds, built a no-nonsense ranch house: the main roof was much steeper than it is today, gabled instead of hipped, with shingles instead of red tiles; the two wings were flat-roofed, without covered walkways; the courtyard was a barren work area faced by storerooms, a kitchen, a laundry, a blacksmith shop and a foreman's office. Even the entrance was reversed: a front gate, in a long wall between the wings, opened into a dusty enclosure, and that famous Monterey welcome looked out on the backyard. The main attractions here were the fifteen thousand head of cattle, the seven thousand sheep, and the three thousand horses chewing on grass that grew as far as the eye could see.

In 1866 the ubiquitous Bixbys, who later owned Rancho Los Alamitos as well, got control of the property and fancied up the ranch house even more. From their many red tiles, brick porches, shed roofs and colonnades, an authentic rancho emerged, with wide lawns that sweep past flowers and shrubs and enormous specimen trees from around the world. In 1955 this was all turned into a pleasant museum.

B · RANCHO LOS ALAMITOS
6400 East Bixby Hills Road, Long Beach; entrance at south end of Palo Verde Avenue
Juan José Nieto, 1806; John W. Bixby, 1878 and after; Fred H. Bixby, 1906 and after
Now a museum; open Wednesday through Sunday, 1–5; closed on holidays; free admission

La Casa de Rancho Los Alamitos (The Sycamores), one of the oldest houses in California, is located on the hilltop site of an ancient Indian village, with ocean breezes, a freshwater spring and views of the mountains, the Los Angeles basin and the Pacific. At present only seven and a half acres of the rancho remain, boxed in by houses and condominiums, but the little ranch house and its vigorous garden are still vivid reminders of a romantic past.

The original adobe, built in 1806 by Juan José Nieto, was a simple one-story rectangular block. In the early 1840s the Yankee Abel Stearns added a wooden bunkhouse wing on the north; in 1878 John W. Bixby built another wing on the south, creating a courtyard; in 1925 Fred Bixby, John's son, put a second story on the original adobe, added two covered porches and refurbished the interior as a suitable environment for a twentieth-century cattle baron. But beneath the wood additions, the four-foot-thick adobe walls still exist, their presence clearly visible in the deep doorways and windows.

Though painted white with red trim, the house is often difficult to distinguish from its garden. Densely planted roses, vines and native foliage have matured along the edges of the walls and the numerous patios. Two enormous Moreton Bay fig trees shade most of a large front lawn, which is encircled on its eastern edge by Mexican fan palms. On the south, the row of palms becomes a fragrant allée of pepper trees that leads up between the house and its red-painted barns and sheds on the west. There are vine-covered arbors everywhere: one, draped in Chinese wisteria, curves out toward the blacksmith's shop; another screens a wire fence beside a pair of ancient tennis courts; one more wraps around the trunk of an old pepper tree, now deceased, near a splashing fountain brimming with koi.

V 19 · NAPLES

The Southern California dream of the good life, with boats, can best be savored at Naples, below Long Beach. Like Venice and most of the rest of Southern California, Naples started (twice) as a gleam in the eye of a real estate developer; only, unlike Venice, this one has worked, and it lays claim still to the luxury-on-a-budget pleasantness that has been Southern California's hallmark and draw for this past century.

It was started the year before Venice, in 1903, by Arthur Persons, whose vision included canals and gondolas in the mud flats; but his bank account did not survive the next downward cycle. Railroad tycoon Henry E. Huntington held it until 1923, when new developers completed the canals and bridges and then treated prospective buyers to free lunch and a band concert on a side-wheeler steamer. The lots must have sold felicitously, but gradually; none is vacant now, and houses representing most of the styles since 1923 jostle one another cheerfully on small lots made to feel spacious by the water, which is everywhere. The layout is carefully structured, with a circumferential canal, the Rivo Alto, and a central grassy circle, Colonnade Park, with a triple-tiered fountain; but the place also becomes highly picturesque, as the canals break the land into a miniature archipelago at the edge of a pretty bay.

Perhaps the most distinguished of the houses is the most modern, the Frank house, at 5576 Vesuvian Walk, designed in 1962 by Killingsworth, Brady and Smith as a Case Study House for the Los Angeles magazine *Arts and Architecture.* This is an elegant Mondrianesque composition in posts and beams, clean wall planes and panels of water, all skillfully disposed on a tiny site to create at once privacy and some mystery, with a sense of great spaciousness.

A number of Spanish houses sit well in the sunshine—usually simple and small, with occasional stair risers that gleam with patterned tile. Even shingled houses of Cape Cod persuasion seem at home along the edge of the bay; out of the California of the movie sets, they may stir up memories of cheerful films seen long ago or late at night. Some of the angular contemporary houses of the 1960s make pleasant neighbors, too, though others so vividly show off their architects' enthusiasms that they become aggressively prickly in such close quarters.

This isn't by any means the most lavish neighborhood we describe, nor the

V 19 · *Naples*

most architecturally distinguished, nor the most convincingly located; but it is one of the most pleasant, and with its low-cost Southern California foibles, perhaps the most endearing of them all.

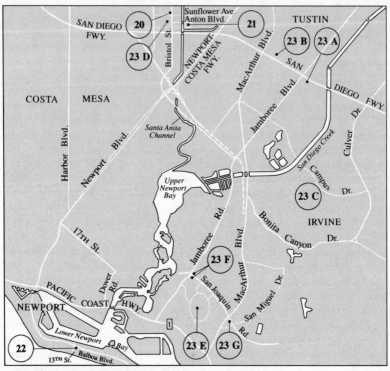

V/PACIFIC COAST HIGHWAY (INSET 1)

V 20 · WORLD SAVINGS
3820 South Bristol Street, Santa Ana
Kamnitzer, Cotton, Vreeland (Thomas Vreeland), 1979

This World Savings office, sited near the lackluster South Coast Plaza (page 138), on the edge of a vast parking lot that services a dismal series of fast-food stands and supermarkets, is an elegantly formal outpost of pure Modern architecture. It has great presence in its slightly slipped foursquare simplicity, reminiscent of an early-nineteenth-century neo-Classical pavilion. Its strong geometry recalls the work of the great Philadelphia architect Louis Kahn, with whom Vreeland worked in the 1950s. Alternating strips of ceramic tiles, light gray and white, thick and thin, wrap continuously around the building; second-story windows run in a single, deeply incised band. This powerful rectangular block is cut away at the base, between four strong piers that clearly define the building's corners. Among these piers, connecting three of them, is a glass box, triangular in plan, that houses the public or "served" spaces, as Kahn would have called them. The square piers contain the private service functions of the bank (the "servant" spaces): elevator, vault, safety-deposit boxes, and toilets. The interior, airy and bright under a central square skylight, is sophisticated and lively, with dominant cool grays and blues contrasted with vivid pink. One of the few pieces of serious, unpretentious Modern architecture in Los Angeles, this little building is a masterful combination of grace and strong logic.

V 21 · A CALIFORNIA SCENARIO
**Two Town Center, at the southeast corner of Anton Boulevard and Park
Center, near South Bristol Street, Costa Mesa**
Isamu Noguchi, 1982

Off in a corner of Costa Mesa, two green glass high-rises (too blunt to scrape the sky) help an L-shaped parking garage to enclose a big squarish space in which the great modern sculptor Isamu Noguchi was asked to do something. (The commission must surely have included the word "Art.") A California Scenario is the result.

Now, I am a fair-weather fan of Noguchi: some of the places I like best in the world bear his imprint, as do some I find the most deadly. His own house in Takamatsu, in Japan, where he has placed his own paper lanterns and stone sculpture simply in an exquisitely plain—but enveloping—traditional Japanese farmhouse, is for me one of the most serenely magic places on this planet; on the other hand, his Cobo Plaza on the Detroit riverfront, is, I think, bleak, uninhabitable and pointless. A California Scenario lies somewhere in between: inhabitable it is not; beautiful it sometimes is. It is better, certainly, to see it not as an open space meant to be inhabited by urban dwellers, like a plaza/piazza, but rather as an object of art stretched to cover a vast empty space and (maybe this is part of the Art) make it seem, by the stretching, even emptier.

It's so big it gets a scenario, as the title says. The scenario, explained on a plaque in one corner, includes: 1) a long, flat granite block on a grassy hill called Land Use; 2) a fountain with lots of water shaped as a cylinder on a hemisphere with an anemometer on top, called Energy Fountain; 3) a mound with startlingly pretty tall grass and flowers and a horseshoe-shaped walk past a bench, all called the Forest Walk; 4) a pile of rocks called the Spirit of the Lima Bean; 5) a much bigger pile of earth with cactus, called the Desert Land; and, most notably, 6) a triangular water source with water flowing over rocks down a chute to 7) a stream meandering across a flat sandstone plateau, ending under 8) a large, flat pyramid called Water Use.

V 20 · *World Savings*   **V 21** · *A California Scenario*

The sinuous curve of the stream is arresting: it seems like a gash in the stone plain, and has rocks strewn on its flat bottom, against which nozzles squirt water, all in the same direction, to suggest a much more vigorous brook than is actually there. Then there are cubes and other shapes of stone, which conceal lights and ashtrays. The line of the water course is hauntingly beautiful, evocative of lots of things and at home in the space (though it looks as if the plumbing subcontractor rather than the sculptor had placed the rocks along the stream bottom), but the other objects seem desperately lonely. The two blank walls of the parking garage that faces the space have been rendered bright white and dead simple, like a background for a work of Luis Barragan; this is an extremely powerful foil to the inanity of the green high-rises, but nothing acknowledges it, nor sets it to work. A great sculptor (like Noguchi) at his best invests strong shapes with energy so powerful that they positively crackle with it and beam it out across space. Here there is maybe too much space and too little energy, and the pieces don't seem beamish enough.

In the corner of the square between the green behemoths are some low buildings, including most notably the Copa de Oro restaurant by Lee and Sakahara Associates (1982). Now *there* is some energy, almost more than you can handle, with blocks falling at the top in a way recollective of the Mayan civilization at its height, or those wonderful black-and-gold flamboyances of the thirties (the Crocker Bank, page 272), though this one is beige. Inside are upside-down stepped pyramids and eyeball-searing murals with camels and palms, I think. It's such a relief to feel the juices flowing after you've strained so to discover them outside.

V 22 · LOVELL BEACH HOUSE
1242 West Ocean Front (a walkway), on the northeast corner of Thirteenth Street and the Pacific Ocean, Balboa Peninsula
R. M. Schindler, 1922–1926
Private Residence

Mies van der Rohe summed up one of the continuing controversies of modern architecture when he announced, "I don't want to be interesting; I want to be *good.*" David Gebhard, who wrote the book on the great architect R. M. Schindler, granted that his Lovell Beach house is "a key work of twentieth-century architecture," but he thinks it cannot match other key works (Neutra's Lovell house [page 254], Gropius' Bauhaus at Dessau, Le Corbusier's Villa Savoye at Poissy, and Mies van der Rohe's German Pavilion at Barcelona) "as an art object." That continues, it appears, the Mies distinction between "interesting" and "good." I'm more inclined to an opposite assertion that "interesting" is an important and useful description of art, and that Schindler's Lovell Beach house, "as an art object," beats those others hollow (except maybe for the Barcelona Pavilion, which is no longer around for comparison).

The Lovell Beach house is interesting, even fascinating, and complex (though direct), ambiguous (though fairly polemical) and full of surprises and wonders that play well with most notions of purity. It sits on five concrete constructivist cradles that hold its two upper floors off the sand, to leave the site free for a playground and to let the wide beach (just across a walkway) appear to continue under the house. The first floor up is a long, rectangular open living space, with fireplace; service rooms are at the end opposite the ocean. On the floor above that, four bedrooms, each with sleeping porch, nestle between the five cradles, offset from the living room so that the latter is mostly two stories high, with a balcony leading to the bedrooms along one side of the high space. The arrangement of all these spaces is altogether natural, direct and easy, but (and

V 22 · *Lovell Beach House*

maybe it's in the shape of the concrete frame cradles) there is a latent air of fiendish ingenuity, of energy crackling on this relaxed and sun-drenched beach.

The details, especially of the windows and the screens, come rather as a surprise: their delicate geometry is almost at the point of being fussy, though they make a splendid foil for the grandeur of the concrete frames. They owe something, probably, to Piet Mondrian and certainly a great deal to Frank Lloyd Wright, whose Los Angeles office Schindler had come to California to run. But for me the expressive triumph, the most "interesting" element of the house, is at the middle scale: the stairways, which go from near the center of the long side of the house gently up, on the right, to the living room, and more steeply up, on the left, to the kitchen. The stairs are detailed similarly and simply, but they describe eloquently, talking directly to human muscles, an invitation to guests to sweep upstairs to the main entrance, or to the delivery man to make the more arduous trek up to the kitchen door.

Already in 1926 this house was an architecture for people in motion, a ride as well as a masterful building. As always with a real masterpiece, continued looking reveals endless surprises and confirmations and delights.

V 23 · IRVINE
William Pereira and Associates, original plan, 1960

The low hills of Orange County lie languidly in the sun, sheltered by the high Santa Ana and the higher San Gabriel Mountains and cooled by the Pacific Ocean. The rich soil, ample water and benign climate have made this a singularly inviting place for human habitation for millennia: 250,000 Indians, about one-fourth the population of the medieval pre–United States, once lived here. After their decimation, their homesites were transformed in the 1860s and '70s by James Irvine, Thomas Flint and Llewellyn Bixby into a sheep ranch of well over one hundred thousand acres stretching from the mountains to the sea. For almost a hundred years only sheep and a few farmers enjoyed the good life along this stretch of Southern California. James Irvine ended up with a large part of the property but never succumbed to the lure of the place, preferring San Francisco. His son, similarly disinclined, was only persuaded to move here by the 1906 San Francisco earthquake.

In 1960 the Irvine Company retained William Pereira to make a master plan for developing the eighty-eight-thousand acres that remained of the ranch. This plan, typical of its time, incorporated the most up-to-the-minute, state-of-the-art urban-planning principles. Despite this, it was not wholly vapid in execution. Still, there are the expectable, carefully integrated communities of single-family and multiple-unit residential components, site-specific within the parameters of the greenscape and the infrastructure of the landscaped, enviro-morphic vehicular connectors (streets); industrial parks were systematized sequentially along interurban connectors (freeways) to contain any hyperpenetrable network edge conditions, to interface within the matrix of existing transportation corridors, and not to impact the exurban configurations; a one-thousand-acre donation was targeted for a branch of the University of California to effect and potentiate a cultural and socioeconomic focus; shopping and commercial facilities and complexes were organized at interurban connector intersections, becoming synergistic, multinodal termini, secondary collectors and tertiary focal points.

The tracts of expensive houses are interposed among orange groves, eucalyptus windrows, and ancient clumps of native oaks and sycamores on streets named Sierra Santo, Sierra Calmo, Sierra Bravo and Sierra Majorca, or alternatively, Leatherwood, Satinwood, Tanglewood and Pebblewood. But they turn out to be mostly just a more expensive and up-to-date version of the San Fernando Valley sprawl of the 1950s and '60s.

The industrial parks bristle with huge architectural statements best seen from the San Diego Freeway at fifty-five miles an hour. The Fluor Corporation (23 A) (on the south, east of Jamboree Boulevard) combines an oddly angled, mirrored-glass high-rise office building with a lower factory building; at the corners are concrete mushrooms that look like prison-guard towers. The Occidental Petroleum Research Center (23 B) (on the north, east of MacArthur Boulevard) is a leering black box supported on aggressive concrete columns that press up to the edge of the freeway.

The University of California at Irvine campus (23 C) suffers now from the optimism of the 1960s. Its diagram of millennial perfection contains a circle around which bland behemoths of the future were to be regularly arrayed. But as we all know, the sixties dream faltered. Only some of the slabs were built, so the master plan of a place that was not going to be all right until it was finished (on the myth of perfectibility) resembles now not so much a way station to the goal as it does a comb with numerous teeth broken out. Though if you don't try to get the formal idea of the place, the texture of it, the step-by-step inhabitation is seductive indeed.

Irvine's two commercial clusters, South Coast Plaza and Newport Center, suffer from the heavy burden of their own pretensions. South Coast Plaza (23 D) (on the northwest corner of Bristol Street and the San Diego Freeway) is just about the ultimate in suburban shopping malls; inside its windowless walls are nearly every high-fashion chain boutique and department store available as well as a great number of specialty stores, from Mark Cross to Gucci. But even the Joseph Magnin's designed by Frank O. Gehry and Associates, the Jewel Court covered in a stained-glass dome (designed by the Judson Studios and Green Associates), an array of fountains and a merry-go-round have not brought it to life.

Newport Center (23 E) to the southwest, a Corbusian wolf cub in Pereiran woolens, is one of the most self-consciously grand assemblages in the region, a veritable Piazza Potpourri. High-rise office buildings set on a hilltop are strung along an oval drive whose centerpiece is Fashion Island, a high-class open-air shopping mall surrounded by parking. The streets are so wide that it would take the vanished aboriginal population of Orange County to fill them up. As it is, they seem lonesome. The shimmering new office buildings on display in their little landscaping stand each one alone, with no habitable space formed between them. One of the region's most magnificent panoramic views—of the San Gabriel and Santa Ana Mountains, the Santa Ana River and the Balboa Peninsula, and the long Pacific coastline—somehow got missed.

There are two projects in this area that get our merit badges. The first is at the south and east corners of Jamboree Boulevard and San Joaquin Hills Road (23 F), where two gas stations make up the welcoming gates to Newport Center. Their flat roofs inscribe arcs which, if they were not pierced by San Joaquin Road, would form a semicircle. Each crescent appears to be cantilevered from a central gas station office, though auxiliary support is discreetly supplied at each pump island. The symmetrical siting, the sleek, low-slung forms and the machine-made materials—bronzed steel, glass and beige concrete block—reflect the automobile aesthetic and combine to form a 3-D gateway to nothing in particular.

The second award-winner is Roger's Gardens (23 G) (2301 San Joaquin Hills Road, Newport Beach, at the southwest corner of MacArthur Boulevard, 1974). The theme park approach is applied here to a landscape nursery, even to its enclosure within a Disneyesque berm. Winding concrete pathways connect a variety of "plant lands" including Sherwood Forest, a collection of trees and shrubs, Bush Gardens, thick with shade plants, and Central Park, an amphitheater for planting demonstrations. One ramada is draped in hanging baskets; another houses great staghorn ferns and cycads, plants presently enjoying enormous popularity. Fountains, retaining walls, arbors and gazebos (one is a castoff from Disneyland) are cleverly configured to set off particular plant groups and floral displays that change with the seasons. Sod-roofed buildings are set into the berms and are so engulfed in plant life that they disappear into the landscape. The gardens even qualify as good for pilgrimages, except that instead of your bringing something to the shrine as most pilgrims do, from here (for a price) you take something away.

V 24 · LAGUNA BEACH

Laguna Beach is a colorful artists' colony with the sort of natural good looks that have inspired Sunday and serious landscape painters since it was settled in 1904. The foothills run close to the coast here, falling away in sycamore-filled canyons and wildflower-covered plateaus before the cliffside plunge into the ocean. Unlike the wide swaths of sand that line so much of the Southern California coast, Laguna's beaches are secreted away in little coves whose neat, sandy crescents are sheltered by rock promontories. Development has only enhanced the natural charms: bungalows and studios wrapped in passion vine, swank Modern villas hidden among glistening banana leaves, posh boutiques

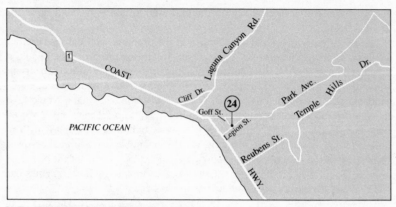

V/PACIFIC COAST HIGHWAY (INSET 2)

around Spanish courtyards, and olde-English-cottage art galleries all cascade down the rolling slopes (sometimes literally, during heavy rains) in the most colorful manner.

Try a stroll along the shore past contorted Chinese-landscape rock pools or a walk down Forest Avenue through the diminutive and rustic commercial heart of the village. Nearby is a particularly dense pocket of picturesqueness, a church called St. Francis-by-the-Sea (430 Park Avenue, at the north end of Catalina Street, 1916 and after). The fairy-tale Spanish-Craftsman styling, though convincing in each part, was apparently pulled out of a hastily packed trunk of architectural elements; scales and details are all casually mixed to mirror the relaxed atmosphere of the town.

Every summer Laguna Beach hosts what must be the major kitsch event in Southern California, the Pageant of the Masters. Carefully cast townsfolk pose as famous works of art in proper costumes and makeup on a stage in front of appropriate backdrops. When the curtains part, the figures are stock-still; then they come to life before a gasping audience. Buy your tickets early.

VI/WILSHIRE BOULEVARD

La Brea Tar Pits

Wilshire Boulevard cuts a wide and fantastic swath on its sixteen miles from downtown Los Angeles to Santa Monica and the Pacific Ocean. It first ran only from the west end of MacArthur Park, near Bullock's Wilshire department store, to the sea; but later it was extended through the park and into the center of downtown in order to relieve congestion. Said to have been the first shopping street in the world that was made with the automobile in mind, the boulevard is lined from the beginning with fabulous, dazzling stores, their big windows visible to motorists driving by, their access from the back, from adjacent parking lots. The Santa Monica end, which started life as Nevada Avenue, had an automobile racing track; and there was another one farther east. At one time there were even two airports along Wilshire. As recently as forty years ago, the boulevard ran through open country from time to time on its route to the sea. But then and now Wilshire Boulevard has been the main street of Southern California—a place for shopping and one of the main places where visitors from the East would obtain their images of the Good Life to be found here.

Wilshire Boulevard was named (and it seems appropriate) after an extraordinary fellow, one H. Gaylord Wilshire (1861–1927), "a capitalist, socialist, monopolist, and golfer of Los Angeles," as he is described in one of the histories. He invented something called the I-on-a-co, a magnetic horse collar, which, when placed around the neck or waist, was said to cure practically all human and some canine ailments and restore gray hair to its original color by magnetizing the iron in the blood. It sold for $58.50 cash, or $65 on time. The claim was finally disputed—not, however, until Wilshire had made enough to develop his boulevard, which was, at the time, in the midst of California's great "Boom of the '80s," just an unpaved road in a tract of land that he planned to improve; Wilshire named both the road and the subdivision after himself. His statement about the area tells a lot: "With the increasing comfort and speed of transportation, California is fast becoming a winter playground of the leisure class of Americans. I have no doubt that when we have socialism, and the place of man's abode will be determined by his will rather than as it is now by his job, Southern California will be the most thickly settled part of the American continent."

Wilshire's boulevard, anyway, is certainly thickly settled. It is said to be the longest, widest boulevard in the country, intersected by 202 streets; one of them, Veteran Avenue, creates with Wilshire the busiest intersection in the world not on a superhighway. The first experiments with synchronized traffic lights were conducted here, as were the first Christmas street decorations and the first parking limits. And the drive-in phenomenon was born and died here.

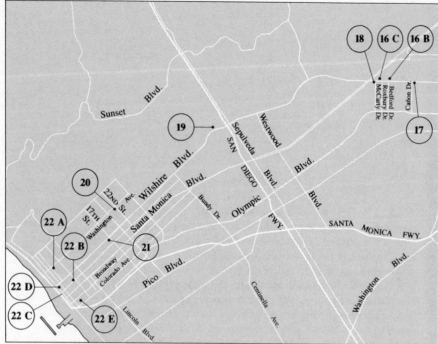

VI/WILSHIRE BOULEVARD

There were at one point forty-three drive-in businesses along the boulevard, although now the initial format of dazzle in the front and access at the rear has come back; the exception is Beverly Hills, where entry is from parking lots underneath the buildings. Along the boulevard are monuments of the 1920s and '30s and the decades since, from such early masterpieces as Bullock's Wilshire and the Elks Club, near the eastern end, to the latest Cesar Pelli tower near the ocean.

VI 1 · ELKS CLUB
607 South Park View Street, on the west corner of Sixth Street, across from MacArthur Park, Los Angeles
Curlett and Beelman, 1927
Now the Park Plaza Hotel

This is one of three particularly endearing buildings in the post-Ramona idiom of growing-up Los Angeles. The great one among the three is the Los Angeles Public Library (page 18); the second is its baby brother, the National Bank of Commerce Building (page 22). This one is a little more monumental than the other two—half mastaba, or squared-off Egyptian pyramid, and half nine-story, fairly straightforward hotel that rises out of the mastaba without in any way lightening it. The Elks Club, like the other two buildings, is encased in crystalline plinths that rise in a straight line to become molded architectural angels— angels of death or of mercy. A pair of these plinth-*cum*-angels rises up at each face of every corner, which is surmounted finally by a squashed urn that looks as if it has some highly religious or at least symbolic function. Even the hotel

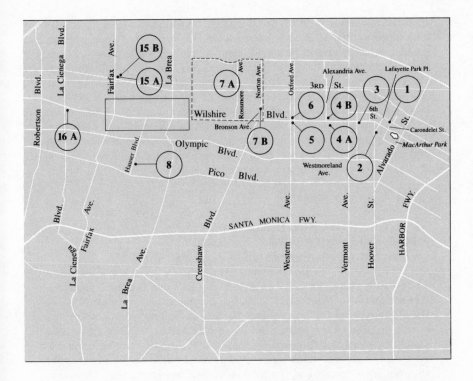

mass, which comes soaring out of this monolithic base, has stern angels, about twice as high as the others, guarding plinths along each side.

Although the walls are made of reinforced concrete, they seem happy to have all this buttressing, for the plaster skin is etched and scraped to look like giant blocks of ashlar stone. At the level of the heads of the lower angels is an extraordinary gallery of torsos, each niche filled with a different fierce soldier, pressed into the smooth wall like a set of dentils intaglio—a really stunning enterprise. The gallery becomes an almost two-dimensional, curiously Egyptian frieze as it crosses colossal piers that grow up from the bottom of the tower. In the center is a three-story glassy entrance arch with giant Corinthian columns and piers on each side and a strange head for a keystone, a sort of Medusa with what might be electrified snakes for hair. Under her is a mandala with twelve numbers, which could also be seen as a clock, with an elk's head emerging from a central disk like an Egyptian animal god.

Inside, from whence the Elks have long gone, linger the scents of three thousand years of cigar smoke, ancient, archaeological, genuine—the cigar smoke of

VI 1 · *Elks Club*

the ages. Just inside the door, past a marble-floored lobby, is a steep and very wide stairway that sweeps up toward a wooden barrel-vault ceiling, darkly painted, lightened up a bit by a window at the rear; overhead is a series of huge, strange, throbbing chandeliers. On each side are Composite-columned loggias that lead to other mysterious rooms, many with intricately painted wood ceilings. All the walls are decked out in somber theatricality with dark wood wainscoting and vast expanses of white cut-stone veneer. Somehow the old Frank Lloyd Wright joke comes to mind: When Wright was in Rome and went to see St. Peter's, the work of his archrival Michelangelo, he looked at it for a while and then asked, "Is it hollow?" In some way, a look at the Elks Club brings on the same question. But the cigar smoke inside makes any answer inconclusive.

VI 2 · GRANADA BUILDING
672 South Lafayette Park Place, Los Angeles
Franklin Harper, designer and builder, 1927; restored, 1982

The Granada Building reeks of panache among Southern California's architecture and design community. It has a curious resemblance to other places across the Mediterranean world, from Santa Barbara to the Costa Brava, which also attract designers. Required, apparently, is 1) a number of intimately scaled structures, which 2) constitute a simple, strong place with 3) an interesting sequence of small and middle-size spaces, 4) simple walls on which dance the shadows of lush plants and 5) a little bit of fascinating ornament. The white-walled Spanish Colonial Revival style seems particularly capable of producing this vision. The Granada Building does it within an unusually formal plan in which four structures, each containing two layers of two-story offices and apartments, are arranged around a T-shaped circulation corridor to appear as one building and to allow each of the units an outside entrance. The short shaft of the T runs perpendicular to the street, providing entry, while the long crossbar is an open-air corridor. Twin stairways flanking the entry court and a free-standing elevator tower in the middle lead to third-story wooden walkways and bridges, which provide access to the upper offices. The tight, brick-paved courts, with ficus trees and a lily pond, are quiet retreats from the street.

VI 2 · *Granada Building*

VI 3 · *Bullock's Wilshire*

Massive white walls, covered in a compendium of stucco surfaces, step forward and back along the street, incorporating a great variety of playful Spanish Colonial Revival elements—turrets, wooden balconies, metal grilles, blue awnings, projecting bays, and round, flat, oval and pointed arches—in scales ranging from tiny to huge. The interior walls are simpler, but the variety of window and door openings manages to give each set of offices a special character. With space this grandly and intimately cascading around the visitor, the place was a joy even during its long downhill slide into tacky oblivion. Now it has been fully restored, and it is a thrill.

VI 3 · BULLOCK'S WILSHIRE
3050 Wilshire Boulevard, on the south side, between Wilshire Place and Westmoreland Avenue, Los Angeles
John and Donald Parkinson, architects; Eleanor Lemaire, Jock Peters, Feil and Paradise, interior; Herman Sacks, ceiling mural of porte cochere, 1929

Bullock's Wilshire is one of the masterpieces—perhaps *the* masterpiece—of Los Angeles' golden age of Art Deco in the late 1920s, when the country was still prosperous and the architecture of a department store could reflect high aspirations, a sense of good feeling, and even art. The building is full, as well, of superior planning ideas and attitudes that put it at the beginning of the next era, which would be dominated by the automobile and suburbia. Bullock's, which is said to have been the first suburban department store, rose up in a bean field at the east end of what was then an isolated, though rapidly developing new stretch of Wilshire Boulevard, for the road had not yet been cut through Westlake (now MacArthur) Park. John Bullock figured that he could lure wealthy customers in their cars away from the fashionable downtown stores; to fulfill his vision, he created the first building that recognized the importance of the automobile: the front, along Wilshire, is at a scale that makes window-shopping possible for drivers; the back, the sunny south side, has a far grander entrance than the one in front and opens directly onto a big (now two-level) parking lot edged by ginkgoes and palm trees. So Bullock's manages to live in both worlds, to have the easy accessibility from the automobile prized by post–World War II shopping centers, and to front on a street, which lets it be a part of an urban fabric, even though this particular fabric is of the loosely woven sort demanded by the automobile.

The building itself is dazzling, a five-story pile with a ten-story tower, both with lots of copper spilling over the parapets like a generous crème de menthe topping on a parfait, all green over the beige cast stone of the walls. The tower's tall piers, which don't quite fit into the ice cream image, rise unbroken to a point near the top, where copper crème de menthe spills over them, too. The building has everything—the stone, the copper, exquisite ornament, inside and out, and beautiful murals. There is even a theme, the spirit of transportation—fast, streamlined transportation, which shows up first in the magnificent painted ceiling of the south entrance's porte cochere; here are Mercury and ships and planes and even the *Graf Zeppelin,* all done in glowing, brilliant colors, with hard-edged Art Deco assertiveness and elegance. Bullock's Wilshire is all art, all full of energy and life and conviction and spirit; perhaps because it is so full, that when further layers of energy are laid onto it, such as the greenery at

Christmastime, it doesn't resent the overlay, but gets richer and more wonderful than ever.

On the Wilshire Boulevard entrance, a part of the message is written in words as John Bullock tells us that his goal is "To Build a Business that Will Never Know Completion." The heart-on-the-sleeve and the love in all of this makes it hard to know whether Mr. Bullock was talking to the customers at all with his high-minded message. It is somehow heartening to look back on this from our pinched and more narrowly commercial times, hemmed in as we are by the graduates of all the business schools with their energy reserved for the bottom line.

The elegance and the completeness of the design go on and on inside, too. Two related persuasions of chandeliers—disks and branched torches—work their motifs in room after room against exotic tropical wood veneers in some places and gorgeous modernistic collages in the clothing salons. Images of flight are everywhere, a part of the whole building's continuing theme. Still, the powerful theme doesn't prevent a number of submotifs from surfacing, such as the tops of palm trees at the entrance to the men's department or even the mechanical grilles, which, instead of being some dirty anemostat in an acoustical-tile ceiling as we've grown to expect, are careful developments of similar themes in Art Deco patterns made lovingly for the job. The light fixtures do it, too, and so do the frosted glass doors with their big clear-glass plants; even the *Graf Zeppelin* appears again, along with Mercury and ships and smaller boats. All of it is aggressive and energetic and generous, but all of it is sumptuous as well, not the hushed sumptuousness of the money-colored Beverly Hills French of the years that were to follow, but excited, almost explosive, and celebratory—celebrating a way of life that is altogether worth celebrating. So excited were the designers by this flexible and high-spirited idiom that it seems as if they couldn't bear to stop.

VI 4 · AMBASSADOR HOTEL
3400 Wilshire Boulevard, on the south, between Catalina Street and Mariposa Avenue, Los Angeles
Myron Hunt, 1921

The Ambassador (4 A), Los Angeles' first grand resort hotel, is one of the prime reasons Wilshire Boulevard became the extended Main Street of Los Angeles. When construction of the hotel began in 1919, Wilshire was a dirt road running between bean and barley fields on the fringes of rather tentative residential subdivisions. Nonetheless, from opening day, January 1, 1921, the hotel was a success and quickly became a tourist attraction, a fashionable winter residence and a prominent local social center. Its activities moved the city's center of gravity westward and spurred the commercial development of Wilshire Boulevard.

The Ambassador was designed as a classic resort hotel of the period: a many-storied but sprawling big building attended by smaller ones in vast landscaped grounds. All the buildings have salmon-colored plaster walls with red-tiled roofs and recall the charm of Italian villas. The main structure has a flared H-shape plan and contains public and service rooms at the ground levels with guest rooms above. Two-story bungalows, U-shaped in plan, lie secluded in the gardens.

The grounds are filled with flowers, lawns and lavish diversions. A great greensward stretches back and back, from Wilshire to the hotel; gardens along the side and in the rear contain pergolas, a putting green, fountains, tennis courts, a health club, a wooden jogging track, and a swimming pool with its own sandy beach. There used to be a lot more, including the original and sensational Coconut Grove nightclub. The club, alas, was remodeled in 1957; but the rest of the hotel was spared. Some changes have been made over the years, but the good-time elegance of 1921 remains surprisingly intact.

An undeniably poignant part of the atmosphere of the Ambassador's neighborhood was provided by the Brown Derby (4 B) restaurant (1926) across the street, shaped like a brown derby hat, and famous, therefore, across the world, a kind of bellwether of pre-Disney Los Angeles chic. It may have vanished by the time you read this (there are itchy fingers on the wrecking ball), or just maybe it will be saved.

VI 5 · PELLISSIER BUILDING

3790 Wilshire Boulevard, on the southeast corner of Western Avenue, Los Angeles

Morgan, Walls and Clements; Stiles O. Clements, designer; G. A. Lansburgh, theater; Anthony B. Heinsbergen, murals, 1930–1931

Two attributes make the Pellissier Building memorable: it has, on a major corner, 1) a tidy little Zigzag Moderne tower, just twelve stories high but with enough apparent soar to entice King Kong; and 2) it is turquoise blue. It has shops along the streets it faces, a floor of offices above them, a squat octagonal tower (on the corner of Oxford Avenue) roofed in green copper and its main tower on the busy corner of Wilshire and Western. Buried in the block and virtually intact (therefore, almost automatically gorgeous, so architecturally splendid was 1930) is the famous Wiltern movie theater, with enough razzle-dazzle Zigzag Moderne ornament and steaming jungle colors on the walls to make the movie as incidental as the popcorn.

The main tower, which faces diagonally onto its corner, is a lesson in the amount of drama that can be wrung from a little building given the withholding of devices to suggest any particular scale, until the very top. The almost miniature windows rise in continuous slots between long shafts of terra-cotta tile, which form, finally, into ziggurat mounds with little projections of more turquoise tile that sparkle in the afternoon light. To the left, a little tower goes just a bit farther toward scraping the sky.

The two towers and the intervening commercial space of the Pellissier Building now gleam from a recent restoration, while the Wiltern Theater has been dusted off as well to become a performing arts hall. However, some of the sparkle will be dimmed when a proposed thirty-story mixed-use slab rises up, a few feet to the south, to blot out the sun.

VI 6 · McKINLEY BUILDING

3757 Wilshire Boulevard, on the northwest corner of Oxford Avenue, Los Angeles

Morgan, Walls and Clements, 1923

Across Wilshire Boulevard from the Pellissier Building, the McKinley Building is a smaller commercial work designed by the same firm a few years earlier.

Here the architects demonstrate how effortlessly a standard three-story commercial block can be transformed into a Spanish Churrigueresque fantasy. The walls are smooth concrete painted a deep terra cotta. In contrast, every window and door receives special attention: important openings, like the archway to an interior courtyard, are framed in unpainted, heavy, modeled-concrete ornament; less significant openings are set deep into the wall surface below unpainted concrete lintels or ironwork grilles. A grand tower at the corner erupts through the red-tiled roof.

VI 7 · HANCOCK PARK

Bounded approximately by Wilshire and Beverly boulevards, Bronson and Highland avenues, Los Angeles
1910–1940
Private residences

Hancock Park, Windsor Square and New Windsor Square (7 A) were the last of the fancy residential tracts developed on the flatlands of the Los Angeles Basin and are the only ones that still maintain their original splendor. This property, once part of Rancho La Brea, was purchased by Henry Hancock when he arrived from Maine in 1860. It proved rich in oil and became the foundation of the Hancock family fortune.

In 1910 Henry's son, Captain G. Allan Hancock, laid out these subdivisions around the Wilshire Country Club, with broad streets, lavish planting along the sidewalks, and city-sized lots that were just large enough for the grand houses in town of people rich enough to own, as well, beach cottages in Santa Monica or Hermosa, or ranches in the valleys. Oddly, most of the mansions were constructed following the Crash of 1929, but their owners—Van Nuys, Doheny, Banning, Huntington and the rest, who also owned land and oil—were free from want and free from fear. Though done up in a variety of elegant period styles, the houses form a congenial neighborhood unified by similar scale, siting and landscaping. Bronson Avenue (7 B) between Fifth and Sixth streets is a curiously shrunken version of these effulgences, made perhaps for poorer millionaires.

VI 8 · DUNSMUIR FLATS

1281 South Dunsmuir Avenue, Los Angeles
Gregory Ain, 1937
Private residences

Dunsmuir Flats, a classic of the 1930s, has been used repeatedly as a model of the burgeoning International Style in Southern California. Indeed, the lean appearance of the much photographed north side of this long, white stucco apartment building would satisfy the most doctrinaire Modernist: above a street-level garage, the two-story rectangular volumes step cleanly up a gentle slope, at a slight angle from the property line. Each of the four apartments then can slide to the right a bit, to evince its own identity and to shelter its neighbor's one-story entry. The slab roofs over these entries seem to have scraped along the walls, leaving a neat trail of narrow strip windows, which are repeated in a continuous band of glass just below the flat main roofs.

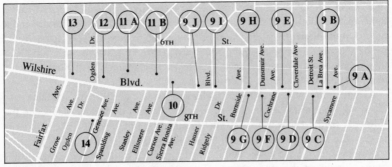

VI/WILSHIRE BOULEVARD (INSET 1)

The south side, however, is a much looser composition of large windows and glass doors that open onto garden patios on the first level and bedroom balconies above. Such willingness to compromise with pure form—in this case, to take advantage of the California sunshine—is doubtless one of the main reasons Gregory Ain was never elevated to the top ranks of the Modern Movement by the keepers of the list. How could they know, in New York and Northampton, that there would be an advantage in admitting the California sunshine? But this one design has become famous, and it still seems an intelligent and pleasant way of dealing with a modest apartment house on a small lot. Although the paint has peeled and the boards have warped and the spare detailing of the period has weathered badly, the hedges have grown very tall, so the Dunsmuir's sunny gardens are even more private than they started out to be. The stark lines of almost half a century ago have mellowed behind growing plants into comfortable middle age.

VI 9 · MIRACLE MILE
A ride going west on Wilshire Boulevard, from Sycamore to Masselin avenues

In the early 1920s a Mr. A. W. Ross determined that automobiles would shape the future of Los Angeles and that four miles would be a satisfactory automobile commute. Placing a circle with a four-mile radius on a map, he discovered he could encompass four of the area's wealthiest residential districts—Beverly Hills, Wilshire, Hollywood and West Adams Heights—from a center on Wilshire Boulevard between La Brea and Fairfax avenues. Along here, Wilshire was merely a two-lane dirt road lined with eucalyptus trees and bean fields, but Mr. Ross had visions of a great commercial center.

While everyone laughed, Ross bought eighteen acres along the south side of the street for the outrageously high sum of $54,000 and began negotiating for the north side. He set up a real estate office to sell lots for $100 a front foot in what he called Wilshire Boulevard Center. Others called it Ross's Folly. By 1928, however, business was booming to such a degree that Ross's Folly was respectfully rechristened the "Miracle Mile."

This was one of the first commercial strips in Los Angeles designed especially to appeal to the motorist. To accommodate the cars, Ross widened Wilshire to six lanes and encouraged buyers to acquire additional land behind their buildings for parking. To accommodate the commuter shoppers, he pioneered a number of commercial firsts: ornamental street lighting, synchronized traffic lights, parking limits, Christmas street decorations, crosstown bus service and a district trade show. Even the fronts of the buildings were designed to be visible to the shoppers driving down the boulevard at twenty miles an hour. Art Deco in style, these simple, streamlined volumes were elaborated with stepped walls and parapets, towers, bands of ornament, or windows and reveals.

Although the buildings shared similar styles and a fairly continuous low profile along the street, they often formed a rich pattern of ins and outs along the sidewalk; their façades were all trying to make a point, designed like billboards to grab the motorists' attention in an instant. Even today, when high property values have forced the newer buildings to square up to the setbacks and height limits, enough of the old buildings remain to make a drive down the Miracle Mile an animated one.

At 5209 Wilshire, near the northwest corner of Sycamore Avenue, is the Kohram Building (9 A) (Morgan, Walls and Clements, 1929). Although this building is only one story high, it makes its presence felt on the street with one of the last remaining façades of black and gold terra-cotta tiles, the ultimate showstopper of the 1920s; a similar black-and-gold motif was used by these same architects on the unforgettable Richfield Building downtown, demolished in 1968.

A few doors down, at 5225 Wilshire, on the northeast corner of La Brea Avenue, is a stepped ziggurat, the Wilson Building (9 B) (Meyer and Holler, 1930). A four-sided Mutual of Omaha sign now masks the buttressed top of this Zigzag Moderne colossus, but you can still see its dirigible mast, a device employed by a number of these tall buildings to advertise themselves beyond the old 150-foot height limit.

On the south side, at 5370 Wilshire, is the Dark Room (9 C) (Marcus P. Miller and Associates, 1938). Although this little store is now called Yalle International Brass, its display window is still the front of a super-scale camera, a giant version of the miniature cameras that were all the rage at the time. Just as plaster over wire mesh seem appropriate materials for giant hot dogs and doughnuts elsewhere, glass block and vitrolite seem comfortably at home here.

At 5410 Wilshire, on the south side between Cloverdale and Cochran avenues, is the Dominguez-Wilshire Building (9 D) (Morgan, Walls and Clements, 1930). This elegant tower seems taller than its ten stories, with vertical strip windows that dramatize a glassy, recessed entrance from which you can look right through to the parking lot behind. The ground floor has been remodeled, but the cast Zigzag ornament is still visible above, on the tower and on a two-story wing, which slipstreams down the block, curves around a corner and then slides along Cloverdale Avenue.

Across Wilshire from here is a one-story block of stores (9 E), each one interesting, the ensemble a special treat. Sweeping around the northwest corner of Cloverdale, at 5401 Wilshire, is Chandler's shoe store (Marcus P. Miller and Associates, ca. 1938), now called Tru Line Litho Service. An energetic display of Moderne elaboration erupts from the top of its smooth plaster walls: various curved forms, including half- and quarter-round pylons with capitals like accordians, leap up from dentil or diamond-patterned string courses; a chimney-shaped pylon marks the corner entrance. The store next door has been remodeled out of its place in the line, but the four shops at 5407 through 5411 Wilshire call attention to themselves with a marquee composed of horizontal stripes and a little fret of flowers with stylized leaves. Next, at 5413 Wilshire, is Roman Foods (ca. 1935), which is a very simple building except for rows of horizontal lines along the upper plaster wall; on the right, a large pylon trimmed with smaller horizontal lines spells out a vertical MARKET. Then comes Brown's Bakery, at 5423 Wilshire, which is in Beverly Hills French. It slips in just before this block-long roadshow comes to a halt at 5425 Wilshire, on the northeast corner of Cochran Avenue, where the tiny Flying Saucer Barbeque serves up fast hamburgers and chickens under a bright red roof.

At 5458–5480 Wilshire, ending at the southeast corner of Dunsmuir Avenue, is a standard, two-story Zigzag Moderne commercial building (9 F) (ca. 1928) with store fronts on the first floor and offices on the second. At each end a small tower flaunts with gay abandon ornament of the Churrigueresque pastry-tube persuasion.

At 5514 Wilshire, on the south between Dunsmuir and Burnside avenues, is the Wilshire Tower (9 G), formerly Desmond's (Gilbert Stanley Underwood,

VI 9 · *Miracle Mile*

1928–1929). This block-long, two-story Zigzag Moderne building, with an eleven-story tower that steps up from the center, even has its ground floor in original condition, with rounded corners, marquees over the entrances, and display windows lined in maroon ryolite or black-and-red granite. Desmond's, A. W. Ross's first customer, established with this building the precedent for parking spaces in back and an Art Deco enthusiasm in front that was to streamline much of the boulevard and make it work.

Across the street, at 5517 Wilshire, is El Rey Theater (9 H) (W. Cliff Balch, 1928), which is a tiny Art Deco extravaganza; its smooth walls break into inset panels of somewhat straightened-up botanical ornament, overlaid by wavy lines and then zigzag ones; three ribbed towers fortify the marquee, while a vertical, fluted panel grows out of it. Everything has been painted gray now, except for the silver leaves that still gleam on an extraordinary box office in the center.

The buff-colored walls of the two-story building (9 I) at 5615–5631 Wilshire, on the northeast corner of Hauser Boulevard, swarm with Plateresque-Churrigueresque details. Although the first floor has been remodeled, the upper walls, which rise to a small tower on the east, are still covered in stonelike blocks in a random ashlar pattern that blooms with ornament around doors and windows and along the cornice. This confluence of insets and outgoes, all beneath a variety of shed and pyramidal red-tiled roofs, is altogether dazzling.

One block west, at 5665 Wilshire, on the northeast corner of Masselin Avenue, is an undistinguished 1950s sort of building that used to be a Van de Kamps bakery (9 J). It still supports a huge, blue billboard-size sign with the Van de Kamps windmill on it, only now the blades are gone and other signs, MEXICAN CUISINE—LA MALAGUENA and DISCO, have been added. This one sign seems to say a lot about the whole Miracle Mile, of high-spirited extravagances in more prosperous times and tacky low-budget adaptability in the face of decline.

However, most of the buildings along the Miracle Mile still have their original exteriors, especially above the first floor. The businesses within prospered until the 1950s, when the wealthy residential districts shifted west to avoid the smog; new shopping areas developed, first in Beverly Hills, then in the malls near the freeways. Retail business along the Miracle Mile has been good enough generally to stave off demolition, if not good enough to merit restoration. Given the notions of restoration prevalent since World War II, we should be grateful.

VI 10 · PRUDENTIAL BUILDING

5757 Wilshire Boulevard, on the north, between Masselin and Curson
avenues, Los Angeles
Wurdeman and Becket, 1948
Now called Museum Square

This is a surprisingly pleasant building from the mild-mannered forties, an asymmetrical composition of great rectangular blocks covered in salmon and cream-colored terra-cotta tiles. Horizontal louvers protect long bands of windows on the south side, which faces Wilshire. The largest block is on the right, a stone-clad office wing that reaches out toward the street; a lower department store wing on the left protects a landscaped entrance plaza with giant and shiny Art in a round fountain. Several palm trees have attained wonderful heights and ficus trees have grown to a size that would startle an Easterner trying to raise an expensive little one in a pot in his apartment. While the building makes a Modern monumental statement all its own, it still responds to the same themes established along the boulevard: the main entrance is at the back, facing a large parking lot; elements along the front echo the low scale of the other buildings along the Miracle Mile, each of which is, of course, making its own Modern monumental statement as well.

VI 11 · LA BREA TAR PITS
· GEORGE C. PAGE MUSEUM OF LA BREA DISCOVERY

5801 Wilshire Boulevard, in Hancock Park, near the southeast corner of
Curson Avenue
Thornton and Fagan Associates, 1976
Open Tuesday through Sunday, 10–5; free admission

Remains of the recent past are in fairly short supply in this new city, and archaeological evidence is negligible; but in the realm of the very distant past Los Angeles shines, thanks to the extremely ancient contents of La Brea Tar Pits (11 A). These pits are actually pools of asphaltum and crude oil (*brea*), the largest over three hundred yards long, which have been seeping from subterranean sources for thousands of centuries. During the Ice Age huge prehistoric beasts—mammoths, giant sloths and bears—were deceived by the layer of water over the ooze and became helplessly mired. Predators—dire wolves and saber-tooth tigers (*Smilodon californicus* is the official California state fossil)—would pounce on their struggling victims and become trapped themselves. The tar preserved the skeletons, making this the world's largest find of Pleistocene remains.

Eons later the Indians used the tar for waterproofing their canoes and baskets; the Spaniards and Yankees put it on their roofs. In 1905 oil geologist W. W. Orcutt discovered that thé real worth of the pits was not petroleum but fossils. So rich was the find that ten years later, when the owner, then Mayor G. Allan Hancock, donated this land to Los Angeles County, the Museum of History (only one of a stampede of collectors) had recovered over six hundred thousand bones.

Today the thirty-two-acre preserve, landscaped with lawns and shade trees, like a typical American city park, encompasses a number of fenced observation pits and the George C. Page Museum to display the cleaned skeletons; the large and lackluster Los Angeles County Art Museum is on the grounds, too, because the county already owned the land. A life-size reproduction of an imperial mammoth, half submerged in a great tar lake alongside Wilshire Boulevard, trumpets desperately to her poignantly dismayed mate on the boulevard shore. Glimpsed from the busy street, this sight is one of the city's most bizarre.

The George C. Page Museum (11 B) is set partly underground and partly within grassy berms, so only its entrance, which looks something like an Egyptian tomb, and the wraparound frieze of its space-frame roof are visible. The frieze consists of repeating panels of prehistoric scenes cast into antiqued bronze fiberglass. The underground museum wraps symmetrically around a square open-air atrium filled with tropical foliage and a splashing waterfall. Since most of the museum's daylight is filtered through the space frame and the plants, the interior illumination resembles the muted greenish glow found in artists' renderings of dinosaur-ridden jungles. The exhibits range from predictable but still awe-inspiring skeletons to the holographic transformation of bones to flesh (before your very eyes) of a saber-tooth cat and an Indian maiden. An orange backlit wall of 404 dire wolf (*Canis dirus*) skulls steals the show.

VI 12 · LOS ANGELES COUNTY MUSEUM OF ART

5905 Wilshire Boulevard, in Hancock Park, at the northeast corner of Ogden Drive, Los Angeles
William Pereira and Associates, 1964
Open Tuesday through Friday, 10–5; Saturday and Sunday, 10–6; closed on major holidays; admission fee

Sited on the edge of the La Brea Tar Pits, this bleached-white modern behemoth, which looms over the bones of mastodons, mammoths and the other monsters of the past, is actually, on the inside, one of the finest museums in Southern California. Giant panels, built up in narrow strips of a kind of mosaic material, glisten from within thin frames of molded concrete to achieve a sort of pink elegance against the sky. A balcony, which would be monumental in scale except that it has no scale at all, overlooks what once tried to be an urbane moat. It leaked, so now grass with sculpture on it surrounds the block on your left, called the Ahmanson Gallery, the Armand Hammer Wing straight ahead, and the Bing Center on the right. It's about what you'd expect here: that a wing would be in the center, and a center would be on the right.

VI 13 · MAY COMPANY
6067 Wilshire Boulevard, at the northeast corner of Fairfax Avenue, Los Angeles
Albert C. Martin, Sr., and S. A. Marx, 1940

The May Company is distinguished for putting everything it's got right up front in the manner of the Spanish Churrigueresque, but in the altogether different idiom of the popular Late Streamline Moderne style of the 1940s. The best bet is to approach this four-story building from the west, for most of its energy has been invested in an enormous tower at the Fairfax corner, visible for many blocks, announcing the west end (or beginning) of the Miracle Mile. This quarter-cylinder signpost, glittering with one-foot-wide bands of gold mosaic tile, rises from the corner entrance to the lip of the store's flat roof; just to make sure of your attention, there's a concave black marble frame with MAY CO in gold letters down the sides. The rest of the building, with its plain, porous stone walls, which were once white, and its rows of slightly projecting, intermittent strip windows, doesn't try to compete with such virtuoso showmanship. The first-floor windows along Wilshire and Fairfax keep to their business as well, but they are made urbane by a continuous, projecting marquee with flags waving above. The result, though it lacks the richness of Sullivan's ornament, is a marvelous openness to the street similar to that of the famous Carson Pirie Scott department store in Chicago. In the tradition of Wilshire Boulevard, the more ample entrance is at the back, facing the parking lot, where another marquee and more black marble with gold embellishments turn customers into patrons.

VI 13 · *May Company*

VI 14 · *Buck House*

VI 14 · BUCK HOUSE
On the southwest corner of Eighth Street and Genesee Avenue, Los Angeles
R. M. Schindler, 1934
Private residence

The Buck House is one of R. M. Schindler's most sophisticated, most resolved, most beautiful and best-preserved works; the house sits close to the front of a corner lot in order to allow a generous courtyard garden behind, so it is one of the most visible of Schindler's buildings as well. It is also a splendid example of the possibilities of an architecture composed almost entirely of white stucco walls. With only one material in use (windows manage to remain voids), the play of light over it becomes the design. Smooth rectangular planes shift and slide, up and down, forward and back, and become enclosing or freestanding walls, parapets and overhangs. The eye is led from one plane to the next and back again. Throughout the day and the year, the sunlight changes the assemblage from flat to three-dimensional and back.

Schindler designed this house at the height of the Miracle Mile development, whose center on Wilshire is just a few blocks away. Perhaps in deference to this, the roof of the Buck House resembles a miniature version of the Streamline Moderne pylons and towers on those commercial structures. But more historically important than the external sculptural effects is the easy continuity of the interior spaces, from one to another and through the glass walls to the courtyard around which they are organized. All of this presages the development of the relaxed, outdoor-embracing California houses of more recent years.

VI 15 · FARMERS MARKET
On the northeast corner of Fairfax Avenue and Third Street, Los Angeles
James Dolena, 1934–1937 and after
Open Monday through Saturday, 9–8

Approximately ten million locals and tourists visit the Farmers Market (15 A) each year, only one million fewer than go to Disneyland. The place is well known for the exceptional quality and variety of the produce sold here, but it is better known for being by far the liveliest pedestrian environment in the city, a sensual maze of food stalls, shops and cafés. All manner of fruits, vegetables, nuts, meats, seafood, baked goods, teas, coffees and jams beckon from open-air stalls and stands. Outdoor kitchens fill the air with the aromas of Chinese, Mexican, Middle European, Italian and American home cooking in this giant sidewalk café. Chocolates are dipped, pies are taken from the oven and cakes are decorated. The non-food shops offer an exotic assortment of baskets, toys, clothing, souvenirs and even pets.

The market first opened in 1933, during the Great Depression, as an ordinary marketplace for local farmers whose fields were then as close as the San Gabriel and other adjacent valleys. The farmers paid fifty cents a day to sell whatever they could from handcarts and the backs of trucks. After real estate promoter Roger Dahljolm persuaded the landowner, oilman Earl B. Gilmore, to transform this modest gathering into a showcase for California's produce, the market evolved slowly over the next decade into a permanent institution.

All of the stores, stalls and stands are collected into two main buildings ringed by an enormous parking lot. The cluster on the north is a typical 1940s

VI 15 · *Farmers Market*

and '50s shopping-center scheme: a walkway surrounds a long island of shops. The more exciting cluster on the south, a small-scale precursor to the shopping malls of the 1960s and '70s, is just the opposite: the shops surround a pedestrian court. Here the food stands are jammed together in an intricate jumble of narrow passages lined with goods, much in the manner of a Middle Eastern souk. Closely spaced awnings, overhangs, umbrellas and a few scattered trees filter the sunlight and provide haphazard protection in case of rain. The architecture is gentle, even casual, a sort of western American builder's dream of New England with a slight Spanish accent: white-trimmed, putty-colored clapboards cover most buildings; a clock tower with a peaked roof and a tiny balustrade announces the market and serves as its logo.

At the northeast corner of the parking lot, behind a mysterious adobe wall and luxuriant foliage, is the old Gilmore adobe (15 B) (1851), which was one of the early buildings on the vast Rancho La Brea. This single-story house, comfortably nestled into its oasis, now serves as offices for the Farmers Market. There is a pleasant glimpse of it through its front gate.

VI 16 · THREE BANKS
A · GREAT WESTERN SAVINGS
8484 Wilshire Boulevard, on the southwest corner of Hamilton Drive
William Pereira, 1972

B · SECURITY PACIFIC PLAZA
9665 Wilshire Boulevard, on the east corner of Bedford Drive
Craig Ellwood Associates, 1969

C · MANUFACTURERS BANK
9701 Wilshire Boulevard, on the west corner of Roxbury Drive
D. J. Anthony Lumsden, DMJM, 1973

Combining the fun-filled chutzpah generally expected in Los Angeles, especially along gala Wilshire Boulevard, with the stern dignity usually associated with banks could produce some truly questionable miscegenations. We are probably fortunate that the offspring are as well-behaved as they are, though mostly they don't seem to have inherited their parents' strength. These three, each by a different architect, all date from the most recent period of financial optimizing and share a blandness that is too slick to be really chunky, but too simple to be very stirring. An architectural problem of these times is, of course, that the medium is the message; and the medium, in the case of corporate architectural practices these days, is a tiny plastic model, beautifully made. The trouble is that it has probably one ninety-sixth the dimension of the finished building, and any detail or visual delight too small to show at one ninety-sixth scale seldom makes it to the finished work.

Great Western Savings, Security Pacific Plaza and Manufacturers Bank are steel-frame buildings with slick skins of dark glass divided by grids of steel mullions. Though they are tall, they do not change as they rise, but are simple extrusions of their plans. Great Western, oval in plan, looms like an enormous squashed dirigible, upended and moored to the corner of Wilshire and La Cienega boulevards. In the street-level plaza that surrounds its base, fat geyserlike fountains splash between shaggy sycamore trees. The plan of Security Pacific is a simple rectangle pulled back from the sidewalk behind a small boulevard plaza. Its surface is a medium brown. Manufacturers Bank, a descendant of Mies van der Rohe's amoeba-shaped tower of 1928, rises up sheer, extruded from its plan, which undulates in rolling curves like a massive 3-D piece of a jigsaw puzzle.

VI 17 · BEVERLY THEATRE
9404 Wilshire Boulevard, on the southwest corner of Canon Drive, Beverly Hills
B. Marcus Priteca, 1931; restored, 1982
Originally called the Warner Theater

This high-spirited intermingling of Zigzag Moderne and Churrigueresque persuasions, only two blocks east of Rodeo Drive (page 212), is one of the most sophisticated pieces in Beverly Hills' chic downtown. The Beverly Theatre was designed as a cinema by Los Angeles' virtuoso theater architect B. Marcus Priteca, who had just completed the Hollywood Pantages Theater (page 245), one of the most extravagant Art Deco interiors of all time. In 1982 new owners finished a monumental restoration of the Beverly and reopened it for concerts and stage shows.

The most stirring part of the façade is a six-story tower that thrusts above the central marquee as a series of thick pylons that break off at different heights to form a stepped top; above that is a cornice of zigzag lines and pastry-tube floral shields, which give way to a ziggurat roof topped by a giant artichoke of a finial. Two-story sections on each side of the tower echo the excitements above with gushing cornices, stepped and zigzagged pilasters, and a series of elaborately ornamented upstairs windows surrounded and made even more throbbing by enormous indentations in the walls.

The interior lives up to this flamboyant introduction. The lobby has white walls trimmed in gilded ornament and ceilings painted in rich floral patterns; even the wood beams are decorated in gold tendrils. The theater itself is an Art Deco bombshell, of ornament piled on ornament, with zigzag and curving shapes exploding from every surface, all in muted reds and blues and outlined in gold; a scalloped gold frieze frames the ceiling, whose feverish patterns seem touched off by a golden starburst in the center. Still, one of the grandest moments in the Beverly Theatre takes place in its least extravagant room, a small downstairs lobby with wood-paneled walls and just a fringe of gilded ornament around the top. Here the modern theatergoer can relive a quiet moment of Hollywood's Golden Age, sipping champagne by a black marble fireplace or drinking water from an elegant brass seashell.

VI 18 · HOME FEDERAL SAVINGS
9720 Wilshire Boulevard, on the southwest corner of McCarty Drive
Edward D. Stone, 1962

I thought this was the most painful building in the world when it was built for Perpetual Savings; the new tenants have done nothing to alter my opinion. Although this eight-story building is very small for a skyscraper, the relentless rows of strange, space-age medieval, identical parabolic arches, each in its own gleaming white precast concave panel, make the walls ripple in the sunshine and help the building to seem agonizingly taller. It is curious how Piacentini's arcaded building in the E.U.R., Mussolini's Third Rome, which looks similar and may have been the inspiration for this one, manages to be fairly straightforward, while this one, with all of its kinkiness and curling and coming and going, looks more than faintly sinister. The west side is blanked out, but the arches on the north, which faces Wilshire, have thick vines, achieving a quality somewhere between hirsute and pubescent. The pain is not eased by the token small plaza in front with its standard fountain and a few trees. They just couldn't let it alone: the parabolic arch motif continues around a one-story parking garage at the back; here the arches are completely filled in by greenery except for a merciless ogival number at the end, an automobile entrance, which is still too narrow for drivers to enter without dread.

There are, by way of compensation, some wonderful houses on the street behind.

VI 19 · SAWTELLE VETERANS CHAPEL
On the southwest corner of Bonsall and Eisenhower avenues, just north of
Wilshire Boulevard; take the Veterans Administration Hospital exit
from Wilshire
J. Lee Burton, 1900
Interior is usually closed; for permission to take photographs, call (213) 478-3711

Just west of the San Diego Freeway, Wilshire Boulevard curves through the vast Sawtelle Veterans Center, whose great lawns are dotted by shade and palm trees. Up to the 1960s, the grounds looked much like a nineteenth-century summer resort with white-painted shingle and clapboard structures that bristled with Gothic picturesqueness, but nearly all of these have been replaced by an assortment of anonymous government-issue behemoths. The only early one to survive is the Catholic-Protestant Chapel, a building with exceptional verve.

This dedicated mixture of Colonial and Gothic revivals, with its creamy white clapboard walls, steep gable roofs and fancy woodwork, seems to have started off on a rather straightforward cruciform plan. However, as the name might suggest, there are two separate chapels inside, each with its own entrance—one entered on the east, the other on the south. This duality forced its way out to the exterior and altered things considerably: there are doorways for every occasion, from a grand arcade to a cute little porch with a peaked roof,

VI 19 · *Sawtelle Veterans Chapel*

while three bell towers fill up nearly every hollow in the plan and point sharply (if not accusingly) up to heaven, each in its own energetic way. And then the scroll-saw man went to work, inspired by the breathless ambiguity: intricate moldings of every persuasion frame rectangular windows, arched windows, lancet windows and lunettes; ornate brackets drip from the eaves, while endlessly enthusiastic little balustrades spring up at every opportunity. The result is a church that has stood here for the whole of this century without ever seeming to stand still and has served as a remarkably cheerful distraction from the horrors of five wars and their sad aftermaths.

VI 20 · GEHRY HOUSE
1002 Twenty-second Street, on the south corner of Washington Avenue, Santa Monica
Frank Gehry, 1978–1979

Frank Gehry is one of Southern California's most distinguished architects, with a reputation that rockets around the world. Here he has taken on a perfectly ordinary house on a perfectly ordinary street and added overtly and aggressively ordinary pieces to it to make the whole thing into a Statement about his views on the Art that his friends, the major artists of Southern California, are making, and about his views on life and society and the ordinary and the complex and, again, Art. His repertoire of the ordinary enjoys, especially, corrugated metal sheets, cyclone fencing and two-by-four studs. Gehry finds a continuing pleasure in throwing these pieces together in ways that are meant to look casual but then hit you in the back of the head with their extraordinariness and their qualities of surprise and, with any luck, delight.

It seems to me that delight is especially strong in this house, which is, for all its astonishing differences with what's around it, a cheerful and pleasant addition to a cheerful and pleasant neighborhood. The neighbors aren't so sure, but it has that same kind of "Maybe it seems naïve but you know it isn't" apparent ingenuousness that makes houses built out of bottle glass or broken plates or other unusual materials become monuments that people travel halfway around the world to see.

What Gehry has done here is to take a polite house on a corner lot and partly tear it apart, revealing its innards, then surround it with a new skin of his materials—corrugated metal, glass, exposed studs and, in the kitchen/dining area outside the original house, an asphalt floor. I would have thought the last would be asking too much of one's wife, but I have had dinner there, and Mrs. Gehry seemed to walk across the asphalt floor with elegance and grace. (The floor, it turns out, was her idea.) As we've said over and over, a place like this is not so much a building as a ride, an experience, and so, as in any ride, the criterion has to be, not what formal standards it meets, or does not meet, but how you feel there. I have to report, having spent some time in this house, that while I'm in it and looking around at it I feel just fine. I will allow the architect his artistic statement, his whole idiom, even, if it comes off as an experience to be cherished; and this time, I think, this one does. I'll even listen a little bit to all the things he's trying to tell me as he celebrates his ordinariness, his unfinishedness, his laid-backness and his appreciation of how things are.

VI 21 · PACKARD SHOWROOM
1626 Wilshire Boulevard, on the south corner of Seventeenth Street, Santa Monica
Edwell James Baume, 1928
Now Simonson Mercedes-Benz

This Spanish Colonial Revival automobile showroom is just a big rectangular box that lets everyone know exactly what's inside: on each side of a giant, elaborately detailed Moorish archway are huge, two-story curtain walls of glass. The great size of the panes and their aluminum mullions indicate recent remodeling, but the 1960s ratio of window to wall was here from the beginning, in 1928. Perhaps surprisingly, the glass looks right at home in its Spanish-flavored frame of beige plaster walls, spiral colonnettes and red-tiled roofs. The building's finest moment, in fact, is an intermingling of picture and frame, an intricate wrought-iron screen along the top that recalls the Baroque reredos of Mexico and Spain. Still, there is no question about what is most important. From either direction the passing motorist can ogle the fancy cars displayed inside, their shiny surfaces twinkling beneath the lights of three Spanish chandeliers. The far wall, not unlike the backdrops for car ads today, is a Castilian castle stage set of little Moorish windows, romantic stairs that sweep up through a huge archway, and entrances to the back that look like walk-in fireplaces.

VI 22 E · *Santa Monica Place*

VI 22 · SANTA MONICA DOWNTOWN

The survey plot for the City of Santa Monica was filed with the Los Angeles County Recorder on July 10, 1875, by developers Colonel R. S. Baker of San Francisco and Nevada Senator John P. Jones. The city opened for business a few days later, when Thomas Fitch announced the public auction for the newly laid-out lots with these remarks:

> At one o'clock we will sell at public outcry to the highest bidder the Pacific Ocean, draped with a western sky of scarlet and gold; we will sell a bay ... a southern horizon ... a frostless, bracing, warm, yet unlanguid air ... ordered with the breath of flowers. The purchaser of this job lot of climate and scenery will be presented with a deed of land 50 by 150 feet. The title to the ocean and the sunset, the hills and the clouds, the breath of the life-giving ozone, and the song of the birds is guaranteed by the beneficient God. ...

Despite Fitch's eloquence, however, the bidders were far more interested in Santa Monica's possible future as the port of Los Angeles, a city without a natural harbor. To this end the developers had constructed a mile-long wharf, and a railroad line from Santa Monica to Los Angeles. Nevertheless, after a fierce five-year battle that went to the Congress, San Pedro became the port and Santa Monica became a resort.

Growth was gradual until the 1920s, when many Hollywood movie stars built summer villas along the beach and brought glamour, while the opening of Donald Douglas's aircraft company brought employment. Santa Monica boomed. During the next twenty years, the vaguely nautical, vaguely resort, vaguely midwestern character of the city was established. Blocks and blocks of modest Streamline and Zigzag Moderne, Spanish, Moorish and a few English-Cottage bungalows and courts were constructed on the city's flatland lots; similarly styled four- to eight-story commercial blocks and civic structures were built; resort hotels and more courts went up along the view strip of Ocean Avenue. And countless palm trees were planted everywhere.

Some memorable buildings from the period before World War II include: the Embassy Apartment Hotel (22 A) (Art Harvey, 1927), at 1001 Third Street, a particularly handsome garden apartment building whose smooth concrete walls are enlivened by rich Moorish and Spanish details and flowering vines; the Santa Monica Post Office (22 B) (Robert Dennis Murray, 1937), on the west corner of Fifth Street and Arizona Avenue, blending Streamline Moderne with American Indian motifs in the same understated elegance as Union Station in downtown L.A.; and the Streamline Moderne Shangri-La Hotel (22 C) (William E. Foster, 1939), on the east corner of Ocean and Arizona avenues, which sports shipshape massing and hardware to offer an evocative background for a seaview structure.

Since the 1950s, the smog to the east has made Santa Monica with its ocean breezes increasingly valuable, and pressure to develop higher densities along the coast has escalated. Bungalows have been replaced by cheap apartment buildings jammed into those original 50-by-150-foot lots, while period-styled medium-rises have given way to glass and steel towers. Fortunately, a number of the new structures recall the special character of the city.

The most noticeable is the General Telephone Building (22 D) (DMJM, Cesar Pelli, 1973) at 100 Wilshire Boulevard, on the east corner of Ocean Avenue. Alternate bands of windows and twenty-two white concrete floors curve continuously around the corners of this Streamline Moderne skyscraper. On every side huge pilasters rise the full height of the building, while at street level the floor is cut back to leave columns standing free in front of a monumental arcade. This creamy white tower is considerably higher than surrounding structures and becomes the axial end to Wilshire Boulevard.

Santa Monica Place (22 E) (Frank O. Gehry and Associates, 1980), at the north corner of Second Street and Colorado Avenue, is another regional shopping center with a predictable formula—an enclosed mall lined with franchise shops, department stores to anchor the ends, and voluminous parking lots. Still, the designers have managed to add an overlay of upbeat surprises. The walkways are angled and meet in the center at a piazza, a high basilica volume drenched in natural light from abundant clerestory windows. Even glassier expanses at the entrances allow them to be light and airy. Galleries recede as they rise between floors so that people can circulate at each of the three levels and can enjoy yet more natural light. From each entrance a catalog of up-to-the-minute elements unfolds: greenhouses, shed-roof appendages, celebrations of vertical circulation, freestanding walls with cutouts, and eye-catching accessories such as brightly colored awnings and artful lighting fixtures. Even so, the parking garages are the strongest feature. The one on the north corner is covered by a huge green metal grid. On the south, chain-link screens run floor to roof line; they echo the hazy light of the beach and softly announce the name of the Place with misty letters twenty-eight feet tall.

VII/SUNSET BOULEVARD

Beverly Hills Hotel

If you could have just one drive through Southern California, Sunset Boulevard is probably the one you should take. It doesn't have the commercial splendor of Wilshire Boulevard or the pathos of Route 66 or the breathtaking views of the Pacific Coast Highway; but in its 27 miles from the plaza where the city began to the Pacific Ocean and the sunset, it traverses at least the most various and certainly some of the most fascinating pieces of Los Angeles. In the first few miles it goes out of the resurrected hoopla of Olvera Street (page 8) through areas where Vietnamese refugees and very poor Chicano families live, past a dense cluster of Victorian houses on Angelino Heights, Los Angeles' first suburb, and a pretty lake in Echo Park. It then goes through the heart of Hollywood's entertainment industry, past some of the old movie studios and the newer studios for television and music recording. There's still a lot of the expected color and tumult along here, much of it rather old by Los Angeles' way of keeping time, including Crossroads of the World, one of the earliest and still one of the most appealing shopping centers, Hollywood High, the backdrop for countless late-show reruns, and Tiny Naylor's, the last of the big-time drive-ins.

After Crescent Heights Boulevard, Sunset crosses into an isolated section of Los Angeles County to become, for a little less than two miles, the Sunset Strip, where especially dazzling aspects of life in Southern California have happened, from the Golden Age of movie stars and F. Scott Fitzgerald's days at the old Garden of Allah to the psychedelia of the sixties to the amazing billboards, which are now the most visible and often the most exciting art forms in Los Angeles. When the Strip crosses an imaginary line and becomes Beverly Hills, it changes dramatically again, this time to luxuriant plants and huge houses, some of them behind high fences, others that should be. Special attention has been given in recent years to the mansion (on the northwest corner of Sunset and Alpine Drive) of an Arabian sheik who pointed up the frontal nudity of his Classical statues with a realistic paint job. As of this writing, the house has been gutted by fire and boarded up, but the statues remain.

A little farther on, Sunset passes in front of the Beverly Hills Hotel, which is even more thickly landscaped than the rest of this celebrated garden city; then it begins to curve sharply through further greenery, with the UCLA campus (page 199) on one side and the hills of Bel Air, another enclave of great wealth and movie stars, on the other. Past palatial gates and up a beautiful canyon is another grand hotel, the Bel-Air, one of the world's most wonderful places. Across the San Diego Freeway, the scenery becomes only slightly more modest as the boulevard passes through Brentwood, home of only slightly less well-known

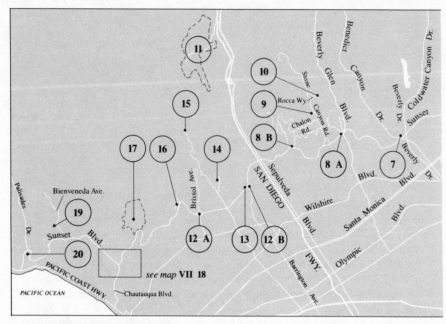

VII/SUNSET BOULEVARD

and well-to-do people. Sunset becomes more rural as it sweeps by Will Rogers' ranch and Rustic Canyon and enters Pacific Palisades, famous for its artists and writers and its views of the sea. After several more miles Sunset curves down one last hill in a giant, near-360-degree loop and comes to an end at the Pacific Coast Highway, next to a little Spanish Colonial Revival gas station, across the street from the Pacific Ocean.

For all the rushing traffic and urban chaos alongside, most of Sunset Boulevard is surprisingly pretty, with more than its share of gorgeous landscaping. Even the seedy parts toward the east have a sun-drenched quality that bleaches out some of the darker aspects of poverty. The commercial activities along the Strip are especially cheerful, small-scale and laid back, but lush, with a kind of energetic extension of a style that is locally called French but was surely born in Beverly Hills. The gentrified charms of the super-rich communities at the end are less pressing, but the trees seem to come at just the right moment to soften the clamor. Indeed, it often seems that this most varied ride through Los Angeles has been rigorously choreographed from east to west by some movie director or screenwriter or Walt Disney or even Busby Berkeley—anyone but the opportunistic developers who are said to have built up the route. Every possible kind of vista or landscape or building or economic condition or way of life in this vast city seems to have been compressed and laid out like some gripping novel along the length of Sunset Boulevard. Don't forget your bathing suit for the denouement.

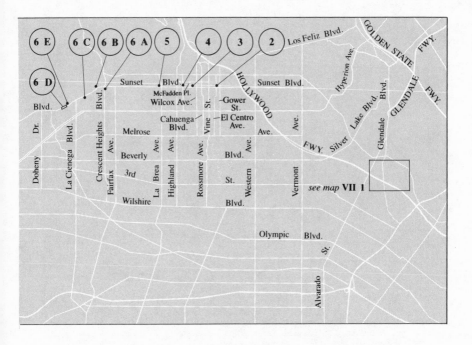

VII 1 · CARROLL AVENUE VICTORIANA

**A walking tour of the 1300 block of Carroll Avenue, Angelino Heights;
from Sunset Boulevard, go south on Douglas Street for six blocks**
A tour of the interiors is given once a year

With the arrival of the Southern Pacific Railroad in 1876, Los Angeles began to shed its relaxed Ramonaland demeanor in earnest. Easterners, with their Yankee ways and Yankee architecture, flocked into town, lured by feverishly written accounts of palm trees and blue skies. Most eagerly read of the breathless publicists was Charles Nordhoff, who wrote *California for Travellers and Settlers* in 1873 and *California for Health, Pleasure and Residence* in 1882. And then, of course, there was Helen Hunt Jackson's *Ramona* in 1884. In 1885 the Santa Fe Railroad completed the second transcontinental line into Los Angeles, which started a hard-fought rate war that suddenly made the Promised Land affordable to anyone; at one point in 1887 the price of a ticket from Kansas City to Los Angeles dropped to a single dollar. And so began the remarkable real estate "Boom of the '80s," which lasted only from 1885 to 1888, but saw as many as a thousand new arrivals a day, all of them given a warm welcome by real estate promoters. Colored flags that marked new subdivisions and whole new towns fluttered across much of the Los Angeles Basin; land prices went up 500 percent a year. The boom went bust in 1888 and many newcomers went home, but Los Angeles was changed forever. The early adobes and the vast ranchos had been quickly surrounded and then engulfed by the familiar ever-widening rings of Yankee suburbia.

Angelino Heights, an upper-income subdivision overlooking downtown, was Los Angeles' first suburb, reached by a mile-and-a-half-long trolley line. Carroll Avenue was its finest street, lined with large wooden houses in the most up-to-date Victorian styles, Queen Anne and Eastlake, or most often a mixture of the

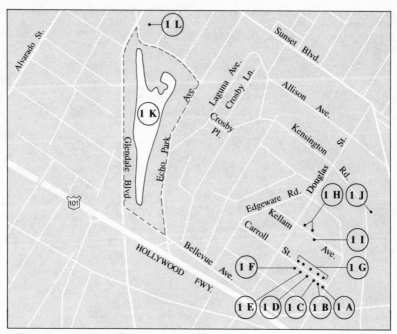

VII 1 · CARROLL AVENUE VICTORIANA

two; so the irregular massing, Classical details, high turrets and sweeping porches of the former were given even more life by the delicate, sticklike structure and the profusely scrolled and turned ornament of the latter. When the boom ended, this tiny island of high-spirited Victoriana was cast adrift, gradually encircled by less expensive houses, and allowed to decline.

But in the mid-1970s local residents organized themselves into the Carroll Avenue Restoration Foundation, which has produced, in a remarkably short time, the densest and most handsomely restored collection of late Victorian houses in Los Angeles: the little lawns and flower beds are as bright and cheerful as the authentic Victorian paintwork and the globed street lamps. So a stroll down Carroll Avenue today, especially at dusk, is laden with dreams of an Old California as mythical and heartwarming as any conjured up by Charles Nordhoff or Helen Hunt Jackson.

At 1300 Carroll Avenue, on the southwest corner of East Edgeware Road, is the Phillips house (1 A) (1887), a lacy white Queen Anne monument with a touch of Eastlake agitation; its *de rigueur* turret is composed of a gable-roofed, two-story bay window at the entry. At 1316 Carroll, the Russell house (1 B) (1887–1888) is much more wholeheartedly Eastlake, with dark green rectangular panels emphasized by beige sticklike trim. At 1320 Carroll the beige-painted, brown-trimmed Heim house (1 C) (1887–1888) sports such major Queen Anne elements as corner turrets and a wraparound porch, though Italianate brackets bristle along the eaves. 1325 Carroll, the Scheerer house (1 D) (1887–1888), is a tiny pale blue and white-trimmed cottage with Queen Anne frills along every edge; it looks a little like a doll's house, wedged between its towering neighbors.

At 1330 Carroll is the avenue's grandest and most exuberant structure, the Sessions house (1 E) (1888–1889) by one of the period's most famous architecture firms, the brothers Samuel and Joseph Cather Newsom. This studiously

VII 1 E · *Sessions House*

asymmetrical blend of Queen Anne and the Orient, made up of brick and clapboard and various kinds of shingles, was the Newsoms' version of the long
sought-after indigenous California Style. In the Queen Anne tradition, an intricately carved veranda wraps around a turret on the right, while a multitude of
gables makes up the roof. The most striking element is a two-level porch in the
center, most of which seems to have arrived here from China, though each level
is capped by a flamboyantly shingled, Classically molded pediment. The lower
porch is reached by a sort of half-moon bridge, past Chinese lion-dogs and
through a giant latticework arch; the three sides of the upper porch are protected by abacus spool screens, each with a large moongate circle cut out of the
middle.

The Haskin house (1 F) (ca. 1895), at 1344 Carroll Avenue, is the last Victorian to be built on the 1300 block, though this time a full-fledged, hellbent for
leather Queen Anne style with all the trimmings. This yellow-painted, white-
embroidered fantasy looks like everybody's vision of a cute little Victorian
house, partly because it has been the backdrop for scores of movies and television commercials. It has everything: a first-floor veranda slides around beneath
a tiny second-story turret, which is itself an open porch covered by a fairy-tale
cone roof; the clapboard and fish-scale shingle walls angle in and out, forming
two-story bay windows that look like more towers; and everything is outlined in
sinuously carved brackets and columns and intricate spindlework that erupts
from balustrades, screens and a spiky fan above the front porch.

The houses across the street, at 1321, 1325, 1329, 1345 and 1355 Carroll Avenue
(1 G), are all various intensities of the Eastlake persuasion and are, for the most
part, as full of affectionately restored charms as the ones on the south. The first
two are recent arrivals, refugees from other parts of Los Angeles. The streets
north of Carroll Avenue were developed later and therefore are lined with a
great many Mission Style houses and California bungalows, though a few Victorian dowagers still hang on. At 1343 and 1347 Kellam Avenue, one block
north of Carroll, are two nearly identical Eastlake houses (1 H), both built for
the Hall family in 1887. The Funnell house (1 I) (1902) at 1334 Kellam is a one-
story, wildly eclectic transition between Queen Anne and the California bungalow, with every manner of Classically inspired decoration. Three blocks north
of Kellam Avenue, at 824 East Kensington Road, is the Weller house (1 J)
(1880), which was brought here in the early 1900s from Bunker Hill, off which
wealthy residents were already moving. It's easy to understand why Weller

brought his gingerbread masterpiece along with him in the move. This romantic mixture of Queen Anne forms and Eastlake ornament is a Valentine's Day card of gable roofs and little porches laced with frilly balustrades and screens and delicate Moorish arches. A high turret in the middle is a heart-rending tribute to the picturesque.

Just west of Angelino Heights is one of Los Angeles' prettiest and oldest parks, Echo Park (1 K) (donated in 1891), a forest of native and ornamental trees wrapped around a fifteen-acre lake. Here you can walk across an arching footbridge to a little island and observe one of the nation's largest stands of Oriental lotuses, which bloom bright pink in late spring and summer. They are said to have been started by superstar evangelist Aimee Semple McPherson, whose quarter-round, five-thousand-seat Angelus Temple (1 L) (1923) still stands near the northwest end of Echo Park. One of the best ways to enjoy the park is to glide around in a rented paddleboat and gaze out past giant turn-of-the-century palm trees to the skyscrapers of downtown.

VII 2 · CBS BUILDING
6121 Sunset Boulevard, on the north side between Gower Street and El Centro Avenue, Hollywood
William Lescaze, architect; Earl Heitschmidt, associate architect, 1938
Not open to the public

The CBS Building is truly a wonder. It has been important to me since my childhood, when it was new and first published; I took it then as the heart of International Style modernity, as thrilling as the cathedrals of Europe. There have been some additions and remodelings over the years, but the elegance of the structure and all the wonderful 1930s friendliness is still here. And, CBS being CBS, the building has been kept up beautifully; the kind of staining and deterioration that we're used to seeing on those clean, moldingless buildings of the early Modern period has simply not been allowed to happen.

The big event here is the absolutely forthright, five-story main volume, which lies in the middle of the block, perpendicular to the street. This reinforced-concrete rectangular volume has a smooth skin of soft beige stucco (surely it used to be white) with regular bands of strip windows that barely scratch the surface and form those tiny corner recesses that seemed so important in those days. The windows, with their alternating casements and fixed sash, set up a rhythm that reflects very satisfactorily the sky and, in a way, dematerializes the building. The appearance of lightness is set up already by the way the top four floors seem to hover in the air above fat round columns, the pilotis of Corbusian doctrine; the solid ground-level walls, which used to be glassy, are set in a couple of feet from them. The only exception to the absolute rectangular simplicity of it all is the CBS sign, which is a flat flange of beige stucco, perpendicular to the street, with a curvy top and diagonal bottom.

The CBS Building came from that part of the 1930s that had developed a great scorn for streets and for what was regarded then as the terribly limiting condition of having buildings that showed only a street face and were not seen, as Le Corbusier had learned in Greece they ought to be seen, from all sides, like a Greek temple. So Lescaze made his gesture against the street by turning the main building at right angles to it. This unexpected twist allowed the building to be seen from three sides and also provided an impressive courtyard in which people could alight from their exciting automobiles. Today, in a more hostile era, the driveway is gone and a big fence cuts across the once welcoming mouth of the courtyard; where sleek automobiles used to be are tables that look a touch forlorn on the concrete pavement. Three other two-story wings fill out this block of Sunset Boulevard: the ones on the east, next to and behind the courtyard, have the same clean details as the main building (although the middle wing has lost its glass); the one on the west is, and always has been, an unrelieved stucco box.

VII 3 · HOLLYWOOD ATHLETIC CLUB

6525 Sunset Boulevard, on the northeast corner of Hudson Avenue, Hollywood
Meyer and Holler, 1924
Now the Berwin Entertainment Complex

This half-block-long building, two stories high on the west and seven stories higher in a fat tower on the east, was one of the most sumptuously outfitted and populated city athletic clubs in America during Hollywood's golden years; almost everyone in the movie business, it seems, was a member. The Athletic Club was designed during the fever for Spanish Colonial Revival by Meyer and Holler, the same showmen-architects who did Grauman's Egyptian (page 243) and Chinese (page 242) theaters; so it is to be expected that a few out-of-the-ordinary flourishes would be added to the standard pink-tinged plaster walls and red-tiled roofs. The two-story wing is straightforward, with Moorish arched windows on the street level and rectangular windows above, all shaded by maroon awnings. The base of the tower, which serves as the main entrance, is faced in an elaborate but unremarkable version of Italian Renaissance stonework.

The one really grand moment happens at the highest part of the tower. After six uneventful floors, the tall top story, sliced off at the corners to become an octagon, erupts into a four-way symmetrical Classical extravaganza: each side sports a deep-set Palladian loggia in the middle, surrounded by pilasters, blind arches, intricate moldings and diminutive balustrades; each corner opens onto a little triangular porch, shaded by a maroon awning; and then the whole is

VII 2 · *CBS Building*

VII 4 · *Crossroads of the World*

topped by a red-tiled roof with an American flag waving from the center. As in the Chateau Marmont (page 178), farther up on Sunset, and in Patriotic Hall (page 395), the Athletic Club's most extensive and carefully crafted signs of inhabitation surprise the passerby by taking place way up in the air. Seen from below, this strange Renaissance stage set looks tiny and delicate and almost enchanted, as if some fairy tale were being acted out high above the boulevard.

VII 4 · CROSSROADS OF THE WORLD
6671 Sunset Boulevard, near the northeast corner of Las Palmas Avenue, Hollywood
Robert V. Derrah, 1936

Of the same period and just as startling as the CBS Building, only eight blocks away but poles apart from it, is the Crossroads of the World, a high-spirited eclectic free-for-all of little shops grouped around a Streamline Moderne building that looks like a cross between a diner and an ocean liner. This charm-drenched shopping center was designed by Robert V. Derrah in the same year (1936) that he launched his famous Coca-Cola Bottling Plant (page 30). The ship, in the case of Crossroads, has portholes, pipe-railings and rounded ends, but it doesn't go so far as the Coca-Cola one; it is, in fact, a small-scale abstraction of the perspective drawing Derrah had made, in a corner of the Crossroads site plan, of a cruise ship tied up next to a Moroccan village, where exotic shops beckon the passengers to disembark.

The ship, as built, does have a large number of nautical features, all trimmed in red, white and blue, and all unbelievably shipshape. But it is itself a group of shops and it's rather small, for the most part only one story high, with a two-story section at the front. And it faces Sunset Boulevard with a giant, four-pyloned tower sweeping up from its bow; spinning around the top is an eight-foot-diameter globe, symbolic of the worldwide assortment of shop fronts around it. Placed in front of the bow (at some later date) is a tiny, astonishingly out-of-place Spanish fountain, symbolic, perhaps, of the oceans this liner came in on.

Unlike the ship, the little one- and two-story buildings around it are surprisingly literal fantasies. These miniature fragments from the world's most romantic villages (with or without harbors) are extremely convincing, going all the way to cute and back, arranged, something like Disneyland, in little architectural lands of their own. Here is a truly astonishing collection of teeny turrets and bays and oriel windows and odd chimneys and stairways drifting up the outside; there are little towers and big towers and motifs that go from Santa Barbara Hispanic to Beverly Hills French to vaguely Alpine to North Africa. Also like Disneyland, the edges often melt together while the details and the scale seem less inspired by pattern books than by fairy tales.

The area on the east has a Spanish or Mexican theme. The Spanish Colonial Revival building that wraps around to face Sunset has, on the sidewalk, a short arcade with some of the finest columns anywhere. They are no more than three feet high, dwarfed to a sort of minimidget size by big arches on top of which are corbels, on top of which are more arches, on top of which is a tiny second story, a third-story tower and various red-tiled roofs. Next door is the large Church of the Blessed Sacrament, dressed in a half-modernized Churrigueresque, whose tall tower is almost as pure and powerful as the one on the Crossroads cruise ship. Farther along on the right are Spanish roofs and towers and details turned by lathes in a sort of Magic Mountain motif. The shapes are extraordinary, made up of purple tile, blue roofs, little porches, tiny windows, and steps that go up tight to overhangs over front doors. After a while the Spanish theme changes into Moorish or Turkish. There's a one-story building that would seem to be Spanish except for the detail, which is full-blown Moroccan with south-of-the-Sahara tattoos all over the trim.

The buildings to the west of the ship have Italian and French flavors, and are a little calmer, although they sport flamboyantly painted shutters. The second-story walls of the front building have diagonal grooves that suggest a kind of trellis. As you turn the back corner, going west toward a parking entrance on Las Palmas, the buildings become more Victorian and cottagelike with white clapboard walls and a white picket fence, a recollection of Early America and Cape Cod.

The north side of this walk and a large area behind the ship, once projected for more shops, is the site of a parking lot. The part of the main walk behind it, called Continental Villa, remains intact. Its flanking rows of shops, with trees and brick planters down the middle, are a particularly vivid evocation of Northern European persuasions. Somehow it doesn't seem odd that the mood is introduced by a little Spanish fountain, a big eucalyptus tree and a handsome Victorian-Americana five-globed street lamp. The possibly Swiss Alpine buildings on the left get more dreamy and woozy as they go, while the perhaps French Alpine buildings on the right start off rather woozy but become sort of country Provençal, like the Beverly Hills version of French. The tiny shops along the ground floor have extremely romantic stairways that curve up to even more quaintly considered suites on the upper floors. On the left end this goes all the way to a particularly explosive Hansel and Gretel manifestation which is probably French, though no one in France ever saw anything like it. Across the walkway, on the right end, is a tiny one-story building with a complicated shingled roof that curves at the bottom, suggesting its French persuasion. Behind it is a lighthouse, complete with light and a balcony where even a midget couldn't fit.

Everywhere you look are steep roofs and odd little dormers and half-timbered walls next to Classically detailed plaster ones. And the scale gets flipped around as much as the details: there are tiny panes in big bay windows, small roofs supported on enormous brackets, and miniature balconies with overscaled posts. The astonishments never end. A white-plaster turret has a Russian Orthodox sort of onion dome that rests on some of the world's strangest columns. There are chimneys shaped like you've never seen them shaped before; but perhaps they're not chimneys at all. The effects are somewhere between that of a quaint village in the south of France and appropriate decoration for a wedding cake. And, not surprisingly, everything fits right in with everything else in this high-spirited architectural traffic jam at the crossroads of the world.

VII 5 · TINY NAYLOR'S
7101 Sunset Boulevard, on the northwest corner of La Brea Avenue, Hollywood
Douglas Honnold, 1950

One block west of Hollywood High is the classic high school hangout of years past, a drive-in hamburger stand of the kind where carhops (preferably on roller skates) bring out your hamburger and your milkshake on a little metal tray that fastens onto your car's door. The craze for this kind of place had swept the nation in the years bracketing World War II, when the automobile seemed so wondrous and had just become an essential part of the youthful social scene. It started in California and was particularly suited to the California good life. The drive-ins quickly became a destination, if one were necessary, for a major nighttime activity in Los Angeles—cruising. In faster-paced times since, these gathering spots have been all but replaced by the drive-throughs; Tiny Naylor's is just about the last of the real drive-ins in Southern California.

It is still a fine place to hang out. It remains a gleaming oasis on this busy corner, in the middle of a large parking lot, twisted forty-five degrees to catch the traffic from two main streets. All the traditionally zoomy 1950s materials are here, and in excellent condition, from the terrazzo pavement to the steel wedge-shaped columns to the vast expanses of glass. Most wonderful of all is the enormous rocket roof that extends way out over everything; it sweeps up from an indoor coffee shop at back to become a giant, high-flying porte cochere above the parked cars in front. The white-stuccoed ceiling underneath is studded with recessed spotlights, so at night Tiny Naylor's becomes a dazzling blaze in the glitter of Sunset Boulevard.

VII 5 · *Tiny Naylor's*

VII 6 · SUNSET STRIP
Sunset Boulevard between Crescent Heights Boulevard and Doheny Drive, Los Angeles County

Commercial strip developments are endemic to the western United States, but there are only two in the world-class category—the ultra-flashy casino connector, the Las Vegas Strip, and Los Angeles' own, the Sunset Strip, once the playground of Hollywood and now, among other things, the rock-and-roll and popular music capital of the world. Here, on a 1.7-mile-long segment between Hollywood and Beverly Hills, Sunset Boulevard changes dramatically: everything becomes suddenly bolder and brighter, packed with glamorous billboards, racy store fronts and boundless energy. The Strip has become synonymous with night life, excitement and cruising; it is a kinetic destination in itself, where you can become a spectator and a participant at the same time. While much of the magic happens after dark, when the exuberant buildings and signs come alive with powerful lights, the ride is still a thrill by day.

For the most part, this section of Sunset became the way it is because it goes along the north edge of an anomalous, unincorporated piece of Los Angeles County, where activities are less encumbered by the law. But the Sunset Strip owes much of its appeal to its geography, for the roadway has been cut into the lower elevations of the Santa Monica Mountains and winds in and out of ravines to create constantly changing vistas of the hills above and the vast city below.

As a reflection of the temporality of the entertainment business, the buildings and especially their façades change as quickly as the latest trends, from rock to punk, from cabaret to comedy, from steaks to hamburgers to nouvelle cuisine. By the late 1950s, the famous nightclubs—the Trocadero, the Mocambo and Ciro's—had gone. And so had most of the movie stars; great numbers of them used to shop and carouse along here, for the Sunset Strip was once the trunk line from home (Beverly Hills) to work (Hollywood). As on Hollywood Boulevard (page 241), the 1960s brought the drug addicts and the pornography and a near disastrous decline. But by the 1970s the record companies began to move in, followed by a number of television and movie production companies, followed by new shops and fancy restaurants to serve them. The chichi and the flash have returned, almost as dazzling as ever.

The flashiest sights along the Strip, and the most temporary, are the enormous billboards, which are cleverly sited and beautifully painted glorifications of the momentarily famous. Gleaming with polychrome and neon, sometimes mechanically activated and sometimes blasting out of their frames, these signs are hardly ever the mass-produced variety; rather, they are one-of-a-kind originals rendered by skilled painters, often in celebration of one person. It is said that this egomaniacal tradition began in Las Vegas in 1953, when the Sahara Hotel advertised itself with a traffic-stopping sign that included as part of the act a real swimming pool and real bathing beauties. Shortly afterwards an aspiring starlet rented a billboard on the Sunset Strip to exhibit her portrait and name; she didn't go over, but the idea did. From then on, a long procession of big-name actresses, from Mamie Van Doren to Julie London, began to smile down on their fans, edged out finally by musical luminaries such as the Beatles, the Grateful Dead and Rod Stewart. Soon the most coveted status symbol in the music business was not a platinum record but a personal salute on the Strip. At night the celebrities thus honored are indeed superstars, the most brilliant objects shining in the Hollywood sky.

Although the Los Angeles County line and the official beginning of the Sunset Strip occur in the vicinity of Marmont Lane, just west of Crescent Heights Boulevard, the pace begins to quicken a little before that. One early throb is the famous Schwab's Pharmacy (6 A) at 9024 Sunset, near the southeast corner of Crescent Heights, where, later facts have revealed, Lana Turner was not discovered. However, this was, and still is, a place for stars and aspiring stars to hang out. Architecturally, Schwab's is undistinguished in its very 1950s mode, but the most interesting things to look at on the Sunset Strip anyway are the people—all of them flexing whichever muscle is appropriate to get them into the movies. Here, though, are a handful of buildings that might catch your eye as well.

B · CHATEAU MARMONT
8221 Sunset Boulevard, on the north, at Marmont Lane
1927

This big hotel, as famous and long-enduring as anything else along here, acts as a gateway to the Sunset Strip, which was a dirt road when the hotel went up in 1927. Since then almost every movie star in the world has either stayed or lived here, in an atmosphere known for its relaxed and rather tumbledown elegance. There is not much to say about the architecture of this enormous, L-shaped block of reinforced concrete except that it has allusions to a sort of Norman Gothic, and that almost all of these allusions occur at the top, seven or so stories up in the air. So, like the old Hollywood Athletic Club down the boulevard, most of the signs of inhabitation—in this case, wide terraces with traceried balustrades and striped awnings—go on their merry, somewhat eerie way at the place where such a straightforward high-rise is expected to have a flat parapet. Steep roofs with elaborate chimneys and dormers and a pointed tower in the middle all add to the surprise of this frothy-headed white behemoth that rises up against a dark green hillside. At the bottom is a handsome Gothicky entrance arcade with ribbed vaulting, brick paving and a little fountain at its end.

C · SUNSET TOWER
8358 Sunset Boulevard, on the south, opposite Kings Road
Leland A. Bryant, 1929–31
Private residences

The Sunset Tower apartments, along with the CBS Building and Crossroads of the World, has been a favorite of mine since I was a child and is surely one of the great places along the boulevard. Gebhard and Winter call it "a first-class monument of the Zigzag Moderne and as much an emblem of Hollywood as the Hollywood sign." This eleven-story, reinforced-concrete Hispano-Deco extravaganza rises up all by itself on the south side of Sunset on a site that plunges down from the sidewalk, so it's blessed with a magnificent view of the Los Angeles plain. It is roughly square in plan, with rounded corners and rounded corner windows and with a remarkable shifting in and out of planes on each wall surface. It piles up past statues and friezes finally to an elevator tower worthy of a world's fair, with great cavetto cornices high on top of a strange series of engaged pylons that look something like multiple umbrellas or the howdahs of elephants in distant civilizations. There are a number of large panels emblazoned with flat, almost Plateresque versions of the local toothpaste-tube Churrigueresque ornament, and there are even some brackets with statues flattening themselves against the wall. But more than the parts, there is something about this building, a charismatic chutzpah, that sets it apart and makes it special.

At present, Sunset Tower is under restoration and looks like the battered old wreck it is—a little bit like an aging movie star in a mud bath. But when it's fixed, it will surely have that same dazzle that the refurbished stars achieve.

D · SUNSET PLAZA
On both sides of the Strip, 8589–8711 Sunset Boulevard (on the north) and 8600–8720 Sunset Boulevard (on the south), at the intersection of Sunset Plaza Drive
Charles Selkirk, original architect, ca. 1932; Honnold and Rex, 1934–36

This group of swank shops, which line both sides of the boulevard with parking behind, has been called the commercial center of the Sunset Strip. It seems to try very hard to be chic, in the manner of Rodeo Drive (page 212), and employs a mixed idiom that is special to Southern California, especially to Beverly Hills. The little shops, all one-story and very much alike, have aimed for individuality with fronts that are variations on neo-classical, Colonial Revival and Regency Moderne themes. The roofs have different heights and different slopes, and there is a broad range of bay windows, planter boxes, quarter-round awnings, and tasteful signs with names like Optique Boutique and Tutto Italia Grocery And Delicatessen. There are flagstone walkways and trees and well-trained shrubs, and there is even a narrow formal garden down the center of Sunset Boulevard. The ambience gets strained at times, but the façades are considerably calmer in their elegance than those on Rodeo Drive. And, like Beverly Hills and Westwood Village (page 206), and very unlike the new enclosed shopping malls, Sunset Plaza has taken advantage of the possibilities in Southern California for a relaxed sophistication in the open air.

The eastern gateway to Sunset Plaza, though it was surely not meant to be that, is a restless little coffee shop on the north side of the Strip called Ben Frank's (6 E) (8585 Sunset Boulevard, 1962). It is recollective of Googie's On The Strip, which isn't there anymore, but which started a whole jazzily unorthogonal style of architecture in the 1940s. This version is made of what seem to be long, super-scale strips of red shingles fastened down by a series of A-frames. The roof has been tilted crazily down at the middle, so what starts out to be a contemporary Alpine statement, sliced off at the bottom to provide a glassy entrance, becomes a South Seas dream of rum-drenched afternoons. It's only a coffee shop, but it has an air of drunken abandon. Googie's had it, but few others have had it quite so fully as this one.

West of Sunset Plaza, all the way to where the forests of Beverly Hills bring the Sunset Strip to an instant conclusion, the older landmarks have given way to a highly charged and nearly indistinguishable array of sparkle and bright colors. The pace is so fast along here that you can almost watch the shops and restaurants and nightspots changing hands and becoming more glittery still. Individual descriptions would be beside the point, for the medium here is the montage, which gets more interesting by the day.

VII 7 · BEVERLY HILLS HOTEL
9641 Sunset Boulevard, on the north, between Beverly and Benedict Canyon Drives, Beverly Hills
Elmer Grey, 1912
Group tours are not encouraged; no photographs

The Beverly Hills Hotel, which Burton Green, the developer of Beverly Hills, had built to attract land buyers to his new town, is one of the most celebrated hotels in the world. However, it is not known for its architecture, neither the original Mission Revival structure nor the Modern additions; nor is it particularly well-known for its erratic, though sumptuous trappings. What affords this place such universal acclaim is the fact that, since it opened in 1912, almost every one of the richest or most powerful or most famous people on earth has stayed here. Its 325 rooms and bungalows and its fancy gathering places are engulfed by an aura of wealth and glamour as heavy as its pink plaster walls and as thick as the twelve-acre jungle that surrounds them.

The foliage is so dense that the walls, already trimmed in forest green, have all but disappeared. Throughout this oasis, which is in the heart of the larger oasis of Beverly Hills, the overgrown landscape is the dominant theme. Here is an exotic garden gone wild, where every tropical plant imaginable has been nurtured to abundant excess: tall Mexican fan palms are choked with the scarlet blooms of bougainvillea; long tendrils of ivy have climbed to unbelievable heights on other palms and eucalyptus; narrow pathways to secluded bungalows (Howard Hughes used to keep several) appear to be hacked out of every pink shade of hibiscus; even interior corridors are wallpapered with life-size banana trees.

VII 8 · BEL AIR
Mostly north of Sunset Boulevard, approximately between Beverly Glen Boulevard and the San Diego Freeway

The wooded hills of Bel Air are home to vast numbers of movie stars as well as the rich and famous in general. Ever since this strictly residential community was developed by Alphonzo Bell in the late 1910s and early '20s, the residents here have consistently hired California's finest architects to build their opulent estates. Unfortunately for the sightseer (though maybe in the end it's for the best) they also employed the finest landscape architects, whose overgrown work is about all we ever get to see. The first architect was Mark Daniels, who was hired by Bell to plan the development. He also designed a Spanish Colonial Revival administration building (ca. 1928) on the northwest corner of Chalon and Stone Canyon roads, which is now part of the Bel-Air Hotel (below). This was the first of many Spanish-flavored buildings here, often designed by such grand masters of the idiom as George Washington Smith, Wallace Neff, Roland Coate and Gordon B. Kaufmann. The other kinds of houses by other famous architects are as numerous and wonderful as they are impossible to see.

Two neo-Baroque entrance gates, on Sunset Boulevard at Bel Air Road (8 A) and at Bellagio Road (8 B), both by Carleton Winslow, set the stage for the sequestered luxury in the hills behind. The streets bear romantic names like Siena Way, Chantilly Road and Strada Vecchia Road; but most descriptive of itself and of the entire street system is Tortuoso Way, for all the roads go through treacherously picturesque contortions as they wind around hills and ravines or the edges of the Bel Air Country Club. The roads curve through jungle-like tunnels and pass between densely planted hedges and trees or stone walls covered in vines. Even though most of the architecture has to be imagined, the drive through here is still enjoyable. Like a visit to the Beverly Hills Hotel (page 179), a ride in Bel Air is a well forested one, rich with the fragrance of exotic plants and great wealth.

VII 9 · BEL-AIR HOTEL
701 Stone Canyon Road, Bel Air
Burton Scott, 1945 and after

Stone Canyon Road sets the mood as it ushers you off the traffic of Sunset Boulevard and winds slowly through the dense undergrowth of a steep and peaceful ravine; it opens up at last at the Bel-Air Hotel, one of the most wonderful places in Southern California. At first glance the hotel looks like just another big stand of trees, though fragments of pink plaster and red tile peek out from the foliage. The most visible feature, rising out of a courtyard, is a large silk-floss tree, which blooms a bright pink-purple in the fall.

There's a parking lot in front with gentlemen in green blazers. Your car is taken away and you find yourself walking under a very simple, almost rustic green awning across a stone bridge. Below is a little stream and all around are twisted sycamores, Chinese elms, Australian tree ferns, purple bougainvillea, and palms—the works. In the distance, bordered by rocks and flowers and a tiny lawn, is a green pool with swans gliding by. The walkway, still canopied, divides, passes by clipped hedges and then crosses through a pretty arcade with soft pink walls and half-circle arches trimmed in white. You go through a short corridor, past a pleasant and intimate lobby, and come out in an open courtyard surrounded by green plants, pink and light gray walls, and red-tiled roofs. A walkway on the right takes you through another corridor, past a *trompe l'oeil* fountain, to a terrace in front of the dining room. Below is the garden where the swans play, the setting for endless weddings and bar mitzvahs, and beyond are more shaggy-edged walkways that lead to the swimming pool. The dining room and adjoining bar are elegant and dark, their windows shaded by banana palms and ferns and scarlet blooming camellias. The main delight is a fireplace set in what seems to be a rocky cliff and surrounded by skylit ferns and ficus, a sharp and exciting contrast to the merry northernness of the glowing embers.

It soon becomes clear, as you look closer at everything, that this is one of the most significant examples in the world of the sum being greater than its parts. One of the great L.A. attributes of the Bel-Air is that if you look at every single detail, it's wrong; there isn't a noble gesture in the whole place. Walkways are made of the plainest concrete, planters of the plainest concrete block; patios are covered in corrugated plastic over two-by-six frames over the thinnest of columns; grillwork, railings and furniture are insistently from the 1950s; and even the delicate arcades that slip around everywhere are awkwardly proportioned. The rather handsome coffered ceiling in the dining room is made of combed plywood, and the textiles on the walls seek pathetically to extend the ambience of the fireplace with a kind of Renoir or Mary Cassatt enthusiasm. What isn't just ordinary is done up in a mild sort of Beverly Hills French.

And yet the hotel comes off as a solid piece of paradise; for all its clumsy parts, the place is seen as a whole, united by a number of elements that please. There are the Spanishy walls and the red-tiled roofs, but more important is the paint, the subtle tones of pink and gray and the crisp white trim. And more important than that is the luxuriant landscaping, which overshadows the buildings and ennobles the spaces but still allows vague hints of the good but misdirected life. And there is a unity, not really of ineptitude, but maybe unschooled innocence, one of the most interesting phenomena to have graced the Southern California scene during these last dissolving decades. And then there's the greatest factor, the extraordinary amount of love and caring that everyone from owners to guests has invested in every inch of this place. One way or another, the people here have performed the magic of turning the ordinary into the extraordinary.

VII 10 · NILSSON HOUSE

10549 Rocca Place, off Stone Canyon Road, Bel Air; can be seen only
from across the canyon at the end of Somma Way
Eugene Kupper, 1979
Private residence

This house for singer-composer Harry Nilsson is one of the most complete, sophisticated, witty and handsome of the exercises (of which there have been
many during the seventies) in forming a set of plain walls with plain openings
placed with sufficient syncopation, surprise and highly disciplined whimsy to
recall without detail a traditional building. It is post-Modern, but in a very different sense from the way that word is usually used. The references to other
forms seem clear enough: to Luis Barragan in the simple plaster walls colored
mauve, pumpkin, an ocher and some white; and to traditional naves and barns
in the gabled central spine. One of the reviews of it (*Progressive Architecture*,
December 1979, by Suzanne Stephens) expresses the hope that from this combination of shapes, colors and influences a strong choreography can emerge: "The
use of vernacular materials, archetypal forms, and certain Modernist principles
indicates that the synthesis and development of these manipulations promise yet
to take us 'beyond Modernism.' " The house is a big one, something over five
thousand square feet, and is designed to be a good neighbor in the very special
architectural landscape of Bel Air.

VII 11 · MOUNTAIN GATE

A residential subdivision on Mountaingate Drive, west of Sepulveda
Boulevard, in the Santa Monica Mountains overlooking the San Diego
Freeway
Carl McClarand, 1978 to present
Private residences

Mountain Gate is one of the most extraordinarily grandiose exercises in the restoration of a garbage dump that has ever taken place on this planet. After the
developers got possession of some deep and sharply sloped ravines that fed into
Sepulveda Canyon, they managed somehow to get permission from the City to
use them as refuse fills. For years the garbage was brought here by armies of
trucks and mixed in with earth taken from the tops of the hills, so that hilltops
became mesas that could serve as flat sites for town houses, and filled-up ex-
canyons became, with a little sod on top, a golf course; the only giveaways are
the pipes that stick up through the greens, burning off the methane gas that
bubbles up from fermenting garbage below. This is regarded, however, as not
more than peripherally unsightly, and rows of giant town houses have popped
up all around.

The town houses have been built, so far, in five clumps called the Crown, the
Crest, the Terrace, the Vista and the Promontory—all much the same, designed
by the same architect, and selling for $675,000 and up in 1983. For the most
part, they are made up of a tawny-colored stucco under red-tiled roofs but have
been variegated in style to reflect the pluralistic heritage of Southern California;
the thinness of the details, though, is much more recollective of modern trailer
courts. The exteriors are done in Spanish, Beverly Hills French, late-Midwest-
ern and some other style for which no sobriquet comes to mind. The buildings

are huge and neatly sandwiched onto narrow sites so that almost everyone can have a view down over the edge, past the golf course with its flaming pipes, to Sepulveda Canyon and the wide San Diego Freeway. The interiors are astonishments of a kind of down-home late Catskill persuasion with swags and chandeliers and gold-plated fixtures.

Sometimes there seems to be a rhythm between the themes and subthemes that animate the designs; the Beverly Hills French theme might include, for instance, a Great White Hunter subtheme with animal skins and poison arrows on the walls of the den. Usually, however, the inner rhythms that marshal these energies are thickly disguised. One of the themes seems to be Old South–*cum*–Charleston or Savannah; another is more sort of Fort Worth Suburban; then others are cosier, but only a few are as fully defined as the Spanish Colonial Revival and Beverly Hills French. The golf and tennis clubhouses are grander in scale and simpler in detail, suggesting that the lack of cosiness is meant to express their public character. The parking lots surrounding them help in that regard. There is surely material for a Ph.D. thesis mediating between the expansive verticalities here of fifteen-foot-high mirrors over marble fireplaces in two-story living rooms and the homier expansive verticalities of the entrance doors of West Hollywood (page 226).

VII 12 · BRENTWOOD
Bounded by the San Diego Freeway, San Vicente Boulevard, Rustic Canyon and the Santa Monica Mountains

Brentwood, which lies to the west of Beverly Hills and Bel Air, is the third of the alliterative upper-crust communities lined up along Sunset Boulevard. It is a little less luxurious than the other two, but it has a full measure of celebrities and expensive houses. Like the others, Brentwood was laid out from the start (in 1906) as a home for the élite; even its streets are said to have been patterned after those in San Francisco's Golden Gate Park, with landscaped roundabouts at thirty-four of the intersections. Only a handful of these traffic circles have survived, mostly along Bristol Avenue; the biggest one (12 A), at Bristol and Sunset Boulevard, is still there, but Sunset Boulevard has lately broken through the middle.

Unlike Bel Air, Brentwood was relaxed enough to allow shopping within its borders, mostly along San Vicente Boulevard. One of the oldest groups of shops, from about 1935, is on the south side of Sunset Boulevard on Barrington Avenue. Most of the Spanish façades have been updated over the years, but a Spanish Colonial Revival gas station (12 B) at 110 Barrington is as glorious as ever with a many-faceted and finialed tower erupting from red-tiled wings.

VII 13 · EASTERN STAR HOME
11725 Sunset Boulevard
William Mooser and Company, 1932
Private residence

Just up the boulevard from the Barrington Avenue shopping center, on a gentle rise above a broad lawn, lies the Eastern Star Home, a particularly large and devoted exercise in the Spanish Colonial Revival. This fine retirement home (for widows of Masons) was designed by the architect who had, three years earlier, concocted the grandest Spanish Colonial Revival structure ever built, the Santa Barbara County Courthouse. Naturally, comparisons leap to mind.

Here a long white-plaster façade, one story high in the middle and two stories at the ends, employs, like that Santa Barbara extravaganza, a great many elements to rivet your attention. There's even a two-story version of the famous courthouse tower near the middle. Next to the tower an entrance archway opens onto a wide front porch, which extends on the left as a series of arches on thick piers and on the right as a colonnade with rectangular openings. The windows, too, come in a variety of sizes and shapes. Red-tiled roofs cover it all: the two-story portion on the right combines hip, gable and shed roofs, while the one on the left, which sports a grand outside stair, has a low-pitched Swiss chalet roof that projects forward on large concrete brackets; these brackets, like big corbels and beams elsewhere, are painted rather nicely to look like wood.

The lively parts all add up to a romantic building with a bit of verve, but there is none of the vitality of the Santa Barbara work, none of the wit or the fantasy or the mind-boggling jumps in scale; the rhythms here are pleasant, but they don't really stir the soul, and seldom emerges a melody. It makes you wonder if Mooser had been wrung dry by the Santa Barbara Courthouse or if the rumor might be true that he had gotten help from some unknown hand on that earlier masterpiece.

VII 14 · *Sturgis House*

VII 14 · STURGIS HOUSE
449 Skyewiay Road, off North Kenter Avenue, Brentwood
Frank Lloyd Wright, 1939
Private residence

This grand sculptural statement from Frank Lloyd Wright's Late Period is extraordinarily easy to find, poised as it is in a row of unassuming houses. As you look up from the sidewalk, all you can see is the front end of what looks like a gigantic wooden balcony, wide as a house, cantilevered way out above an ivy-covered slope. Underneath, deep in the shadows, is a red brick wall almost as wide and just as massive as that strange wooden thing that slammed into it and then froze so mysteriously in midair. After hiking up a steep curve in the road, you look up at what must be a driveway, and the suspicion that this all might be a house begins to grow on you. The red bricks pile up to look rather like exterior walls and become finally a kind of chimney. Another horizontal slash of wood could be a main roof; another could cover a carport. But no windows or doors can be seen, nor any sign of human life.

VII 15 · RODES HOUSE
1406 North Kenter Avenue, near the end, Brentwood
Moore Ruble Yudell, 1979
Private residence

This is another building in which I had a hand, so it will have to go uncriticized. The Rodes house had to bridge across a canyon filled in with structurally worthless soil, so it represented a difficult and, for us, very interesting problem: how to celebrate the act of bridging and at the same time celebrate the tastes and interests of the owner, a bachelor professor whose field is seventeenth-century English literature. Original schemes called for a huge two-story truss, or bridge, to go from side to side of the canyon, where solid ground for foundations could be found; a convex façade, symmetrically fenestrated, was to penetrate the truss. It turned out that such an elaborate bridge would be far more expensive than an underground concrete grade beam, so the latter was adopted, and now a trellis much more delicately performs the service of making a plane for the two-story convex façade to penetrate.

Behind this front wall, entered by any one of five French doors, is a double-cube living room with reminiscences for the owner of the double-cube rooms by Inigo Jones, the seventeenth-century English architect. Just inside, the plane of the trellis continues along as a high grid for mounting theatrical lights. Behind the living room, reached from either side of a central fireplace, is a tall, octagonal dining room with proper Georgian dining furniture. Other spaces are miniaturized and tucked into corners.

The house has been extensively published, praised and criticized for being Classical or Palladian or trying to be more than the simple stucco box that it is. This is seen as either pretentious and horrid or aspiring and grand. The front wall of the stucco box and, indeed, the whole atmosphere of the place came directly from the owner's extensive collection of pictures of houses; modernized eighteenth-century houses in the south of France prevailed in the pictures and in our scheme. The stage-set demeanor is intentional, for Mr. Rodes has plans to perform plays on the half-circle stage of his front terrace, with actors entering and exiting from the five front doors. Further, the front yard has been planted as a miniature orange grove so that the audience might stretch out in the fragrant shade of an orangerie and be transported far from the hills of Los Angeles.

VII 16 · CLIFF MAY RANCH HOUSES
Riviera Ranch Road and Old Oak Road, Brentwood; take Riviera Ranch Road off Sunset Boulevard
Private residences

Cliff May is considered to be the grand master of the California ranch house, that well-known persuasion of long and rambling one-story wings, low-pitched and overhanging shake roofs, and interior spaces that merge into one another

VII 16 · *Cliff May Ranch House*

and with the out-of-doors. The real importance of this idiom, apart from its ubiquity, is its full-blown homage to the relaxed heritage of Southern California, of living close to the bountiful landscape or at least looking at it through vast expanses of glass.

Many of the California ranch house features can be found in any number of frontier buildings, but the open plan, the access to the outside, and the ground-hugging forms beneath wide roofs can be traced, as well, to the immensely popular California bungalow (page 331). The bungalow itself, however, owed a great deal to the early California rancho, whose linear arrangement of one-story rooms was connected by a covered porch; as the dons grew wealthier, their long

VII 16 · *Cliff May Ranch House*

adobes began to sprout wings, usually around courtyards, where, of course, Ramona used to spend a lot of time.

During the late 1930s and after, Cliff May and a number of other architects began to combine and experiment with the bungalow, a closed box on the outside with an open plan within, and the rancho, composed of closed rooms but open through generous verandas to a courtyard outside. What they came up with might be that elusive Indigenous California Style (if millions of houses built is any indication) that had been so sought-after by architects here since the Mission Revival period. After World War II, when great waves of Americans descended on Los Angeles, the California ranch house had been perfected and lay waiting. By the 1950s, builders and developers were turning out ranch houses by the thousands, often honed down or disguised by Cottage or Contemporary façades, so their true personality was not always apparent. But the majority of tract houses in California are versions of the ranch house persuasion. And the phenomenon spread across the United States as well, faster and more fully even than the bungalow (and horribly disfigured, by the time it reached the other coast, as the Raised Ranch or Split-Level Ranch or boxy Ranchette).

Here, just off Sunset Boulevard, is a little enclave of ranch houses that represent the best of the genre. These are clearly the upper-income variety, each sitting in the middle of a large lot as if it were the main house of some vast spread. The luxuriant planting, which all but conceals the houses from the roads and from each other, adds to the feeling of spaciousness. The little roads are lined by adobe walls and trees, and they end in cul-de-sacs with more trees in the center; as you drive down these green tunnels, the most noticeable ranch house appurtenances are the horses in front. But enough can be seen down the long driveways, past rustic wood gates, to observe the qualities they share: all the houses follow the accepted format of low and stretched-out wings, covered porches and adjacent gardens; all of them are mixtures of Old West materials, from board-and-batten or clapboard siding to adobe or local stone, though there is plenty of used brick and stucco; and almost all of them were designed by Cliff May, who, if not the George Washington, was the George Washington Smith (page 343) of ranch houses.

Of the few houses you can really see, the most comfortable and the most characteristic one is at 1520 Old Oak Road (Cliff May, 1940). Along the front, a shaggy mass of bougainvillea separates a white horse in a white corral from a rough-sawn main gateway; steer horns hang from the crossbeam. A little beyond this, the driveway branches at a front lawn, which is just what it looks like—a small putting green. The right fork heads off to the entry; the left one follows a split-rail fence out to a big garage and a breezeway. The one-story board-and-batten house, painted a cheerful pale yellow with white trim, is shaded by a covered porch that appears to run along the entire front. The visitor can't tell just how far this goes on, for the side wings angle back and eventually disappear into the foliage. But there's plenty of room on the shake roof for all the necessary equipment: a number of brick chimneys, a weather vane, and the sine qua non of ranch houses—a pigeon coop. Ramona would have loved it, especially if she played golf.

VII 17 · WILL ROGERS RANCH

14235 Sunset Boulevard, Pacific Palisades
1924 and after
Now Will Rogers State Historic Park: open daily, 8–7 in summer, 8–5 in winter; house tours, 10–5; parking fee

The ranch houses of Brentwood are a good introduction to Will Rogers' comfortable spread, which ambles up from Sunset through a eucalyptus forest planted by Rogers himself. Here, on 186 acres in the foothills of the Santa Monica Mountains, is the California Dream become real, the perfect example of the relaxed but sophisticated outdoor living that has been the goal of all the other ranch houses, from the tracts to Cliff May. This one has it all: picturesque stables and old-fashioned barns, a rambling house with vine-covered verandas, even a polo field for a front yard; everywhere there are rolling lawns and white fences and eucalyptus trees; to the north is a wilderness of chaparral, to the south is a view of the Pacific Ocean. For the most part, everything has been maintained as it was before Will Rogers died in 1935.

In 1922 Rogers moved to Beverly Hills, built a mansion and became a silent-movie actor. With the arrival of talkies, which captured the personality behind the affable grin, Rogers became a number one box-office attraction. He was, at the same time, one of the nation's most popular radio and newspaper commentators. In 1924 he built his Pacific Palisades ranch as a weekend retreat and kept adding onto it as he spent more time there. By 1928 he had moved there permanently, so he could keep horses and play polo and throw barbecues and ride the long trails behind his house. Today you can hike these same trails, to an impressive view at Inspiration Point or far into the wilderness.

The ranch house, a rather odd assortment of unassuming parts, is not a remarkable piece of architecture. Rogers put it together as the need arose, one homey piece after another, rather in the endearing way in which he remodeled the English language. Still, the house is as straightforward and good-natured as its owner. It is a long, linear building, mostly two stories high, with white-painted, board-and-batten walls and gently sloping shingle roofs. Notched out of the

VII 17 · *Will Rogers Ranch*

middle is a small patio with an outdoor fireplace where the Rogerses ate dinner and entertained. The south part, which came first, is filled up mostly by a wood-paneled living room, which Rogers had raised to two stories in 1932 so he could practice his rope tricks inside. Every surface is covered by cowboy paraphernalia, Western art and Navajo blankets. The north wing contains bedrooms, a library and Rogers' study, with a globe still marked by the route he would take to Alaska, where he was to die in a plane crash. The three parts of the house, which look like the disparate additions that they are, are united by a covered porch along the front: it begins as a pleasant shed-roofed veranda on the south, becomes a bougainvillea-covered pergola at the patio, and winds up, on the north, as the space beneath a shallow Monterey balcony. The main attractions, though, are the robust and brightly colored plants—the tangles of trumpet vines and the enormous succulents, the marigolds, azaleas, roses and geraniums. Shrubs and trees have now almost obscured the house and have made it an intimate part of the landscape.

The happiest architectural moment on the ranch is the stable barn, north of the house. Rogers found this elegantly shaped barn in Hollywood, cut it in half and moved both halves here. They flank a big rotunda that he built, with arched openings at each end and a flurry of sticklike trusses under its low-pitched dome. The magic layer of nostalgia is thicker here than anywhere: horses still prance around in the stalls and in the rings outside, for this is now the home of a polo and hunt club. It would no doubt please Will Rogers, who loved polo playing even more than roping, to know that on most Saturday afternoons the vast field below his house thunders again with his favorite sport.

VII 18 · RUSTIC CANYON
South of Sunset Boulevard on Brooktree Road, Pacific Palisades
Private residences

Rustic Canyon is a heavily wooded part of Santa Monica Canyon, the dividing line between Santa Monica and Pacific Palisades, which is the last outpost of great wealth on Sunset Boulevard before it ends at the ocean. Pacific Palisades is named for its shoreline cliffs and is probably most famous for the expensive houses that slide down these cliffs when it rains. In the 1910s Thomas Ince built a movie studio at the end of what is now Sunset, but the area wasn't settled until the arrival in the early 1920s of a group of Methodists who dreamed of creating an art colony around a grand chautauqua. The Methodists' vision never got off the ground, but the artists came anyway, from around the world; during the 1920s through the '40s, Pacific Palisades was thickly populated by famous artists and writers and, of course, movie stars. They lived on curving streets laid out by the Olmsted brothers and in houses designed by many of that era's most distinguished architects.

Rustic Canyon, more than the fancier parts of Pacific Palisades, still recalls that original art colony spirit. It is reached from Sunset Boulevard by Brooktree Road, which actually follows a bubbling brook and is lined by trees—acres and acres of them, for this was the site, in 1887, of the nation's first experimental forestry station. These enormous groves of redwoods and oaks and eucalyptus were first inhabited in the early 1920s by the Uplifters' Club, a group of wealthy businessmen and well-known writers who wanted a sylvan retreat from the city. Along Latimer and Haldeman roads, they built woodsy little houses, often de-

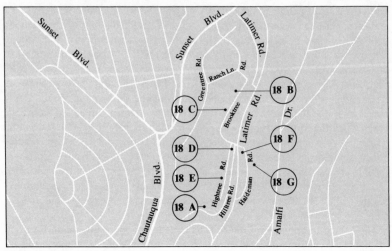

VII 18 · RUSTIC CANYON

signed by that most prolific of bungalow builders, Alfred Heineman (page 331). The members of this élite colony played polo on their own field and socialized in a Spanish Colonial Revival clubhouse (18 A) (701 Latimer Road), which is now part of a beautiful eight-acre public park.

As you drive down Brooktree Road to this old retreat, you will find a number of newer houses in various brands of modern, rustic, and not so rustic. Near to each other are two relatively recent ones, elegantly spare, by Raymond Kappe. The first, at 739 Brooktree, is the Katzenstein house (18 B) (1973), a Late Modern exercise in posts and very long-span beams and layers of redwood and glass. The simple rectangular exterior, now enveloped by foliage, belies a thrilling interpenetration of the interior spaces and an absolute mastery of the cantilever; look, for instance, at the deck above the carport. The second, at 715 Brooktree, is Kappe's own house (18 C) (1968), a handsome blend of clean, rectangular volumes mostly made of redwood and glass, though there's a concrete-walled tower on the right. It's all piled up on an ivy-covered hill, almost hidden behind an enormous sycamore.

On Hightree Road, off Brooktree, are two slightly more visible modern statements by Craig Ellwood (page 320). The Anderson house (18 D) (1950), at 656 Hightree, is about as minimally pure as architecture can get, at least on the façade. All that's visible is a corrugated aluminum garage door next to a one-story brick wall; this is softened, however, by thick foliage all around. The Elton house (18 E) (1951), at 635 Hightree, is a spacious and crisp contemporary bungalow bathed in the dappled light of sycamores and oaks. A wide, almost flat gable roof, which spreads over both the house on the right and a carport on the left, opens up to let light onto an entrance patio in between.

Brooktree Road ends where the old Uplifters' Club begins; it crosses Latimer Road and becomes Haldeman Road, which snakes around on the hillside behind Latimer. Both roads are lined by the original houses as well as a number of newer ones. While this is no longer a private club, the atmosphere hasn't changed much; the little houses are just buried a little deeper in their romantic forest.

Two of the most evocative houses are fairly visible. Heather Hill (18 F) (1922–1923), at 7 Latimer Road, was probably designed by Alfred Heineman. It sits firmly planted on a little mound and looks as if it would be equally at home in the Cotswolds: small-paned windows peek out from red-stained, shaggy-shingled walls; green shingle roofs, even more shaggy, curl over at the edges like thatch; and the surrounding garden, though almost as thick as the forest around, has an air of being ever so slightly tamed. High on a hill behind this house, at 38 Haldeman Road, is the Marco Hellman log cabin (18 G) (interior by Alfred Heineman, 1923–1924), which was owned by a prominent Los Angeles banker. It is said that this cabin and its two neighbors (nos. 36 and 37) were built as movie sets and were moved here afterwards. They look the part, made of bark-covered logs on fieldstone foundations; the vertical logs on the garage do, indeed, look a bit like a movie cavalry fort. Another log house on Latimer, now almost invisible, is said to have been the Norwegian pavilion at the 1915 San Francisco Fair and to have been barged down here afterwards. The rest of the houses around here, or what parts you can see of them, are pleasant though mostly unremarkable. What *is* remarkable, especially apparent along the northern stretches of Latimer Road, is how wonderful even the most dingbat little cabin can become when it's placed in a remote forest just off Sunset Boulevard.

VII 19 · ST. MATTHEW'S EPISCOPAL CHURCH
1030 Bienveneda Avenue, Pacific Palisades
Moore Ruble Yudell, architects; Campbell and Campbell, landscape architects, 1982

This is a recent replacement by Moore Ruble Yudell (that's us) for an earlier, delicate A-frame wooden church (by A. Quincy Jones, 1953) that burned in a forest fire. A very special, possibly unique attribute of the new church is that it was designed in a series of workshops by the entire parish, so that it reflects, as closely as we could manage, the wishes of the people who are to worship here. The plan came from an extraordinarily spontaneous set of decisions by seven groups; when the decisions were presented to the whole group, seven separately designed schemes were found to coincide almost exactly. The parishioners de-

VII **19** · *St. Matthew's Episcopal Church*

VII 19 · *St. Matthew's Episcopal Church*

veloped, as well, the building's mass and texture, arrived at in part from a slide show of churches around the world (Bernard Maybeck and Alvar Aalto were the big winners). They pressed toward a familiar Latin cross shape, which syncopates in what we thought were exciting ways with a half-ellipse of seating, done to get the congregation close to the altar. A prayer garden, left over from the fire and of special importance to many of the older parishioners, is visible through windows on the left of the altar. The walls are plaster to make good acoustics for an anticipated organ, but they are painted and trimmed with wooden battens so as to re-create the wooden feeling of the older church. A chapel to the left of the nave, as well as colonnades and other shapes outside, performs the additional service of bringing the edges of the building close to the ground. This helps to maintain a scale that is rural, quiet and relaxed, recollective of the smaller buildings nearby, including a handsomely picturesque Parish House left over from an estate built in the 1920s; equally important, the scale of the new church tries to recall its smaller predecessor, which is, like the prayer garden, dear to the memories of many.

VII 20 · LAKE SHRINE

17190 Sunset Boulevard, just south of Palisades Drive, Pacific Palisades
Paramahansa Yogananda, 1950
A garden retreat of the Self-Realization Fellowship; open to the public, 9–5; closed on Monday; free admission

As Sunset Boulevard sweeps down a giant curve on its last half-mile to the Pacific, an astonishingly luxuriant sight can be glimpsed through thick hedges on the left. Here, in a small ravine engulfed by flowering plants, is an odd assortment of little structures situated around a little lake. The place turns out to be as mystical and exotic as it first appears, for it is the much loved-over sanctuary of the Self-Realization Fellowship, a religious sect that believes in, among other

VII 20 · *Lake Shrine*

things, the universality of all religions (which allows anyone to visit) and the glorification of plants (which makes its gardens the main reason to visit). The Fellowship was founded in Los Angeles in 1920 by Paramahansa Yogananda, an Indian mystic who, in 1950, bought this ten-acre site with its spring-fed lake and turned it into his own vision of paradise, supervising the landscape construction himself while he lived in a two-story houseboat that is still moored by the shore.

A little walkway winds around the lake in the manner of a Japanese tour garden so that, at selected points, the foliage opens up to reveal and frame particular vistas. Usually a bench is provided for the occasion. In this way, you are allowed to gaze at and reflect on some of the strange events along the route: an authentic replica of a Dutch windmill (a chapel), a series of white-stucco posts and beams with gold-painted domes (the Golden Lotus Archway) or that odd little houseboat (now a guest cottage). From tiny piers placed around the shore, you can observe the many fish, ducks and swans, and a bird refuge that floats out in the lake. A pleasant combination of native chaparral and exotic plants, of bright flowers and little lawns and dense jungle, creates a large number of special places and manages to make the whole garden seem much bigger than it is.

All this should get you in the mood for the biggest attraction of all on Sunset Boulevard, the Pacific Ocean. After one last architectural effort, a Spanish Colonial Revival gas station (page 118) on Pacific Coast Highway, and one last stoplight and one last park named after Will Rogers, this time a wide stretch of white sand, it's all just water and sky and maybe sails. When there are no clouds, some people watch for a green flash as the sun drops below the horizon.

VIII/WESTWOOD AND BEVERLY HILLS

Beverly Hills City Hall

West of Hollywood and the Miracle Mile, along Santa Monica and Wilshire boulevards, lie the two centers on the west side of Los Angeles: Westwood and Beverly Hills. The more western of the two is Westwood, part of the City of Los Angeles, between Santa Monica and Sunset boulevards, just east of the San Diego Freeway; its commercial center, Westwood Village, lies north of Wilshire, on and around Westwood Boulevard. Westwood was established as a real estate development in the 1920s by the Janss Investment Company, which performed the extraordinary coup of offering, at a discount, to the Regents of the University of California a small but highly developable site for UCLA. This ensured the inordinately high value of the surrounding Janss-owned real estate for decades to come. An architectural review board loosely enforced a Spanish-flavored persuasion, though red brick, Classical details, cupolas and flourishes that were doubtless thought to be Italianate were encouraged as well.

From the beginning, Westwood Village has been one of the most popular places in Los Angeles to shop; it bustles even more today as shiny office towers and movie theaters pack themselves between the refurbished boutiques. The streets are thronged with shoppers, younger than the ones in Beverly Hills, for even with its increasing elegance this place is still considered to be a college town. But people come from all over to shop here and to be a part of the excitement; even the ones who cruise the streets forlornly looking for places to park find that they, too, have become part of the California Good Life.

Just east of Westwood, still within the city limits, is Century City, later and denser and far, far duller than Westwood and Beverly Hills with their varied charms. It is reached by a phenomenon known as the Wilshire Corridor, along which high-rise condominiums sporting superexpensive penthouses rise up at what has seemed for decades like a daily clip. They are beginning to densify and to cast Wilshire Boulevard and the little houses to the north into shadow.

At the eastern end of this corridor, forming an odd jigsaw-puzzle piece that lies mostly north of Wilshire Boulevard, is Beverly Hills, one of the world's wealthiest places, a self-consciously separate municipality—some would say a club—of 28,000 people. It is surrounded by the City of Los Angeles (though its eastern neighbor, West Hollywood, is an unincorporated part of the county) and is studded with beautiful trees and gorgeous houses. It was meant from the beginning to be an upper-income community, with its wide streets and large lots laid out in 1906 by the Rodeo Land and Water Company (hence Rodeo Drive), after a turn-of-the-century oil company failed to find anything here but water, great quantities of it. It was the unusual wealth of water, even more than that of the residents, that ensured Beverly Hills' independence from Los Angeles; most of the other towns, including Hollywood, had to give up their cityhood in order to share in the water of the Owens Valley Aqueduct (1913), owned by the City of Los Angeles. The president of the Rodeo Land and Water Company was Burton Green, who came from Beverly Farms, Massachusetts (hence Beverly Hills), and who had the presence of mind to build the Beverly Hills Hotel in 1912 to attract wealthy Easterners to his slow-moving subdivision. The boom began in 1919 when Douglas Fairbanks and Mary Pickford built their fabulous estate, Pickfair, here, and nearly all the other famous movie stars of the period rushed in.

Santa Monica Boulevard, with a beautiful park alongside, and Wilshire Boulevard, lined mostly with commercial buildings, form a sort of horizontal X through the lower part of Beverly Hills and function rather like class boundaries: south of Wilshire are the houses of the merely well-to-do; north of Santa Monica are those of the very rich; while in the real hills of Beverly Hills, north of Sunset Boulevard, are the mansions of the fabulously rich, with the focus on movie stars. (Mostly inaccurate maps to their houses are hawked for high prices on street corners, although the same maps, just as out of date, are available for only $1 each at the Chamber of Commerce.) In the acute triangles of the X, particularly in the eastern one, lie the commercial buildings of downtown and, to the far west, the Los Angeles Country Club, which adds an even larger and more luxuriant swatch of green to the already paradisiacal landscape.

Not long ago all this was potato fields and bean fields and without trees. The first brilliant step of the developers was to line each of their generous, curving streets with a characteristic type of tree—jacaranda, pine, acacia, oak, sycamore—and sometimes to name the street after its trees. So the shaded splendor was already established by the time the houses filled in behind. And the houses, from the start, have been lavish. Harold Lloyd, whose acreage has recently been broken up, was the proprietor of one of the grandest spreads; it included a canoe stream and a waterfall, a nine-hole golf course, a handball court, a swimming pool, and kennels for Great Danes and Saint Bernards—the works. Groucho Marx lived not far away, as did Edward G. Robinson and Lionel Barrymore and Marion Davies and Charlie Chaplin; Fred Astaire, as of this writing, is still in the neighborhood. For a while, before his death in 1935, Will Rogers was honorary mayor. He wrote in 1923:

> Lots are sold so quickly and often here that they have been put through escrow made out to the 12th owner. They couldn't possibly make a separate deed for each purchaser; besides, he wouldn't have time to read it in the ten minutes that he owned the lot. Your having no money didn't worry the agents if they can just get a couple of dollars down, or an old overcoat, or a shotgun, or anything to act as down payment. Second-hand Fords are considered A-1 collateral.

It all sounds a good deal tackier than the place looks now—high walls and hedges equipped with every possible security device. In the middle, the commercial area is replete with some of the most elegant boutiques in the world; they have made Rodeo Drive, the main street of Boutiqueland, one of the really dazzling shopping experiences on this planet.

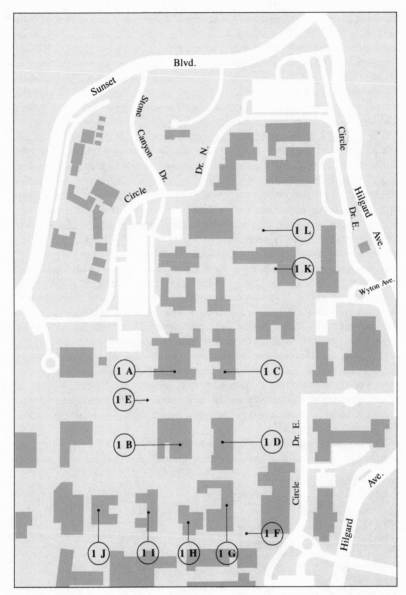

VIII 1 · UCLA

VIII 1 · UCLA
Bounded by Sunset Boulevard and Hilgard, Highland, LeConte, Gayley and Veteran avenues, Westwood
1929 to present
Parking is often difficult; it is therefore best to visit here on late afternoons and weekends; campus maps are available free at entrance kiosks

The Los Angeles campus of the University of California started out as a State Normal School in 1881 on a five-acre site now occupied by the Los Angeles Public Library. In 1925 the Janss Corporation, which was developing Westwood at the time, gave the Regents of the University of California a discounted price for 200 acres of the present campus, a series of canyons just north of Westwood Village (page 206). Alphonzo Bell, the developer of the much fancier Bel Air (page 180) just north of here, arranged a similar deal for 183 acres more. By 1929 the first four of UCLA's now 130 or so buildings were completed. The University of California at Los Angeles soon became the cultural focus (as well as the developers' drawing card) for the little Mediterranean-styled village at its feet and for the opulent houses in the hills above.

The original four buildings, paired across a grassy quadrangle called Dickson Plaza, are Royce Hall and Haines Hall on the north, Powell Library and Kinsey Hall on the south. All four were built in particularly rich and spirited versions of an Italian Romanesque style that was then extremely popular on American college campuses. They are all of red brick with bands of beige stone and Byzantine detail, and are now surrounded by mature trees and shrubs. The four buildings have great charm and are, in the minds of many of us, the first and practically the last distinguished buildings at UCLA. Indeed, most of the buildings since 1930 are pallid and tedious beyond redemption, but it is clearly worth making a few exceptions to the blanket condemnation of blandness that gets leveled against this campus. A handful of buildings, erected shortly after the first ones, and at least two or three since, are easily worth consideration. And the grounds themselves are extremely pleasant, often beautiful, thanks to the landscaping by Ralph D. Cornell, from 1937 until his death in 1972, and by his firm—Cornell, Bridgers, Troller and Hazlett—since then. The landscaping is rich and thick; it arches over and shades the walkways and roads and jogging paths and manages, thank heaven, at least partly to conceal most of the buildings. The grounds are full of extraordinary specimens duly labeled, but placed in arrangements that are artistic enough and dense enough to transcend the limits of a botanical garden; the whole campus comes off as a genuinely bountiful California landscape.

The original four buildings are handsome and joyous affairs that are, by themselves, worth a trip. Josiah Royce Hall (1 A) (Allison and Allison,

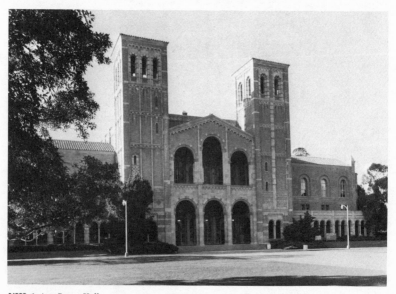

VIII 1 A · *Royce Hall*

1928–1929), which contains a 2,000-seat auditorium in the center and class-rooms on the sides, is the most elaborate of the four. With its twin towers flank-ing a three-arched portico beneath a high, pedimented loggia, it is certainly the most ecclesiastical. Royce Hall's main delight is its arcade, along the entire fa-çade, which rests on paired columns and brick-and-stone striped piers. The building's most prominent features, though, are its two almost maniacally de-tailed towers. Though identical in shape to its mate, each tower is picturesquely unsymmetrically disposed. Each begins with a tiny pair of arches in a thick base. A slightly recessed stone rectangle above the arches has crockets that are partly Lombardic, partly Saracenic. Above that are panels with all kinds of strange irregular brick patterns. Each main shaft then rises up, with either two narrow pilasters or a single wide one, past freely placed lancet windows to a belfry, which has either three or two arched openings.

VIII 1 B · *Powell Library*

Directly across the quadrangle is Powell Library (1 B) (George W. Kelham, 1928), now the undergraduate library. This great pile of bricks is about the same size and almost as ebullient as Royce Hall, but its proportions and general lines are altogether different. As on Royce, there is a central entrance façade with a gable-roofed loggia, but the entry is a single grand arch, and the towers on each side are narrow piers with little temples at the top, capped by sharply pointed cones. The base of the entire building, a full half of the height, is a heavy com-position of horizontal stripes, thin lines of brick alternating with thick stone, pierced by only a few small windows and capped by a blind arcade. On the up-per half of the building, the tall Lombardian-Romanesque arched windows, the thick brick piers in between and the incised cornice seem almost light and airy. A single fat octagonal tower lumbers up the middle in two tiers to a low red-tiled roof and a narrow lantern that echoes the fairy-tale turrets beside the en-try. Beneath all this is a vast rotunda, which is reached by a grand stairway and supported on tall arches in ornately patterned and stenciled brick walls.

Just east of Royce and Powell, Haines Hall (1 C) (George W. Kelham, 1938) and Kinsey Hall (1 D) (Allison and Allison, 1928–1929) also face each other across the quadrangle. Although they were built by the same architects as their neighbors to the west, with the same materials and with the same colorful leaping back and forth from red brick to beige stone, they are much calmer and considerably more workaday buildings than Royce and Powell. Still, they both seem filled with life, stirred up by all sorts of incised decoration and terra-cotta ornament with bears and suns and fishes and lightning bolts and snakes. The back (west side) of Kinsey Hall has a very pretty double flight of stairs that cascades around a half-rotunda.

At the west end of Dickson Plaza is a semicircular terrace (1 E) paved with brick and concrete and lined with a Classical balustrade. From here a long flight of stairs with wide landings (called the Janss Steps after the developers) goes down to a lower terrace, which is flanked by the men's and women's gymnasiums. The axial view from the upper terrace ends in a bright green playing field, which has been impinged on by a number of lackluster buildings, including high-rise dormitories on the hills to the west.

An extension of one of the early grid lines, straight south from Dickson Plaza, leads to one of UCLA's finest moments, the Inverted Fountain (1 F) (Jere Hazlett and Howard Troller, 1973). This big round basin, with a wide masonry rim that easily accommodates sitting and dangling of feet inside, has water—a great deal of it—that surges up (at ten thousand gallons a minute) from the perimeter, splashes across a riverbed of stones and then plunges into an off-center, frothing and churning vat that suggests the power of even greater quantities of water. The outer ring is stone-lined, still and deep; next a narrow masonry surface allows the kinds of smooth, sinuous curves of water you might expect to see running over a weir; and then the rocks break up these patterns and create a highly charged tumult as the water rushes headlong toward the vat. The only part that seems less than wonderful is the hole in the middle, which, by virtue of being round and simple and fairly big, has the hint of storm drains or sewers to it. Still, the fountain's really generous action and its closely packed stones make for a convincing recollection of powerful rivers in the foothills of the High Sierra.

Most of the newer buildings that rise up around the Inverted Fountain are insipid beyond hope. Knudsen Hall (1 G), on the northwest, is a fair example. It features square columns outside bland brick walls with mosaics of utmost triviality that describe, apparently, some scientific themes. On top is a multistory block, typical of the buildings on campus, that ends with a multibarrel-molded blind arcade of the 1960s persuasion, for which the Detroit architect Minoru Yamasaki is usually assigned the blame.

However, the Placement and Career Planning Center (1 H) (Frank O. Gehry and Associates, 1976), which lies just west of Knudsen Hall, is much happier, a pleasant and modest but still interesting insertion onto its site, at the corner of two walks on the grid. Red brick walls, free-standing and sometimes fragmented, stand in front of almost Schindleresque beige stucco volumes; but Gehry's forms are simpler, plainer and less frenzied than Schindler's, and represent this architect at his most assured. The interior is filled with Gehry enthusiasms from that period when exposed round ducts sailed across the spaces overhead. A very ordinary wood joist and plywood ceiling (no need in this one-story building to worry about fireproofing) is held on glu-lam beams atop steel-pipe columns.

West of here is a pair of early buildings by the two architects who did the original four. The first is Moore Hall (1 I) (George W. Kelham, 1930), which continues the Lombardian-Romanesque tradition with less verve than Royce or Powell Hall, but there is still a great deal of tapestried richness to its red brick and beige stone façades. West of Moore Hall is Kerckhoff Hall (1 J) (Allison and Allison, 1930), the only Gothic building on campus. It is a rather flat version of East Coast Collegiate Gothic, with a few leanings toward Tudor, made up of the early UCLA format of brick and stone.

North of Dickson Plaza is Bunche Hall (1 K) (Maynard Lyndon, 1964), which is the campus' most controversial building, partly because it is so big, partly because it actually demonstrates a point of view. It is a nine-story rectangular slab lifted, on its western half, two stories above grade on thick, round columns, so an original north-south axial walkway can go underneath and allow a view of the Murphy Sculpture Garden on the north. The north face of the building is a glass curtain wall, while the south side, which bridles people the most, is smooth purplish beige granite with even rows of dark square windows, over which shades stick out from the granite like sunglasses to allow air to flow behind. Although this is the most severely criticized structure at UCLA, it is easy to argue that, outside of Gehry's Placement Center, it is the only newer building with any architectural distinction at all. The others are banal to the point of inanity, while this, though it is unquestionably brutal and unflinching in its single-mindedness, is clear and clean; and though it may be going too far to call it attractive, it is a tolerably good neighbor. There is a great space underneath it, and a pleasant indoor garden fills a lower wing on the east.

The axis to the north, passing through Bunche Hall, continues along a curious walkway that seems to be a bridge, for it has a low railing on each side and it narrows in the middle. At night an eerie light glows from a thin slot in each railing. There is no question about it; we have just crossed over to the world of Art.

Ahead and to the east is the Franklin Murphy Sculpture Garden (1 L) (Cornell, Bridgers and Troller, 1969), where objects by twentieth-century Modern Masters are sprinkled around five acres of lawns and trees and thick ground cover beside curving walks. On the west is a whole grove of jacaranda trees that cause the place to be altogether magical in June; the rest of the time it is much less magical. The Dickson Art Center, a nine-story block with an art gallery attached, occupies the northwest corner. MacGowan Hall, with the Theater Arts Playhouse inside, takes up the northeast corner. In front of MacGowan is a terrace lined with coral trees and famous works of art. Past the Rodin, past the Maillol, past the Henry Moore is, on the east, a long panel of water with a stack of gushing cubes, by George Tsutakawa (1969), as its source.

The pieces of sculpture, in most cases, don't seem to carry the moral responsibility they're supposed to, and often seem lonesome standing all by themselves. The catholicity of taste is interesting: on a terrace below the Maillol and Henry Moore, for instance, are a pair of narrow columns capped by two tiny figures, very thin and very realistic, by Robert Graham; in front of them is a horizontal work by Anthony Caro, a collection of orange I-beams of an altogether different scale and demeanor. It seems an unhappy arrangement to have the figures, especially those that are somewhere near life-size, put up on circular bases, although these are not very high off the ground. If they could just be standing in the grass, they might come across as more accessible and friendly. The Rodin comes perhaps the closest to this idea: even though the figure is on a little base, he strides right by where you walk and where you can touch him. At times, though, the Murphy Sculpture Garden seems to function well as a UCLA campus in miniature, with various kinds of Modern Statements sticking up here and there, on firm bases, surrounded (and made more palatable) by a verdant Southern California landscape.

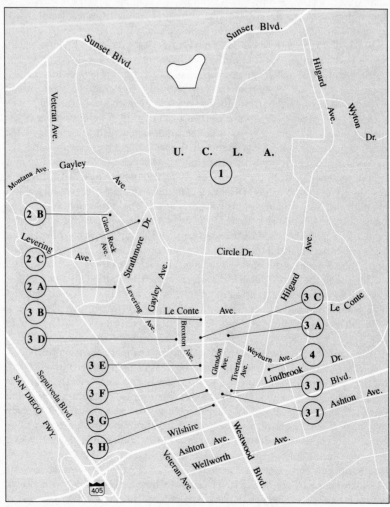

VIII/WESTWOOD AND BEVERLY HILLS (WESTWOOD)

VIII 2 · AVANT-GARDE HOUSING
Three apartment buildings near the southwest boundary of UCLA

After UCLA arrived in its midst in 1929, Westwood quickly became known as a college town, although it was, and continues to be, a solid upper-middle-class community, out of the price range of most students and now of most professors. Westwood was also one of the prettiest places to live in Los Angeles, with little streets that curved around its rolling hills and filled up rapidly with generously landscaped houses of almost every picturesque persuasion. Among the Spanish and American Colonials and the various English and French revivals is an occasional glimmer of Modernity. These three apartment buildings were the zenith of Modernity when they were built; two of them now provide low-cost housing for UCLA students.

A · STRATHMORE APARTMENTS
11005–11013½ Strathmore Drive, Westwood
Richard J. Neutra, 1938
Private residences

Here Richard Neutra applied the cleanest of International Style lines to the relaxed format of the popular Southern California bungalow court; and he did it, during those stringent times, with Southern California's cheapest construction method: wood frame and stucco. Beginning with a row of garages at the base, two angular masses of white stucco and glass work their way up a steep hill. The four apartments on each side are reached by a long stairway up the middle. Each dwelling has an air of individuality (the two-story buildings at the top are even detached from the rest), but variation was clearly secondary to the smooth purity of the rectangular volumes. The long bands of windows lie flush with the wall planes, while balconies and doorways are hollowed out from these undisturbed surfaces. Today thick mounds of foliage soften the disciplined forms and help to evoke that pleasant vision of a courtyard that Neutra had used as a model.

B · LANDFAIR APARTMENTS
10940–54 Ophir Drive, on the south side of Ophir, between Landfair and
   Glenrock avenues, Westwood
Richard J. Neutra, 1938
Now called Robison Hall; private residences

Of the same vintage as the Strathmore Apartments, this apartment house is a more formal arrangement, a textbook example of the International Style. Originally constructed as eight apartments, the building has been sliced into "torpedo tubes" for eighty students, and is at the edge of collapse. It's all one flat-roofed, two-story, white stucco and glass building that forms an L around a small backyard. The long end, along Ophir Drive, is slightly staggered to express the nature of each apartment group, which is unerringly modular. The elevations are straightforward and direct: strip windows, flush with the walls, wrap uninterrupted around the entire building; balconies appear scooped out of the rectangular mass; pipe columns hold up De Stijl porches; and six identical penthouses, which cover stairwells, seem to try to do what chimneys did in more romantic times.

C · SHEETS APARTMENTS
10919 Strathmore Drive, Westwood
John Lautner, 1949
Private residences

While Richard Neutra, with the Strathmore Apartments, made an International Style landmark out of the Southern California bungalow court, John Lautner (page 240) applied his own notions about architecture to that form and came up with one of the strangest buildings in Los Angeles. The Sheets Apartments are a volatile and truly bizarre mixture of the rustic with the futuristic. Enormous white stucco wings thrust out from this hillside site to serve either as platforms or as roofs for four huge redwood cylinders, inside of which people live. The first two of these giant hot tubs spring up from a platform cantilevered over a lot-wide carport. The others, with spiky fins and rocket roofs spinning off them, prepare to launch themselves up the hill. In the middle is an incongruous little forest where a stairway winds past trees and a trickling waterfall— placed there, perhaps, to help quiet the expected roar of the blastoff.

VIII 3 · WESTWOOD VILLAGE

As we have seen (pages 199–203), the early buildings and grounds of UCLA had considerable domestic charm and fit well with the scale of the houses that were being built around Westwood's commercial center. The format for Westwood Village, which was laid out by planner Harland Bartholomew in 1928, was also small-scale and, for that time, striking, though very Californian. For the most part, it consisted of one- and two- and occasionally three-story commercial buildings of stucco or brick—the stucco generally off-white, the brick dark red —and red-tiled roofs. Shoppers arriving by automobile were considered from the beginning: display windows were made large enough to be seen from the street; handsome towers, large enough to be spotted from Wilshire Boulevard, sprouted up from the roofs to advertise the presence of gasoline stations, the Fox Theater, the Bank of America and other important institutions.

The initial glories of both the university and the village have been considerably submerged in the construction that has occurred since the late 1940s, when architectural review ceased, especially in the behemoths that the UCLA Medical School unloaded between the town and the main campus. More recent buildings have gotten higher and duller and, along Wilshire, extremely dense. In the photographs of Westwood in the 1930s, the area around Wilshire Boulevard shows up as a landscaped foreground for the delicacies of the village. Now it's all tightly packed with skyscrapers, though that word is a misnomer: these lumps don't really scrape the sky, they clout it. The traffic count at the corner of Wilshire and Veteran Avenue (83,139 cars per 24 hours in 1982) is said to be the largest in the city or perhaps in the world. (The distinction between city and world is not carefully made by most Angelenos.) Westwood Village has recently become one of the most popular nighttime hangouts for the young and rich, and it is now *the* movie theater district for all of Los Angeles, with premieres and long lines, even in the morning, for some thirty-three cinemas. Along with the movies have come boutiques and fancy restaurants and other glittery establishments, which have gradually replaced the more ordinary kinds of businesses. The last supermarket left several years ago.

Still, a view down Westwood Boulevard, the main street, remains an attractive one. The street is lined with ficus trees; the medians, though less wide than before, are filled with palms and oleanders. The village's recent influx of wealth and glamour, which arrived with the skyscrapers, has also brought about the restoration of a number of the older buildings; and some of the newer ones have managed to maintain the original village character. The mostly two-story shops have second floors as thoughtfully disposed as the first, with glassy loggias, and a few arcaded third-floor loggias, some modern skylights, sloped walls, tiled roofs, arcades and the occasional corner tower or turret. The scale is larger than that of Rodeo Drive, the stores are more collegiate and far less expensive, but the air of the Southern California good life is as powerful and as pleasant here as it is in Beverly Hills.

VIII 3 E · *Glendale Federal Savings, with the Fox Westwood Village Theater in the background*

Bullock's Westwood (3 A) (Welton Becket, 1952) at 10861 Weyburn Avenue, at the end of Glendon Avenue, is one of the newer buildings that fits into the charm and domestic tranquillity of the original format. It is, as well, a great visual success. A two-story concave façade follows the curve of Weyburn and helps to make that piece of the street remarkably intimate and sheltered and contained, even though there is at present a very large parking lot across the street. Part of Westwood Village's famous attention to the needs of motorists was a system of parking places in the center of the blocks. Bullock's Westwood adheres to this idea with an elegant entrance at both the front and back, much as Bullock's Wilshire had pioneered a few years before (page 147). The front wall is a set of concrete pylons that cantilever out to support the second story in a manner curiously recollective of Schindler's Lovell Beach house (page 136), but without the constructivist brio. Between the pylons of the second floor are panels of glazed tile; on the first floor there are sections either of rough stone or of glass. The stone parts could be accused of not providing enough display space, but the plantings in front of them are attractive. The glass entry doors are surrounded by enough windows to make the store seem inviting, unlike the standard latter-day shopping fortress.

Along Le Conte Avenue, on the north edge of the village, opposite the campus of UCLA, are a number of elegant buildings with courtyards. The Spanish Colonial Revival building (3 B) at the southwest corner of Westwood Boulevard and Le Conte (originally Holmby Hall; Gordon B. Kaufmann and John and Donald Parkinson, 1930) is particularly redolent of the charm of the old paradigm, with arches on the first floor, shuttered windows on the second and an arcaded loggia on the third. At the end of this richly Spanish block, at the northwest corner of Westwood and Weyburn Avenue, is a tall, Gothically capped Classical clock tower (3 C) that thrusts up above the New Wave entrances of recently remodeled boutiques.

One of the most prominent towers, and one of the first, is that of the Fox Westwood Village Theater (3 D) (P. O. Lewis, 1931) at 961 Broxton Avenue, on the northwest corner of Weyburn Avenue. Its smooth, white-plastered, six-sided walls rise up, Spanish, with an occasional cartouche, to a ring of six somewhat

Classical columns with winged lions at their feet; the top is a vertical flurry of Streamline Moderne metal ornament. The big white plaster box of the theater itself has a spiky-topped Churrigueresque cornice and more winged lions on top of corner turrets. At the base of the tower is a big marquee above a tiny box office and a flagstoned garden with hedges and one last surviving palm.

At the sharp corner of Broxton Avenue and Westwood Boulevard, where the latter veers off to the northeast, is the centerpiece for Westwood, now the Glendale Federal Savings building (3 E) (Allison and Allison, 1929), long the Bank of America and originally the sales office for the Janss Corporation. This clean-lined mixture of Spanish and Classical is dominated by a big glassy-arched entrance and a colorful tiled dome. It's all rather tiny, but so is everything that matters in Westwood, so its focal prominence has never been upstaged. With its bright and shiny surfaces, it is fully monumental in its Southern California way.

A number of the buildings along Broxton Avenue are now gone in favor of parking lots, so the mood of the street, which is less decorated than Westwood Boulevard, is being little by little dissipated. One of the interesting buildings that remain (3 F) is at the corner of Broxton and Kinross avenues, opposite the Glendale Savings dome. It has a small three-story-high courtyard space, entered from both streets, with lots of little details—iron balconies, awnings, a central fountain with palm trees, and colorful tiles everywhere.

The whole west side of the 1100 block of Westwood Boulevard, between Kinross Avenue and Lindbrook Drive, is a new red brick building (3 G), two stories high, with lots of parking underneath, the legislated burden of newer buildings. It has almost no details, but it steps back on the second floor so as to keep the domestic tranquillity and small scale of the earlier works. Across Lindbrook, on the southwest corner of Westwood Boulevard, is a smaller version of this clean brick persuasion (3 H), with a second-story restaurant that steps back to form an outdoor dining terrace.

The northeast corner of Lindbrook and Westwood has always been a prominent one, thanks to a fat turret with an elaborate cavetto cornice and a curved and Classically pedimented entrance. The building behind the turret (3 I), with its handsome blind arcades, used to be Ralphs Grocery Store (Russell Collins, 1929), which once was sheathed in white plaster. The sand-blasted brick you now see was revealed by nostalgic archaeologists of the 1970s.

Next door, at the northwest corner of Lindbrook and Glendon drives, is another building (3 J) whose brick walls have been laid bare. It is mostly one story high, with another turret at the corner and a number of galleries and bay windows and small-scale charms. It wraps around one of the village's most attractive courtyards, octagonal in shape, with patterned tile all over and a flowering tree in the center; there are tables here for a Mexican restaurant, a cast-iron balcony on one side, and vines growing overhead. Looming up across the street, at the northeast corner of Lindbrook and Glendon, is, alas, one of the blockbusters from Westwood's middle age of very high densities.

VIII 4 · 28TH CHURCH OF CHRIST, SCIENTIST
1014 Hilgard Avenue, on the east side of Hilgard between Weyburn Avenue and Lindbrook Drive, Westwood
Maynard Lyndon, 1956

The 28th Church of Christ, Scientist is a block-long sweep of cleanly detailed concrete; its rigorous horizontals and verticals play off a concave curve, in plan, that follows a gentle bend in Hilgard Avenue. The building is painted in soft shades of gray as cool and understated as the design by Maynard Lyndon, one of the important Los Angeles architects of the generation just after World War II. The entrance, on the sharp corner of Lindbrook, is marked by a fountain in front of a curved, free-standing wall that protects and almost hides a wall of glass. Glass doors in the glass wall open into a formal but airy lobby whose wood surfaces are detailed with a masterful Spartan hand. Straight ahead are doors to the sanctuary, while on the left is another glass wall that looks out on the beginning of a long gallery; the open colonnade, with tall piers, a thin entablature and a flat roof, extends along Hilgard and connects the church to a Sunday school—a separate building, similarly restrained, on the corner of Weyburn—that was once the main church and was remodeled by Lyndon to fit in with the new work.

Behind the colonnade, in the open space between the two buildings, a luxuriant garden serves as a vibrant contrast to the pure geometries everywhere else. At the rear of the sanctuary, near big windows shaded by an ample overhang, the level of the garden sinks down while its foliage bursts up, in a jungle free-for-all of palm trees and tropical plants, all visible from inside the church. The interior is lined with fine woods and travertine, composed as simply and consummately as the concrete outside; a dark ceiling intensifies the warm apricot color of the carpet and the upholstery of the seats, which face down on a pulpit that is clearly upstaged, on each side, by vast terrarium-like windows and that organic insurrection going on behind them.

VIII 5 · PSYCHOANALYTIC ASSOCIATES OFFICE
1800 Fairburn Avenue, on the southeast corner of Little Santa Monica Boulevard, Los Angeles
Charles Moore Associates, 1972

Farther east, on the south side of Little Santa Monica Boulevard (the smaller, southern stripe of the boulevard), is a building in which I had a hand, for Psy-

VIII 5 · *Psychoanalytic Associates Office*

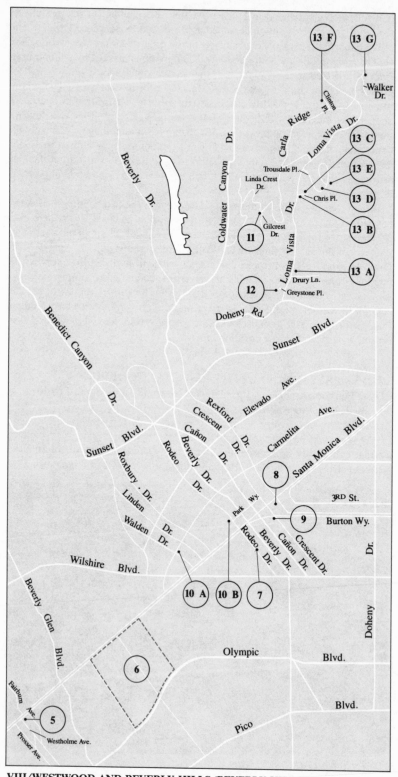

VIII/WESTWOOD AND BEVERLY HILLS (BEVERLY HILLS)

choanalytic Associates, Inc. Inside are two-story central galleries lit by large skylights and interlaced with open corridors and bridges to the suites of twenty-two psychiatrists. The inward-facing, softly lit arrangement is meant to heighten the sense of privacy and to calm apprehensions. On the outside, this corner building looks something like the many condominiums all around it, built of the stuff of ordinary structures in Southern California, beige stucco on a wood frame. Each of the two street façades is made up of two parallel planes, about six feet apart, filled in with balconies and bays, and penetrated by windows, unglazed openings and a semi-grand entrance stair on Fairburn Avenue. In between these walls, as well, are little gardens tended by the psychiatrists, who, by the nature of their profession, spend long days indoors at the head of a couch looking out over their plants.

VIII 6 · CENTURY CITY
Bounded by Santa Monica and Olympic boulevards, Century Park East and West
Welton Becket and Associates, master plan

In the late 1950s, 20th Century–Fox Film Studios, which still produces movies behind its old entrance north of Pico Boulevard and Motor Avenue, decided to turn its unused 180-acre back lot into cash. Along behind the goal of making a great deal of money tagged the noble concept of turning the futuristic visions of this century's best urban planners into reality. This was to be an ideal twenty-first century city, made from a choice, unencumbered chunk of real estate next door to Beverly Hills. The grand planners would have—oh, rarest of opportunities—complete control of this vast site. They could build utopia, a city within a city, without a thought to the unplanned, small-scale neighborhoods around it. This, at last and all at once, was the big time.

And the dream was fulfilled. Private developers, aided by some of the finest high-rise architects in the world, have managed to change this place, once the backdrop of a thousand movie fantasies, into a futuristic fantasy of their own. There is still an air of movie sets here, something like the superrealistic science fiction settings of late, where, say, extraterrestrial giants tried to colonize a forbidding planet but had to live indoors and died. Some scenes from *Planet of the Apes* were, in fact, filmed here, though the University of California at Irvine shares that distinction. This City of Tomorrow is said to be a great financial success. What is thoroughly puzzling, though, is why so many people write about it as such a success in all the other ways that matter, and why they see it as such a positive addition to the Los Angeles scene.

Our heaviest reservations about Century City come from what seem to be its complete denial of the open-air relaxed heritage of Ramona, of the romance of Southern California, in favor of a hard-bitten, supercommercial urbanity, or, more accurately, excessive density. These bland and blank, completely faceless high-rise buildings are arranged in some order that must have made sense on the drawing board, but it is very hard to comprehend what that order might be when you're in or around them. Of course, you're never actually around the buildings anyway, for the only access is through underground pedestrian tunnels or parking garages as confusing as they are cavernous. The place does not seem to have been designed with people in mind, at least as we know them on earth, where they are less than thirty feet tall and breathe air.

Entrance to Century City is by means of a wide utopian expressway called the Avenue of the Stars, with a strip down the middle for flowers and monumental fountains. From here, with all the shiny slabs popping up on either side, the view brings to mind, in a sort of anguished déjà-vu, the drawings for a City of Five Million by Le Corbusier and the other visionary schemes of his contemporaries and successors, which, for obvious reasons, were never built. Most of the slabs are rectangular, on the orthogonal or the diagonal; some are triangular, and a few seem to have started off as rectangles but had sections sheared off in spasms of playfulness. Most sit on strange sorts of plinths, some are taller than others, and each one gleams a little differently in the sun.

Off to the east lies what is billed as the focal point of Century City: the Century Plaza Towers (Minoru Yamasaki, 1975), which are two particularly tall skyscrapers, triangular in plan, that loom up from a vast plaza swept clean by the winds they create. The buildings seem, often, to come in pairs. There's another pair in front of the last one, only four stories high this time, with a lighted marquee that says "ABC Entertainment Center." These four behemoths line up on each side of an axis that ends, on the west side of the avenue, with the giant concave curve of the Century Plaza Hotel. A walkway runs along this axis, partly subterranean to make it under the Avenue of the Stars. The buildings here, like all the others, rise up as independent objects, with no visible relationship. The spaces in between are big and amorphous, arranged, typically of their time, apparently for the benefit only of those who fly in helicopters or draw plans.

VIII 7 · RODEO DRIVE
Between Wilshire and Santa Monica boulevards, Beverly Hills

Rodeo Drive, a middle-size street with flowers and small trees down the center and fancy one- to two-story boutiques on each side, is one of the grandest and ritziest and most famous places to shop in the world. Here, packed shoulder to shoulder, are all the earth-shaking names of high fashion—Gucci, Hermès, Celine, Courrèges, Ted Lapidus, Ralph Lauren, Saint Laurent, Bottega Veneta, and on and on. Although almost every one of these shops is grievously narrow, each one has employed every artifice to look bigger and more elegant and more expensive than the rest. The latest gimmick is a tiny sign on the door that says "By appointment only."

But even with its excesses, Rodeo Drive is a pleasant enough place: the grandiose little shop fronts are interesting to walk by, and they appeal mightily to the shopper, whether on foot or driving; the consistent low scale helps to soften the continual surprises; and, a little oddly in our time, what this very high-class street seems to do best is to take advantage of the relaxed out-of-doors nature of Southern California, as against the particularly oppressive business of being enclosed in one of those placeless, faceless malls, such as Beverly Center (page 230) a few blocks east.

The commercial part of Rodeo Drive is a short and very limited street, which may be part of the urban design clue to its success. It is just a little over two blocks long from Wilshire to Santa Monica Boulevard, where it changes suddenly into an upper-crust residential street that looks, on the map anyway, like a funnel for the great wealth of Beverly Hills. The Wilshire end is visually closed off, not by some big department store anchor, but by one of the world's

VIII 7 · *Rodeo Drive, Anderton Court*

premiere hostelries, the Beverly Wilshire Hotel (9500 Wilshire Boulevard; Walker and Eisen, 1928). This eight-story, U-shaped slab, which is almost on axis with Rodeo Drive, sports a flurry of typical Southern California Classical and flat Churrigueresque details: there are engaged columns, balustrades, arcades, shields, garlands, human and lion heads, trees on a second-story terrace, and a central tower. It has all been kept up superbly and seems very much a part of the exuberant local scene, though its architecture has never been accused of winning any prizes.

There is, in fact, so much exuberance around here that the buildings which come off most elegant are the simple ones, with simple materials, a few well-placed canvas awnings or a shiny metal door flanked by straight-edged display windows. The least simple boutique is Anderton Court (328 North Rodeo Drive, 1953–54) by Frank Lloyd Wright. This little-known (with good reason) late work by the master is a three-story eruption of angular forms and dangerously sharp ornament with a zigzag spiral ramp up the center and a tinkly-tinkly tower at the top, all painted a blinding bright white. Some call this sort of thing the product of Wright's maturity, but it's more the result of a very jazzy old age. It has all the spiky detail and frantic energy of his last works, such as the Elkins Park Synagogue in Pennsylvania and the Marin County Civic Center north of San Francisco, and yet it is somehow thinner and sillier, more chintzy and ill-considered than the rest. It is interesting to compare Anderton with another of Wright's commercial buildings, the V. C. Morris Store (1949) at 140 Maiden Lane in San Francisco, which has a cool brick face with one arch in it and a spiral ramp inside; at Anderton the shapes and the human movement are jerky and uncertain.

Up the street, at 431 North Rodeo, is the instantly famous Rodeo Collection (Olivier Vidal, 1982), a group of shops behind one big façade that has countered with superscale details the fidgeting of Frank Lloyd Wright: the new building's white front wall has an almost relentless row of gigantic glass arches with enormous glass medallions in between. But this bold effulgence has been kind to the street by continuing the low scale across the front and by opening up at each end for a pleasant little walkway to more shops behind; still, like so many of the high-fashion statements along here, it seems to falter under the burden of a couture too haute to handle.

VIII 8 · BEVERLY HILLS CITY HALL
450 North Crescent Drive, bounded by Santa Monica Boulevard, Rexford Drive and Burton Way, Beverly Hills
William J. Gage and Harry G. Koerner, 1931

The Beverly Hills Civic Center is a bunch of buildings that seem to face away from the center and have almost nothing to do with each other, though they are all built near a wonderful city hall—a two-story, H-shaped, symmetrical edifice that piles up to three stories at the center and then bursts into an eight-story tower; a colorfully tiled dome gleams from a big cupola on top. This centerpiece for one of the world's richest cities is mostly rather simple: it rises up with a kind of commercial sub-Deco austerity, ornamented with a fairly flat and restrained brand of Hispanic froth around the openings, more vigorous at the main entrance and at the top of the tower. But for all its never having any magic moments in detail, it comes off as a remarkable building, thanks to its graceful tower and its dome, and thanks, too, to the relaxed and self-assured way that Spartan restraint shifts without visible effort into Hispanic heavy breathing. Also, there is some fine landscape, with brightly colored flowers, clipped hedges, royal and sago palms, and softly splashing Spanish fountains.

VIII 9 · UNION 76 GAS STATION
427 North Crescent Drive, on the southwest corner of Little Santa Monica Boulevard, Beverly Hills
Pereira and Luckman, 1965

Diagonally across Little Santa Monica Boulevard from City Hall is a gas station that people of some persuasions would say is the most eligible of all the neighboring works for inclusion in the *National Register of Historic Buildings.* It's all just one huge triangular canopy that thrusts up at the corners and is supported (or held down) by only three sweptwing piers. It looks like a three-cornered stool that's been sat on by someone of unusual heaviness, except that it's *big*—about a hundred feet long from cantilevered corner to cantilevered corner. It covers the whole of this large site and completely overwhelms the nasty little concrete-block service building underneath. A blaze of neon light against the white-plastered sweep of the ceiling heightens the space-age theme, while a frieze of big orange squares along the edges seems to try (but not hard enough) to make this intergalactic visitor fit in with its red-tiled Spanish Colonial Revival neighborhood.

VIII 10 · TWO FILMLAND FANTASIES
On Walden and Rodeo drives, just north of Santa Monica Boulevard, Beverly Hills

---

In Beverly Hills, where haciendas, villas, castles and chateaux of every possible excess cry out for our attention, theme houses are more usual than unusual.

Only the most striking or monomaniacal fantasies even get us to slow down. Here are two with the power to stop you in your tracks.

A · SPADENA HOUSE
516 North Walden Drive, on the southeast corner of Carmelita Avenue, Beverly Hills
Henry Oliver, 1921
Private residence

Here is the quintessential Hansel and Gretel house, which has taken the fairy-tale English Cottage, all the rage in the 1920s, as far as it could go. The sharp angles and the nightmare exaggerations and the thick atmosphere of mystery and evil make it immediately apparent that only a wicked witch could possibly live inside. Small-paned windows (which appear crooked though they are really straight) pockmark the lumpy plaster walls that look yellowed by centuries of gloom. Crude shutters seem ready to fall off, as do the shingles on the various hoary roofs that hang, steep and sinister, almost to the ground. The steepest and highest roof, an impossibly peaked gable above the entry, sweeps down three full stories, supported by a huge witch's broom; a similar dormer nearby and two spindly chimneys look equally precarious. The house is surrounded by a poisonous-looking moat and a rickety picket fence, and in the overgrown garden hollyhocks and other candy-colored flowers wave like bait for little children.

VIII 10 A · *Spadena House*

VIII 10 B · *O'Neill House*

Although it looks like a movie set, and was probably used as one, the Spadena house was originally built as the office for Irvin C. Willat Productions, a movie studio in Culver City, and was moved here later. Two long, one-story wings, camouflaged by the spiky foliage and the vertical madness in front, have helped to turn this wonderful little horror story into a sizable house. Whoever lives here now has maintained it impeccably.

B · O'NEILL HOUSE
On the alley behind 507 North Rodeo Drive, just north of Santa Monica Boulevard, Beverly Hills
Don M. Ramos, 1978 to the present
Private residence

In this land of impressive façades it comes as some surprise to find that the hands-down strangest house in Los Angeles is hidden away at the intersection of two alleys, behind an unremarkable Spanish house on Rodeo Drive. Here, for only a few neighbors and the garbage man to see, is one of the most energetic and inspired and utterly outrageous displays of Art Nouveau in the world. The house is really two buildings, a pavilion and a guest house, one story on the north, two stories on the south, connected by a narrow doorway, but the whole thing is woven inextricably together by giant whorls of sculpted organic ornament that writhe and twine and blossom out of the blinding white plaster walls. On the north building a great mass of light blue tiles forms a melted mansard that swells above one door and two windows; this waving roof becomes the background for a mosaic of white clouds and black geese that migrate across its full length.

The south building, on the corner, has a more modest, but still undulating orange-tiled gable roof, which is hardly noticeable above balconies that sink into or branch out from the protoplasmic walls; a few startled fish, which tried to leap clear, were stung into gargoyles, while stained-glass windows in their glistening mahogany frames are being swallowed whole. The two doors, also mahogany, seem to be changing back into the trees they came from, aided by cocoons of thick, clear varnish. It's natural to hesitate before you go very near this house, lest it strike out and make you part of the next addition.

VIII 11 · SCHULITZ HOUSE

9356 Lloydcrest Drive, near the southwest corner of Gilcrest Drive, Los Angeles
Helmut Schulitz, 1977
Private residence

Just as the De Bretteville–Simon duplex (page 239), a set of steel-and-glass industrial cubes in the hills west of Mt. Olympus, is a tighter version of the Charles Eames house (page 118), the Schulitz house, a set of steel-and-glass industrial cubes in the hills west of Trousdale Estates, is a tighter version of the De Bretteville–Simon duplex or, according to many architects, a more intellectual or conceptual composition. The controlling philosophy here is the reverse of most house construction concepts, though similar to that of factories and

VIII 11 · *Schulitz House*

warehouses: rather than employing custom-building techniques for a standard plan, Helmut Schulitz used standard, off-the-shelf industrial parts to create a custom-designed, altogether unique house for himself. So the rectangular forms, clad in gray corrugated aluminum- and metal-framed windows, are allowed to terrace down an extremely steep slope with some degree of abandon. The three levels are locked into a precisely modular steel skeleton, which is painted dark blue and fastened onto deep caissons, but they are relaxed enough to allow interior spaces and their openings to be where they want to be. There's room, as well, for a number of balconies and for two large decks, which bask in the sunshine and look out over a smashing view of Los Angeles behind bright red railings. A shaggy landscape helps to soften the crisp geometries and the assertively unromantic materials.

VIII 12 · GREYSTONE MANSION
In Greystone Park, 905 Loma Vista Drive, Beverly Hills
Gordon B. Kaufmann, 1925–1928
Interior of mansion closed to public: surrounding park, owned by the City of Beverly Hills, open daily, 10–5 in winter, 10–6 in summer; free admission

Beverly Hills is almost as famous for its grand estates as it is for the movie stars who live in them. There are hundreds of both. Rather than try to make any sort of survey of millionaires' houses, it seems better to visit just one, Greystone Mansion, because 1) you can see it, which you can't say about most of the others, and 2) it is the grandest of them all. You can no longer tour the opulent interior, but you can walk all around this vast building and look in the windows and stroll through the gardens on the sixteen acres that remain of the estate. It once went on for 400 acres, but the rest has been sold off, mostly to Paul Trousdale, who developed Trousdale Estates (page 218) from it.

Edward L. Doheny, the man who introduced the oil well to Los Angeles, is the person responsible for this castlelike pile of gray limestone, although he didn't even build it for himself. He was happy to live out his days in the quirky Victorian extravagance he had purchased on Chester Place (page 279). Greystone, all forty-six thousand square feet of it, was a gift for his son, Edward Jr., whose family lived here until 1955. In 1964 the City of Beverly Hills bought the mansion and the hillside immediately around it in order to excavate an enormous reservoir; the roof for some 40 percent of the city's water supply is now a parking lot behind the house. The rest of the property is now a beautiful and well-maintained city park.

Near the parking lot you can get a map and take any of three self-guided walking tours through the formal gardens, the mansion gardens or the lower grounds. All of these involve pleasant journeys down grand stairs and little paths that lead through lawns and forests; there are terraced gardens filled with statues and pools and tranquil memories, perhaps, of Italy in the cinquecento. Along the way are long balustrades, clipped hedges, flower beds, and little pavilions hidden in the trees.

The mansion, the largest house in Beverly Hills, lies halfway down the hill between the parking lot and Doheny Road. It is a rambling Revival of everything from Tudor on and looks as if it had been moved here from the English countryside. It was aptly named; but the endless grays of the stone walls and slate roofs and slate terraces have been lightened up considerably by a romantic jumble of gables, twisted Jacobean chimneys, bay windows and intricately carved ornament. The luxuriant landscape and the fountains help, as well, to subdue the baronial monumentality and to adapt the house even a little for its arrival in Ramona's paradise.

VIII 13 · TROUSDALE ESTATES
A residential subdivision at the north end of Beverly Hills; Loma Vista Drive is the main street and major access
Paul Trousdale, developer, 1955 to present
Private residences

Trousdale Estates is one of the earliest and largest cut-and-fill housing tracts in the hills of Southern California. It represents, like the Chrysler Imperial of that same era, a particular peak of late 1950s taste. The same pre-energy-conscious description serves them both—curvaceous as Jayne Mansfield, whimsically aerodynamic, loaded with extras, ultra-long, ultra-low, ultra-luxurious and, above all, up to date, though whether that date is Middle Minoan or post-Modern is hard to tell.

The houses of Trousdale have a variety of themes—Roman, Greek, Hawaiian, French, Tudor, Ranch, or Space Age—but they share a common format. All are sited carefully for privacy and views on pads that range from 20,000 square feet to four acres, although many of the lots are agonizingly small. All the utilities, including television, are hidden beneath wide streets; the houses, too, are partially concealed behind generous setbacks thickly planted with palms, bananas, ivy, philodendron and dramatic rows of Italian cypress—no lawns here. All this manages to create an air of spaciousness, for these are, after all, not mere houses in gardens, but estates. Carports, which serve as showcases for the Mercedes and Rolls-Royces, are prominent features, often just extensions of the houses' roofs; and most driveways sweep right up to the front door. Construction, for the most part, is wood frame covered in stucco and adorned with marble, crushed rock panels, and latticework; and almost always there are casement windows, sliding glass doors, double front doors, and lots and lots of statues. Roofs are usually flat, and colors are muted, often just black and white, for these houses are, in spite of everything, Modern.

The best way to discover the ambience of this place is to cruise past the estates and pick out your favorites. Here are a few of ours:

409 Drury Lane (13 A), on the northeast corner of Loma Vista Drive, seems to have a number of long, low wings that spin off a round clerestoried roof behind the entry. Everything is white. The most conspicuous walls are done up, Las Vegas style, with stones so white they sparkle.

410 Chris Place (13 B), on the southeast corner of Loma Vista Drive, has a vast, overhanging, rock-covered roof in the shape of an artist's palette, a favorite shape of the 1950s; palm trees grow up through the hole where the artist's thumb might go. A Corinthian-columned fence, made up entirely of reinforcing bars, and a row of topiary marshmallow trees complete the vision. Next door, 400 Chris Place (13 C) is an excellent example of trabeated neo–Beverly Hills Classical, with creamy white and dark gray planes that intersect to form an entrance portico almost as wide as the garage door. Two columns before the huge

VIII 13 · *Trousdale Estates*

front door are the only literal elements, except perhaps the topiary ficus trees being trained as Palladian windows.

The 300–400 block of Trousdale Place (13 D) has an exceptionally high concentration of Greek-like columns and statues. By contrast, 400 Trousdale Place (13 E), behind a high, worm-eaten wood fence with volcanic rock piers, is a sort of A-frame Hawaiian vision.

630 Clinton Place (13 F) is a residential-scale version of the Pasadena Art Center College of Design (page 319). This black steel-and-glass truss of a house spans between massive stone piers. As at the Art Center, there's a driveway underneath, but this one is screened by a condominium-scale garage door.

Sited almost at the top of Trousdale Estates, 1960 Carla Ridge (13 G), on the east corner of Walker Drive, is an assortment of white stucco boxes tied together along the front by a lurching Ionic colonnade. The circular drive, however, has a distinguished row of ten little white-painted lions, each with a paw raised in greeting. Across the street, at the cliff-edge end of Walker Drive, there is a splendid view, high above the swimming pools, toward the northwest; here, in the middle of Los Angeles, the chaparral-covered peaks of the Santa Monica Mountains seem to go on forever. This sight comes as a particularly pleasant surprise after so grueling a climb.

IX/HOLLYWOOD, WEST HOLLYWOOD, AND SILVER LAKE

Hollywood Boulevard

The most famous romance in Ramonaland has been one of its most ephemeral, or at least has left some of its slummiest remains: Hollywood, the presumed locus of the Magic of the Movies, mostly just housed the workaday part of the movie industry and afforded some cheap housing for the aspiring unemployed. Nathanael West's *Day of the Locust* sets the stage in an appropriately sleazy manner, and Raymond Chandler's private detective, Philip Marlowe, gumshoes through scenes of commanding seediness. Hollywood has for a long time been the place where devout searchers after glitter can measure, as nowhere else, the astonishing thinness of the shimmering substance. Hollywood was also one of the centers of action in Los Angeles during the era when great architects were gathering here—Frank Lloyd Wright, his son Lloyd, Rudolph Schindler, Richard Neutra, then Harwell Harris and Gregory Ain, with an extended all-star cast that included cameo appearances by, for instance, William Lescaze from the other coast. So the premises contain a wealth of architectural treasures, which are often very small, often very difficult to find, and apt to leave you not sure when you've found them. Occasionally, now, they are to be found in neighborhoods where your concern for personal safety may outstrip some of your architectural or detective enthusiasms.

For our purposes, there are three parts to Hollywood: the middle, called Hollywood by most people, though it's really just another part of Los Angeles but is bounded, they say, by Vermont and Melrose avenues, Crescent Heights Boulevard and the crest of the Hollywood Hills; the eastern reaches, called Silver Lake, another part of L.A., with steep hills that wrap around the Silver Lake Reservoir; and the western extension, this time a part of Los Angeles County, predictably yclept West Hollywood, in order to lay claim to some of the glamour. The middle contains the urban streets, most of which seem long overdue for strong catharsis, urban renewal, or perhaps earthquake. The hills of Silver Lake, which have great views of the reservoir, the Los Angeles Basin and the mountains behind, provided the sites, mostly just before World War II, for some of Los Angeles' most spectacular little houses. To the west of Hollywood there are unusually small houses, their tininess reinforced by the superscale ministrations of their inhabitants, who flaunt their miniature grandeurs in the very faces of adjacent monoliths.

The history of this magic land, like most local histories, is short. At the turn of the century it must have looked like a passage out of *The Mark of Zorro,* with pepper trees overhanging dusty trails and a God-fearing population of about four hundred scattered around in the chaparral on a few farms. But the first years of the twentieth century changed all that; a particularly rotten winter in

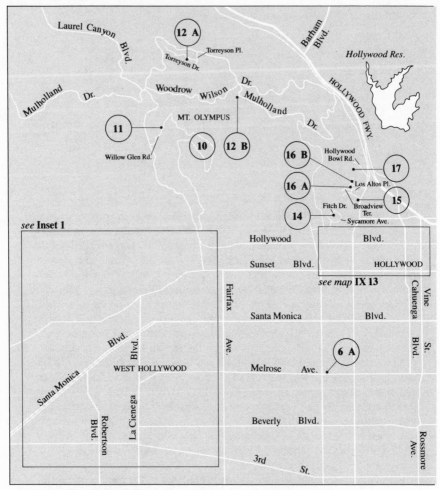

IX/HOLLYWOOD, WEST HOLLYWOOD, AND SILVER LAKE

Chicago in 1907 hastened the move of a fledgling movie company to the sunshine and the multiple scenery of Southern California. Then in 1913 Cecil B. DeMille, Jesse Lasky, Samuel Goldfish (later Goldwyn) and Arthur Friend, after arriving in Flagstaff, Arizona, from New York to make the movie *Squaw Man,* found the Western atmosphere in Flagstaff deficient and pushed on to Hollywood to begin its most glamorous era.

The 1920s was the great decade of silent movies, the '30s the decade with sound. The '40s and '50s and '60s and '70s and the subsequent years have witnessed an elaborate decline (of the industry and the town) decorated with triumphs and reprieves—mostly the latter and hardly ever the former, usually involving television. These recent years would do justice to the last centuries of Rome or Byzantium, though the older cities, on the whole, left better ruins.

Because this is L.A., a visit is a ride, usually in a car. Our trip moves from west to east, for convenient driving rather than for any historical or dramatic development. You have to start somewhere, so let it be Beverly Hills.

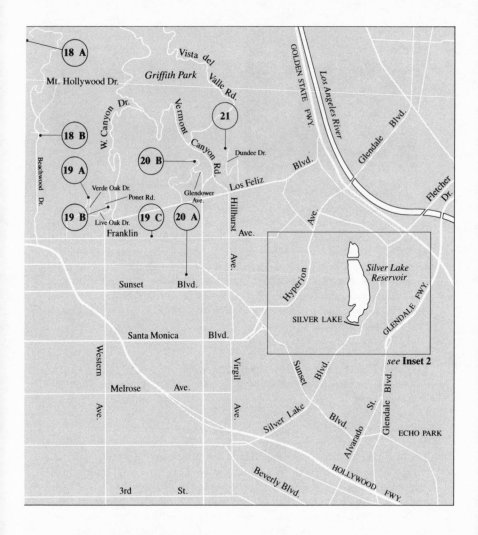

IX 1 · LLOYD WRIGHT HOUSE

858 North Doheny Drive, on the southeast corner of Vista Grande Street, West Hollywood

Lloyd Wright, 1928

Private residence

Frank Lloyd Wright's son, Lloyd Wright, rates more space later in this chapter (page 250), but almost the first house to attract our attention coming on Hollywood from the west is his own. It is especially apparent here that Lloyd Wright had been a landscape architect before he began to design buildings. His house is a two-story Mayan masterpiece that fills up a prominent corner on Doheny Drive, but it is almost obscured by its well-placed forest. A dense canopy, composed of only two enormous pine trees, keeps the entire site in perpetual shade, while thick shrubs and vines cover most of the buff-colored plaster walls. Even the occasional bursts of ornamental concrete blocks have a stylized Joshua tree pattern that amplifies the botanical theme.

The house itself, unlike the architect's Wayfarers' Chapel (page 130), did not

IX 1 · *Lloyd Wright House*   IX 2 · *West Hollywood Houses*

require three decades of growth to complete his vision. Even before the foliage took over, the structure was a deft arrangement of rectangular volumes that managed, at once, to be very private and to use every foot of the small lot. It is hard now to know where the house leaves off and its garden walls or planters or parapets begin. A courtyard and an upstairs terrace face directly onto Vista Grande Street, but they are hidden behind sizable walls; these plain surfaces play against walls of ornamental concrete blocks, screen the windows of a grand two-story living room on Doheny and drip like crystalline stalactites from a dark cave of an entrance.

IX 2 · WEST HOLLYWOOD HOUSES
Along Dicks Street, between Doheny Drive and Hilldale Avenue, West Hollywood
1950s to present
Private residences

The Lloyd Wright house on Vista Grande, for all its special qualities, is the last outpost of the familiar on this street. As you head east, you enter a sort of twilight zone of houses (or house fronts) that encompasses some of the most surprising architectural acrobatics on this planet. These little houses of West Hollywood have received a good deal of press lately, including a number of magazine articles and even a few books. Some of the attention is titillation about the preponderance of males among the inhabitants, and the preponderance of interior decorators among the males, but the interesting parts are the staggering changes of scale that these tiny buildings allow; it is as if in each telephone-booth-size living room some mild-mannered Clark Kent of a decorator were changing into his Superman suit, so as to leap several jumps in scale with but a single bound. During the 1920s the streets of this blue-collar neighborhood were filled in with rows of supermodest bungalows, mostly of the Spanish stucco persuasion. Since the 1950s, the format has been for professional decorators, especially, to move in and add the grandest possible gestures to the little front walls. For the most part, their palettes have worked in three popular themes: Beverly Hills French, Trousdale Estates Classical (page 218) and Contemporary—all done at least double the size you might expect. The most prevalent characteristic, regardless of the stylistic tilt, is a two-story front door in a one-story façade.

A mere two blocks of Dicks Street, between Hilldale Avenue and Doheny Drive, offers the aesthetic gourmand the opportunity to gorge himself on this idiom. Here the flashy little false fronts are packed tight together in something like a residential version of Rodeo Drive (page 212); each house tries desperately

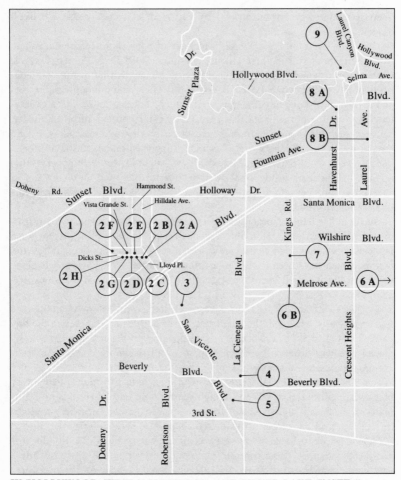

IX/HOLLYWOOD, WEST HOLLYWOOD, AND SILVER LAKE (INSET 1)

to outdazzle its neighbors on a bit of land not much wider than the Mercedes or BMW that sparkles out front.

8936 Dicks Street (2 A) sports the most up-to-the-minute Contemporary look, an industrialized study in dark brown. A driveway, a walkway and a low wall, all in brown brick, introduce this gleaming Hi-Tech box whose front is nothing but windows and steel mullions and Levelor blinds—everything in subtle shades of chocolate brown. A silvery steel frame in the glass front door serves as accent.

Next door, 8940 Dicks Street (2 B) is, on the other hand, Contemporary on a much lower budget. An extremely plain, free-standing wall (made of eight-foot-high panels of vertically grooved plywood) with only a simple door in the center has been positioned about four feet in front of a little Spanish bungalow. The house itself, even its modest landscaping, has not been touched. This may be false-front art at its most sublime.

8952 Dicks Street (2 C) is a rather simple French chateau, almost hidden behind a high, vine-covered fence. A mansard-roofed box, with just a normal-size central door and two carriage lamps, begins to conceal a steep-roofed cottage in back. But the owner, perhaps fearing that his studied restraint had gotten out of hand, has painted everything a rich terra-cotta red, so his house now acts like a beacon.

There are, even on Dicks Street, a number of Spanish stucco or Craftsman wood bungalows still in their original condition. 8968 Dicks Street (2 D) is, however, an original Spanish Colonial Revival bungalow that is more outlandish than any of the updated ones. Behind a tiny lawn with miniature palm trees and a mound of bougainvillea, this white stucco cottage looks like a twenty-foot-wide version of the Santa Barbara County Courthouse: a turret on the left has a progression of slit windows that reappear on the right, cascading around the corner; in the middle, a striped awning, supported on conquistador spears, sweeps over a front porch that has, where you might expect a lamppost, a little mission bell hanging inside a hollowed-out plaster pier; and all of this moves cheerfully along beneath a gigantic parapet wall that swells above the roof line like the surf at Malibu.

On the other hand, 8969 Dicks Street (2 E), directly opposite, is a straightforward Craftsman bungalow that remains relatively untouched, except for a few picture windows and an elegant veneer of redwood siding. These horizontal boards, which have been rubbed to a rosewood luster, actually continue along the side walls, where, it seems, most people in this neighborhood are not expected to look.

9015 Dicks Street (2 F) is a sort of rustic Contemporary whose clean lines are made up of used brick—in the false front, in the entry stair and even in the tiny yard. The redwood latticework in a large opening on the left and the artfully placed greenery around the edges help to recall the more extensive spreads around a thousand country clubs.

9016 Dicks Street (2 G), across the street, is a return to the Contemporary blank wall, with vertical grooves, a high central door and carriage lamps. This understated façade and its symmetrical mounds of tamed shrubbery must be seen as a perfect backdrop for the maroon Mercedes parked in front.

Next door, 9020 Dicks Street (2 H) is almost impossible to identify, for it is completely engulfed, from top to bottom and on every side, by vines. Only a tiny white garden urn gives the stylistic signal for French. As if the mystery were inadequate, closely spaced iron bars cover the few still visible windows and a tall hedge conceals the front yard.

If you still have an appetite for this sort of thing, you can find dozens more examples on the streets nearby. As you drive past these flashy little houses, you can often glimpse the bright blue Pacific Design Center looming up a few blocks away; the view from here makes you wonder why some critics complain that the Blue Whale, as it's called, doesn't fit in with its neighborhood because of problems of scale.

IX 3 · PACIFIC DESIGN CENTER
8687 Melrose Avenue, at the northeast corner of San Vicente Boulevard, West Hollywood
Gruen Associates; Cesar Pelli, 1975

Just as the residential streets of West Hollywood are filled with the strange little houses of interior designers, the major streets here, most famously Melrose Avenue, are lined with interior design and furnishing firms, one of the largest concentrations of such businesses in America. In the early 1970s it occurred to the

IX 3 · *Pacific Design Center*

real estate branch of the Southern Pacific Railroad, which owned a sizable chunk of Decoratorland's heart, to pull many of these design shops together into one great big building. They hired Cesar Pelli (then of Gruen Associates) to do it, and Cesar Pelli did it up blue—out of dark, highly reflective, almost cobalt-blue glass. It's huge—245 feet wide by 530 feet long, with 750,000 square feet, or over 100 million cubic feet in its tall seven stories. And for all the glass, there are hardly any exterior windows; contrary to the design of most buildings, almost all the windows are inside, in the form of glassy fronts for the shops that line interior hallways.

With its hangarlike dimensions and its lack of human-sized elements, the building occasioned immediate outbursts from the architectural community and especially from the community of little bungalows and one-story shops all around that were forced suddenly into its shadow. In 1975 John Pastier, architectural critic of the Los Angeles *Times,* compared the Design Center with "an attempt at hiding a whale in a backyard swimming pool," and the nickname Blue Whale was seized upon. But in recent years the sobriquet has been used more affectionately as people have begun to think of this flashy behemoth as a focus that has helped to draw the design neighborhood together. Even Pastier later called it "a quintessential Los Angeles structure" that serves as a symbol for "this unusually fragmented and individualistic city" and for the lavish interior decorating industry; and it becomes a shimmering glass "metaphor for a place long known as a city of illusion"; the building, he continued, even has its main entrance in back, to accommodate the automobile.

The Pacific Design Center has also received, from the beginning, a great deal of favorable reaction because of its elegance and because, as usual in a Cesar Pelli building, it's got some special quality—call it wit. There's a kind of strangeness to it that makes a visit a joy even though the format of many floors connected by escalators and elevators leaves the spatial delights untouchable until you get to the very top, where a big, two-story, barrel-vaulted gallery allows the chutzpah to show. Still, there are other kinds of delights along the way:

the shop fronts on these dark and twisting internal streets are the last word in sophisticated splendor, for behind them are the wholesalers of style.

There is a particularly L.A. sort of amusement along the Melrose Avenue side, which some might call the entrance façade even though the parking lot is on the opposite side. When the developers were buying up land for the project, they couldn't get one little lot with a one-story shanty of a house on it; so, alongside the vast undifferentiated sweep of this blue whale, there is a tight little grove of trees shielding a small festering slum. Otherwise, the building is made up of billions of rectangular plates of blue glass with thin, nearly flat mullions, though a kind of bronze glass was used in a cylindrical escalator tower on the left end of the Melrose façade. A marquee that runs the full length is formed by a tilting up of the glass wall, which happens again at the very top. The back wall undergoes similar cantilevers and also sports a 530-foot-long terrace, where outdoor restaurants frequently get lost. The end elevations are the characteristic and, some say, the strange ones, with almost barnlike sheds topped by the half-circle of the barrel-vaulted gallery. From this view it's easy to see how someone once compared the building to a giant extruded architectural molding.

IX 4 · TAIL O' THE PUP
311 North La Cienega, near the northwest corner of Beverly Boulevard, West Hollywood
Milton J. Black, 1938

This tiny hot dog and hamburger stand, built in the shape of a giant hot dog in a bun with oozing yellow mustard ornament, has for some time been seen as one of Los Angeles' most important architectural works; pound for pound, it is certainly one of its most spirited. A Pop Art plaster blowup, it's something like the wax-food displays in the windows of Japanese restaurants, where what you see is more or less what you get.

For an aggressive little hot dog stand, the Tail o' the Pup has been, from the beginning, more than just high-caliber advertising art. Near the corner of two major boulevards and only fifty feet from the Beverly Hills border, it has served as a highly visible satire of the self-important buildings nearby, especially the ones along La Cienega Boulevard's famous restaurant row; even its name is a parody of the celebrated Tail O' The Cock restaurant just down the street. Today, now that the gargantuan Beverly Center blots out the sun to the south, the Tail o' the Pup's giant-killer image is more poignant than ever.

IX 5 · BEVERLY CENTER
8500 Beverly Boulevard, bounded by Third Street and by San Vicente, Beverly and La Cienega boulevards, West Hollywood
Welton Becket Associates, 1982

This most recent of Los Angeles' indoor shopping centers is housed in a remarkably *big* building, eight stories of almost blank plaster walls extruded from the sidewalk edges of an entire city block and made even more overpowering by the most negative neutral brown-gray that human color sense has yet devised. This great mass looks at first glance as if it might have fallen out of the sky, but then an uneasy suspicion begins to grow that it was built with the expectation of human occupancy. Long horizontal slots on the first five floors seem to have been scooped out and inset with a kind of pastel rainbow of railings; zigzagging up two sides are glass-covered escalators, meant presumably to share in the élan of their predecessors on the Pompidou Center in Paris; a small number of big letters spell out BULLOCK'S and THE BROADWAY; and black street-level caverns have ominous red neon signs that say ENTER. But other than these, there are few suggestions of human inhabitation or even of the likelihood that this object is hollow.

Those adventuresome enough to drive inside discover that it *is* hollow, that it *is* a building and that the first five levels of it are a parking garage. At this writing the first-floor façades are blank, though there are plans to befriend the sidewalks with street-level shops and restaurants. The main stores are all on the top three levels, recollective of Le Corbusier's ill-fated "shopping streets in the sky" in his famous Unité d'Habitation at Marseilles; but of course Corbu didn't have outside escalators. The ones here are of the same uncleanable persuasion as their Parisian brethren at the Plateau Beaubourg, but they are a bit grander; their chief attribute is that they are in the open, which at least allows you to figure out—for the only time in this shopping experience—where you are. Once inside, your first impression is of hopeless confusion, augmented by claustrophobia, which never really goes away; curiously, the format is a recognizable, old-fashioned 1950s one, with a department store at each end, long rows of shops in between, and light coming down from above. But here the sun filters through high light wells sealed off by translucent skylights and the store fronts all look the same, for three levels up and down and for as far ahead as you can see, which is not far: the shopping street curves according to the plan of the building, which turns out to be shaped like a boomerang (with a big bite taken out of the San Vicente Boulevard side in order to avoid some 50 working oil wells).

The place looks like a science fiction movie set—not the kind where anything good happens to anybody, but the kind where the bad guys have taken over the galaxy and everyone else is trapped in some building of the future. The shops are maybe a little classier or flashier than those in the other indoor shopping centers, but it would take a real connoisseur to spot the difference. Compared, for instance, to the Galleria in Houston, which is grand and lush, Beverly Center seems very hard; compared with the underground streets in Osaka, very drab and mean. Halfway down the boomerang is an expanded light well that tries to give a sense of center to the whole with glassy elevators and escalators outlined by rows of tiny lights; in the middle is a sunken, carpeted conversation

IX 6 A · *Danziger Studio*

IX 4 · *Tail o' the Pup*

pit, arranged to fend off any possible conversation; nearby are big vats of plastic flowers.

This one central space is an example of how the new indoor shopping center mode can allow a good deal of three-dimensional play—though very heavy and somber play indeed. Here escalators angle overhead in a kind of post-Piranesi fantasy, but there's something so leaden about the whole experience that the fantasy goes unnoticed. It's hard to be sure precisely why it's so grim. Perhaps it's because all the parts are an antiseptic white and look molded out of plastic even when they're not, or because there is no detail. Still, there is a kind of unremitting level of—not really energy—but stirred-up-ness about these shaved-off shapes that gives them the air of having been all made by a nonhuman superintelligence.

The sense of wonder comes at last when you make it back to the loading dock of the outside escalators and see a window and know that there is still a world out there that has not been blown away. After that, the escalator tube, which seemed so inhuman on the way up, now seems like a happy escape into the realm of humankind. Some years ago a new movie was advertised around town by billboards that said, "I have seen the future and it won't work." They knew.

IX 6 · TWO STUDIOS BY FRANK GEHRY

Frank Gehry has always viewed himself as an artist and his buildings as sculpture. But his now celebrated ripping apart of things as we know them, accompanied by sorties into the ordinary worlds of cyclone fencing, corrugated siding and exposed studs, has come about gradually. These two art studios, a mile and a half apart on Melrose Avenue and eleven years apart in time, record this shift in philosophy, from the unknown architect who moved confidently within the tenets of Modernism to the world-famous one who answers now to much more syncopated inner rhythms.

A · DANZIGER STUDIO
7001 Melrose Avenue, on the northwest corner of Sycamore Avenue, Los Angeles
Frank O. Gehry and Associates, 1965

This little art studio demonstrates Gehry's early-on mastery of the Modern persuasion, taking architectural minimalism about as far as it might want to go. The view from Melrose is of two adjoining two-story boxes, sheathed in almost windowless light gray stucco, the left one pushed back to form a front courtyard; this tiny open space, filled up now by a big tree, is protected from the sidewalk by a one-story, free-standing stucco wall. Entrance is on the left, through a narrow door that becomes a high window. The Sycamore Avenue side is just one big stucco wall with a dark gray garage door set into the lower right corner, though a large window, enclosed by a stucco cube, peers out from the roof. On the north, facing the alley, the building lets go a bit with two near-curtain walls of glass. It is one of my favorite buildings in Los Angeles.

B · GEMINI G.E.L. STUDIOS
**8365 Melrose Avenue, on the northwest corner of Kings Road,
Los Angeles**
Frank O. Gehry and Associates, 1976

A decade later, when the sounds of a different drummer had become audible to him, Gehry designed a 5,000-square-foot addition to this prestigious fine arts gallery and lithography studio. At first glance his two-story cube doesn't appear much different from the one-story, L-shaped original that it fits into; the earlier one is stuccoed dark gray, the new one, white. The details of the addition are clean and unselfconscious, something like those of the Danziger Studio and recollective as well of the work of William Lescaze forty years before (page 172), though these are cheaper and simpler and a little quirkier. The windows on both the Melrose and Kings Road sides are restrained vertical or horizontal slashes, almost flush with the walls.

Closer inspection, however, reveals that Gehry's new spirit, wild and joyously subversive, is thrashing around just inside. There are rows of exposed studs behind every clean sweep of window, and even more disquieting are the two connections with the older building: both are sheathed in panels of unfinished plywood, now weathered dark brown, with big windows that reveal tilting skylights, exposed rafters and studs, and raw stairways that create forced perspectives—a favorite Gehry device—by climbing up at a slightly different angle from the building. Aside from an artful patch of chain link on a parking-lot gate, the cyclone fencing of the new Gehry idiom is missing, as is the corrugated metal, so it is particularly noteworthy how much energy Gehry has managed to stir up here by merely shifting or uncovering the most basic building materials.

IX 7 · SCHINDLER HOUSE
833 North Kings Road, West Hollywood
R. M. Schindler, 1921–22
*Now the California Office of Historic Preservation; open for tours Saturday,
11–4, Sunday and Wednesday, 1–4, and by appointment; admission fee;
call (213) 651-1510*

One of the most extraordinary things about seeing Schindler's own house for the first time is at once what a monument and what a mess it is. It's a *real* shanty, its own version of the Bel-Air Hotel (page 180), just a bunch of thin concrete panels and little boards, too small in most cases to stand firm, all tacked together and now working themselves apart. The sort of ad hoc construction, the extremely small scale and the openness of everything to the outdoors are the characteristics, in America and in Europe, of summer cottages; indeed, Schindler is said to have had the idea for this place while spending part of a summer in a rented cabin in Yosemite. He had recently arrived from Vienna via Frank Lloyd Wright's Taliesin studio in Wisconsin and was very excited about living in such a salubrious climate. Schindler thought, for instance, that it would be okay to sleep outside in California the year round, so he built what he called "sleeping baskets," or open sleeping porches, on the roof; after a while, of course, they were closed in because the out-of-doors in California on most nights, especially in winter, is too awful. But the whole house is part of this summer house excitement, full of the kind of pleasure people in this country and Europe have for a long time gotten out of making buildings that were not meant to stand up against the stern requirements of heavy winter weather and of formal Victorian or Edwardian lives. So here we have a kind of Bohemian shack; at first it was on a street, but later, as various trees and bushes and remarkably huge bamboo grew up, it became a shack in a jungle. Visitors come for the Important Modern Architecture they've read so much about (most critics agree with Schindler that this and his Lovell Beach house [page 136] are his two greatest works), so they have the opportunity to be surprised to see what a wonderful, low-key, ad-hoc, nail-it-up-yourself shack in a jungle it really is.

The house was a place for Schindler to experiment with ways of making things as simply and directly and as modern as he could, with a budget so small that he had to do much of the construction himself. His materials—concrete, redwood, glass and canvas, all kept in their natural colors—created a number of vivid contrasts. Between light and dark, hard and soft, machine-built and hand-crafted, permanent and temporary, or, as Schindler himself said, between a solid permanent cave and an open lightweight tent.

This was a place, as well, for Schindler to take his theories on the cohabitation of man and nature about as far as they could go. The three-winged sort of pinwheel plan allows each wing to wrap around a grassy courtyard, where a little concrete terrace flows directly into the floor of each room; big sliding doors, filled once with canvas but now with glass, open wide to make each room and its garden seem part of the same space, a space enclosed by concrete walls at one end and hedges at the other. Schindler continued the lines of the house out into the landscape with the simplest and most impermanent of materials, shrubbery, so that the unroofed part of his 100-by-200-foot piece of Eden became, over time, a series of shaggy green rooms. A few even have outdoor fireplaces, as do most of the interior rooms, though Schindler never felt obliged to install any other form of heating.

The house was also a laboratory for Schindler's ideas on the cohabitation of man with himself as well as with Nature. He designed it to be lived in by himself and his wife and their friends, Mr. and Mrs. Clyde Chase. Each couple had their own suite, patio and entrance, but shared the kitchen, guest room and garage. This arrangement worked out exactly as well as the outdoor bedrooms did, and the Chases moved out. Ironically, after the Schindlers stopped talking to each other, the house was flexible enough to allow them to live entirely separate lives in the separate halves—for sixteen years.

But more than the landscaping and the sociology, the technological innovations and the Modern forms are the reasons for the house's fame. Schindler was a Viennese, so we expect, somehow, that his work, like that of Richard Neutra or such later Germans as Helmut Schulitz (page 216), might be devoted to Teutonic cleaning and tightening up and making more neat and precise the vocabulary for doing ordinary things, using, like Schulitz, supposedly ordinary off-the-shelf industrial parts. Schindler seems to have taken it the other way around, to have been interested in tilt-up concrete panels and experiments with thin boards or canvas or whatever to see how easy and directly responsive these materials and techniques could make things. The problem with the cleaner, tighter and neater versions is that in time they too will crumble and lean and crack and twist and stain. Both the Lovell house (page 254) by Richard Neutra and the Schindler house have fallen apart, but somehow the latter, like a summer cottage, becomes more endearing as it peels and crumbles and warps and falls; it's sufficiently complex to let its shadows stand up in decay. The striking difference in these two houses comes in part from the initial attitudes of the two architects. Perhaps it's not too grossly oversimplified to see Neutra as the kind of architect who starts from the idea and later, almost reluctantly, builds it (although Neutra built a lot). Schindler is an example of the kind of architect who starts with the act of building and the pleasures attached to that, and then works up a dialectic about why to do it one way and not another. The enthusiasms inherent in Schindler's approach to design can produce a number of mistakes along with the inspired solutions, but the architect's own house, at least, reveals so openly the love and the struggle that went into it that the flaws seem unimportant. The cracks in the blank walls of the Neutra Lovell house, however, seem to echo out across the canyon.

IX 8 · HOLLYWOOD APARTMENT COURTS

As tourism increased in Southern California, the California bungalow, a determinedly individual house in its own little garden, begat the bungalow court, a group of individual houses (often for Easterners to winter in) placed around a shared central garden. As automobiles increased, the bungalow court begat the motel, but it also gave rise to a unique courtyard apartment scheme that began in Hollywood and flourished through the 1920s and '30s. Despite an increase in density, these residences allowed everyone from retired Midwesterners to movie stars to live year round in the warm climate. Two-story apartments were wrapped around a richly planted central courtyard, with garages close at hand but unobtrusive. The apartments were attached to each other, but, as in the bungalow court, each one expressed its own personality and enjoyed substantial privacy. This phenomenon took place at the height of the Spanish Colonial Revival, so most of these buildings had white plaster walls and red-tiled roofs and gorgeous details, from hand-carved beams and balustrades to wrought iron and colorful tiles to fountains and turrets. The idea of the garden apartments caught on and spread through California and beyond, often decked out in other styles. When the format migrated north and east, much of the design seemed to freeze up. Today almost any developer's dismal stucco box that has a hole in the middle can trace its origins to the pleasant little courtyard apartments that bloomed for two decades in Los Angeles. Many of them are still around, with waiting lists far longer than for any of the newer versions. Below are two of the best.

A · ANDALUSIA APARTMENTS
1471–75 Havenhurst Drive, West Hollywood
Arthur and Nina Zwebell, 1926
Private residence

Arthur and Nina Zwebell arrived in Los Angeles in 1921 and, with no formal training in design, began to build apartment houses—some of the most beautiful in the world, all wrapped around richly planted courtyards. With Arthur as architect and builder, and Nina as interior designer, they created eight of these little Spanish-style oases in Hollywood in fewer than eight years. It is not surprising that, after the Crash of 1929, they became studio set designers, for their apartment designs had as much fantasy about them as any Hollywood movie. Indeed, these buildings were so appealing that they served as prototypes for all the rest of the courtyard apartments in Southern California. It was the Zwebells, more than anyone else, who started the phenomenon of the garden apartment.

The Andalusia, named for the Spanish architectural style adopted by the Zwebells, is in many respects their most resolved and most endearing building, constructed when they and their team of craftsmen had reached full stride. A long walkway, which begins at the street, passes straight through the center of the symmetrical two-story structure and its three courtyards in enfilade, each more private than the last. First, behind a driveway in the front wall, is a wide, red-tiled courtyard, so pleasant a place that the garage doors in the side pavilions seem not to be made for automobiles. But this is, indeed, where the residents' cars are stored, conveniently next to the main entrance, which is a small archway beneath a long second-story balcony. This leads through a gallery that opens onto the largest outdoor space, a verdant garden with a fat turret in the far right corner, an outdoor fireplace beside a little patio on the left, and, in the center, a brightly tiled fountain that was copied from one in Seville. Narrow paths lead to apartment entrances on either side, while the main walkway continues through another archway at the back. Here stairs climb up to more apartments or down to the last courtyard, which is really just a backyard enclosed on three sides by tall hedges. This is, though, the most private outdoor room of all, a tiny place (with a large swimming pool) where the many movie star residents, including Clara Bow, John Payne, Cesar Romero and Marlon Brando, used to catch up on their tans.

The picturesque details in the Andalusia, as well as the rich materials and the loving way they were crafted together, belie a little the straightforward symmetry of the plan. At every turn, hand-carved eaves and hand-wrought brackets support uneven red-tiled roofs; dark balconies with hand-hewn timbers and elaborately turned balustrades project from thickly plastered white walls; terracotta tiles gleam from the walkways, while smaller, hand-painted tiles with bright glazes sparkle from the fountain and the stair risers and make special places on the walls; small-paned windows glisten from slate-gray frames, while tiny statues in round niches look out on this tamed jungle of tropical trees and shrubs and bright flowers. And it all comes together, delight after delight, with no fuss at all and with impressive economy of means: there's not one flourish too many. Helen Hunt Jackson herself could not have dreamed up a more seductive place.

B · VILLA D'ESTE APARTMENTS
1355 Laurel Avenue, West Hollywood
Pierpont and Walter S. Davis, 1928
Private residences

At the sixteenth-century Villa d'Este near Rome, a long walkway climbs up a hillside while the world's most spectacular waterworks spout and crash and cascade beside it; the villa at the top of the hill seems almost an afterthought. The twentieth-century Villa d'Este in Hollywood is a little different: here the Italian Renaissance villa itself climbs up a hillside while only an intermittent water course runs down the center; and much thought must have been lavished on it. This Classically detailed, two-story apartment house, whose white plaster walls and red-tiled roofs wrap around a luxuriant garden, is one of the most inspired places in all of Ramonaland.

Like the Andalusia, the Villa d'Este is symmetrical; it starts from a central walkway that begins as a forecourt between two garages, then passes through an archway to a main courtyard. But here the spatial events take place on four progressively higher terraces, and the overall demeanor, set up by convincing Renaissance details, is more formal.

Indeed, this villa convinces you of its ties to Rome before you even leave the sidewalk. On each side short driveways ease down from the sidewalk to a garage pavilion, each with a low red-tiled roof above faded white-painted brick walls; along the front of each pavilion an arcade on Composite piers frames three elaborate wooden doors. Between these garages a short flight of palazzo-scale steps leads up to the projecting forecourt, where thick rows of windmill palms bristle along the sides and a stone lion spouts water into a narrow pond at the center. Behind this four more steps rise between two enormous eucalyptuses to a high archway in the front of the building. The large, stony voussoirs of this arch protrude grandly from the white plaster wall, which steps forward itself from two flanking wings. All three parts of the façade, though, are brought together by a windowed loggia beneath intricately carved eaves and by large quoins that fortify every corner.

The courtyard behind the archway is even more wonderful. Past a vaulted corridor with its authentically faded rich colors and up four more steps, this open-air room is engulfed by tropical shrubs and trees that form a dappled green ceiling above the red brick floor. A tiny Moorish water channel down the middle is fed by a tiered and brightly tiled central fountain, which is ringed by four large olive trees. Other trees grow from planters along the sides, in front of little brick walls that create private entrance patios for the apartments. On the second floor another row of windows like a loggia lies just behind a row of tiny Composite columns, which hold up pergolas when the walls cut back to form upstairs porches. At the back of the courtyard a few more steps lead up to a small terrace in front of a final dark archway. In here the restrained water theme turns into a grand, if frozen display of fluid form as the shiny dark blue and frothy white tiles of a long staircase cascade out from the shadows.

IX 9 · STORER HOUSE
8161 Hollywood Boulevard, West Hollywood
Frank Lloyd Wright, 1923
Private residence

Here is the second in Frank Lloyd Wright's Mayan concrete block series that began with La Miniatura in Pasadena (page 318). The Storer house went up in the same year (1923) as that first masterpiece and recalls just a little of its magic: the plain gray block, which blossoms into ornament around the windows and other edges, has some real power as its tall, rectangular volumes climb up through the dense foliage of a steep canyon.

First comes a ten-foot-high retaining wall that serves, at its top, as the railing for a front terrace. The rooms of the house form an L behind this patio, with a one-story wing on the left and a two-story living room at the back. Floor-to-ceiling windows, separated by narrow piers and delicate wood mullions, help to make the volumes appear even taller than they are. More windows on the back side of the living room open onto another terrace and a forest of eucalyptus.

The Storer house is a good example of Wright's ability to make a small structure seem large by continuing some of its walls out into the landscape. His impulse from the decades before, of course, was to make the house appear to hug the prairie, so extensions into it were usually horizontal. Here, however, Wright took advantage of the mountainside and extended the walls vertically. The tiny house looks like a castle, and it fits into this rugged hillside as if it had been carved out of the rock.

IX 9 · *Storer House*

IX 12 A · *Chemosphere*

IX 10 · MT. OLYMPUS
A residential subdivision; main entrance at Mt. Olympus Drive, off Laurel Canyon Boulevard

The Mt. Olympus subdivision, which spreads down a hillside just east of Beverly Hills, is a sort of low-budget Trousdale Estates (page 218); it overlooks the odd little houses of West Hollywood (page 226) in much the same way that Trousdale overlooks Beverly Hills. The parallels between Mt. Olympus and Trousdale, with the former always a bit tackier and more pretentious even than the latter, go on and on. Mt. Olympus is another big earth-moving project with pads cut deep into the hillside, this time so brutally that vegetation has not been able so far to hide the scars. The large houses on the tiny lots are, for the most part, puffed up versions of tract houses, coated with enough decoration to suggest one fantasy or another. Like the houses of Trousdale, and like the West Hollywooden miniatures below, most of the fantasies on Mt. Olympus are concocted out of Contemporary, French and especially Classical Greek persuasions, though here the allusions are particularly thin and the houses often just look like apartment buildings.

As in Trousdale, rows of Italian cypress march around everywhere—there are undoubtedly more cypress trees per capita here than anywhere else in the world. They were planted by the developers as part of their own fantasy, which became the subdivision's theme, a garden residence for the Greek gods. That the landscape of Greece is even more barren than the chaparral-covered hillside they started out with was scant bother, so the trees of Italy and Beverly Hills and Palm Springs line most of the steep streets, which were all given names like Venus, Apollo, Zeus and Achilles drives. The entrance to the main street, Mt. Olympus Drive, is announced by a trio of free-standing, abstractly ordered columns that sparkle with a veneer of white stone tiles, recollective of casinos on the Las Vegas Strip. Farther up this street, near the intersection of Electra Drive, a stone grotto with a black pool inside tries to evoke the shaded corners of Italian Renaissance gardens, only this one is five feet from a hot curb. Up a little farther is a tall pile of boulders that once functioned as a fountain. In fact, almost every intersection sports a fountain, usually made of materials that gleam in the sun, usually not working. A rustic waterfall at the northwest corner of Vulcan and Hercules drives combines shiny pebbles, shards of white marble, and flat planes of concrete.

IX 11 · DE BRETTEVILLE–SIMON HOUSES
8067–71 Willow Glen Road, off Laurel Canyon Boulevard, Los Angeles
Peter de Bretteville, 1976
Private residence

These two heavy industry–inspired houses, lying end to end in a forested ravine, are nearly identical two-story rectangular volumes, clad in corrugated steel and enormous expanses of glass. Designed on a precise four-foot module as prototypes for limited mass production, the houses combine an assortment of mostly middle-tech parts to appear decidedly High-Tech, recollective of the post-and-beam work of Los Angeles' early Modernists of the *Arts and Architecture* Case Study House era. In particular, they look like later, more taut versions of Charles Eames's off-the-shelf masterpiece in Pacific Palisades (page 118); like the Eames house, these are enveloped in a luxuriant landscape, which manages to take the edge off the sharp lines, though here the buildings are still visible through the foliage.

The houses confront the street as one continuous, vertically ribbed wall, three stories high, relieved only by two partially disguised garage doors, two high blocks of windows, and a gap in the center where a low part of the wall frames two stairways. The stairways lead (if you can get permission to use them) to a little courtyard between solidly corrugated end walls; the back walls and the other end walls, in marked contrast, are made up almost entirely of glass, in large panes with thin white-painted mullions. Running the full length of each back wall is a sort of Monterey Style porch, a metal-grated catwalk with white canvas sunshades tied to red-painted pipe columns. Inside are airy volumes lined by skylight-washed walls, with smaller rooms tucked away in corners or on mezzanines. Here the structure reveals itself as a gradual transition—from floor to ceiling—of concrete to steel to wood. But more immediate and more satisfying is the transition from these taut industrial geometries, through the glass, to the still-growing woods outside.

IX 12 · MULHOLLAND DRIVE
Along the ridge of the Santa Monica Mountains between the Pacific Ocean and Cahuenga Pass

The vast area of the Santa Monica Mountains, which is mostly wilderness, cuts an astonishing cleavage almost through the middle of America's third largest city. Among its peaks along the length of the range weaves Mulholland Drive. A journey on this forty-mile-long road is often a thrilling sequence of surprises as it traverses forested enclosures, passes a number of the strangest houses in Los Angeles, then opens onto some of the most spectacular views in the world —on a clear night you can watch the lights of the Los Angeles Basin on one side and the San Fernando Valley on the other twinkle almost endlessly to the horizon. Indeed, this road was built primarily as a scenic highway in 1923 and

1924, when William Mulholland, the chief engineer of the Los Angeles Aqueduct, still enjoyed a good press; but the secluded view-points along the way have also been favorite places for countless backseat romances and other adventures, from the fictional rendezvous of Philip Marlowe or Sam Spade to equally exciting real-life intrigues.

Development of this wilderness has been limited by the rugged terrain, the isolation and the threat of brush fires (this is real chaparral, the local oily brush that literally explodes into flame during the long, dry summers), so most of the inhabitants are coyotes, skunks, raccoons and deer; the rest are, for the most part, a hardy and independent breed of humans who build their houses any way they feel like it. Their architectural fantasies, many visible from Mulholland Drive, include everything from sprawling ranch houses with Polynesian backyards to glass boxes perched out on stilts to any number of space-age peculiarities. Those closest to the centers tend toward the slick; farther west, in Topanga Canyon, the homelier arts of the wood butchers prevail.

Below are two of the farthest out futuristic models. There are hundreds more, of every persuasion, and almost anything might lie behind the next bend. But none can measure up to the main delight of this ride: the panoramas over much of this endless city.

A · CHEMOSPHERE
7776 Torreyson Drive, Los Angeles
John Lautner, 1960
Private residence, but can be seen from a number of streets, including
   Mulholland Drive; closest view is on Torreyson Drive about 100 feet past
   the driveway

It's easy to see why the Malin house, called the Chemosphere, has been mistaken for a UFO. Only a tall concrete column with a collar of radiating struts attaches this large one-story octagon to a nearly vertical site, so from the distance a glassy gray flying saucer seems to hover against the dark green mountain behind. This is the most famous of a long line of dramatic houses by John Lautner, who, like Schindler and Neutra, started out with Frank Lloyd Wright and then made his own reputation in the pursuit of a very personal vision. His specialties have been structures of surprising geometry—somewhere in mood between Frank Lloyd Wright's Prairie and Outer Space, which often manage to touch gently onto otherwise unbuildable sites. Within this context the Chemosphere is an unqualified success: the only things that touch the impossible terrain are long stairs, a small cable car and that one column, which carries the utility lines as well as the entire structural load; floor-to-ceiling windows, in a continuous band, provide panoramic views while, at night from outside, their glow combines with red and yellow spotlights from below to hasten many impressionable newcomers toward the conviction that the War of the Worlds has begun.

B · CARLING HOUSE
7436 Mulholland Drive, Los Angeles
John Lautner, 1950
Private residence

Here is another John Lautner work, which in this case looks like a thin slice of a Quonset hut just beginning to fall off a cliff. From the road it appears to be only a tiny one-story house with a garage door on the left, a high stone wall on the right and an open slot in the middle, all covered by a great arching roof. A spiral staircase, however, winds down the central gap to reveal that the bulk of the square footage lies below, propped up against the mountainside on giant steel columns. Everything, including the mailbox, is painted a light slate-gray, but there are just enough plants in front and enough large windows and careful details beneath that government-issue roof to make this futuristic statement a home—or, at the very least, a homey docking station for the Chemosphere.

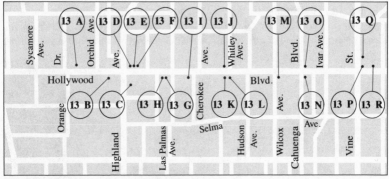

IX 13 · HOLLYWOOD BOULEVARD

IX 13 · HOLLYWOOD BOULEVARD
A walking tour of about ten blocks, going east from 6925 to 6233 Hollywood Boulevard

During the golden age of movies, in the 1920s and '30s, Hollywood was famous around the world as the home of filmmaking, movie stars and all that was glamorous. At the same time, Hollywood Boulevard was built and billed as everybody's image of the motion picture capital become real: if there was a boulevard at the end of the rainbow, this was to be it. Though most of the buildings were only two stories high, almost every one of them was decked out in energetic versions of the latest styles—Spanish Colonial Revival, Churrigueresque and both kinds of Art Deco, as well as a lighter rendition of the Chicago Style for the tall buildings. Hollywood Boulevard, or some ten blocks of it, became lined with elegant shops and famous restaurants and premiere movie theaters, which were themselves fabulous stage sets, inside and out; motion picture executives filled the offices above and movie stars were everywhere, or so the tourist hoped.

Sightseers have always been disappointed by the workaday world of the real Hollywood; Hollywood Boulevard used to be the closest thing to their expectations, but now it could be the biggest disappointment of all. After many of the studios and most of the stars left town, Hollywood and particularly its boulevard began a long decline. Beginning in 1958 terrazzo stars, inlaid with the names of famous entertainers, have been placed in the sidewalks (there are now over 2,500 of them), but they only seemed to attract the Hippies of the sixties and their hard-core counterparts in the seventies. Echoing the change, many of the elegant façades were cheaply remodeled, though usually only on the first floor, and the stores began to cater to the new kind of street life. City boosters say that a rebirth is at hand and point to the rows of new lollipop trees and the refurbished Hollywood sign (page 249), but rejuvenation has been slow in arriving. Still, most of the old buildings, especially on the upper floors, are in good condition and manage to recall a poignant era that is no more and, when you get right down to it, never really was—at least not right here.

The walk down Hollywood Boulevard starts, like most people's images do, at Grauman's (now Mann's) Chinese Theater (13 A) (Meyer and Holler, 1927), no. 6925. For half a century this has been one of Los Angeles' biggest tourist attractions. It was built by the consummate showman Sid Grauman, who had earlier masterminded the lavish Million Dollar Theater downtown (page 25) as well as the Egyptian Theater just up the boulevard. Here, for decades, movie stars attended gala premieres (more here than at any other theater) and they still put their footprints in the concrete forecourt. This tradition began, it is said, when Sid Grauman stumbled into the wet concrete and called up his friends Mary Pickford and Douglas Fairbanks to suggest that they do the same.

IX 13 A · *Grauman's Chinese Theater*

The façade, like most stage sets, is more concerned with astonishing the audience than holding strictly to its theme—in this case, Chinese. A pair of two-story pavilions flank a central courtyard, which enshrines a central tower that owes something, maybe, to a feverish recollection of Angkor Wat. The walls of the flanking pavilions are smooth and green with a huge pier-pinnacle at each end. Each pier has bands of grottolike ornament and, at the top, a tall copper obelisk that erupts from flames; there are more flames at the peak. Between the piers, spiky Oriental longhorn steer motifs cover slightly mansarded windows (it's amazing how close to French or to Churrigueresque the Chinese style turns out to be in Southern California) while much more recently run-up dragons cavort across flamboyant marquees. The famous forecourt is an open, nicely Californian space, partially closed off by the pavilions' wing walls, which act as teasers at stage front; it has curving back walls—like the Villa Giulia in Rome—that end in the aforementioned grand central entry beneath a huge Sino-Polynesian sort of Tiki copper roof. This high mansard, rising up steep sides in ways that surely never have been seen in China, is supported on bright red columns with dragon-mask capitals and cornices that skyrocket out of friezes apparently copied from ancient Greek vase paintings. Elaborate doors lead (for the price of a movie ticket) to an interior of equally blithe eclecticism, while a doorway in the surprisingly thin wall on the left of the courtyard leads abruptly to the parking lot. Here you can see how the great bulk of this movie prop is just a big green box, and somehow this discovery helps endear the enterprise.

Across the street, at 6834–6838 Hollywood Boulevard, is the seven-story Paramount movie theater (13 B), formerly El Capitan (Morgan, Walls and Clements, 1935). El Capitan started out as a legitimate theater, the most deluxe on the boulevard, but its East Indian interior by G. Albert Lansburgh is gone and mirrored witch's balls now sparkle above the marquee. The controlledly frenzied Churrigueresque façade, a kind of Baroque in Bondage, however, is intact. Pastry-tube ornament oozes out above and below four-story window slits across the upper floors; the thin piers in between the windows are a cross between Mexican church columns and elaborately turned table legs. The first floor has elaborate cast-iron window frames; the cornice sports statues of famous thespians.

Just south of the boulevard, at 166–168 Highland Avenue, is the lavishly outfitted Max Factor Building (13 C) (S. Charles Lee, 1931). The Max Factor cosmetics firm, which has improved the faces of countless movie stars, had its own façade made up in a sort of Regency Art Deco: swags and medallions ornament etched marble panels, fluted white plaster piers and jewelry-box display windows. The showroom inside is a curious blend of Classical Greece and Streamline Moderne with curving walls in delicate shades of cream and light salmon.

On the northeast corner of Hollywood and Highland is the Hollywood First National Bank Building (13 D) (Meyer and Holler, 1927). This big, white cleaned-up neo-Classical block of a building lumbers up to a twelve-story octagonal neo-Gothic tower with eight flying buttresses, all designed, oddly enough, by the same architects and completed in the same year as Grauman's Chinese. The bank building was once the second tallest structure in Los Angeles; it still comes close to marking the center of Hollywood.

Next door to the bank is a two-story Spanish Colonial Revival (13 E) (6765–6773 Hollywood Boulevard) with frothy ornament under the eaves and above the second-floor windows; two first-floor arches, at the entrance to the Hollywood Wax Museum, are all that's left of what used to be a handsome arcade. There are a number of pleasant, now sort of sleazy, Spanishy buildings like this one along the boulevard. Next door (13 F) is an Italian Renaissance façade with rusticated arches on the first floor and Classically detailed arches on the second; everything has been painted white, except the pilasters and balustrades, which are black.

At 6712 Hollywood Boulevard is the Egyptian Theater (13 G) (Meyer and Holler, 1922), Sid Grauman's first Hollywood extravaganza. It was inspired, as was the whole Egyptian Revival architectural style, by the discovery and later opening of King Tutankhamen's tomb in the early 1920s, but, typically for Meyer and Holler, a number of other excitements were thrown in. This mostly Egyptian theater, with its red-tiled roof, was reached by walking down a long courtyard filled with mummy cases, big vases and pagodas, perhaps Chinese. The walls on each side were made to look like massive stone blocks; on the right, between the banana palms, were cages filled with wild animals; on the left were six little Middle Eastern shops that sold Oriental wares behind striped awnings. Most of this is gone today; a two-story 1950s sine curve, frozen in beige stucco, now waves above the entrance to the courtyard, which itself has been covered by a 1950s canopy. But a number of details remain: next to an old side entrance, sphinx heads continue to stare down from tapered piers; along the front, a cavetto cornice with a jelly-bean molding still has Moorish tiles hanging down in ways the Egyptians never quite got to; painted in the lobby is a temple of Hatshepsut above a sphinx as someone who may be Nefertiti offers libation to the great god Hathor; a lotus frieze with hieroglyphics rims the popcorn counter.

On the right side of the entrance to the Egyptian courtyard, at 6714 Hollywood Boulevard, is a one-story Churrigueresque exuberance that used to be a Pig 'N' Whistle restaurant (13 H) (Morgan, Walls and Clements, 1927) and is now occupied by Hollywood Sportswear. The elegance created by this particularly well-done ornament out of a toothpaste tube was meant to complete the moviegoing adventure next door; it even had a fancy marquee of its own. Much still remains, including a resplendent ceiling and a cartouche, on each end, of a pig playing a whistle.

At 6652–6654 Hollywood Boulevard, on the southwest corner of Cherokee Avenue, is the Shane Building (13 I) (Norton and Wallis, 1930; now called Hollywood Center). This Zigzag Moderne masterpiece makes the most of its four stories with a burst of ornament along the top. The lobby, on Cherokee Avenue, is a silver-and-red Art Deco explosion.

One of our favorite buildings along here (though it has to be taken just a little at a time) is the Bane Building (13 J) (Gogerty and Weyl, 1926; now U.T.B.) at 6605 Hollywood Boulevard, on the northwest corner of Whitley Avenue. It is in the sophisticated Costa Brava–*cum*–Santa Barbara style of the thirties, but cheap. This mostly two-story, white stucco fantasy has a balconied third story on the corner, a tower in the middle and a little Palladian sort of church façade on the left, covered in toned-down but gilded, Churrigueresque ornament. The entrance is set into the corner beneath a scalloped molding that engages in a frenzied adolescent lurch up and out.

Across the street, at 6606–6612 Hollywood Boulevard, is the famous purveyor of sexy nightwear, Frederick's of Hollywood (13 K), formerly S. H. Kress and Company (Edward F. Sibbert, 1935). This classic Art Deco building, designed by one of that style's New York masters, has been painted purple; the stylized plant ornament and the new awnings above the display windows are pink, like so much of the merchandise. Next door to Frederick's, at 6600–6604 Hollywood Boulevard, is an even louder Art Deco building, the J. J. Newberry Company (13 L) (1928), which was designed by an anonymous Newberry staff architect. It continues to sport its original colors. The second floor is a series of long piers and mullions that gleam with turquoise tile; the windows in between are capped by gold and glittery chevron-patterned panels.

There's a splendid early Zigzag Moderne building (13 M) (1931), now occupied by Mandels shoe store, at 6436–6440 Hollywood Boulevard, on the southeast corner of Wilcox Avenue. The second story is some sort of National Treasure with aluminum spandrels cast in high relief, naturally finished, set between piers of ceramic tiles. On the southeast corner of Cahuenga Boulevard, at 6380–6384 Hollywood Boulevard, is another splendid Art Deco building, this time an early Streamline Moderne, designed for the Owl Drug Company (13 N) (Morgan, Walls and Clements, 1934; now called the Julian Medical Building). Although there's an original shop front at no. 6382, the fast-paced second story is the main attraction. The glassy, rounded wall at the corner, a quarter-cylinder within a concave frame, surely must have influenced the one on the Wilshire May Company (page 156). A curved pylon, set asymmetrically behind the corner, thrusts up another couple of stories, while big piers between the windows on Cahuenga Boulevard manage to clear the roof as well.

Directly across the street, at 6381–6385 Hollywood Boulevard, on the northeast corner of Cahuenga, is Hollywood's first high-rise, the six-story Security Trust and Savings Bank (13 O) (1921; now called Security Pacific Bank). It was designed by John and Donald Parkinson, who would go on to stun this city with Bullock's Wilshire (page 147), though here they settled for a reprise of an early Louis Sullivan skyscraper with a dignified glassy first floor, a grand bracketed Renaissance cornice and, in between, big windows set between thin, flat columns that join to form an arcade at the top. Even so, narrow Solomonic columns twist up between the windows in ways the folks would not have tried back in Chicago.

Two blocks east is, at last, the world-famous intersection of Hollywood and Vine, which, those in the know all agree, is not the center of Hollywood. The enormous buildings on three of its corners seem to suggest, however, that it must be the center of something. The Pantages Building (13 P) (Aleck Curlett, 1929; now called the Hollywood Equitable Building), on the northeast corner, is the most interesting of the three. This dignified, U-shaped pile of white terracotta tile, put together in a sort of genteel Art Deco skyscraper style, rises up twelve stories to a nicely domestic green copper roof. There are a few balconies along the way and a bit of flutter at the top, but mostly it just goes up, with no fuss at all.

Just north of Hollywood and Vine, at 1750 Vine Street, is that great landmark of the 1950s, Capitol Records (13 Q) (Welton Becket and Associates, 1954). This was the world's first circular office building, fourteen stories high, with visorlike sun screens on every floor, all the way around, and orientation be damned. It is probably the world's largest self-descriptive building as well, on the order of giant hot dogs and doughnuts, for it was meant to look like a colossal stack of 45 r.p.m. records with a stylized stylus on top—and it does.

Next door to the old Pantages Building, at 6233 Hollywood Boulevard, is the fabulous Pantages Theater (13 R) (R. Marcus Priteca, 1930). This was America's premier Art Deco movie palace, the largest (seating capacity, 2,812) and most ornate theater in Hollywood. Now used for stage plays, it is almost as grand as ever. But for all the excitement on the interior, the front façade is a surprisingly straightforward essay in Zigzag Moderne. Black marble on the first floor glistens around shop windows and lines the central entry. The second floor is a mild-mannered, two-dimensional Mayan temple, molded out of reinforced concrete and painted white. Enormous windows, with bas-relief panels above and flat grillwork below, seem etched away to form wide piers and wider towers, which are slightly stepped and have Indian maidens pressed into their tops. A flamboyant marquee held up on spiky chains and the gleaming shaft that sprouts up from a central tower begin to hint at the spectacle within. The lobby and the women's powder room are the most famous pieces, but almost every surface is a dazzling, overflowing, mind-boggling exaggeration of an already extravagant style. "One of the most dramatic statements ever made," David Gebhard called the interior. We think so, too.

IX 14 · YAMASHIRO RESTAURANT
1999 North Sycamore Avenue, Hollywood
Franklin M. Small, 1914
Open daily

The Yamashiro, which means "castle on the hill," is a vision of a sixteenth-century Japanese palace that seems to have sprung up magically from the top of

Hollywood's most scenic promontory, just above Hollywood Boulevard, overlooking most of the Los Angeles Basin. This carefully detailed mansion was built in 1914 by the brothers Adolph and Eugene Bernheimer, who were wealthy importers of Oriental antiques; they also imported an army of Oriental craftsmen to create their Japanese fantasy and its seven-acre garden that included over thirty thousand exotic shrubs and trees. The walls of the large two-story house, wrapped around a central courtyard, are made to seem less overpowering by the overhang of an enormous gray-tiled roof with eyebrows arching above a central entry and over a number of bay windows; the building's substantial bulk has been relieved by ornate timber columns and latticework in the white plaster walls and by intricately carved brackets and rafter ends along the roofs.

During Hollywood's golden age the mansion was a clubhouse for "in" members of the entertainment industry, and then, in 1960, it was opened as a posh restaurant. Most of the garden is gone now, and too many glassed-in dining porches have grown out from the walls, but the elaborately crafted interior and the views it offers, especially at night, still have the power to amaze.

IX 15 · *American Legion Headquarters*

IX 16 A · *High Tower Court*

IX 15 · AMERICAN LEGION HEADQUARTERS
2035 North Highland Avenue, Hollywood
Eugene Weston, Jr., 1929

The façade of this two-story, flat-roofed fortress, with a squat, pyramid-capped tower that steps up behind, is a foursquare, no-nonsense display of military might. A series of low steps lead up, past a howitzer aimed at the street, to riveted metal doors in the middle of a blank white-painted wall made of reinforced concrete with the form marks left showing; the corners are softened with swords. Like many military uniforms, this merciless wall serves as a foil for the attached decorations, the brightly colored, straightened-up Churrigueresque effulgences that gleam around the entry and along the cornice. The latter is a ribbonlike frieze emblazoned with colorful shields of World War I army divisions. An architrave beneath this says "For God And Country We Associate Ourselves Together For The Following Purposes: To Uphold And Defend The Constitution Of The United States Of America." These thoughts continue on, becoming a densely worded paragraph above the entrance, which outsparkles the rest; then there are more shields in a very snappy pediment and a gold American Legion seal that bursts from the top. The first level of the tower says "In Peace As In War We Serve," with dates, while the second level remembers Generals Foch and Pershing. Then a metal flag demonstrates a steadfastness not normally associated with flags. But our description, perhaps too picky, makes the building seem perhaps too prickly. It doesn't adequately suggest that the American Legion Headquarters in Hollywood is curiously beautiful, even moving.

IX 16 · HIGH TOWER COURT
North end of High Tower Drive, above Camrose Drive, Hollywood
Private residences

High Tower Court (16 A), set high on a hill and deep in Raymond Chandler country, is a strange Hollywood sort of marriage between a Streamline Moderne bungalow court and an Italian hill town. What's more, this group of little houses, which wrap around the top of a steep canyon, is reached by an elevator inside a tall campanile of the kind you might find on a piazza in northern Italy. The piazza in this case is the dead end of High Tower Drive, which is lined on each side by tiny garages just visible beneath dense foliage spilling down from the mountainside. After parking here, residents walk through a short tunnel at the end of the street to reach the base of a reinforced-concrete tower that rises up against the greenery with remarkable austerity: its plain, buff-colored plaster walls frame a row of three rectangular windows, which allow stroboscopic views of Hollywood from the open-cage elevator; the slightly recessed belfry (or machine room) is delimited by subtle, machicolated stringcourses and capped with a pyramid of red tile.

Just below the belfry, a door opens onto a bridge that ends in a maze of sidewalks, stairways and more bridges leading to the houses, which, for the most part, are not nearly as memorable as the tower. Most noticeable is a collection, in the center, of stark white cottages (Carl Kay, ca. 1966–1956) whose curving walls cling to the hillside with a certain slipstream panache, though the well-worn wooden surfaces seem to have grown weary from the burden of such taut attention. There are a number of stucco houses with mildly Spanish intentions on either side of the compound, while a few rather more opulent places lie farther up Broadview Terrace, the main walkway that winds through this mountaintop thicket. The Otto Bollman house (16 B) (2200 Broadview Terrace, 1922), one of Lloyd Wright's first designs, is a remarkable exercise in impossible angles and zigzag detail, but it is almost obscured by tropical plants and vines.

For all the absence of an architectural Great Moment, the arrangement of these little houses on this almost unbuildable aerie remains an inspired solution: all of them enjoy sunlight and air and extraordinary views; the separation of the residents from their automobiles and from the rest of the world is brought about with remarkable ease—as long as the elevation works. And the dense foliage adds some poetry to the notion of Urban Jungle.

IX 17 · HOLLYWOOD BOWL

2301 North Highland Avenue, in Cahuenga Pass, Hollywood
1921 and after
Grounds open daily; for concert information, call (213) 876-8742

The Hollywood Bowl is a vast outdoor amphitheater where the Los Angeles Philharmonic Orchestra performs summer "Symphonies Under the Stars" and where, too, almost every well-known musician or singer of the last fifty years has played. Like the Hollywood sign, the Bowl is a landmark of considerable dimension: 17,619 seats look down on a 100-foot-wide band shell surrounded by 120 acres of trees and thick shrubs in a natural depression of the still wild Hollywood Hills.

In 1919 this naturally resonant hollow, then called Daisy Dell, was purchased as the site for religious plays, but the first owners quickly lost faith and sold out after their architect suggested one million dollars' worth of improvements. Although Easter sunrise services are still a big event, starlit concerts by superstar entertainers have been the main draw since the formal dedication in 1922. In 1924, to keep the Bowl from foundering, the next owners deeded it to Los Angeles County—which promptly dynamited Daisy Dell into symmetry and poured yards and yards of concrete into the stage and under the expanded seating. Since then, the place has never sounded quite the same.

From that day until now, a number of famous architects have tried to correct the acoustics by rebuilding the band shell and by constructing walls to dull the roar of the Hollywood Freeway, which moved in next door in 1954. In 1924 Lloyd Wright had built perhaps the prettiest-sounding band shell—an enormous Mayan pyramid that was slapped together in ten days out of the set he had designed for the Douglas Fairbanks movie *Robin Hood*. It was, however, thought to be so ugly that Wright was asked to design another one for the 1928 season. His next effort was left out in the rain and ruined, so in 1929 Allied Architects designed the one that remains today; it is made of white-painted transite on a steel frame that endures the weather but does little for the quality of sound. Oddly, this last design has served as a prototype for a great many of America's band shells, which tend to sound just as bad. In recent years, Frank Gehry has tried a number of modifications, from fearsome-looking speakers to a

IX 18 A · *Hollywoodland sign*

cardboard-tube stockade to huge spheres suspended from the ceiling, to try to recapture the sounds from those old days in the tall grass.

The setting, though, is still magical. On a balmy summer evening, after a picnic in the surrounding park or after the ritual climb from the parking lot past Italian cypress, birds-of-paradise and fragrant eucalyptus, the visitor passes through a short tunnel and comes out in the Hollywood Bowl, a mysteriously enclosed valley where time seems to have stopped. Although the Bowl is less than a mile from Hollywood Boulevard and only a few hundred feet from the freeway, the chaparral-covered slopes recall more romantic days when Indians and then wagon trains traveled past here through Cahuenga Pass. When the sun goes down and the music begins, and the huge white band shell glows against the black hills and the sky, the elusive Hollywood enchantment slips back into place.

IX 18 · HOLLYWOODLAND SIGN AND GATES
The gate is on Beachwood Drive, just south of Westshire Street, Hollywood; you can't miss the sign
1923 and after

Even the high-powered hoopla of the Hollywood movie industry was outdistanced, in 1923, by a local real estate syndicate. The promoters of Hollywoodland, a 500-acre subdivision in the foothills above the business district, put up a Gothic stone gateway at the south entrance and an enormous $21,000 sign that spelled out HOLLYWOODLAND across the chaparral-covered mountainside behind; the white-painted, fifty-foot-high, sheet-metal letters, outlined by 4,000 twenty-watt light bulbs, could be read from twenty-five miles away, day or night. Unlike most of Hollywood's other stage sets, these two early examples of inspired showmanship still exist.

The Hollywoodland sign (18 A), minus its last four letters, has become Los Angeles' most conspicuous landmark, famous around the world. The LAND was removed after the sign and its vast site were donated in 1945 to the city, which, until recently, could do little more than watch the huge letters fall apart; despite occasional attempts to fix it up, the sign became a grim reminder of the deterioration in the community below. But by 1978 the citizens of Hollywood became convinced that a rebuilt sign could spark their town's own resurrection. A new sign, constructed on the latest principles of billboard technology, was put up, with various celebrities donating $27,700 apiece for the letters: Gene Autry paid for an L, playboy Hugh Hefner threw a benefit party for the Y, and rock star Alice Cooper bought the last O in memory of Groucho Marx.

The Hollywoodland gates (18 B)—on a direct axis with, but far below, the Hollywood sign—look like two tiny pieces from some fairy-tale castle as they arch over the sidewalks on each side of Beachwood Drive. The thickness of their gray sandstone walls adds an unexpected substantiality to this promotional fantasy. The gate on the west, a simple cube with a low gable roof, seems to serve as a guardhouse or as a foil for the high-spirited keep across the street; the sides of this narrow tower are just wide enough to contain a long, iron-barred slot, a working clock and a phony chimney that jerks its way up past the stone pyramid of a roof.

Just north of these gates, across the intersection of Westshire Street, lies a cute little English cottage with steep gable roofs and tiny dormers. It should come as no surprise that this brief essay in quaintness was, in the 1920s, the sales office for those inspired hucksters of Hollywoodland.

IX 19 · THREE HOUSES BY LLOYD WRIGHT

Frank Lloyd Wright, Jr., known as Lloyd Wright, has received far less attention than he would have if he had not worked in the shadow of his father or if he didn't have the same name as the best-known architect of recent centuries. Although he was influenced enormously by his father's work, Lloyd Wright developed, over time, a remarkable personal style that was concerned mostly with a harmony between man and nature—a predisposition that is not surprising, since he started out as a landscape architect. In fact, he came originally to California to help Olmsted and Olmsted design the grounds for the Panama-California Exposition of 1915 in San Diego. He stayed to supervise the construction of a number of his father's houses and then in the 1920s began to design richly landscaped houses of his own.

The three examples below are from that early period. Although all three have become famous, they reveal Lloyd Wright's restless uncertainty with forms handled by his father (who, Lloyd said, copied the shapes from him) with far greater conviction. The houses here don't yet have the composure and self-assurance of either Lloyd Wright's own house (page 225) or his masterpiece, the Wayfarers' Chapel (page 130).

A · SAMUELS-NOVARRO HOUSE
5609 Valley Oak Drive, Hollywood
Take Van Ness Avenue to Briarcliff Road to Verde Oak Drive to Valley Oak Drive
Lloyd Wright, 1926–1928
Private residence

Valley Oak Drive is almost impossible to find, as it winds through thick, upper-income forests where every street is named some kind of Oak Drive. But once you've found the street, you'll never miss the Samuels-Novarro house. This four-story slab of white stucco thrusts up from a bend in the road like a sheer plane of the San Andreas Fault; skinny globs of green ornament sprinkle along this wall like plants carried up in some eruption but crystallized before they made it back down. This single-family house, which is even wider than it is tall, has the bulk of an apartment building as it dams up the end of a sizable ravine.

There is a hint of Zigzag Moderne in the hesitant steps of its massing, as well as in the green copper panels that cling to the numerous windows and slide down a kind of tower in the middle. The house was, in fact, designed shortly after the 1925 Exposition des Arts Décoratifs in Paris, which had introduced Art Deco and made Machine Age architecture suddenly popular. So (or maybe anyway), Lloyd Wright transformed the Mayan concrete-block visions of his father into thin sheets of pressed copper. More than anything else, this house is a movie set, built for a movie star (Ramon Novarro), and it reflects—according to the historical plaque out front—"a great era of Hollywood cinema."

B · TAGGART HOUSE
2158 Live Oak Drive East, at the northeast corner of Black Oak Drive, Hollywood
Lloyd Wright, 1922–1924
Private residence

Although the Taggart house rises up two stories high on a steep hillside, it manages, for the most part, to hide itself in the dense foliage all around. Lloyd Wright accomplished this vanishment by means of a simple though heavy emphasis on the horizontal lines. Each of the two stories divides sharply into two bands: each lower half is white plaster, while each upper half is layered even further into a corbelled mass of dark-stained horizontal boards. From the bottom of the hill, the house appears as a series of light and dark stripes, from its long retaining wall to its flat roof.

But then the horizontal spell is broken, on the right, by an explosion of verticality: a huge, two-story window in a three-story frame lunges upward past tall mullions and taller moldings, and ends, at last, in a little red-shingled peak roof, fuller of youthful exuberance than of mature control.

IX 19 C · *Sowden House*

C · SOWDEN HOUSE
5121 Franklin Avenue, Hollywood
Lloyd Wright, 1926
Private residence

The Sowden house is straightforward: it's a big pink stucco box with a Mayan courtyard cut out of the center and what appear to be the concrete-block jaws of a dragon yawning out of the entry. Some say Lloyd Wright's father must have had a hand in such a disciplined design, but maybe time was just short.

IX 20 · TWO HOUSES BY FRANK LLOYD WRIGHT

In 1917 Frank Lloyd Wright was in Wisconsin, without much work, when Aline Barnsdall, an eccentric oil millionaire in Los Angeles who had heard about his Prairie houses, invited him to come out west and design a house and a cultural center on top of a little hill she owned in Hollywood. Wright decided to celebrate the change of venue by vastly altering the idiom in which he worked: his own version of the California Dream would be based on the massive forms of pre-Columbian temples. And so began Frank Lloyd Wright's famous Mayan concrete-block houses, which took advantage of this laid-back land of sunshine by being, for the most part, huge and monumental and very dark. The Barnsdall house is actually stucco over wood frame, but it looks as massive as the ones to follow. The rest, made of square concrete blocks, a mixture of plain and ornamental, were the Millard (page 318) and Storer (page 237) houses in 1923 and the Freeman and Ennis houses in 1924.

Of these, the Millard house, which we will see in Pasadena, is our hands-down favorite. It is cavelike, as are the others, and like a fortress, too; it seems built to last forever. At the same time, it is delicate and light and approachable, partly because it's so small. You feel every kind of pleasure and no pain in getting up close to its walls. This is not the case with the Barnsdall and Ennis houses, which are the least congenial of the five; you can't help but feel a real hesitation in approaching very near. Their huge shapes seem ponderous and coarse and grim; from the outside they don't really give the appearance that they were meant for human inhabitation. The Ennis house, for instance, keeps being referred to as a mausoleum.

It is easy to forget that Frank Lloyd Wright, the apostle of an organic new world, was after all an Edwardian architect. His first work was done in the days of the British Queen Victoria, and his major Prairie houses date from the reign of King Edward VII—a period of massive drawing rooms and overstuffed furniture and corseted dress, with a corpulence to just about everything reflecting that of the monarch himself. It was not an era of brightly sunlit Modern architecture, suntanned bare limbs, and cuisine Minceur; rather, it was, by our standards, one of darkness and gloom, port and cigar smoke. And though Wright's California houses were built a decade or so after Edward VII's reign was over, they cannot help but carry the stamp of those confident and confining times.

Barnsdall House

A · BARNSDALL HOUSE
4808 Hollywood Boulevard, in Barnsdall Park, Hollywood; entrance is opposite Berendo Street
Frank Lloyd Wright, 1917–20
Now a museum, administered by the Los Angeles Cultural Affairs
Department; tours given Tuesday and Thursday, 10, 11, 12 and 1; also
every Saturday and the first and third Sunday of each month, 12, 1, 2
and 3; admission fee; call (213) 485-2433

Aline Barnsdall bought Olive Hill, an olive-covered mound in the flatlands of Hollywood, in order to found an experimental theater and an art colony. There would be a 1,200-seat theater, and studios and apartments for visiting artists and actors; her own house was to be the centerpiece. The full scheme never came off. Most of the buildings were never built, and she moved out of her house three years after it was completed. In 1927 she deeded part of the property to Los Angeles for a "people's park," and allowed the rest, including the house, to go to seed. Then in 1967 a Junior Arts Center was built, and in 1971 the Barnsdall Municipal Art Gallery, both in a neo-Wrightian persuasion. People began to picnic on pleasant lawns shaded by ancient olive trees and the other mature trees placed here by Lloyd Wright in 1920. A modified version of Aline Barnsdall's dream seems to be coming true. In 1975, $500,000 was allocated to restore her house.

So the place now looks remarkably new, still sort of half buried in its lawns, as if the long retaining walls that reach out from the corners are the tops of even more disconcerting things. Much of the house is just one story high, with bedrooms and sun decks and a tall living room hidden behind a high Mayan mansard roof. Sheets of seamless beige stucco rise up from a cornice, all the way around, of stylized cast-stone hollyhocks—after Aline's favorite flower, which has given the place its most used name, the Hollyhock house. The building forms a U around a courtyard where a colonnade sports hollyhock capitals; there are hollyhock finials on the roof. This was the start, they say, of Wright's excitement over ornamental concrete block. And there *are* windows and doors, sometimes big ones.

The brooding impenetrability of the exterior, however, belies what goes on inside. It *is* hollow, and Wright's special mastery of intermingling and surprising spaces, which began in the Prairie houses, continues here: a low entry hall introduces the high living room; all the rooms, which are separated more by stairs or changes in ceiling height than by walls, flow into each other and outside as well; special views in light present themselves repeatedly as the visitors move along, and sometimes, with the help of the giant retaining walls or light that comes from unexpected places, these glimpses give the impression that the house might go on forever. Still, the house doesn't seem easily inhabitable or very friendly. Perhaps it's the wall-to-wall carpeting over the wood floors or the tacky new tiles around the fireplace or the other vaguely sinister touches left by the remodelers.

Probably the most important effect of the Barnsdall house is that it brought Rudolph Schindler to Los Angeles. Wright had him supervise the construction while he went off to work on the Imperial Hotel in Tokyo. Schindler also designed Studio-Residence A (1920), a garden wall (1924) and much of the landscaping. And then Schindler brought out Richard Neutra. Together they designed a very pretty wading pool and pergola (1925) at the end of the courtyard. After that, it is said, they started Modern Architecture in California.

IX 20 B · *Ennis House*

B · ENNIS HOUSE
2607 Glendower Avenue, Hollywood
Frank Lloyd Wright, 1924
Private residence; tours given on occasion

About a mile north of the Barnsdall house, on a steep hillside overlooking Olive Hill and the rest of the L.A. Basin, is the Ennis house, the last in Wright's Mayan series in Los Angeles and by far the hugest, most monumental and most frightening. Like some ancient castle, this complex jumble of gigantic masses piles up in ways that seem meant to confound and overwhelm the viewer; openings appear to be dark slots carved out of solid rock. From below, in the distance, it's not so threatening—a little Machu Picchu, perhaps, terracing up the mountain. But from the street, the fortress image is complete; faceless towers thrust up behind an enormous wall, blank save for a rampart-protected iron gate that leads to the keep. It's a Mayan dream after an Aztec bloodletting, become at last an Incan doom. Even the ornamental block has been eaten away by the elements to look melted and run together, agglutinated by a recent coat of thick beige paint.

IX 21 · LOVELL HOUSE
4616 Dundee Drive, off Commonwealth Canyon Road, Los Angeles
Richard S. Neutra, 1929
Private residence

Richard Neutra's Lovell house, one of the great monuments of Modern Architecture, is a crisp composition of steel and glass and gleaming white concrete panels that thrusts out from its green hillside like a Mondrian painting come to life. It was America's first all-steel frame residence and one of its earliest and most influential International Style buildings, and it was the turning point in Richard Neutra's career. Upon its completion, the house was widely publicized

IX 21 · *Lovell House*

by the architectural press, helped along by the owner in his widely read column on health in the Los Angeles *Times* and by the architect in his second book, *Amerika,* finished shortly after the house was. Soon after that, Neutra returned to Europe on a visit and was hailed as a conquering hero. This meant, back in California, that he was now an international celebrity (very important hereabouts), and the commissions flowed in.

The house was also the cause of a lot of complex controversy between Neutra and his (up to then) close friend, Rudolph Schindler. The two architects were both from Vienna by way of Taliesin and Frank Lloyd Wright; they had been partners for a while and were even sharing Schindler's communal house on Kings Road (page 233). This relationship grew considerably less cordial when it seemed to Schindler that his partner had stolen one of his prime clients, for whom he had designed the Lovell Beach house (page 136), another great monument in Modern Architecture. Some say the accusations came only after Neutra's Lovell house became an even bigger Modern monument than Schindler's.

Whatever the undercurrents, Neutra's Lovell house is very different from Schindler's Lovell Beach house. It's about as pure and powerful a piece of Neutra as there is, with continuous bands of strip windows, smooth spandrels, flat roofs and rooms all very simply lined up; its detailing is squeaky clean. But it suffers the problem of most buildings in this idiom: without moldings and the shadows they cast, and the other reasons for forgiving the signs of wear and tear and old age that come to any building, they look like the very devil when they start to go. This sort of architecture is one to be conceived and drawn, and not much one to be nailed up out of recalcitrant stuff, to be rained on and weathered and to develop character with its wrinkles and cracks. It is not growing old very gracefully.

Even so, the house has the remnants of a stern and beautiful vision; it's like seeing some famous beauty at the very end of a long life. When she was young, this siren seduced generations of architects around the world, especially in Southern California. It could certainly be argued that the pure, spare buildings of Craig Ellwood or the Case Study houses by Pierre Koenig and the rest got their start from the clean, simple lines of the Lovell house far more directly than they did from Schindler's more complex or ad hoc constructivism. So, even in her semiderelict old age, the lady commands respect.

IX 22 · TWO APARTMENTS BY SCHINDLER

In his 1912 manifesto, written while he was still a student in Vienna, Rudolph Schindler summed up the whole of architectural history as "the use of a plastic structural mass material" to enclose usable space; the quality of the material determined the quality of the space. But by 1912, he reasoned, new building technologies (reinforced concrete in particular) had freed the architect to focus not on the container, but on the contained. "The architectural design concerns itself with 'space' as its raw material and with the articulated room as its product .... The architect has finally discovered the medium of his art: SPACE."

Schindler's manifesto would later be modified by diverse influences from two continents as well as by idiosyncrasies of his own, but he did seem always to remain loyal to this vision, to the preeminence of space. It was the beginning and the end of every Schindler design; the excitements he could conjure up by means of some spatial tour de force were, for him, the main reason to build. It was this notion of volumes sliding and shifting, from indoors to out, from positive to negative, from rigorously defined to ambiguous, that determined his shapes more than anything else. The following two apartments are particularly good examples of this lifelong pursuit.

A · SACHS APARTMENTS
1807–1817 Edgecliffe Drive and 1826–1830½ Lucile Avenue, Silver Lake
R. M. Schindler, 1926–1940; 1807–1809½ Edgecliffe and 1826–1826½
Lucile built by others in 1923, then remodeled by Schindler in 1926 to
conform to the rest; 1815–1817 Edgecliffe added by Schindler when he
remodeled all of the buildings in 1939–1940
Private residences

This assortment of beige stucco boxes and their connecting planes tumble down a steep hillside between Edgecliffe Drive and Lucile Avenue. Schindler designed them for artist-designer Herman Sachs, who would later paint the famous "Spirit of Transportation" on the ceiling of the porte cochere at Bullock's Wilshire (page 147). Perhaps the client helped to inspire this elaborate abstraction, but in the mid-1920s Schindler was already arriving at a personal vision, blending the pure forms of his German mentors with the planes and sculpted volumes of the De Stijl movement and with the surface patterns of Frank Lloyd Wright.

Here, these surface excitements, the lively window patterns and all the wood, especially the vertical battens and balcony outriggers, contrast so sharply with the plain stucco volumes that they partly disguise the graceful way the volumes step down the hill. Still, it is a thrill to walk down the steep staircase that winds through this assemblage and connects the two streets. There is, indeed, a feeling here that is less one of walls than of the spaces that the walls create, of roof gardens defined by their trellises, and of courtyard volumes that press against the stucco walls and slide into corridors before they slip down stairs beyond. Today these spaces are enriched by a new dimension, a thick layer of trees and tall shrubs, which speak of the romantic naturalist that was also in Schindler; the greenery softens the hard sculpture and calms the nervous wood trim.

IX 22 A · *Sachs Apartments*   IX 22 B · *Falk Apartments*

B · FALK APARTMENTS
On Carnation Avenue between Edgecliffe Drive and Lucile Avenue, Silver Lake
R. M. Schindler, 1942
Private residences

The enforced austerity of World War II had its effect on Schindler's Falk Apartments, built for only $6,000 on a steep corner lot almost next door to the Sachs buildings; they are considerably less ornate than their neighbors. Here the wood trim, which is reserved mostly for garage doors and trellises that extend the roof planes, is painted a near match for the beige stucco walls. The walls, however, have made up for the plain materials by leaping into a frenzied free-for-all of cut-out volumes and jagged planes; they build up from thick vegetation to form a building closely resembling a five-story-tall abstract sculpture. The volumes step down quietly along the two sidewalks, but above that they twist and angle with an abandon that recalls Moshe Safdie's Habitat of 1967, and with the same intent: each of the five apartments has a splendid view, sunshine and privacy, as well as a secluded garden and roof terrace. Large walls of glass with thin mullions make the outdoor patios seem a part of the double-height interiors.

IX 23 · MICHELTORENA STREET
1856 to 2404 Micheltorena Street, Silver Lake
Private residences

Micheltorena Street winds just below the crest of a hill that rises up west of the Silver Lake Reservoir. Its houses, which are either above or below street level, are generally small, built with inexpensive materials, on narrow, often steep sites; all of them scramble around, one way or another, to catch the stunning views of Los Angeles, all the way to the ocean, while the houses on top can often look east as well, down to the reservoir. An extraordinary number of these little houses were designed by some of Los Angeles' finest architects.

At 1856 Micheltorena is the Daniel house (23 A) (1939), one of Gregory Ain's best, which employs a combination of modern and traditional forms against a steep hillside. At the front, large yellowish stucco planes frame a cut-out for a first-level garage, step forward to become planter boxes, and step up to protect a central entry as well as to form a De Stijl composition with strip windows along the top. Although the hip roofs floating above this modernity seem almost abrasively mild-mannered, they dissolve, as Frank Gehry might have dissolved them forty years later, at special places to become open rafters or sky-

lights. The small, glass-filled hole above the entry only hints at the large dis-
solves at the back, which has been wrenched around as well to make room for a
patio and to let in the view.

At 2007 Micheltorena is the house John Lautner built for himself (23 B) in
1939. On Mulholland Drive (page 240), Lautner later demonstrated how anti-
gravitationally he can handle a cliffside site, so it may come as a surprise to see
how tamely his own little house is perched on the edge of its chasm. In fact, this
low, flat-roofed structure looks like something by Schindler at his most relaxed-
ly domestic, with mostly horizontal walls, large windows and a mixture of concrete and dark wood. About all that's visible, before the house begins to vanish
down the mountainside, is a carport and a corrugated wood fence that wraps
around a sunken entrance patio and an enormous eucalyptus tree. There is,
though, a little of that Lautner drama: the front fence, somewhat resembling a
hand, seems to grasp desperately onto the tree as if it were its last chance before
being swept over the edge.

The driveway at 2138 Micheltorena climbs up great mounds of foliage to Sil-
vertop (23 C), where in 1957 the passion for levitation in an older John Lautner
was allowed to reach its apogee. This enormous concrete-and-glass spaceship of
a house, with swirling flat roofs and walls that slide at the push of a button,
looks as if it has landed temporarily on this six-lot aerie in order to observe, or
maybe to feed on, the little houses of Silver Lake below. The best view is from
the east side of the reservoir or from Redcliff Street, where a back driveway, a
swimming pool and an aerial tennis court all cantilever out from a mountain
covered with vegetation.

At 2236 Micheltorena is the Oliver house (23 D), another classic by R. M.
Schindler, from 1933. Like much of Schindler's work in the 1930s, this house
explores the dynamic possibilities of ambiguity. Beige stucco rectangular volumes lie on three levels of a jungled hillside: a garage and an entrance vestibule
and the twisted prow of a living room all form parts of a dynamic De Stijl composition of solids and voids. It looks very vertical, but the living spaces are all
on a single level; the top one, which forms a rather modest L, is angled to capture views in three directions. The formal excitement comes where it is least expected—from the main roofs, which, seen from the back, are a lively assortment
of sheds and gables that create complexly changing axes and ceiling heights and
continual surprises.

The Alexander house (23 E), at 2265 Micheltorena, was designed in 1940 by
Harwell H. Harris, who produced some of the handsomest houses in Los Angeles (page 260). His two-story composition here of buff-colored stucco boxes
forms a T whose end, with a garage in its base, faces the street behind two large
pine trees. These trees seem to divide the house into two personalities: the right
half, with few openings beyond the garage and entry doors, has an International
Style simplicity to its tall, flat-roofed volumes and to its one-story stucco wall
that extends the plane of the back wall. On the left, the house relaxes into Prairie Style horizontality with more openings and with Frank Lloyd Wright's low
hip roofs covering a Greene and Greene sort of open porch.

At 2323 Micheltorena is the Tierman house (23 F) (1940), the best-known .
work of Gregory Ain. It is certainly the purest: this unassuming one-story cottage, barely visible behind thick hedges, forms a perfect square beneath a forty-
five-degree pyramid roof. The house was built just as the leading edge of
California's Modern Movement was beginning to soften (even Richard Neutra
was turning to wood and masonry). The Tierman house, true to its time, relaxes
its purity with traditional materials and manners: white stucco walls are topped

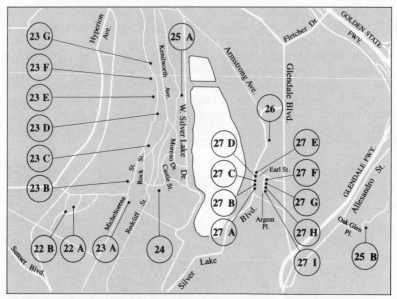

IX/HOLLYWOOD, WEST HOLLYWOOD, AND SILVER LAKE (INSET 2)

by a band of windows trimmed in slate-gray-painted wood just beneath the eaves (for there *are,* traditionally, eaves); asphalt shingles on the steep roof give way to a skylight at the peak, which is shaded by a massive brick chimney. Although the interior opens up, wide, light and beautiful to the view in back, this little house, with its matching garage on the left, looks more like an exquisitely detailed tract house than a Modern masterpiece; yet the Historical-Cultural bronze plaque out front reassures us that it is the latter.

Just up the street, at 2404 Micheltorena, is another Ain house (23 G), designed in 1941 for one Alice Orans. It begins oddly, even a little pretentiously: the front yard is a semicircular driveway with a drive-through carport in the center. But the house itself seems agreeable as its various rectangular volumes and low-pitched roofs terrace up the hillside, and its buff-colored stucco and dark wood trim mingle handsomely with foliage. Still, after the Tierman house, there's something disquieting here. Perhaps it's just the lollipop ficus out front.

IX 24 · DROSTE HOUSE
2025 Kenilworth Avenue, Silver Lake
R. M. Schindler, 1940
Private residence

This three-story composition of bright white stucco boxes and dark panes of glass is one of Schindler's purest De Stijl inspirations; from head on, the house would look like a painting by Mondrian. But the only view of it is from the right, at the base of a steep drive, so the numerous volumes and the thin roof planes are seen to burst into three-dimensional life, popping in and out of the picture plane (wherever that may be) with cheerful though Teutonically controlled enthusiasm. Prodigious leaps in scale and apparent weight add to the excitement: a monumental stepped tower on the right plays against tiny, almost fairy-tale balconies on the left; the large openings, two garage doors below and a garage-door-size window on top, are balanced by a band of small windows in the middle; dark-stained eaves on the upper left are lightened up by a white-painted, open-raftered pergola on the lower right. Throughout the day, advancing shadows cast angular patterns of their own on the rectangular forms and create even more life, so this gleaming white vision seems almost to vibrate against its dark green ivy-covered hillside. Affectionately maintained, Schindler's carefully considered sculpture looks as new and as astonishing as the day it was made.

IX 24 · *Droste House*

IX 25 · HANSEN HOUSE
2305 West Silver Lake Drive, Silver Lake
Harwell H. Harris, 1951
Private residence

Harwell Hamilton Harris was a student of some of Los Angeles' most celebrated architects, including Rudolph Schindler, Richard Neutra and Frank Lloyd Wright, and in many cases went beyond the work of his more famous predecessors. The houses he made were just as interesting, but were consistently calmer, simpler, more livable and more responsive to the touch. He was also influenced by the Craftsman movement, by the Greene brothers of Pasadena and by the Japanese architecture that had inspired the Greenes and Frank Lloyd Wright. Again, Harris seemed to understand the Oriental use of wood even better than that earlier generation had (the Greenes probably excepted) and employed it to soften the hard-edged forms of his own times. From Neutra he learned landscaping and how to soften the edges even more, so that most of his houses now are hidden by foliage.

The Hansen house (25 A) is no exception. Although it sits on top of a little hill with a splendid view over Silver Lake Reservoir, most of the house is concealed from the street by layers of hedges. You can see the long horizontal edge of the main roof and a little of the glass underneath, and there's a bit of a jaunty Schindleresque clerestory on top, but the only really visible part is the garage at the bottom—a simple cube of flesh-colored stucco and dark brown trim with a sun deck for a roof. Next to it a walkway slips up between two retaining walls and disappears into the shrubbery. The house is a sharp contrast to its steep-roofed Cottage Revival neighbors, but with its low forms and high plants it seems remarkably relaxed and at home on this street. The only noticeably out-of-the-ordinary features are the Mies van der Rohe sort of incised corners on the garage, but there is nothing doctrinaire about them or about anything else here—just a delicate touch of artful whimsy from a man who got his manifestoes out of the way early and then made beautiful and comfortable houses.

For collectors of Harris buildings we refer once again to Gebhard and Winter's excellent guidebook, which lists many of them. For the real devotee, who doesn't mind getting lost or climbing up a long path on a very steep hillside, we must mention the famous little house that Harris built for himself in 1935, the Fellowship Park Pavilion (25 B). It's less than a mile southwest of the Hansen house, but the route is circuitous: take Glendale Boulevard to Allesandro Street to Whitmore Avenue, then turn right on Alvarado Street and left on Lakeshore Avenue and go a little more than a tenth of a mile to where four mailboxes say 2238–2242 Lakeshore; climb a little stair and go left on a path that heads up through a forest. The path is private property, but small groups of quiet pilgrims are not discouraged.

The woods were planted by the Universal World Fellowship Church, an out-doorsy sect that came and went in the early 1900s; their only legacy is an over-grown hillside garden and the name assumed by this tiny community of rustic houses. Harris had planned to build a number of low-cost houses on this slope, but nothing ever came of it. He did design the first house on the left (no. 2242), a tiny shed-roofed board-and-batten cabin built for the Meiers, who lived on the other side of the path in a large bungalow (no. 2240) perhaps designed by the Heineman brothers (page 331). Near the top of the path is the Harris house. It's just a very small and very simple Japanese sort of wood house, one glassy story high beneath an overhanging hip roof. It sits on a small shelf in the hill, three of its sides engulfed by foliage; the other side looks out over one of the most spectacular views in Los Angeles. Harris' studio (1945), equally tiny and famous, used to be nearby, but it burned down in 1980.

IX 26 · NEUTRA HOUSE
2300 Silver Lake Boulevard; rear portion of house is at 2351 Edgewater Terrace, Silver Lake
Richard J. Neutra, 1933; front part rebuilt with Dion Neutra, 1964
Private residence

With the completion of the Lovell house in 1929 (page 254), Richard Neutra became rather an architectural celebrity—especially in Europe, where he began to be mentioned in the same breath with Walter Gropius and Le Corbusier. On his return visit there in 1930, Dutch businessman C. H. Van Der Leeuw encouraged him to continue the Lovell house experiments in his own house by giving him a check; in gratitude for such unusual generosity, Neutra named it the V. D. L. Research House. As Neutra stated later in his book, *Life and Shape* (1962), he

IX 26 · *Neutra House*

wanted to prove with this house "that man is stable, that new architecture is no passing fad." And within the Modern context he hoped to build an idealized dwelling that would serve and delight generations of inhabitants. To do this, he would try to accommodate essential household needs, both physical and sensory, by means of efficient space planning, innovative building technology, and forms that were unconstrained by historical allusion.

The house, which has become a landmark in Modern Architecture, was indeed a remarkable statement, considering that Neutra had to deal with a number of specific problems as well as the larger philosophical ones. He had a tight budget and a tiny site (sixty by seventy feet), and he had to account for earthquakes, sun exposures and the view of Silver Lake Reservoir across the street; he also had to separate his home-based architectural practice from his growing family. Although the house was, for the most part, just white stucco on a standard wood frame, he arranged it into an elegant composition of vertical and horizontal planes: inexpensive concrete floor joists allowed long expanses of glass, while enamel-coated metal panels, cork flooring and other experimental materials (often donated by manufacturers hoping they would become prototypes) gleamed in profusion. To increase space and privacy, the house became two houses—a large one in front and a smaller one facing Edgewater Terrace in back, both built up high from their setback lines. A long loggia helped to connect them, but a thickly planted courtyard in between gave the two self-sufficient parts privacy from each other. The rooms of both were made to seem larger with mirrors and with glass doors that continued the indoor space into the gardens. The dense foliage separated the houses from their nearby neighbors and from each other, but the roof decks and porches of the larger house still rose high enough above the trees to catch the sun and breezes and views.

Unfortunately, the larger part of the house, which faced Silver Lake Boulevard, burned down in 1963. But Neutra and his son Dion quickly built a replacement that has a little less of the first one's urgency yet is a little more polished and comfortable. While it is laden with mid-1960s accessories, the new house is a cheerful abstract stack of stucco and glass planes that step up from the street in three tiers and wrap around a glass-enclosed staircase. It remains a monument of high-period Modern Architecture, though today there is even more vegetation than ever to relax those Central European hard edges.

IX 27 · NEUTRALAND
Nine houses on Silver Lake Boulevard and Argent Place, near the intersection of Earl Street, Silver Lake
Richard J. Neutra

A · YEW HOUSE
2226 Silver Lake Boulevard
1957

B · KAMBARA HOUSE
2232 Silver Lake Boulevard
1960

C · IVANDOMI HOUSE
2238 Silver Lake Boulevard
1960

D · SOKAL HOUSE
2242 Silver Lake Boulevard, on the southeast corner of Earl Street
1948

E · TREWEEK HOUSE
2250 Silver Lake Boulevard, on the northeast corner of Earl Street
1948

F · REUNION HOUSE
2440 Earl Street, on the southeast corner of Argent Place
1949

G · FLAVIN HOUSE
2218 Argent Place
1958

H · O'HARA HOUSE
2210 Argent Place
1961

I · AKI HOUSE
2200 Argent Place
1962
All are private residences

Just down Silver Lake Boulevard from the Neutra house is a tight colony of nine International Style houses, all designed by Richard Neutra between 1948 and 1962, and all representative of some of his best work. Each of these next-door neighbors is a neat abstract sculpture unto itself, but together they share a number of characteristics: all are variations of stepped rectangular boxes made up of vertical and horizontal, transparent and opaque planes, and all have front decks that seem to float above ivy-covered slopes and mingle with stands of tall eucalyptus. Neutra seems to have been inspired by the problem of fitting nine houses onto one small hillside; his sensitive siting and window placement have allowed each to enjoy considerable privacy as well as a full measure of light and air and a pleasant view of the Silver Lake Reservoir below.

X/WESTERN AVENUE

Mooers House

Western Avenue is a very poor relation to Sunset and Wilshire boulevards, and several shades tackier, even, than its sibling Ventura Boulevard, to which we will shortly pay a visit. But it is long and straight and, perhaps, therefore memorable, even in its frequent squalor, and is in some way characteristically L.A. Like the others, it is a ride, interesting at the appropriate speed (thirty-five miles an hour, with frequent pauses for stoplights), though it would be intolerable at the four miles an hour of a pedestrian. And many—most—of the individual works are not that fascinating: it's the way the kaleidoscope works that makes the trip.

Western starts where Los Feliz Boulevard, which runs more or less along the bottom of Griffith Park, swings around the base of a hill and faces south, 27 miles to the ocean. The first part is downhill, so it all opens up if the day—or especially the night—is clear. Along the way are endless little junky buildings often redeemed by landscaping (but more often not), many, many signs, and utility lines of enormous complexity and magnitude to line the street. The touching, poverty-born early California sense of do-it-yourself is more present on Western than most places: signs, often hand-lettered, announce very small businesses where a few hamburgers are sold, or a few chickens, or a few somethings.

After a while the street changes: it becomes lined with bungalows of uniform setback with wide eaves and columns. After a while longer comes a convincing milk bottle, two stories high, and then increasing numbers of the handsome old spiky double street lights that long ago seemed a special part of the Los Angeles scene. The fanciness fades out and in: just south of Manchester Boulevard is a shopping center that looks spruced up and lively. Because it is California, institutions that are not collapsing are signaled by well-kept bright green lawns: Jesse Owens County Park presents itself, and later there is a pretty golf course (near the northwest corner of Century Boulevard) with green grass smiling, and trees. Then, finally, comes San Pedro, and a beach, and even a lighthouse.

X 1 · GRIFFITH PARK
North end of Western Avenue, north of Los Feliz Boulevard, Los Angeles
Open daily, 5 A.M.–10:30 P.M.

Griffith Park, once the mountainous portion of Rancho Los Feliz, was donated to Los Angeles in 1896 by Colonel Griffith J. Griffith. In subsequent years, Griffith's personal life became so notorious (he spent a couple of years in prison for attempting to murder his wife) that the city fathers refused his offers to construct an observatory until they received the money after his death. The park has many of the amenities traditionally associated with large American urban parks: picnic areas, playing fields, tennis courts, bridle trails, golf courses, a merry-go-round, fountains and a pleasant zoo. There is even a natural fern grotto, Ferndell, where a year-round spring has caused fragrant sycamores and soft green ferns to crowd the bottom of a steep ravine, a place that has been cool and refreshing since prehistoric times, when it was the site of a Gabrieliño Indian village.

However, Griffith Park's greatest attraction is one you won't find in the usual city park: wilderness, over four thousand acres of it. This is the largest urban park in the United States; most of it is covered in virgin chaparral and is home to ceanothus, sage and manzanita, as well as deer, coyote and quail. Southern California's native heath is remarkably prickly stuff, and the Arcadias in this park are few and far between; the surprises are likely to bite or stab, and not to seduce. Prickles aside, however, there are exhilarating walks and astonishing views.

X 2 · GRIFFITH OBSERVATORY AND PLANETARIUM
2800 East Observatory Road, at the northern end of Vermont Avenue, Griffith Park
John C. Austin and F. M. Ashley, architects, 1935; Archibald Garner, obelisk and bas-reliefs, 1934; Hugo Ballin, interior murals, 1935
Open Tuesday through Sunday, 2–10; free admission

Griffith Park Observatory and Planetarium, the backdrop for innumerable science fiction movies and, of course, for Sal Mineo's unforgettable death scene in *Rebel Without a Cause,* is still listed, complete with full face and profile shots, in the City of Los Angeles film location book. The passage of nearly half a century and the present bright haze have failed to dull its aura of galactic mystery and unknown powers, of scientists in white coats conjuring up a dark future.

Sited in the wilderness of Griffith Park on a steep spur that divides the canyons of Vermont and Western avenues, the observatory commands an unobstructed view out over the Los Angeles Basin. Vice versa, its pale gray form rises from the surrounding dark foliage as a dramatic castellar landmark from the plain below.

X 2 · *Griffith Observatory and Planetarium*

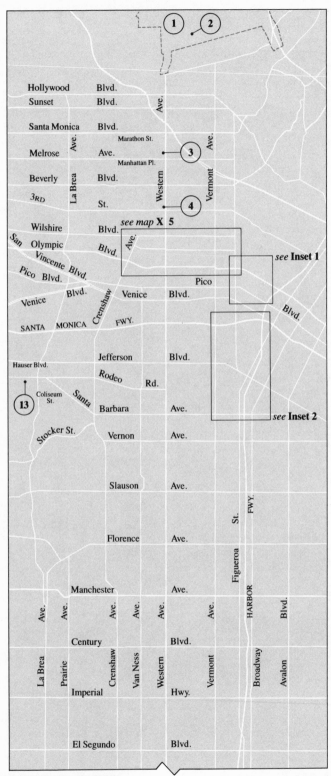

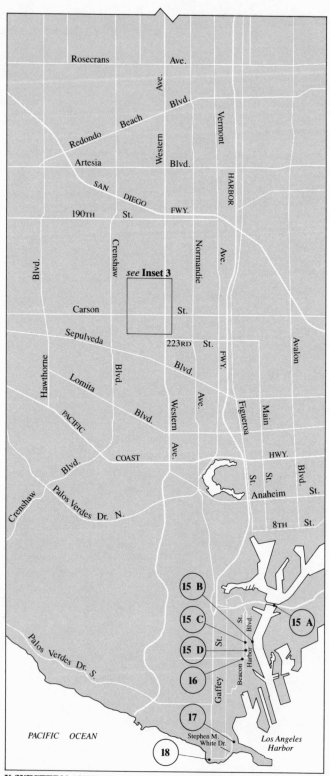

Rosecrans Ave.

Beach Blvd.

Redondo Beach

Western Ave.

Vermont

Artesia Blvd.

SAN DIEGO FWY.

190TH St.

Crenshaw

Normandie Ave.

HARBOR

Blvd.

see **Inset 3**

Carson St.

223RD St.

Sepulveda

Hawthorne

Lomita Blvd.

Blvd.

Blvd.

PACIFIC

Blvd.

Western Ave.

FWY.

Ave.

Figueroa

Main

Avalon

COAST

Anaheim

HWY.

St.

St.

Blvd.

St.

8TH St.

Crenshaw

Palos Verdes Dr. N.

Palos Verdes Dr. S

15 B

15 C

15 D

16

15 A

St.

Blvd.

Gaffey St.

Harbor

Beacon

17

18

Stephen M. White Dr.

PACIFIC OCEAN

Los Angeles Harbor

X/WESTERN AVENUE

Symmetrical, streamlined and stylized, the long, low building of unpainted reinforced concrete is a powerful expression of Depression Modern. The rounded ends of its T-shaped plan are marked by bulging copper domes; smaller domes on the east and west contain telescopes, while the great south one covers a five-hundred-seat planetarium. Stairways curve around the small domes to rooftop observation decks; another viewing terrace around the drum of the planetarium passes through its arching buttresses. Bands of stylized Greek and Deco ornament, deeply incised in the raw concrete walls, wrap around the building to create crisp shadows.

The entry foyer, at the intersection of the T, is a mysterious octagonal volume with astronomical murals by Hugh Ballin that vibrate from the upper walls. In the center, a gleaming forty-foot Foucault pendulum keeps astronomical time by tracing the earth's rotation on a circle in the bottom of a marble well. Around it, three doorways lead to treasure-laden corridors. At the end of the south hall is the planetarium, where a 1934 cut-out skyline of Los Angeles frames the rim of the domed screen. Still, the main attraction at the observatory these days, or nights, is the spectacular view from the terraces out over Los Angeles, whose blazing lights have made the original purpose of the place, stargazing, almost impossible. But the vast city has become its own twinkling Milky Way, through which the lights of our ride down Western Avenue can be traced all the way to the Pacific Ocean.

X 3 · JARDINETTE APARTMENTS
5128 West Marathon Street, on the southeast corner of North Manhattan Place, Los Angeles
Richard J. Neutra, 1927
Now called the Marathon Apartments; private residences

This dingy, four-story concrete box would be easy enough to pass by without a second glance—it blends right in with the other apartments and sad little houses in this rather desperate part of Los Angeles. But the Jardinette is, indeed, the first major building by Richard Neutra, one of the first International Style buildings in Los Angeles and, some say, one of the seminal pieces of Modern Architecture in America. Later in his career, as he warmed to the California sunshine, Neutra became famous for combining innovative materials in original and pleasant ways, but when he designed this apartment house, he had been out of Europe for fewer than four years. The Jardinette began his reinforced-concrete period, when he seemed more inspired by the rationalism of his Austrian mentor, Adolf Loos, than by the organic sympathies of his American one, Frank Lloyd Wright.

It is tempting to wonder what Wright would have thought. These apartments have been much admired, and their cantilevered corner balconies and wide bands of windows, along with the look of terraces at the top of the four-story blocks, certainly presage the elegant—and cheerfully Southern Californian—graces of Neutra's later work. But there is a kind of earnest Austrian post–World War I grimness about the regularity and the density of these blocks that comes off more penitential than sculptural.

X 4 · *Crocker Bank*

X 4 · CROCKER BANK
273 Western Avenue, on the northwest corner of Third Street, Los Angeles
Attributed to Arthur E. Harvey, 1931
Originally designed as a clothing store

This tiny Art Deco bank building, just one story high, fairly erupts from its corner site with a dazzling veneer of black and gold terra-cotta tiles, as flamboyant a color scheme as was devised during that freewheeling period before the Great Depression. Shiny black tiles, divided into patterns that would have delighted Piet Mondrian, cover the columns and outline large, square windows that high-step it around the two streets. The windows are interrupted only by an enormous quarter-cylinder of glass block at the corner entrance. All this goes on beneath a continuous, glittering tiara of an entablature, whose gold tiles form a stylized plant architrave topped by a pointed arch frieze under a star-spandreled, scallop-topped cornice. Such jazz-age high jinks were rare even in 1931 and have grown rarer over the years; with the demolition of the Richfield Building, there are only a few of these black-and-gold extravaganzas left in Los Angeles—one of them is at 5209 Wilshire Boulevard (page 152). How splendid a pastime, to collect black-and-gold façades.

X 5 · KOREA TOWN
Bounded by Eighth and Hoover streets, Olympic and Crenshaw boulevards, Los Angeles

Founded in 1973, Korea Town is already home to the largest Korean population in the world outside Korea. It is five times the size of Chinatown and Little Tokyo combined. Although the residents have not yet decided whether to display their Korean architectural heritage or to blend in with the city around, a number of ventures are ethnic with a vengeance.

The Korean Village (5 A) (1978–1979), an exuberant incarnation of the homeland, is a shopping center with offices and a hotel at the northwest corner of Eighth Street and Normandie Avenue. A sometimes open-air, sometimes closed-in arcade of wooden columns, two stories high, supports a steep and

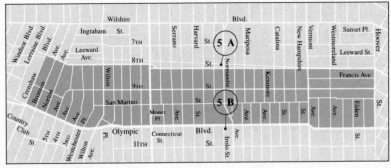

X 5 · KOREA TOWN

elaborate blue-tiled roof. All the structural members, real or not, are exposed and gaily decorated above a never-ending festival of banners, hanging lanterns and Korean signs.

The V.I.P. Palace (5 B) (ca. 1973), at the southeast corner of Olympic Boulevard and Irolo Street, is a wildly extravagant interpretation of a pagoda-style Korean palace. The wood structure is painted in intricate patterns, predominantly red, accented with rose, blue, gold, black and white. Each part, with its special decoration, struggles for our attention and then vanishes in the overall clamor. A splendid tiled roof with dancing gable ornaments adds a great swatch of textured blue. The interior is lavishly decorated with a coffered red lacquer ceiling, hanging lanterns and an elaborate fountain of volcanic rock, colored lights, a splashing waterwheel, plastic plants and koi. There is more passion than balance in the prevalent Korean recall.

X 6 · BONNIE BRAE HOUSES
800 block of South Bonnie Brae Street, Los Angeles
Private residences

These two very flossy houses, full at once of breathtaking splendors and end-of-an-era ennui, carry their burden of décor like a multiple albatross. It becomes easier to understand, in the face of these architectural dowager queens, why the Viennese architect Adolf Loos, in the next decade, would declare that "Ornament is Crime." He would have hemorrhaged over this pair; but in their eighties, and still in good shape, they merit the same respect from us as would human dowagers similarly well preserved and as lavishly gotten up. Displaying respectability and wealth, they also represent a broad sampling of then-fashionable American styles—Queen Anne, Colonial Revival, Moorish and Gothic—and have become a remarkable catalog of Victorian woodworking forms. They sit close together on relatively small lots in the midst of exotic but thoroughly tamed ornamental planting.

A · QUEEN ANNE HOUSE
824 South Bonnie Brae Street
ca. 1897

This, the more conservative of the two houses, concentrates on volumetric elements—porches, roofs, bays and dormers. Its principal feature is a narrow, cy-

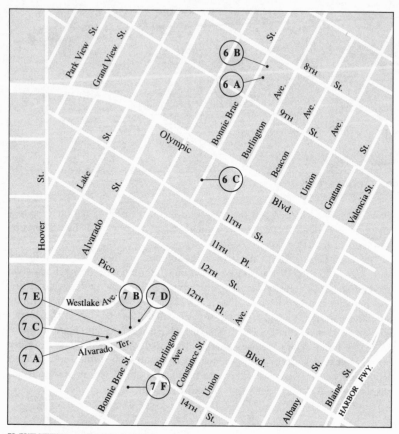

X/WESTERN AVENUE (INSET 1)

lindrical tower wrapped with a circular porch on the first floor and capped with a noble Moorish roof. Slender Ionic columns connected by a little Classical balustrade support the porch roof; layers of curving moldings and a swirling arabesque frieze garnish the upper reaches of the tower.

B · MOOERS HOUSE
818 South Bonnie Brae Street
1894

This much more flamboyant Queen Anne house, which was named for an early owner who had discovered a gold mine in northern California, glories in decorative moldings, shingles, latticework, ornamental plaster work and related charms. An outrageous collision of ornament announces the entrance to the front porch: from ground level, a set of tiny double columns supports a big arch, whose keystone sweeps up to check the flow of a sort of giant melted seashell in a triangular pediment above; cut into the back of the pediment is a half-circle, second-story porch with a fish-scale shingle railing and two disparate columns that hold up part of still another porch, set within an off-center gable end; here a friezed railing supports a lattice with an enormous cutout shaped like an apostrophe; little volutes on each side come menacingly close to the appearance of dowager spit curls. On the right side is a three-story turret ringed by little onion dormers around the base of its Moorish dome.

Down the street, the nineteenth-century 1000 block of Bonnie Brae is virtually intact, with some especially high-spirited Victorian houses (6 C) at nos. 1026, 1033, 1035, 1036–1038, 1047 and 1053 South Bonnie Brae Street. These are, at the moment, in a much more discouraging state of disrepair than the pair at 818 and 824. You have to squint hard to reconstruct the sumptuousness of the turn of this century.

X 7 · ALVARADO TERRACE

South of Pico Boulevard, near Bonnie Brae Street, is a block-long curve called Alvarado Terrace. Along here are no fewer than a dozen houses from the beginning of this century, which is enough, in these parts, to constitute a time warp. The virtually unscathed houses and an adjacent landscaped park recall the days when this street was one of the most desired addresses in the city; it was laid out on the prestigious grounds of the old Los Angeles Country Club and was billed as a "second Chester Place" (page 279). Ten of the houses were built by one man, Pomeroy Powers, who combined real estate speculation with being president of the City Council. He built the houses one at a time, often living in each one until he sold it; finally, his wife refused to move out of the last one. On the north edge of the park is a brick-paved tribute to Pomeroy Powers called Powers Place, the shortest street in Los Angeles. For the most part, these mansions are big, simple two-story volumes sheathed in various styles in vogue during the early 1900s, including Tudor, Queen Anne, and Mission; their great size—suitable for prosperous and populous families—is magnified by their siting above terraced lawns. Sparsely landscaped with only a few specimen trees and shrubs, they are clearly visible from the street below and look down proprietorially on the park—and beyond it, these days—to the glistening skyscrapers of downtown.

A · KINNEY-EVERHARDY HOUSE
1401 Alvarado Terrace
Hunt and Eager; Pomeroy Powers, builder, 1902
Private residence

B · GILBERT HOUSE
1333 Alvarado Terrace
Pomery Powers, builder, 1903
Private residence

C · RAPHAEL HOUSE
1353 Alvarado Terrace
Hunt and Eager; Pomeroy Powers, builder, 1903
Private residence

D · BOYLE-BARMORE HOUSE
1317 Alvarado Terrace
Charles E. Shattuck, 1905
Private residence

The Kinney-Everhardy house and the Gilbert house, at once shingle-style and Queen Anne, both have fat corner turret towers and gambrel roofs, and are rough sandstone below, shingles above. The Raphael house and the Boyle-Barmore house, more or less Tudor, are half-timbered on their upper stories and have deep porches in front of elegant entries; the latter's front door is surrounded by carved wood, the former's by beveled glass, for the owner also owned the Raphael Glass Company.

E · POWERS HOUSE
1345 Alvarado Terrace
Arthur L. Haley; Pomeroy Powers, builder, 1905
Private residence

It is not surprising that the last house built by Pomeroy Powers would steal the show. This daring version of Old California is a mélange of architectural pieces pilfered from the actual and imagined architecture of the missions. The front and right sides of this two-story, gray stucco cube sport false-fronted Mission gables, outlined in big white moldings with Churrigueresque medallions in the peaks. Three of the four corners have towers, each with little classically detailed windows and an overspreading red-tiled roof; the one on the left front corner is much bigger than the rest, allowing room for an extensively decorated Palladian window. Protruding from the front is a massive porch with giant arches below and a lacy railing for a sun deck on top. Almost every kind of carved wood or molded plaster ornament, all painted bright white, outlines every opening. The short terraces of the front lawn are filled with Canary Island palms and other exotic specimens that contribute, as well, to this fanciful rendition of an enriched California past.

F · EGYPTIAN COURT
1428 South Bonnie Brae Street
Edwin W. Willat, 1925
Private residences

This area has one of the largest concentrations of turn-of-the-century houses in Los Angeles, enough to make it worthwhile simply to cruise the streets. But don't overlook the turn-of-the-XXVI-Dynasty apartment court just around the corner from Alvarado Terrace. This ordinary L.A. apartment arrangement of two one-story rows with a long walkway in between has been transformed with only minor adjustments into an Egyptian temenos. The gray stucco on its wood frame is incised to resemble stone blocks or etched with pharaohs and hieroglyphics. The entrance is flanked by massive pylons that sweep up to an entablature with a winged sun disc in the center. Smaller versions of this portal frame the doors to each apartment. The fabled Egyptian everlastingness seems to be missing, but there is a certain undefinable aura.

X 8 · STIMSON HOUSE
2421 South Figueroa Street, Los Angeles
Carrol H. Brown, 1891
Private residence; now a convent

The giant Stimson house is a light Queen Anne fantasy congealed into ponderous Richardsonian Romanesque sandstone and nearly overwhelmed by ivy, shrubs, hedges, banana trees, and palms. The three-story fortress of a house, the four-story octagonal tower, the tall chimneys and the encircling veranda are

X 7 E · *Powers House*

X 8 · *Stimson House*

constructed entirely of rough-cut, rusticated reddish brown sandstone whose weight seems to force the thick ornament to ooze from certain joints. Lintels bulge above the windows, machicolations push out from the tower and porch, capitals balloon from the first-floor columns, and the walls themselves swell out to form bay windows.

In addition to the crenellated tower, a number of defensive positions have been secured above the entry: an elaborate third-floor balcony protrudes from a shadowy archway, and a heavy second-floor bastion-porch grows out of the veranda roof. Although the house is never open to the public, it is possible to see up past the incongruously smooth red marble columns to the ceiling of the veranda, where intricately carved coffers hint at the glorious woodwork within. This Victorian pile was built for Thomas Douglas Stimson, a Chicago lumber tycoon, who had each downstairs room finished in a different hardwood: oak, mahogany, walnut, sycamore, birch and ash. That's to think about, rather than to look at.

X 9 · AUTOMOBILE CLUB OF SOUTHERN CALIFORNIA
2601 South Figueroa Street, on the southwest corner of Adams Boulevard, Los Angeles
Hunt and Burns; Roland E. Coate, 1923

This Spanish Colonial Revival edifice, which wraps around a parking lot, is appropriately enough a salute to the motorist. The roadside elevations, two stories of massive buff-colored walls with arched openings and red-tiled roofs, are sufficiently straightforward to be comprehended at thirty-five miles an hour. A heavy corner tower, capped by a little tiled-roof cupola, forms a handy landmark visible from many streets away. On the east and west sides, driveways lead through high archways to an interior auto court, the best part.

The visitor drives in from Figueroa, past a huge Moreton Bay fig tree and through a high passageway, just deep enough to set up the surprise of a big sunny courtyard enclosed by wings of the building. High up on the walls, little balconies, shaded by narrow red-tiled roofs, extend from arches where shuttered doors and windows must have opened in more fortunate days; arches on the first floor have been filled in by a stonelike mosaic, perhaps to match a 1960s addition that looms up beyond another archway on the west. The parked cars

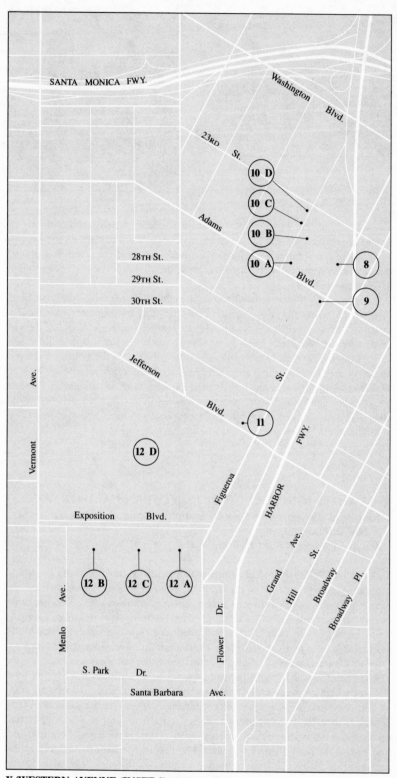

X/WESTERN AVENUE (INSET 2)

are not any great delight, either; the small clumps of palm trees are inadequate really to hold their own, and the little touches high on the building can't quite make it alone.

Still, the courtyard possesses some of that magical quality that the courthouse and other places in Santa Barbara have, of tiny things, like balconies way up high and other excitements that are cut into or sticking out from the great blank walls, to make this, too, a special place. The sun shines easily over the low wing on the south, two fountains splash in a central island, and gentlemen in blue blazers welcome you from a corner entrance; here an iron filigree Automobile Club insignia beckons, and an array of early California flags wave.

X 10 · CHESTER PLACE
Between Twenty-third Street and Adams Boulevard, west of Figueroa Street, Los Angeles
Now the Doheny campus of Mount St. Mary's College; because of private residences, visitors use main sidewalks only; photography limited to professional contracts

Although the West Adams district, in general, has long passed from neglect into advanced decay, the little walled-in oasis of Chester Place, now owned by Mount St. Mary's College, remains in mint condition behind its iron gates, a gracious reminder of the turn of the century, when this was one of the most luxurious residential areas in Los Angeles. In 1895 Judge Charles S. Silent developed this flat twenty-acre site into a residential park where thirteen stately mansions were built in a variety of East Coast styles. But for all their individuality, the mansions share enough characteristics to present a unified demeanor, as if for protection from the local gaucheries, in 1895 as now.

The luxuriant grounds add to the unity and seem, as well, to have arrived intact from someplace else, perhaps New England: huge specimen trees are scattered around spacious lawns that flow across the property lines; strange street lamps, clusters of six round bulbs on ornate standards, provide a constant rhythm along the fronts. But it is the play of structural themes, such as Tudor arches and porte cocheres and thick sandstone bases, which weave through these very different houses in slightly different ways, that constitutes the most breathtakingly sophisticated part of the unification.

The two-story house at no. 10 (10 A) (now the Administration Building) is engulfed by green shingles that flow past little rectangular openings to make an indented balcony and then continue on everywhere, stopped only by the barge boards. A curious Gothic Palladian dormer window keeps unsymmetrical company with a stone chimney, while more stone finds its way into the foundations and the big piers of a front porch. Beautiful trees have grown large over the years, including one mature palm in the front lawn (on the left) that rises confidently—and astonishingly—out of a big urn balanced on a pencil-thin base.

Next door, a hundred or so feet of exotic foliage away, is the main event on Chester Place, the Doheny house (10 B), at no. 8 (Theodore A. Eisen and Sumner P. Hunt, 1898–1900; now Doheny Hall). In 1901 Edward L. Doheny, who had struck it rich nine years earlier with the city's first oil field (at Glendale Boulevard between Beverly Boulevard and Cotton Street), purchased the entire development and, naturally, moved into its most elaborate mansion. The hulking Spanish Gothic version of a chateau that he chose assumes a lugubrious presence in its Victorian garden: stone quoins and dark woodwork line with

X 10 B · *Doheny House*

melancholy its reddish beige plaster walls; the ridges of the steep red-tiled roof have green reptilian, liplike caps and pinnacles; and a relentless row of double-hung windows marches along the second floor.

The air of sobriety is broken, however, by strange events at the entry: on the left a twelve-sided tower, which is topped by a ponderously ornamented pavilion and a crocketed steeple, erupts through the roof; a sharply pointed Gothic dormer seems to have shot up from the other side and nearly cleared the roof as well. In between, two stone lions guard brown marble stairs that lead up to a glass-roofed entrance porch and a fancy iron filigree front door. An airy marquee has a metal Tudor arch that repeats the one in marble above the front door. Along the left side later additions reveal themselves in a fantastic roofscape of colliding dormers, skylights, odd windows, and towers. Farther back it all happens again, in miniature, on a carriage house with the same mournful dormers, Tudor arches and some remarkable colonetted chimneys.

At no. 7 is the Wilson house (10 C) (ca. 1897), a frothy Mission Style giant with some fancy Islamic ambitions that has sprouted a four-story Italianate tower, a Tudor porte cochere and an unassimilated dose of Sullivanesque ornament rendered in plaster. The entry is flanked by two free-form Composite columns, which seem to stagger under the apparent weight of a great gable end-wall with enormous Mission moldings. A large arched opening surrounded by gooey gobs of filigree does not help relieve the weight of this wall. And the pistachio-green paint job, which covers everything, does not manage to unify this jumble of styles and scales.

Next door to the Wilson house, at the end of Chester Place, is no. 1 (10 D), a large house with big beige shingles somewhat more modest than the rest. It is made memorable, however, by the enormous sweep of a roof, all the way down from a three-story gable end on the left to a long one-story porch on the right. Nearby is the beautiful wrought-iron fence that surrounds Chester Place; its thick verticals spiral around each other in ways full of wonder.

X 11 · SHRINE AUDITORIUM
3228 Royal Street, on the east corner of Jefferson Boulevard, Los Angeles
John C. Austin, A. M. Edelman, G. A. Landsbery, 1925

The Shrine Auditorium, when it was built, was the largest theater in the world. It was concocted by the Ancient Arabic Order of Nobles of the Mystic Shrine, as a twentieth-century version of the Islamic architecture built in Egypt during the fourteenth and fifteenth centuries by the Turkish Mamelukes. Something curious, though, seems to have befallen these ancestral memories as they drifted through the mists of time, and the Islamicity bears a close resemblance to the outfits of the Shriners themselves—all business, with a fez and scabbard for show, combining pragmatic minimalism with a discreet sense of the outlandish.

The Islamic manifestations pale a little as they try to compete with the tremendous rectangular volume of reinforced concrete—no courtyards here. However, these forms are still inordinately large and unlikely enough in this neighborhood to create the intended exotic effect. A Moorish dome at each corner sports keyhole windows and a prickly finial. Five enormous horseshoe arches, on massive piers disguised by little paired columns, lurch across the entry, holding up a heavily ornamented cornice, at least five feet deep, that then goes around the whole building. Above this ledge smaller pointed arches with delicate mullions march along beneath another huge molding.

Inside the auditorium a colossal Arabian-tentlike canopy enshrines an opulent scene that was probably inspired by *The Thief of Baghdad,* the popular film that premiered in 1924. If the moviemakers had waited, they could have filmed it here.

X 12 · EXPOSITION PARK
Bounded by Exposition Boulevard, Figueroa Street, South Park Drive and Menlo Avenue, Los Angeles
Wilbur D. Cook, Jr., landscape architect, 1911

Exposition Park is one of the oldest cultural and recreational centers in Los Angeles. Initially developed as an agricultural fairgrounds and horse track, the 114-acre site was purchased jointly by the city, county and state in 1898 and opened as a public park in 1910. Unlike the other major open spaces of the city, which are in the hills or fringes of Los Angeles, Exposition Park is a more conventional big-city garden, sited in the flat inner city, formally landscaped and inhabited by major museums and sports facilities. The most interesting diversions are three of the earliest: the Armory (now the Space Museum), the Museum of Natural History and the sunken rose garden, all strung along the southern edge of Exposition Boulevard.

The Armory (12 A) (1913) is strait-laced, solid and symmetrical, with repeating large windows and massive central portals. Fluted columns, like sentries, guard the entry stairs. At the back, a major addition by Frank O. Gehry and Associates is in the works. Across the rose garden from here, the Museum of Natural History (12 B) (Hudson and Munsell, 1913), which the designers labeled "Spanish Renaissance," is a cheerful example of turn-of-the-century, Beaux-Arts–inspired exposition architecture. Though its cross-shaped plan has been added onto over the years, this triple-domed symmetrical building, with ochre terra-cotta ornament on its blood red tapestry-brick walls, is at once festive and dignified. Its original entry, a grand flight of stairs up to a triple-arched, Classically detailed loggia, was once on axis through the rose garden to the Armory. But this was given up in favor of a new north entrance that possesses all the charm of a loading dock, despite a long pool nearby choked with plants. Inside there are many treasures: along with the expected stuffed animals in front of dioramas are exciting displays of California history and motion pictures and a dazzling collection of gems and minerals presented in miniature landscapes.

Still, the sunken rose garden (12 C), which lies between these two buildings, is the biggest thrill. It is a seven-acre formal parterre that contains over fifteen thousand rosebushes in some 118 varieties, laid out in symmetrical beds flanking grassy aisles. Four white stone pergolas grace the corners, and a reflecting pool with a few splashing jets marks the center. The roses bloom between March and November.

Across Exposition Boulevard from here is the University of Southern California (12 D), which boasts the largest collection of Edward D. Stone buildings on the West Coast. Once a gentle campus consisting of carefully sited, distinguished structures, the school has, since World War II, put up a great number of unremarkable and sometimes downright awful structures in just about every available piece of open space. Today it is a jampacked jumble, in a neighborhood for which the euphemism is "transitional."

X 12 B · *Museum of Natural History*   X 13 · *Baldwin Hills Village*

X 13 · BALDWIN HILLS VILLAGE
5300 Rodeo Road, between La Brea Avenue and Hauser Boulevard, Los Angeles
Robert E. Alexander, Reginald D. Johnson, Wilson and Merrill, architects; Clarence S. Stein, consultant and site planner; Fred Barlow and Fred Edmonson, landscape architects, 1940–1941

Baldwin Hills Village, renamed the Village Green when it became condominiums in the mid-1970s, was an early low-cost housing project that worked. Its great success and wide acclaim have been achieved primarily by clever, generous landscaping, for the buildings are neutral and unassuming. The one- and two-story volumes, clad in stucco and wood siding beneath low hip roofs, contain everything from studios to three-bedroom units, each of which faces a private walled garden. All the buildings are spread out along angled rows, separated by lawns and giant sycamores and oaks. The open spaces lead into three village greens, the middle one big enough for a small golf course, while garages and parking courts nestle into the perimeter. It all adds up to an astonishingly pleasant place to live, thanks to the thoughtful planning and planting, which have put the very simple buildings right in the middle of the California Dream.

X 14 · TORRANCE

Torrance is a blue-collar city toward the southern end of the apparently endless Los Angeles plain, hard to distinguish from all the others nearby except that it has the fragmentary remnants of a center planned in 1913 as a model industrial town by Olmsted and Olmsted, the sons of Frederick Law Olmsted, America's great park designer, with buildings by Irving Gill. Gill, who has already made a relaxed beachside appearance in Chapter V, at the Horatio Court West apartments, is present in Torrance in full seriousness, though his buildings here are not really numerous, were cheap (as well as stern and spare) in the first place, and are mostly in an intermediate state of dilapidation by now.

They seem, in fact, more responsive to the pointed enthusiams of the collector than the more casual pleasures of the tourist. The more of them you see, the more evident it becomes that they are the products of a highly developed point of view, a patient search for simplicity and clarity and rigor. In some Gill buildings, sophistication of color (primaries in the white paint, for instance, so it seems to reflect what is around) accomplishes a kind of prim seduction of the viewer; but in these Torrance remnants there is none of the seduction of the lush and sunny that is so normal a part of Ramona's heritage; rather, there is a boiled-down reticence that leaves the visitor, finally, astonished that so little could suggest so much.

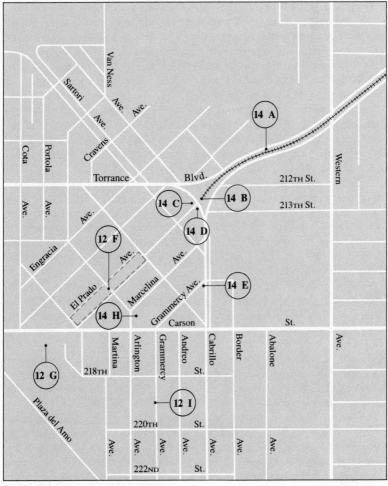

X/WESTERN AVENUE (INSET 3)

Irving Gill had come to San Diego in 1893 from Louis Sullivan's office in Chicago, and had enjoyed a series of successes: the blandishments of the California burgeoning landscape were countered by Gill's almost puritanical devotion to the rationalizing, simplifying and purifying of structures that seem now eerily prescient in their clean-limbed modernity. But about the time the Torrance project was begun, Gill and the times fell out: the labor force, seeing their own jobs in jeopardy, objected to the simplifications in the low-cost houses and stopped the building of more; and the Panama-California Exposition, which was being planned then for 1915, was taken over by the great New York architect Bertram Grosvenor Goodhue, who was later to design the Los Angeles Public Library and the Nebraska Capitol, but in those years was espousing a scholarly but flamboyant Churrigueresque. Goodhue and his style were a runaway success; you can still see why when you visit the fantasies left from that fair in Balboa Park, magical as ever. But it signaled the end of Gill's own successes, and his practice stayed small until his death in 1936.

The best introduction to Gill's original part of Torrance is through one of the six arches (14 A) in his railroad bridge, which crosses Torrance Boulevard between Western and Cabrillo avenues, just east of Bow Avenue. This delicately proportioned, poured-concrete structure serves as a kind of latter-day city gate, accommodating every means of transportation into town as well as the Southern Pacific Railroad tracks across the top. A pair of tall, half-circle arches in the center served Pacific Electric streetcars; on each side of them is a big segmental arch, wide enough for two lanes of automobiles; and then, at each end, is another arch, like the middle ones but lower, for pedestrians. This bridge is typical of Gill's best work, straightforward and bold, with flat surfaces ornamented only by form marks; but with its little arches and big, it seems at once grand and almost fragile. There is, too, a sort of off-center energy in the rhythm of the openings, set against the varying levels of the several roadways, the vines that crawl all around and the groves of eucalyptus at each end. You wouldn't guess, at first glance, that the whole wall is unerringly symmetrical.

The same year he built the bridge, 1913, Irving Gill designed the Pacific Electric Station (14 B) at 1200 Cabrillo Avenue. This is one of his most striking buildings, a sort of distilled Greek temple, mostly just a long, white stucco plane with a long slot hollowed out of it; a row of purified Doric columns supports this restrained entryway; a barely curving, flat abstraction of a Mission gable sticks up just behind it. At least, that's all that's left. Someone seems to have run off with the central dome.

Across the street from this station, on the two corners of El Prado and Cabrillo avenues, are the Murray Hotel (14 C) (1212 El Prado) and El Roi Tan Hotel (14 D), now Apartments (1211 El Prado). Both of these are aggressively bare-bones buildings, just white-plastered, three-story brick boxes with long rows of rectangular windows that have either little variation in their height and placement or none at all. We have arrived at that part of Gill's work in Torrance that only a collector could love. Here the architect manages somehow to be more straightforward than all the other straightforward dingbats in this town, and there is a connoisseur's challenge in telling the difference.

In the same vein is the former Colonial Hotel (14 E) (1607 Cabrillo Avenue, ca. 1913–1914), now just a sleazy old commercial building at the knife-edged intersection of Cabrillo and Gramercy avenues. It's not certain whether Gill designed this triangular, three-story, beige plaster box with its dark brown stripe running between the top two rows of identical windows; but it's a match for the two other hotels.

The Prado (14 F), a central park, is one block north, in the heart of what used to be Torrance's downtown. This narrow, two-block-long lawn, lined with palm trees and little houses, is an especially pretty place, very green. Here is the axis that bred all these diagonal streets: the southwest terminus is the Italian Renaissance high school (14 G), which was insisted on by the school board; the site was supposed to have gone to the city hall. When you look along the axis to the northeast, you can just see Gill's funny little Pacific Electric Station and, on a clear day, Mount San Antonio far in the distance.

At the southeast corner of Marcelina and Arlington avenues is a high-spirited little Spanish Colonial Revival bungalow court (14 H) (ca. 1922), which was not designed by Gill. This U-shaped assemblage of white stucco walls is joined together around a small lawn, with separate personalities for each of the apartments. It is just a little fancier and must have been much more appealing than the stark hotel blocks by the station.

Gill also designed a number of clean-lined bungalows, but few were ever built. The building contractors had little wish to experiment with new materials or time-saving techniques, and the families here much preferred the woodsy Craftsman cottages that were all the rage at the time, rich and as cheap. There is a tight group of the Gill houses (14 I) at nos. 1815, 1819, 1903, 1904, 1907, 1912, 1916 and 1920 Gramercy Avenue. They all began as clean-lined, stucco-over-tile innovations, but most of them have been invested with the inhabitants' energies and visions over the years, which renders them much more picturesque. It's a blessing to the casual sightseer, but makes Gill collecting a bit chancier.

X 15 · SAN PEDRO

San Pedro and Wilmington, directly north, surround the Port of Los Angeles, which, along with the Port of Long Beach on the east, comprises the world's largest man-made harbor, handling 125,000 tons of cargo a day. But even with all the activity nearby, the town of San Pedro still has a small-scale hominess to it. It is a place for seamen and dockworkers to live, on rolling hills that overlook the harbor and the Pacific. During the 1940s a number of important public housing projects were built here for wartime workers, but these buildings have all been remodeled or replaced by more expensive versions; even Richard Neutra's famous Channel Heights apartments is now a cluster of modern town houses. But the town itself has managed to retain its unpretentious charm.

You can enter San Pedro on the Harbor Freeway (11), which, during its last two miles, passes through a weird and wonderful landscape of heavy industry gone berserk. On the right are fields of oil tanks and pipes of a vast refinery; on the left is the port with its huge warehouses and cranes and its acres of new Japanese cars sparkling in the sun; and then comes the biggest sight of all, a handsome green-painted suspension bridge (15 A) (the Vincent Thomas Bridge, 1963), more than a mile long and 185 feet above the water, which crosses over toward Long Beach. After the freeway becomes Gaffey Street, the main street of San Pedro, the atmosphere changes considerably. At first the surroundings look like much of Western Avenue, with wide streets, one-story buildings, few trees and a sometimes blazing sun, but for all that there's something very special about this ordinary port town. Perhaps it's a kind of sea-washed quality that makes it, the smell of the port and ships and of sunshine and fog; it seems in some funny way like northern California, but also like the tropics, and a lot of other pleasant places.

Harbor Boulevard, between Sepulveda and Fifth streets, passes by dockyards and trucks lined up behind a long cyclone fence; but, typical of the scene in San Pedro, at once industrial and Arcadian, the fence is covered by mounds of oleander. There are, as well, plenty of vagrant signs of urbanism in town. At Berth 84, at the east end of Sixth Street, is the Los Angeles Harbor Department Building of 1941, now the Los Angeles Maritime Museum (15 B). This splendid example of Streamline Moderne, with its clock-tower funnel, seems anchored to its site next to the main channel of the harbor. Its interior, too, recalls the swept-wing elegance of 1930s ocean liners. Across the street, at 639 Harbor Boulevard, on the northwest corner of Seventh Street, is the San Pedro Municipal Building (15 C) (1929), a big, Classically detailed block, seven stories high, made of buff-colored brick, stone quoins and a stone base; it's reminiscent, in its foursquare monumentality, of Michael Graves' famous new Public Service Building in Portland, Oregon. Just south of the Municipal Building (15 D) is the beginning of the long and narrow and very pretty San Pedro Plaza Park.

X 16 · MacCAFFERTY HOUSE
1017 Beacon Street near the southwest corner of Tenth Street, San Pedro
Coy Howard, 1980
Private residence

Beacon Street, long a favorite place for seamen to retire, is a handsome line of old wood-framed houses and newer apartments that face San Pedro Plaza Park across the street. This strip of vegetation, between Beacon Street and the edge of a cliff, is not much wider than its thick row of Canary Island palms, which frame the views of big ships and tiny pleasure boats in the harbor below. The neighborhood hardly seems the setting for one of Los Angeles' most aggressively avant-garde houses. But Coy Howard, who does business on the cutting edge of Architecture as Art, has apparently thrived on the contrast.

This narrow, three-story rectangular box, which is half corrugated aluminum and half unfinished plywood, has the dimensions and the flat façade of a row house, only without the row, as if it had been kicked out of some civilized residential street in San Francisco. There's a kind of Classical allusion at the top, where an aluminum-covered broken pediment thrusts itself over a glass prow. From here, the aluminum siding drips down in a zigzag line, something like a silvery sauce on a slightly bowed plywood sundae, and ends above the plywood garage door on the left. A black-painted H-column, with knee braces holding up the floors, sticks out from the center, while on the far left an entrance corridor and a window above it have been gouged away. The south side is all aluminum siding with a number of tiny aluminum-framed windows scattered around; the north side is similar, only its flat wall is mostly plywood and three of the windows are variously sized upside-down Ls. Behind the pediment, the flat roof becomes a terrace with an odd little penthouse that gives onto it.

Inside, the spaces are as arousing as the exterior, especially the floor-to-ceiling stairwell in the middle that serves as a light-filled atrium. The house is sited well with its neighbors and seems, generally, to be a nicely relaxed piece of work within that Southern California 1980s idiom; it's somehow more substantial and more ordinary, in the best sense, than many of the others seem to be. But it's not pretty, and of course it's not meant to be.

X 17 · CABRILLO MARINE MUSEUM

3720 Stephen M. White Drive, San Pedro
Frank O. Gehry and Associates, 1981
*Open Tuesday through Sunday, 10–5; free admission, but there is a fee for
close-in parking*

Cabrillo Beach, at the end of Los Angeles Harbor, is a very pretty place, with
the ocean on one side, a pleasant tiled-roof Spanish building (the old museum)
at the point, and another beach, a little less sparkling, which faces to the harbor.
Shoreward of this latter beach, behind a large asphalt parking lot and up against
a small cliff, is the new Marine Museum, designed by Frank O. Gehry, who
these days is probably Southern California's best-known architect. The museum
is sited in ways that may be perplexing: it seems an odd assortment of one- and
two-story detached boxes, all tangled up in angular nets of cyclone fencing, like
flotsam washed up from a lobster boat. But they are washed up just right, recol-
lecting the guiding philosophy behind Gehry's own house (page 161), something
like "What would this site look like if a bunch of large boxes crashed into it?"
Here the surprisingly positioned boxes are themselves fairly straightforward,
with regular rows of strip windows in walls of off-white stucco or corrugated
metal, which is mellowing nicely in the salt air. Sometimes the walls reverse
field to become one-story skyscrapers covered in squares of reflective glass.

X 17 · *Cabrillo Marine Museum*

The source of much of the brio, though, is Gehry's trademark, the cyclone
fencing, which is everywhere, stretched across fat galvanized pipes. The chain-
link story begins at an entrance courtyard that becomes increasingly narrow as
you pass a big chain-link gate and walk through an enormous chain-link cage,
which is a kind of twisted and sliced-off abstraction of a pergola. Then comes
the main patio, an irregularly shaped open space with a jagged row of offices
along the front and, at the back, the big rectangular volume of the museum,
with an information booth wedged into it. A high-spirited chain-link ceiling
wraps this patio as well.

Frank Gehry, discussing the ubiquitous chain link, says he had grown concerned that, in these days of high security, people were covering up their pretty

buildings with ugly cyclone fences, so he decided to build a group of determinedly bland buildings and put all of his effort into the chain-link wrapper. Here at Cabrillo, ever the enthusiast, he continues the chain-link and pipe through the inside; within a fascinating labyrinth of bright spaces enveloping dark ones, the fencing wends its contrapuntal way. It divides the rooms, allowing glimpses of what's ahead, and it becomes a useful surface to hang things on; but it's a little insistent when the more delicate siren songs of the deep try to sing as well: it creeps up onto the tanks of tiny sea creatures, crosses the ceiling like an exoskeleton and makes barblike projections over the clerestories. The fish tanks are used as room dividers, too, especially exciting when you look from the dark spaces through them or over them to the brightly lit rooms beyond. The fish are fascinating; more fascinating than the occasional glimpses of the bare stomachs of fat men on the bright side of the tanks.

X 18 · *Point Fermin Lighthouse*

X 18 · POINT FERMIN LIGHTHOUSE
805 Paseo del Mar, at the south end of Gaffey Street, San Pedro
1874; closed down in 1942
Now the private residence of the Point Fermin Park superintendent

The Western Avenue ride is one of our longest and, to put it positively, least dense. It seems fitting that it end on a high note, on a promontory high above the ocean in the thick trees of Point Fermin Park, where a pretty little Victorian lighthouse commands one of the finest views in Southern California. The lighthouse is just a two-story board-and-batten residence, painted white, with a four-story tower growing out of its center. It sits close to the cliff edge, surrounded by lawns, dense foliage and a little white fence, one of the few remaining examples in Los Angeles of the spiky Eastlake style, though a bit more relaxed than most. It is the very last of the many wooden lighthouses that once dotted the California coast.

One prominent feature of the Eastlake style was a pleasure in verticality, which worked out particularly well in the design of a lighthouse. The four-sided tower is, of course, the main event here, with vertical boards that run up to a frilly, bracketed balustrade around a tall lantern. In contrast to this and to three high, elaborately capped chimneys, the house below, with its horizontal siding, seems satisfyingly wedded to the ground. It does, however, achieve a full measure of picturesqueness with an assortment of red asphalt shingle roofs and overhangs that ease down on nests of spindly brackets and sticklike struts. Doors and wide window frames are painted light gray; a lacy pergola, painted white, angles back to a tiny garage.

These homey embellishments must have been a welcome distraction for those early lighthouse keepers, for Point Fermin used to be a distant and desolate place. The first residents, two sisters, quit because of the loneliness. You can still get a feel for their problem when you stand in front of the lighthouse and look out over the 180-degree view of the Pacific Ocean. San Pedro Harbor bustles a bit on the left, but the rest looks remarkably untouched: on a clear day, the mountains of Santa Catalina Island appear very close and barren, while the Palos Verdes Peninsula on the right still has only a few houses visible on its grassy hills; and from this height the big ships that have come seem very small, like the whales, which have been migrating past here for far longer.

XI/VENTURA BOULEVARD

North of the hills that line the north edge of the Los Angeles plain lies the San Fernando Valley, known hereabouts as the Valley—flat, with big hills all around, warmer in summer than the coastal plain and a bit chillier in winter. From the beginning of the Spanish occupation, fields were tilled around the San Fernando mission, but past them the Valley was desert, sage and sand, with hardly any human inhabitants. Then in 1913 came Water, in the Los Angeles Aqueduct, from the other side of the mountains, and the boom was on. The water, to be sure, belonged to the City of Los Angeles, and the price of this bounty was annexation, so the area of Los Angeles more than doubled; the city wrapped around the holdouts, Burbank and San Fernando, which, like Beverly Hills and Santa Monica on the other side of the mountains, still have their own wells. But some of the excitement over the arrival of the water is still here: on your right, as the northbound Interstate 5 leaves the Valley, you can see a cascade, a flight of liquid steps that releases the pent-up pressures of the water just rolling into town from the High Sierra. What a blast Bernini would have had with that! But even in its straightforwardly engineered state, the water chute is worth a minor pilgrimage.

The annexation and the attendant arrival of the water more than doubled not only the size of Los Angeles, but also the value of the land in the Valley as orchards and truck farms proliferated; but the big influx of people and their little houses, not to mention light industrial tracts, came in the years after World War II: the Valley filled up, and a loose net of commercial strips to serve the needs of the newcomers was laid across the scatter. Much of it had the rather touching California do-it-yourself sleaziness that we have cast sympathetic eyes on along Western Avenue; but some of the thoroughfares, especially Ventura Boulevard, became somewhat bigger deals, places for a mechanized, linear Los Angeles version of a Latin paseo, where fancily doctored vehicles are used as peacocks might use feathers, or bower birds a nest.

Ventura Boulevard follows the southern edge of the Valley, at the foot of the Santa Monica Mountains. Once it was the main inland route from Los Angeles to Santa Barbara and on to the north. It was bypassed by the Ventura Freeway in 1959 and might have been expected to wither a little. But instead it has burgeoned and looks prosperous: there are buildings along it with themes (the Fiore d'Italia Restaurant, 14928 Ventura); buildings with art added (Home Savings, 17107 Ventura); buildings in a grove of trees (Plaza de Oro, near the northeast corner of Ventura and Louise Avenue); buildings with fountains (Carriage Motor Works, 14315 Ventura, east of Tyrone Avenue); buildings with parking in a row out front (Lingenbrink Shops, 12632–72 Ventura, page 299) or parking hidden in a court (the French Quarter Motel, 11136 Ventura) or enveloped by a sea of parking (McDonald's, 11970 or 13925 or 15301 or 15700 or 17641 Ventura). And, of course, there is an impressive variety of signs—the giant ice cream cone, for instance, above The Creamery (18710 Ventura) or the neon bathing beauty who somersaults into a neon pool at Steele's Motel (13949 Ventura).

A 1981 survey of businesses revealed that from Universal City in the east to Calabasas in the west, Ventura Boulevard sported, among other wonders, eleven coffee shops, thirteen supermarkets, twenty-seven fast-food outlets, twenty-nine motels, forty-nine banks and fifty-eight real estate offices.

XI 1 · CANOGA MISSION GALLERY
23130 Sherman Way, Canoga Park
Francis Lederer, 1934–1936
Gallery open Wednesday through Sunday, 11–5

Francis Lederer, a star from the early days of the movies, built this romantic recollection of California missions as the stable barn for his Spanish Colonial Revival house, which is still just visible in a thick grove of trees on a small hill to the north. Although tract houses have closed in around the back of the stable, and Sherman Way now cuts it off from the ranch house, this miniature mission still brings a certain charm to its new role as a community center for the arts of California and Mexico (with gift shop).

Thick walls of rough-hewn stone and brick and oozing globs of mortar manage to stir up Ramonic visions as they invigorate the straightforwardness of this tiny barn. The picturesque walls build into an elaborate Mission gable at each

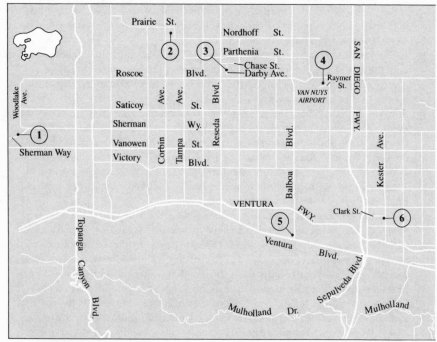

XI/VENTURA BOULEVARD

end, a covered arcade along the right side and a set of pre-ruined arches that increasingly fall apart off to the left. Rustic red tiles cover the barn roof, rustic wrought iron protects the small windows, and rustic wood doors hang in the arched entrances and haylofts. Set in a tiny Old Southwest gravel pit landscape, this little bit of theatricality performs its new part with brio.

XI 2 · TELEDYNE SYSTEMS COMPANY

19601 Nordoff Street, on the northeast corner of Corbin Avenue, Northridge
DMJM, Cesar Pelli with Anthony Lumsden, 1967
Security is tight, but exterior is visible from the front parking lot

The Teledyne Company manufactures its electronic systems and computer hardware behind the greenish bronze, glass and steel walls of a thousand-foot-long, one-story box. The building stretches across almost the full length of its megalopolitan site, with lawns and a small parking lot in front and acres of parking in back. From any of the four bounding streets, however, this enormous incorporation of steel and asphalt looks more like an orange grove—which the site, like much of the San Fernando Valley, had once been. The designers magnanimously preserved a large number of the mature trees, mostly in big squares and long allées along the perimeter, so that the low olive-drab structure almost disappears.

This sensitive solution has worked out remarkably well today, for what was slick and up to the minute in 1967 has faded, with the rest of us, and the shiny metal siding has grown dull while the reflective glass now looks sort of oily. The

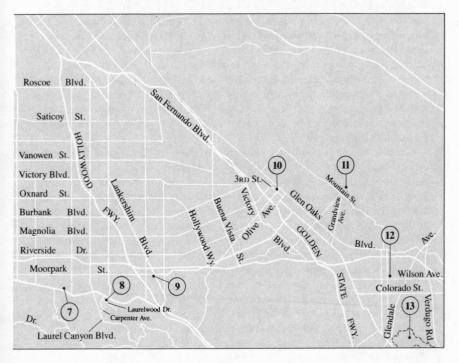

building technology is showing its age as well: in this benign climate, great bands of south-facing windows combine with fourteen thousand light fixtures (which can't be turned off) to produce a heat gain that would quickly melt down most forms of life—and even inert masses—if the air conditioners weren't running all the time. Much more pleasant than the structure is the sight of employees on their lunch hour, picking oranges to take home.

XI 3 · TWO TRACT HOUSES
8433 and 8441 Darby Avenue, near Chase Street, Northridge
Smith and Williams, 1954

After World War II, waves of ex-servicemen with their families and their V.A. benefits arrived in Los Angeles, eager to claim their own hard-won places in this paradise. Waves of equally enthusiastic builders, developers, land speculators, and a few architects and planners responded to the call. They quickly transformed vast expanses of agricultural land, most of it flat and supplied with water, into sprawling subdivisions of affordable, easily assembled, mildly attractive houses on generous lots. By far the most frenzied activity took place in the fertile San Fernando Valley, which grew into one continuous suburb as the population jumped fivefold in fifteen years, from 170,000 in 1945 to 850,000 in 1960. Almost overnight this unassuming farmland, with its miles of orange and walnut groves, blossomed into the undisputed tract house capital of the world.

The rows of one-story, wood-frame, two- to four-bedroom houses, all behind identically large front lawns, are best known for their grinding sameness, but their low-cost, often comical attempts at variation are the chief delight. A diamond-paned bay window in a rickrack frame or a steep roof with one bit sweeping down to the petunias might suggest an English cottage. A front porch beneath an overhanging shake roof with a couple of pigeon coops on top could signal the more common Ranch Style. The least troubling of all were the clean lines of the Contemporary models, so variations on this theme were especially popular. And any of these details could be used in almost any combination. The standard rooms in the open plans were pushed around on their concrete slabs with an easy economy, while the mandatory double garage or carport could be positioned nearly anywhere along the front of the lot. Easier still, the whole plan could be flipped over.

Although there are hundreds of examples of the tract house genre on nearly every street in the Valley, these two next-door neighbors on Darby Avenue represent some of the best. Both are designed in the straightforward Contemporary Style with low-pitched white gravel roofs, vertically grooved plywood siding and standard aluminum-framed windows. Their plans, placed at opposite hands at slight angles to the street, have managed to create a certain amount of privacy and to preserve a number of the old walnut trees. Asphalt driveways curve between the trees, past great mounds of ivy, to the carports at the sides; from here, roof overhangs protect walkways to the front doors.

Despite such traits in common, the two houses hardly appear alike. The one on the left, rosy beige with white trim, emphasizes the horizontal edges of its low roofs and seems pinned to the ground by a prominent chimney. The one on the right, sandy beige with brown trim, tries to rise up from its site with mildly cubist intentions. Even though the rest of the neighborhood is beginning to show its age, these two houses, with their closely compatible but distinct personalities, remain pleasant reminders of that wonderful old notion, which reached its peak by about 1970 in the San Fernando Valley, that every American might own his own home.

XI 4 · 94TH AERO SQUADRON HEADQUARTERS
16320 Rymer Street, just west of Woodley Avenue, Van Nuys
Lynne, Paxton, Paxton and Cole, 1974

Most restaurants serve atmosphere as a complimentary garnish, but a few, like this reincarnation of a U.S. Army Air Corps bivouac beside a runway at the Van Nuys airport, dish it up as the entrée. The courses on this environmental menu include siting, architecture, landscaping, furnishings and even sound effects, which combine to create a fantasy setting that expands mere atmosphere into theater.

The time: 1917, World War I. The place: Normandy. The scene: the 94th Aero Squadron has taken over an abandoned farmhouse to serve as its battle headquarters. The set: a large house and its attached barn, which wrap around an entrance courtyard. Bushy trees partially camouflage the steep roofs and the rustic walls of brick and white-plastered stone. At each side of a central walkway, hay bales hang from lofts above wooden wagons while howitzers stand ready behind their sandbagged emplacements. A windsock flaps from a squat tower that rises from one corner of the courtyard, and olive green bicycles wait by the front door.

Inside, sandbags line the stairs in the small foyer. A half-flight down to the cellar is the Enlisted Men's Mess, a dark timbered lounge bar with massive brick arches and more sandbags. A half-flight up is the Officer's Canteen, the main dining hall, where the walls and exposed beams are covered in remarkably convincing artifacts, from halters and saws and iron cookware to wartime posters and photographs. An intercom plays ballads, interrupted by messages from the CO's office. At the back, large windows look out past a few of the squadron's biplanes to a real runway. The only thing out of place is the dress of the patrons—maybe the management should issue uniforms in the parking lot.

XI 5 · LOS ENCINOS STATE HISTORIC PARK
**16756 Moorpark Street, with another pedestrian entrance on Ventura
Boulevard, near the northwest corner of Balboa Boulevard, Encino**
*Tours of adobe on Wednesday through Saturday, 1–4; Sunday, 1–5; grounds
open Wednesday through Sunday, 8–5; call (818) 784-4849*

This lushly planted five-acre park, with its handful of old buildings and its little springfed lake, is all that is left of the 4,460-acre Rancho de los Encinos, which once covered all of what is now Encino and part of Sherman Oaks. The rancho took its name from the numerous stands of native oaks (*encinos*), but most of the trees were removed to allow the tract houses and the commercial clutter of Ventura Boulevard. Although the back of the park faces directly onto the boulevard, a new adobe wall and layers of well-established trees have managed, just barely, to maintain the aura of this early California oasis. The constantly flowing, 80-degree spring, which has been gushing up here for centuries, was the main reason the land around it was inhabited long before the Spanish arrived. The Indians, who used to soak in the warm mud as a cure, believed that the place had special powers. Occasionally, even now, when the traffic noise dips down, a present-day visitor can feel a little of that magic.

The first white visitors here, the Gaspár de Portolá expedition, camped on this ground on August 5, 1769, three days after they had laid claim to Los Angeles (page 70). They found, according to Father Crespí's diary, "a very large pool of fresh water where we met two very large villages of very tractable Heathens . . . nearly 200 souls."

Several years later a Don Vicente de la Ossa raised large herds of cattle and sheep on this land and, in 1849, built a long adobe ranch house whose simple, linear arrangement of nine rooms, with doors opening onto covered porches along each side, coped ingeniously with the hot summer climate: the ceilings are high beneath a pitched shingle roof, the well-shaded walls are over two feet thick, and the building lies on a northeast-southwest axis to avoid the sun and to allow a prevailing westerly breeze to blow through. Don Vicente's cool adobe, shaded by oak trees, soon became a popular layover for travelers on El Camino Real, and by 1858 it had become an official rest stop for the Butterfield Stage Lines.

Two brothers, Philippe and Eugene Garnier, bought the rancho in 1869 and added a two-story French Provincial hunting lodge out of limestone that was quarried nearby. Their handsome building, complete with quoins, seems a bit homesick in this Old West setting, but so, apparently, were the Garnier brothers. The lodge reminded them of France and served as a kitchen; before that, typically for a Spanish rancho, meals had been cooked outside. The brothers built one of El Camino Real's first fast-food restaurants for the stagecoaches, made a guitar-shaped lake and set about, generally, the serious business of planting a Ramonaland fantasy. Later residents added successive layers of vegetation, so by now the vision is complete: ornamental and fruit trees intermingle with huge oaks and sycamores and ancient olive trees that line the original driveway; manicured lawns have overtaken the customary raked dirt; and a patch of prickly pear cactus, which Don Vicente had started just south of his adobe, has grown into a mountain.

There are a number of other old oak trees still living in the residential areas of Encino. One of the oldest and largest, with a 150-foot spread, is in the middle of Louise Avenue, just south of Ventura Boulevard. The ancient trees are about the only real evidences left hereabouts of Southern California's pre-Ramonic past, now that the chaparral-covered hillsides and the grassy plains have been covered over and the Indians no longer return to their power spots.

XI 6 · KESTER AVENUE SCHOOL

5353 Kester Avenue, entrance near the southwest corner of Clark Street, Van Nuys

Richard J. Neutra, 1951

Visible from the street; visitors' pass required to enter schoolgrounds

Even though this straightforward, economical school design by one of California's pioneer Modernists has been copied all over the state, the one Richard Neutra built in Van Nuys remains not only more elegantly shaped than the others, but a solution perfectly suited to this particular site, where the climate is usually mild yet often hot. Neutra's Corona Avenue School in 1935 had been the prototype for these long, one-story-high, one-classroom-deep buildings connected by covered walkways, but the Kester Avenue School allowed the architect to refine his revolutionary theory that classrooms, especially in elementary schools, should seem like living rooms and should open onto their own patios. Here he extended the patios into tree-shaded lawns, while he carefully positioned the buildings and their openings for natural light and cool breezes on even the hottest days.

Apart from a merciless asphalt playground, the school looks like a park, with low rows of buff-colored stucco buildings that mingle with broad trees and fit easily with the scale of the little houses on the surrounding streets. Each of the rows is on an east-west axis, shaded on the south by open colonnades, with varnished wood ceilings and cheerful red pipe-columns. Except for a high band of hopper windows that admit air and a little light, only the shaded doors penetrate this hottest side. On the north a wide overhang of the low-pitched roof protects great banks of windows and more doors that open onto the patios and lawns.

Near the main entrance, on Kester Avenue, two adjoining kindergarten classrooms face east to their own playground enclosed by a low brick wall. Here Neutra had integrated schoolrooms and garden in a grand flourish with large walls of small-paned windows that slid open. Today the cross ventilation still flows and the morning sun, screened by wooden louvers, still makes its way through similar banks of glass, but thanks to some long-forgotten administrative error the walls no longer slide. This is, however, one of the few alterations; after thirty years Neutra's inexpensive little buildings continue to work well and the setting grows thicker and greener.

XI 7 · *Lingenbrink Shops*

XI 7 · LINGENBRINK SHOPS
12632–12672 Ventura Boulevard, Studio City
R. M. Schindler, 1939–1942

In this row of ten little shops facing the boulevard behind a narrow parking lot, Rudolph Schindler brought his personal brand of Modernism to bear on a local form that is as important to this area as tract houses and apartments—the low-rise, stucco-covered commercial box. Traditionally, its façades are little more than huge display windows below traffic-stopping signs; the simple building in back of the sign, what Robert Venturi and others have taken to calling "the decorated shed," seems often to have been built with the money left over. Schindler, too, employed inexpensive materials and arranged them with the required priorities, but he put them together with heartening verve. Although there is a 1950s veneer on some of the front walls, most of the original design remains intact.

This long one-story building, which becomes two stories in the middle, is an energetic assemblage of rectangular planes and volumes, both positive and negative. Some of the negatives are little courtyards, cut in along the front and filled with shrubs that seem to have spilled down from the steep hillside behind. The front part of each party wall continues up beyond the flat roof to give identity to each shop and to act as a sign that faces the direction of traffic. Most of the stores have now placed their signs along the front, but these variously sized Schindler signatures still hang in the air above roofs that step up and down and in and out to create an agitated skyline. The display windows—glass boxes that stick out like crystals from the walls and intermingle with little planters—have also been treated as abstract sculpture. And, inside, each store has a complex personality of its own, illuminated by an assortment of skylights and clerestories and those crystalline prisms at the front.

XI 8 · LAURELWOOD APARTMENTS
11833, 11837 Laurelwood Drive, Studio City
R. M. Schindler, 1948
Now called Laurelwood Penthouse; private residences

A pale green one-story stucco wall, interrupted only by a gap in the middle for an entrance walkway, stretches across the front of this site. Behind this unpretentious introduction, Rudolf Schindler has made some remarkable improvements on the cheap stucco-box apartment building. Most apparent is the way he has mixed up the normal order of things—the excitements all take place behind the façade instead of on it.

The long front wall conceals carports, which are entered at each end; they are close to the street and to the apartments, and they act as a buffer, but they are out of sight. Behind the carports, two rows of two-story apartments, eleven on each side, climb up the gentle slope of the narrow lot. The row on the left is perpendicular to the street; the one on the right angles slightly inward toward the rear; so the walkway in between is wider in front, where more people use it, while a number of apartments toward the back have room for gardens. The forced perspective created by the angling adds to the appeal of the little walk, which climbs past thick hedges and trees and the doors to the apartments; at the end is a view through more trees to the San Fernando Valley.

A careful application of low-budget building materials increases the appeal. Long two-by-six-inch boards heighten the verticality of the standard concrete stairs, while inexpensive pipe railings curve into artful patterns. Between the floors, panels thicken the walls to break up the flatness, while they protect the lower windows and serve as flowerpot ledges for the upper ones. Overhangs of the flat roofs shade a number of balconies, grow into trellises over second-story patios, and help, as well, to lighten up the boxiness of the straightforward construction.

XI 9 · PARISH HALL
On Moorpark Street, near the southwest corner of Lankershim Boulevard, North Hollywood
Laurence Viole, 1938

Almost next door to the monumental St. Charles Borromeo Church with its wedding-cake tower and outsize Churrigueresque decoration is the stark but beautiful Parish Hall, a little church that looks like it would rather be an Indian mission in New Mexico. Two plump towers with soft-edged pyramidal caps rise up only two stories, little higher than the curving gable of the front wall in between. From the sidewalk the church appears to be a solid, slightly molded mass of adobe covered in lumpy white plaster. The infrequent openings bolster this impression: a small rose window, an unadorned arched entryway, and narrow slots in the towers are all three feet deep. But the design relaxes a little behind the façade: a casual assortment of red-tiled roofs, gable and shed, cover the nave, the short transepts and a number of one-story additions; the walls are still as thick, but the windows are larger and happen more often. Along the sides,

XI **9** · *Parish Hall*

narrow paths lead through tiny gardens to dark wood doors, which are carved with the wiggly Indian symbol for the River of Life. Although this little mission has pleasant next-door neighbors, a Monterey rectory on the left and a Spanish Colonial convent on the right, one would like to grant it more elbow room under a vast desert sky.

XI 10 · BURBANK CITY HALL
275 East Olive Avenue, Burbank
William Allen and W. George Lutzi, 1941

This two-story edifice with a five-story tower in the middle is a high-toned and late example of the Depression Modern Architecture of the 1930s. The Burbank City Hall manages to combine simple reinforced-concrete walls and plain windows with lavish ornament and details to create a powerful focus for a city that is celebrated, even more than the rest of these edgeless towns, for its lack of identity. Part of the building's grandeur comes from its unswerving symmetry, right down to the identical bronze plaques (publicizing the architects!) on each side of the front stairs. The flat-roofed, cream-colored volumes form a shallow U around a central courtyard that steps down to the sidewalk. On each side are planters filled with tropical foliage, while a black-and-turquoise fountain cascades down the axis to the sidewalk. The massive concrete tower, which ends in a gable-roofed belvedere with flagpole, has brass-framed glass doors at the bottom and tall windows above, the latter covered by an elaborate cast-concrete screen. A stylized concrete eagle perches patriotically above the screen, for this was 1941 and the fripperies of Art Deco were firming up for war.

Inside, a well-lit two-story lobby extends this faith in America (and Burbank) with even grander materials and Streamline flourishes. In the center of its gray marble floor, an inlaid winged star commemorates the founding of the city, while travertine marble wainscoting underlines the white plaster walls. On the right is a gleaming brass letterbox with an eagle guarding the bas-relief symbols of mail delivery—a ship, a plane and a train. This echoes, on the left, a brass directory with its own eagle above a torch of freedom and bas-reliefs of office workers at their desks. A central stair at the back rises beside winglike plaster walls inset with large medallions of muscular men fashioning airplanes, the city's biggest industry at the time. A mural above the mezzanine landing depicts DC-3s flying over the back lots of movie studios, the other mainstay of Burbank's business. Sleek brass railings follow the stairs as they divide to reach a second-story balcony that wraps around the room. More brass gleams in the balustrade of this balcony and finds its way into decorative channels that climb the middle of each wall, slide along the ceiling and burst into an imposing brass chandelier at the center. This apparently inexhaustible metal helps out the already sumptuous fluted black marble that trims the jambs of every door.

Back down on the stair landing, glass doors open onto a reflective-glass-covered bridge that crosses a small courtyard to a new addition. This typical glass-and-stucco, curtain-walled box was built during those happy days of 1965 when depressions and wars were not the heavy burdens they had been on the earlier design. It should have benefited from that.

XI 11 · BRAND LIBRARY
1601 West Mountain Street, at the north end of Grandview Avenue, Glendale
Nathaniel Dryden, 1904
Library hours, Tuesday and Thursday, 12–9; Wednesday, Friday and Saturday, 12–6; closed Sunday and Monday; park open daily

Leslie C. Brand was the developer of the original Glendale subdivision. After bringing in the utilities for his new town, and after ensuring its success with an all-important streetcar line from Los Angeles, he built his house, a stark but dreamy white Islamic fantasy in the foothills of the wild Verdugo Mountains, overlooking the little community he had created. On a trip to the 1893 Chicago World's Fair, Brand had been thrilled by the East Indian Pavilion, so he had his brother-in-law design something similar. He called it El Miradero because of the spectacular smogless view. After Brand's death in 1925, his richly land-scaped estate became a city park; in 1956 his house became a public library spe-cializing in music and art with studios and galleries added later.

Brand's Saracenic pleasure palace has accommodated its new role without compromising its strangeness. At the end of Grandview Avenue, the onion-domed minarets and Moorish arches of a white entrance gate still welcome the visitor into a different world, which has grown even more verdant as the town has become more urban. The drive winds up a hill past Mexican fan palms, ter-raced planters and a circular fountain; behind the fountain, long steps (which look scourged by OSHA) climb a grassy hill to the house. From below it looks much larger than its one-story plaster walls might suggest: three high towers with minaret finials reach toward the sky, while open arcades, with layers of elaborate horseshoe arches inside, seem to reach toward the horizon. Mean-while the geometric decoration and the dazzling whiteness create a grandeur all their own; the house seems to shimmer against the chaparral-covered hillside behind and the barely tamed jungle below.

The interior, in contrast, is straightlaced Victorian. There are patterned silk wall coverings above oak wainscoting and intricately carved Classical details around fireplaces and doorways, all of it imported from Europe.

XI 12 · ALEX THEATER
216 North Brand Boulevard, Glendale
Original theater attributed to Meyer and Holler, 1925; front addition
attributed to Arthur G. Lindley and Charles R. Selkirk, 1939

The front part of the Alex Theater, with its undulating white-and-yellow stucco walls, its box office shaped like a three-dimensional C and its impossibly tall pylon erupting out of the center of the marquee, is a real oddity among the stan-dard two-story storefronts of Glendale, a city devoted to conservatism. But the oddest thing about this futuristic façade, which was built in 1939 when the fever for Streamline Moderne and Buck Rogers was at its peak, is that it stands in front of an even stranger design, an exact replica of a Hellenistic movie house. The original theater, with its Greek temple lobby and its portico distyle in antis, opened in 1925, just before Sid Grauman built his famous Chinese Theater in Hollywood (page 242). Despite a thick disguise of yellow paint on the exterior, this elaborately detailed building is still intact. It is reached, as in Grauman's earlier Egyptian Theater, by an open-air walkway behind the box office. A sci-ence fiction stucco roof on rocket-launcher pipe columns now sweeps overhead, managing, at the far end, to conceal the capitals of two mammoth Doric col-umns that hold up the much higher coffered ceiling of the original theater's por-tico; but the rest of the old Greek cinema is all here. Six pairs of double glass doors, etched with floral patterns, are framed by Ionic columns and an entabla-ture that bristles with acroteria. Inside, a large mural covers a far wall, recalling ancient Greek vase paintings. Stairs on each side lead past heroic medallions and victory-wreathed light fixtures to a many-columned balcony. Another cof-

XI 12 · *Alex Theater*

fered ceiling, this time painted gold, once had light bulbs in its rosettes that added a shower of glitter to the architectural odyssey below.

From across the street you can just see a stepped pyramid and large urns that rise above the old entrance of the Greekish theater, standing resolutely in the shadows of that H. G. Wells face lift. It's a little hard to put your finger on it, but there's something extremely L.A. about all of this.

XI 13 · FOREST LAWN

1712 South Glendale Avenue, just north of San Fernando Road, Glendale
Frederick A. Hansen, landscaping and most buildings, 1917 to present
Churches and other buildings open daily, 9–5

Forest Lawn could be seen—indeed, it has been seen, most notably in Evelyn Waugh's *The Loved One*—as a replication of Southern California itself, practically a Garden of Eden, a paradise collaged of lush and beautiful pieces from all over, from Scotland to the Holy Land, diminished just a little by a frontal lobotomy. It reminds the visitor of a sufficient number of real places, but somehow it doesn't have its own reality, as Disneyland does. It is a touch dopey: a critic of my acquaintance compares its look of brainwashed religiosity with that of somebody who has been through Scientology.

But it is a very pretty park, spacious with green lawns, much more like people's expectations of a park than the big real one (Griffith Park) across the way, which is mostly wild and desertlike and scratchy. For "Forest Lawn," it says on the signs, "serves the living"; its Builder's Creed, by founder Dr. Hubert L. Eaton, announces: "I believe in a happy Eternal Life. . . . I therefore prayerfully resolve . . . that I shall endeavor to build Forest Lawn as different, as unlike other cemeteries as sunshine is unlike darkness, as Eternal Life is unlike death." The credo goes on to describe that in the business of undertaking there is no

XI 13 · *Forest Lawn*

XI 13 · *Forest Lawn*

right or wrong, no best way but what's right for "your needs, your lifestyle," and, astonishingly, that no one is turned away for lack of funds.

The format for the place, though there is no serious body of water, is otherwise very like an English park in which strolls (or here, of course, rides) are punctuated with architectural tidbits, not, generally, quite so interesting as the landscape itself. There is, for instance, the Little Church of the Flowers, set up to replicate the church in Stoke Poges that served as the subject for Thomas Gray's "Elegy Written in a Country Churchyard," but so earnestly copied that it ends up seeming to be cast out of plastic, like a hugely blown-up version of electric-train scenery. One's reveries go wrong, especially if the trip is accompanied by the official literature. "When you leave the Memento Shop, you will want to visit [the] Church of the Recessional." Memento shop indeed! It's another of those Southern California pilgrimage places you bring offerings away from, rather than taking the gifts *to* the shrine, as in the previous dispensation. But you do bring dollars, and muse, perhaps, on Perpetual Care. Is there anything about our dollars that can make us sure that these lawns will be mowed until the end of time?

Other wonders attract our attention: Wee Kirk o' the Heather tells "the matchless love story of Annie Laurie" in its stained-glass windows, with their mementoes of Maxwelton. And there's Michelangelo's David, big as ever, and the Crucifixion, the world's largest religious painting, 195 feet long by 45 feet high, big enough for lights to play across its surface to dramatize its story. A museum contains copies of Ghiberti's Paradise Doors from Florence (the copies are impressive, this time) and, they say, perplexingly "copies of rare original sketches by Michelangelo," as well as originals of every coin mentioned in the Bible, also gifts and souvenirs. The Memorial Court of Honor is devoted to the "entombment of world famous immortals" presumably of the sort who had died—John Gutzon Borglum, for instance, and Carrie Jacobs Bond, Rudolf Friml and Hubert Easton himself. Also can be found a 20-by-20-foot mosaic of Trumbull's "The Signing of the Declaration of Independence," accompanied by links from the chain that was strung across the Hudson during the American Revolution. Then there's "The Republic" by Daniel Chester French, which I, for one, admire greatly. A lot of interesting art and architecture and landscape have been collected, but can they bring Eternal Life?

XII / PASADENA

The vast Los Angeles plain, as we've noted, is a wonderfully malleable but essentially featureless desert where the real is phony and exciting rides abound, but fixed places that are at all memorable are widely separated and hard to lodge in the mind or on their sites. The place that has stayed most firmly fixed the longest is surely Pasadena, at the foot of the snow-peaked mountains ten miles northeast of downtown Los Angeles. The vision from the early twentieth century of a day in paradise, which might include breakfast in the sun, a cog railroad ride to the snows of Mount Lowe, lunch in an orange grove and a ride to the beach in Santa Monica, perhaps for a swim, was best centered in Pasadena, perhaps in one of its great hotels. The slide downhill, into smog and urban renewal, started not long after 1925 (I remember having it explained to me in about 1935 how far the place had skidded already). The climb uphill, which started in 1874, didn't take nearly so long. But for all its modest little history, Pasadena has collected an assortment of buildings, especially Craftsman and Spanish Colonial Revival houses, second to none in the L.A. Basin. Berkeley has more Craftsman houses, and Santa Barbara more Spanish Colonial Revival, but Pasadena has them both, and then some.

The city has its present boosters and the boosters write their accounts, which manage often to sound like parodies of a nonhistory. They almost always start with Don Gaspár de Portolá, the Spanish discoverer who almost but not quite looked upon the Valley of the Hahamog-na in 1770. One hundred and four years later, after the local rancho had gone broke an excessive number of times, a group of Hoosier farmers calling themselves "the Indiana Colony" bought the land and settled here. A year sufficed for them to tire of "the Indiana Colony" for a name, and scholarship yielded up the Indian word "Pasadena," which was thought to mean "crown of the valley" in Chippewa. No Chippewa had ever been near the place, but then, when you get right down to it, neither had its founder, Don Gaspár de Portolá.

After the city was properly named, the most noteworthy events came to occur on New Year's Day. In 1890 a pageant called the Battle of the Flowers, combined sometimes with chariot races, developed into an annual Festival of Roses, annexed in 1902 to a notable football game (Michigan 49–Stanford 0), the Rose Bowl, which has been a part of the show ever since. Immigrants of greater than usual age, wealth and cultural attainment were coming already, and being housed in hotels, bungalow courts or their own places, some designed with extraordinary distinction by Greene and Greene and other Craftsman architects. A generation later, about 1925, a new wave of old money was served again, this time by George Washington Smith, Wallace Neff, Roland Coate and

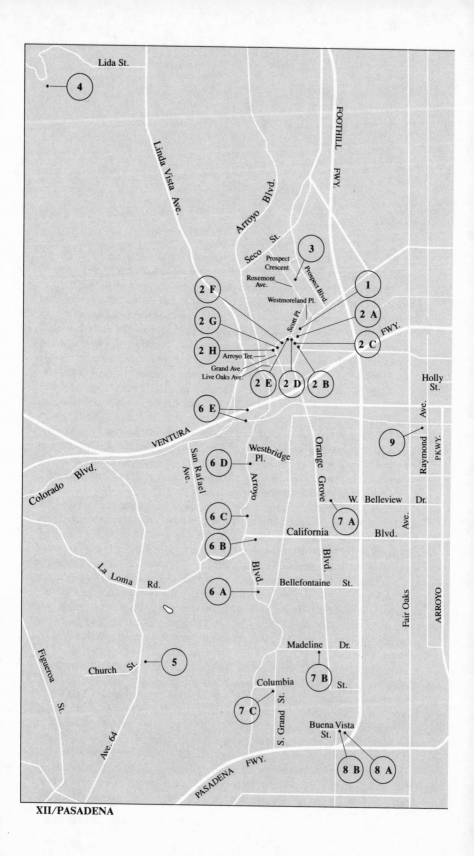

Lida St.

④

Linda Vista Ave.

FOOTHILL FWY.

Arroyo Blvd.

Seco St.

Prospect Crescent

③

Rosemont Ave.

Prospect Blvd.

Westmoreland Pl.

2 F

2 G

Scott Pl.

①

2 A

2 H

2 C

FWY.

Arroyo Ter.

Grand Ave.

Live Oaks Ave.

2 E 2 D 2 B

Holly St.

6 E

Ave.

VENTURA

⑨

Raymond

PKWY.

Westbridge Pl.

Colorado Blvd.

San Rafael Ave.

6 D

Arroyo

Orange Grove

W. Belleview Dr.

6 C

California

7 A

Ave.

6 B

Blvd.

ARROYO

La Loma Rd.

6 A

Blvd.

Bellefontaine St.

Blvd.

St.

Fair Oaks

Figueroa St.

Madeline Dr.

Church St.

⑤

7 B

St.

Columbia

Ave. 64

St.

7 C

S. Grand St.

Buena Vista St.

PASADENA FWY.

8 B 8 A

XII/PASADENA

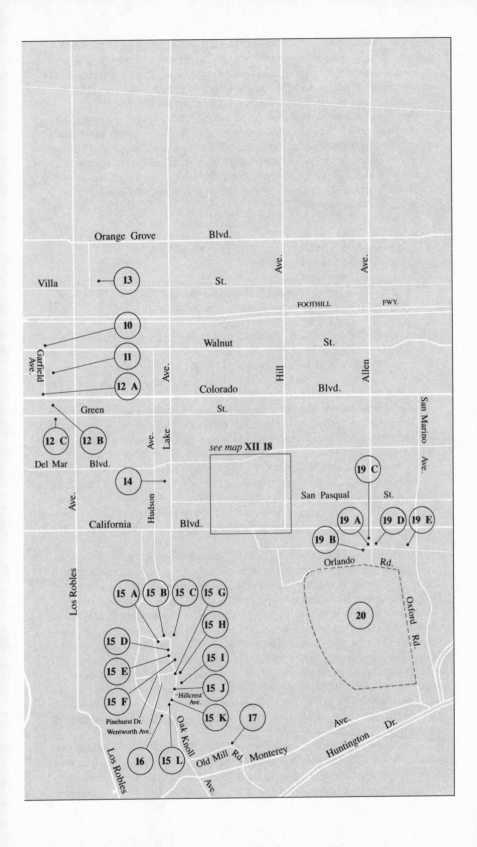

others, who were devising the Golden Age (all white, actually) of the Spanish Colonial Revival. Meanwhile, people who had made it big in chewing gum and streetcars were building more monumental palaces, and civic and industrial self-assurance paved the way for a masterful, airy city hall, a gorgeous Hispanic college campus and one of the world's great assemblages of gardens.

Most of the old money has died in the last half-century, or been driven away by the smog, and it is hard to find a new building with much conviction about it; but many of the fine houses are lovingly maintained by their present owners. There are many citizens around who appreciate them, and there is something special still about Pasadena, not in the air (for which watch out) but close at hand: the largest and finest collection of buildings that bear the Spirit of Ramona to be found anywhere.

XII 1 · GAMBLE HOUSE
4 Westmoreland Place, Pasadena
Charles and Henry Greene, 1908
Now a museum; open to the public every Tuesday and Thursday, 10–3, and the first Sunday of each month, 12–3; admission fee

This openhanded masterpiece of Charles and Henry Greene is the clearest evidence we have of what the good life in Southern California's Golden Age must have been about. It is at once mysteriously shadowy and cheerfully candid, at once special to this place and full of the romance of distant Oriental places, at once puritanically reticent in its spaces and colors and textures and shamelessly sensual in its wooden members—every one of which has been loved and sanded and softened and rubbed and rubbed, as if no tools had even been employed, just somebody lovingly rubbing. Some of the best words to describe this extraordinary place are untranslatable Japanese—*wabi* and *sabi* and *shibui*—all of which have to do with naturalness and the urbane elegance of simple understated rustic things, colored the greens and browns and grays of nature. The Greenes never saw Japan, so their Japanese inspiration was already transformed in books by the time it came to them, and they transformed it further; the Gamble house is far different from the noble houses of Japan in every way except in mood.

The continuing, enduring theme of the house is a love—a passion—for the materials of which it is made, a delight in the way they are joined together, with some of the most poetic hardware in the world. Charles Greene was a craftsman, who might himself have made the first dining-room chair, then have the others copied from it; the whole fabric of the house extends that minute attention usually reserved for fine furniture to the very rafters. The David B. Gambles were heirs to the Procter and Gamble fortune from Cincinnati, and their house cost just over $50,000 in 1908, which bought them a full portion of craftsmanship and care; though the requirements of their relatively unpretentious retirement in the relaxed atmosphere of Southern California are in marked contrast to the Marble house, a Vanderbilt vacation mansion in Newport, Rhode Island, built about the same time, which is supposed to have cost around $11 million.

The Greene Brothers had come West after M.I.T. to join their parents in Pasadena. It was 1893, and they had stopped in Chicago to see the fair, where they had been particularly impressed by the scale model of a Japanese temple. Descriptions of things Japanese were to prove, for them as for others of their generation, a simplifying release from the accumulated stuffiness of the late Victorian western world. In the Greenes' case, this excitement was immediately transmuted into the joining of pieces of well-loved wood, but Oriental images were retained, too: a stylized cloud motif is a continuing theme in the Gamble house; and overhangs and lanterns, as well, recall specific Oriental precedents.

By the time the Gamble house was under construction, the Greenes had been in Pasadena almost fifteen years and had made a number of extraordinary houses, with increasingly free and adventurous plans. The Gamble plan, to the disappointment of historians, presses no innovations and is even a little retro-grade: the plan reads (on paper: it's not particularly clear on the premises) as a long rectangle on the left and a latin cross on the right, with a generous L-shaped entrance and stair hall between. On the ground floor, the left rectangle contains a guest bedroom, kitchen and dining room; the latin cross contains a living room on the back facing a garden-terrace, with Mr. Gamble's den on the front giving onto a large covered porch outside the house.

XII 1 · *Gamble House*

Upstairs, the rectangle houses two big bedrooms and two small ones, while the latin cross, much eaten away by sleeping porches, accommodates two more bedrooms. Once again, a long foyer connects the two portions. Nestled within the roof on the third floor is a billiard room, which was an expensive anomaly for the Gambles, who hated billiards; but the Greenes, with Japanese temples in mind, persuaded them that the extra eave lines of this upper room were essen-tial. The three upper sleeping porches were also more form than function: their skeletal structure and deep shadows expand the house onto the site and prevent the compact, almost stodgy plan from turning in on itself. All of the house's rafters, so thick they had to be tapered and rounded to fit in with everything else, are stout enough to project far beyond the overhanging roofs, so they cre-ate crisp shadows that move across the dark shingled walls and make them come alive.

Two of the most winning attributes of the Gamble house are its near-perfect condition and the fact that it is sometimes open to the public. Detailed and sym-pathetic tours are led by volunteer docents who are under the aegis of the University of Southern California, which owns the house. The tours start at one of the most memorable entrances in the world: a low, very wide wooden door with Tiffany glass panels is flanked by smaller doors, compressed versions of the central one, topped by a clerestory. The stained and leaded glass, green and brown against a milky background, fills every opening to form the continuous tracery of an oak tree.

Inside, the intimate openness of the spaces overpowers any rigidity of the plan. Though the hardwood floors are covered with the Gambles' Persian rugs, the low ceilings speak of Japan. The prominent beams over the low, broad openings closely recall the *nageshi,* which call out, just a little above six feet, the heads of the openings in the rooms of a traditional Japanese house. A beautiful stair makes its way up behind an interlocking banister, a particularly wondrous outcropping of affectionately joined and rubbed wood. In the cross-shaped living room, some more *nageshi* leap across two openings to create an inglenook on one side and a bay with a view on the other. The latter is covered with rugs designed for the room by Charles Greene, rendered in watercolors, then woven in Austria. It does not work to press the Japanese parallel too far, and it is tempting to wonder which of William Morris' works Charles Greene saw during a long trip to England; Morris' house, Whitwick, has a splendid living room, far higher than the Gamble living room but with the same organization; yet the Greenes' softened and loved-up beams are like none of their predecessors', in England or Japan.

The tour looks in on the ground-floor guest room, important to me because a stay for a few days in 1974 persuaded me to come back to Southern California, after thirty-five years of living elsewhere. It's hard to dispute the power of really great architecture. Behind this room is the kitchen, a most congenial place, warm and light, with southern windows through which the sun streams, beautifully crafted worktables, and sinks with the gleam of pewter. The dining room has a view down to the Arroyo Seco just below and such subtleties as a fireplace inlaid with tiles to match a Tiffany urn the Gambles had brought to California.

Outside, an expansive quarry tile and brick terrace embraces, as does the house itself, an enormous eucalyptus tree, one of a pair that was the original focus for the design. A hole in the roof reveals where the other tree used to grow. The terrace ends in an extraordinary little pond with clinker brick walls and edges, about 15 percent Japanese and 85 percent pure Greene and Greene, with a soul-stirring nastiness that occasioned some harsh early reviews but adds some essential grit to the sybaritic Southern California landscape. Past all this a lawn sweeps to the edge of the arroyo and a panorama of the green hills beyond.

Inside again, up those wonderful stairs, the tour goes on to some more bedrooms. The master bedroom, with the wide west view, contains some exquisite light fixtures and maple furniture with silver-and-ebony inlay. The son's room has a fireplace of brick that has been rendered as soft as the wooden beams downstairs. This room, from the beginning, was furnished in craftsman furniture, not Greene and Greene. On up some more stairs is the sheltered but breezy billiard room, now a seminar room, and one of the best examples of a readily habitable space that I know.

The tour goes on out to the garage, where the visitor can these days buy some of the good books about the Greene brothers. This exquisitely crafted house for automobiles becomes a suitable way station; it takes a bit of decompressing to come back from the Golden Age to smoggy present-day Pasadena.

XII 2 · GREENE ENCLAVE

Along Arroyo Terrace, from North Orange Grove Boulevard to North Grand Avenue, Pasadena

Except for the Cole house, all are private residences

As you walk down Westmoreland Place toward Arroyo Terrace, you will notice a certain shingled sameness to the lushly planted terrain, for this is the densest assemblage of houses by Charles and Henry Greene anywhere. Although this tight group of next-door neighbors displays a wide range of the architects' maturing talents, it was once known as "Little Switzerland" because of its consistent homage to the chalet. Before a few of these houses were buried by later alterations, they shared a number of characteristics: all were two stories high with shingle walls and gable roofs; all were built or remodeled during the period just before the great Robert R. Blacker (page 333) and Gamble houses (six were being worked on in 1906); and all were connected by a patterned brick sidewalk and extremely lively retaining wall. The latter was constructed in what became known as "the peanut-brittle style," a Greene invention composed of many-hued clinker bricks and assorted fieldstones that had been carried up from the Arroyo Seco.

A · COLE HOUSE
2 Westmoreland Place
1906
Grounds open to the public

Now the office for the Unitarian Neighborhood Church next door, this carefully maintained house, one of the Greene brothers' best, sports their first porte cochère, which springs forward and lands on two enormous fieldstone posts. These stone mounds in front are relatives of chimneys on the side, made of cyclopean boulders heaved into place with an assurance that causes them, in their wild irregularity, to blend with the gentler shingled shapes of the two-story house. The regular plan of the house is enlivened by porches cut into the front and back of the first floor, by a number of spiky low-pitched roofs over tiny wings and by tall plaster caps on the chimneys. Some recent buildings, a church on the left and a school on the right, seem to have tried to slip into this élite society by wearing fish-scale shingle coats, but their restless manners and their beach ball street lamps give them away.

B · RANNEY HOUSE
440 Arroyo Terrace, on the corner of North Orange Grove Boulevard
1907

Mary L. Ranney, the only employee of the Greene and Greene office to be billed as a designer, did most of the work on this, her own house, which is modest and elegantly restrained: the second floor eases forward slightly to relieve the shingled regularity, and only the purlins project from the simple, overspreading roof. Oddly, a wing on the right has replaced the one she had built at the back, and concrete blocks now line the front yard. But the brick of the sidewalk, the stairways and an entrance wall remain to hint at the virtuoso stonework soon to come along this road.

C · HAWKES HOUSE
408 Arroyo Terrace
1906

The fieldstone excitements begin here, below a tall hedge along the sidewalk, as a low wall mounds up at each side of the driveway to become brick supports for Japanese lanterns. This driveway, itself a swell of brick and stone, spills into the street after flowing past a large covered front porch. The Hawkes, who had rejected a more expensive Greene design, finally just borrowed the plans from their friends, the Bentzes, whose own Greene and Greene house was going up a few blocks away. The only major modification they made to the Bentzes' squarish, two-story, gable-roofed volume of shingles was to add a pergola-like veranda, whose long, oversize timbers help to make this modest house seem more like an estate.

D · VAN ROSSEM–NEILL HOUSE
400 Arroyo Terrace
1903, 1906

Here the Hawkes' low row of fieldstones has bulged suddenly into the boulder base for a stone-splattered clinker brick wall, which, after a narrow pause for a wooden gate, steps up to nearly eight feet at the brick-paved driveway; turning in to protect a front terrace, it changes into an entrance stairway and becomes, finally, the foundation of the house. The house started out as a simple clapboard rental cottage designed by the Greenes for a Mrs. Van Rossem. The cottage is still there, under the shingle surface of the Greenes' own remodeling into a grander house for James Neill, for whom they also added bold wood detailing and a timbered front porch. They lowered the lines of the house as well, with a horizontal strip of first-floor windows, a second-floor planter box, a front terrace and a wisteria-laced pergola that continues over the driveway. The far end of the pergola sits on triangular wood posts above yet another fieldstone wall, which rolls down the driveway and heads back up the street.

E · WHITE SISTERS HOUSE
370 Arroyo Terrace
1903

The low stone wall ambles along under a neat brick cap, swelling lazily into small entrance posts, when, abruptly, it charges up some stairs and bursts forth as the brick-spangled bottom story of a split-level bungalow, designed for the three sisters-in-law of Charles Greene. The dark brown shingles of this otherwise straightforward one-story structure have been replaced by yellow stucco, but the Greenes' first experiments with bracketed timbers are still visible around the front door. The entry lies high above what has now become a stone retaining wall, suddenly so gigantic that it has grown clinkered buttresses and swallowed a garage door.

F · CHARLES GREENE HOUSE
368 Arroyo Terrace
1901, 1906

The stone wall freezes into a triumphal fan of clinker brick above another garage door and then eases down to reveal a charmingly disjointed house above. As before, brick-veined stone posts become a staircase and then a raised foundation, but here the fieldstone capers have been upstaged by a main event, the house of Charles Greene, where he tried out many of the Greene and Greene innovations before passing them along to clients. In 1901, after a honeymoon in England, then the center of the Arts and Crafts Movement, and a love affair with the English country house, Charles Greene was stirred to build this house, called Oakholm. Its front walls still wrap around an enormous live oak whose twisted branches seem to have inspired the design.

The house is a condensed history of the Greenes' development, composed of their favorite materials, from fieldstone and brick to yellow-ocher gunite (a kind of sprayed-on plaster) to shingles and expressed timbers. As it piled up over the years, the unusual geometries became more rectilinear and the details more forceful and refined: the second-floor study, once octagonal like the first-floor living room, was later squared up and given a more characteristic overspreading gable; the frenzied diagonal sheds around the entry were overshadowed in 1906 by a third-floor tower with projecting rafters and a low-pitched roof. This roof became the most distinguishing feature of the Greenes' greatest works, and it served here as the prototype for the extraordinary Duncan-Irwin house, which was soon to follow, next door.

G · DUNCAN-IRWIN HOUSE
240 North Grand Avenue, on the southeast corner of Arroyo Terrace
1900, 1906

The fieldstone wall, low by now, passes by an old reservoir filled in with modern town houses and then continues, covered in vines, around the lawn of a corner lot dominated by one of the Greenes' finest and largest works, the Duncan-Irwin house. Another Greene-on-Greene remodel, this two-story shingled giant, with great overhanging roofs and pergolas and six bedrooms, six bathrooms, six fireplaces, six furnaces and six thousand square feet, altogether overwhelmed Katherine Duncan's little bungalow, the earlier Greene and Greene cottage to which all this was added on. The complex forms and intermingling spaces surround a small central courtyard, which is enlarged by stepped-back balconies and enlivened by a splashing fountain and the crisp shadows of an overhead trellis.

Light streams into the interior rooms through long banks of windows that allow views of the San Gabriel Mountains, the Arroyo Seco and, now, the Rose Bowl. The fieldstone wall has been allowed in along the entrance walkway,

XII 2 G · *Duncan-Irwin House*

where red tiles step up beside an enormous eucalyptus tree. The small stones swell into boulders that support lively masses of clinker brick in the wall of a front terrace, the piers of an entry pergola and the ubiquitous chimneys, whose tops sprout little Orientally roofed houses of their own.

H · JAMES A. CULBERTSON HOUSE
235 North Grand Avenue, at the southwest corner of Arroyo Terrace
1902, 1906–1915; partially destroyed, 1952

On the corner opposite the Duncan-Irwin house lie the remains of one of the Greenes' most unique and carefully crafted houses, which took several years to complete. The Culbertson house once had a mysterious medieval quality to its steep gable roofs and dormers, its half-timbered frame and its rounded bays of diamond-paned or sinuously leaded windows. The interior, a wooden masterpiece, was a mixture of the Orient and Art Nouveau with panels hand-carved by Charles Greene that covered everything. But all this was changed in 1952, when someone lopped off the second story and created an up-to-the-minute California Ranch house. About all that's left are a few well-rubbed beams hiding in corners, an ivy-shrouded pergola and a melancholy peanut-brittle wall.

XII 3 · LA MINIATURA (MILLARD HOUSE)
645 Prospect Crescent, Pasadena
Frank Lloyd Wright, 1923
Private residence

It is against the principles we have set forth to describe in this book a place you can't really see, but it would do even more damage to our principles to leave out the one truly magic Frank Lloyd Wright house in Southern California. La Miniatura, which Wright designed for Mrs. George Millard, a widow, is only a block from the Gamble house, and if you position yourself properly on the sidewalk on Rosemont Avenue you may, through the gate, catch a glimpse of the house from the best-known angle. If you walk around to the other side, on a public drive, you can see the back of the house, pierced only by garage doors and a gate. If the owners are anywhere about, closer approach will be sternly discouraged.

Even from this close, the house keeps to itself, and the published accounts (especially *Frank Lloyd Wright: An Interpretive Biography* by Robert C. Twombley) suggest that the secluded interior is virtually uninhabitable, "a fireproof vault in which casual movement and human clutter seem disrespectful." With all due respect (and I *have* been inside), I don't think so. The two double-height rooms of La Miniatura seem to me among the most superbly habitable spaces in the world, at once grand and hieratic ("like the megaron of a Mycenean lord," as Vincent Scully put it, "opening only in one direction") and, on the other hand, cozy and intimate—partly because it *is* very small, and cared over, inch by inch. Also, an even smaller and more magical two-storied megaron opens in the *other* direction, up the lush miniature canyon on the north side of the house, so that you are not at the edge of somewhere, as a simple megaron might suggest, but right where it all comes together.

None of Wright's houses in Los Angeles has this double-sided richness, though the Hardy house or the Ward Willitts house or the Robie house, back in

XII 4 · *Art Center College of Design*

XII 3 · *La Miniatura*

the Midwest, and numbers of others from Wright's previous decades do it; so you have a fireplace at your back, a view before you, and the chance, with a few steps, to come into another, closely related world that expands in quite another direction. At La Miniatura the first world—solid, space, windows, and arroyo outside—is tiny. The second world is tinier, but complete still, with both high space and low and a grandly monumental opening onto the tiniest of ravines. Of course, it's all made of incredibly fancily articulated concrete blocks, like some crazily impractical concrete lamé that slips it all into the realm of dreams, from which it is half wakened by a nearby guest house by Wright's son, Lloyd Wright.

XII 4 · ART CENTER COLLEGE OF DESIGN
1700 Lida Street, Pasadena
Craig Ellwood Associates, 1976
Open to the public, but no photographs allowed in display areas

You can't miss the Art Center, a sleek black steel-and-glass rectangular mass 627 feet long and 144 feet wide—a two-story truss, apparently, that straddles a 192-foot-wide canyon high up on the chaparral-covered western slope of the Arroyo Seco, looking down on Pasadena. The twisting road to the parking lots in back adds to the tension: it allows an occasional glimpse, and then, abruptly, it sweeps up a deep ravine and passes directly underneath this rigid, unified, simple, serene, bold, clear, controlled, restrained, refined, functional, pure and disciplined box. (Adjectives courtesy of *Progressive Architecture* magazine, August 1977.) The Art Center looks a little as if it had accidentally landed here on this shaggy, impure and specific canyon.

The building, embarrassed maybe by its astonishing contrast with the site, tries to become only one-story high by burrowing into knolls at each end, where the first floors conceal themselves as basements so that the two-story ends look barely higher than the one-story middle. Some of this unity is lost, however, as the middle part expresses itself straightforwardly as a trussed bridge while the ends are forthright glass boxes. But an inexorable beat has been set up, and the whole structure marches to it without a skip—especially the four rows of straight or diagonal members that double-time it across the canyon, sometimes dividing the rooms, sometimes dividing the hallways and sometimes even the doorways of the black-and-white interior.

Though an earlier architect had won an award for a Mediterranean hill town scheme that would have flowed down its hillside, Craig Ellwood triumphed again with this salute to technology and to Mies van der Rohe; this one was built because it was far cheaper, more efficient, less destructive of the environment, and it provided such a dramatic entryway. The building houses, as well, a first-rate art school, so the students' work fairly leaps from the neutral walls; and the carefully arranged views out, especially from open walkways cut in along the bridge, are truly splendid. There is also a special Southern California quality here, very different from the expensively substantial work of Mies himself; this version is pragmatic, realistic, direct, simple, even cheap. From the parking lot the mechanical equipment on the roof all hangs out, and Southern California's prime virtue and vice—its laid-back insouciance—triumphs over the ghost of the taut Teutonic master.

XII 5 · CHURCH OF THE ANGELS
1100 North Avenue 64, on the northeast corner of Church Street, Pasadena
Arthur Edmund Street, Ernest A. Coxhead, 1889
Interior open for Sunday services

The widow of Alexander Campbell-Johnston, a Scot who had developed this area, built the Church of the Angels as a memorial to her husband. She hired the English architect Edmund Street to draw up a version of the Holmbury St. Mary Church in Dorking designed in 1879 by his famous father, George Street. She then retained Ernest Coxhead, a transplanted English architect familiar with the needs of California Episcopalians, to modify the design for the vastly different landscape and way of life in Pasadena. Coxhead made considerable revisions, weaving wit and mystery and a variety of styles into the Victorian Gothic original. Not the least element in this picturesque masterpiece was a reduction in scale sufficient to have made even Walt Disney gasp.

This miniature cathedral of heavy, rusticated sandstone sits with Richardsonian Romanesque substantiality on the small, level part of a hillside above a main canyon thoroughfare. As if by magic, the tranquillity of an English country churchyard hangs in the air, although the shrubs and flowers and chirping birds are pure Southern California; enormous trees, mostly eucalyptus, separate the church almost completely from the nearby houses and traffic.

A massive tower creates a momentary illusion of monumentality, helped upward by long slits of glass, thin columns in narrow belfry openings and a steeply pointed cap; the tiniest of doors, which opens onto a minuscule balcony on the tower's east wall, and the even tinier dormers nearby assist in this vertical fairy tale. But soon the deep horizontal joints in the rough-hewn blocks, the regular bands of smooth, light stones and the rows of shingles on the enormous main roof, which sweeps down to cover a low entrance arcade, bring the eye back down to reality.

A selection of some of the most evocative passages from the catalog of church architecture adds further animation. The great weight of the tan stone wall, the solidity of the red-ochre foundations and columns, and the abbreviation of the openings talk at length of the Romanesque. The half-circle arches agree with this, but hint as well of the California missions; the open arcades and sunny patios are surely Spanish. Around at the apse, the Romanesque arch happens again, bordering a wide-open Gothic display of stained glass and quatrefoil tracery. From here, Tudor half-timbering takes over, all the way around to a half-round baptistry at the back and one last Gothic flourish in the tops of the narrow windows. The heavy wood-shingled roofs, with their tiny dormers, have an Arts and Crafts air, while the intricately joined trusswork underneath recalls the hammer-beams of England. Brass ring pulls and beaten-metal hinges on the thick wooden doors add to the medievalism. The shingled pedestrians' porte cochere, which stretches out from the entry and protects the patio, is perhaps the most remarkable and innovative feature here, with Richardsonian eyebrows arching above the openings.

XII 5 · *Church of the Angels*

Sadly, the church is usually locked up, for the chapel-sized interior is fraught with even wilier wonders. The small pew space, with red-tiled floors and red brick walls, soars up and nearly vanishes in the beautiful dark wood of vaulted sheathing and great semicircular arches. These arches are repeated in a masonry surround, which defines the choir and gives it some distance, and then repeated again in a large window behind the altar. The Gothic dazzle streaming through the stained glass at the end, enhanced by the volumes of darkness overhead, disengages you from the tight plan, and indeed from this whole vale of tears.

XII 6 · SOUTH ARROYO BOULEVARD

Between Bellefontaine Street and Colorado Boulevard, along Arroyo Seco Park, on the west side of Pasadena

South Arroyo Boulevard follows the meandering eastern rim of the Arroyo Seco. Most of the houses along here face west, across the quiet street and the canyon to chaparral-covered hills. Often not much structure is visible beyond the thick foliage made dark by mature shade trees, though enough can be seen to reward a visit.

A · MONTEREY REVIVAL HOUSE
850 South Arroyo Boulevard
Donald McMurray, 1927
Private residence

This Monterey Revival house is surely one of the best examples of its idiom in Pasadena. It is not at all clear whether such a statement carries more praise or question, since the architectural idiom employed in Monterey at the end of the Mexican era was itself a very modest (though endearing) mixture of Spanish, Yankee and probably Caribbean elements. Decades after its genesis, this style became landscaped and prettified, and decades after that it got revived (thus Monterey Revival) and in the process made more elegant but also more denatured; so the most successful examples are often the dullest, like those quintessential Colonial houses of about 1780 in Connecticut, which are almost indistinguishable from WPA-era copies of them.

The Monterey Style is thought to have sprung full-blown from the head of Thomas O. Larkin, the U.S. consul in Monterey, who built a simple two-story house (1834–1937) with a two-story porch all around, also very simple, with a hip hoof. But there are some other houses in Monterey down the street from Larkin's, like the Casa Amesti, gabled and with a balcony on the upper floor front only. It, too, is Monterey Style and was there before Larkin came. Or there is the Abrego adobe, four blocks beyond, one story with a steep, wood-shingled gable roof, adobe walls and a front porch with no rails. It is Monterey Style, too. The upshot is that you can revive any of these, combining the simplicity of the modest adobe houses of Monterey with the understated elegance of American Colonial carried round the Horn. And the further implication is that if you understated it just right, the whole house might just vanish. The character in these places hangs on in a few irregularities and evidences of age, which is very difficult to include in a new house.

So, finally, the Monterey Revival house ought to be modest and pleasant, and a little eccentric. Our Pasadena example is modest and pleasant, and the balcony does droop a little over the driveway.

B · CHEESEWRIGHT HOUSE
686 West California Boulevard, one block east of South Arroyo Boulevard
Jeffrey, Van Trees and Millar, 1910
Private residence

The E.J. Cheesewright house is a shaggy, all-shingle Craftsman cottage (with 3,800 square feet) built for a well-known English interior decorator who must have had Swiss farmhouses or the thatch of the Cotswolds on his mind. Though carefully restored by sensitive owners, the house seems to have fallen under a magic spell in which everything slumbers except the voracious vegetation. Vines have grown everywhere, dripping from the roof, along the walls, over the windows and into the thick hedges and shrubs. A mournful arch in the heavy snubnosed gable roof and the eyebrow dormers above the entrance seem to have joined the vines in this drowsy, picturesque droop. A more cheerful miniature of all this serves as a backyard garage.

C · MANNHEIM HOUSE
500 South Arroyo Boulevard
Jean Mannheim, 1909
Private residence

The small wood sign by the front door still announces, in gold letters, "J. Mannheim Studio," for this comfortable wooden house was also the place of work of the famous Arts and Crafts Movement painter, who designed the building himself. Mannheim's playful ways with texture are initially disguised, first by the light green paint that blends with the robust vegetation, and then by the plainness of this two-story, L-shaped volume beneath its simple roofs; but on the south end there are clapboards on the first floor, shingles on the second, and vertical timbers with plaster infill in the gable, all elegantly crafted and somehow homogeneous. The artful charm, at the edge of prettiness, extends into myriad small-paned windows, a protected front porch and a projecting side pergola, which is a sort of vine-roofed Arcadian porte cochere; all this lies behind friendly fieldstone walls only a few stones high and red camellias blooming in the dappled light of live oaks.

D · BARBER HOUSE
270 South Arroyo Boulevard
Roland E. Coate, architect; Katherine Bashford, landscape architect, 1925
Private residence

The lot here is not very big, but it is very deep, with the house way at the back and a narrow brick walkway shooting toward it. The long front garden recalls at once, in miniature, the inexorable axiality of the Renaissance and that arcane word of twentieth-century landscape architects—ecotone—which glorifies the edge of the forest, where trees and bushes meet the grass, which in this case flanks the little brick sidewalk. The house, just behind a low wall with a white gate, is symmetrical, of two-story New England Colonial persuasion with a Monterey front porch. The simple wood posts and railing of the upstairs balcony, along with white-painted brick walls and a heavy shake roof, create a solid vision of the Old West. But it is the enormous, cleverly tamed forest in front that does the most for the image. The mowed grass on each side of the walkway develops quickly into increasingly higher and wilder shrubs, and finally into tall sycamores that frame romantic views both in and out.

A block north of the Barber house, an opening in the trees reveals two colossal and beautiful bridges (6 E) that carry Colorado Boulevard and the new freeway across the arroyo. The former, the Colorado Street Bridge (John Drake Mercereau, designer and engineer, 1912–1913), is in the Roman aqueduct style, a curving progression of arches whose thin columns make the canyon look even deeper than it is; the newer one attempts to imitate the first but is not half so grand. Together, they form a striking, complex composition that seems to have conquered the rugged terrain as surely as all these houses have grown into it.

XII 7 · PASADENA PASTICHE
Southwestern part of Pasadena

One of the architectural tempests raging these days, sized for a larger-than-usual teapot, is the controversy between those of us who believe that most of the excitement derived from buildings of the past comes in the interpretation, even the transformation, of their imagery and those who believe that virtue lies in fidelity. The fidelitous stuff is hard for us to be particularly gracious about, and these three Pasadena mansions abound in it.

A · STEWART HOUSE
365 West Bellevue Drive, Pasadena
James Rhodes, ca. 1910
Private residence

The Stewart house is either a Swiss chalet or a Bavarian hunting lodge. An enormous, low-pitched gable roof overspreads the simple rectangular volume of the house. Elaborate brackets support a wide overhang and a second-story balcony, which casts long shadows down the dark wood of the south-facing façade. All the chalet details are here, mostly in the matching scroll-saw cutouts of the numerous brackets, the balustrade on the balcony and the trim around the small-paned windows. Bright flowers accent the base of this swelled-up mountain cottage, while the bright green front lawn, spilling down a small berm, works hard at being a meadow. Oddly, this Alpine setting is framed along Bellevue Drive by some of the tallest palm trees in Pasadena.

B · CRAVENS HOUSE
430 Madeline Drive, Pasadena
Lewis P. Hobart, ca. 1929
Now the Pasadena Chapter of the Red Cross; open to the public, Monday through Friday, 8:30–5

The Cravens house is a massive French chateau. It once had grounds more in keeping with its size, but its long drive, which led from a gateway on Orange Grove Boulevard (once lined with mansions), is now the entrance to a gaggle of condominiums done in a brick-and-stucco, mansarded French style. Asphalt parking has closed in to the very edges of the chateau, although the balustraded formal gardens, which terrace down the hill behind, are almost intact.

Its grandeur may have been pinched, but the 24,000-square-foot mansion is still awe-inspiring. Red brick, trimmed in white block relief, covers the two-story structure (of reinforced concrete!). The steep gray Vermont slate roof, hipped on the wings and mansarded across the symmetrical main block, is vivified with two sizes of dormers and a great number of tall chimneys. Enormous French doors march all the way around, opening, on the first floor, beneath two types of arches and, on the second, behind ornamental iron railings.

The Red Cross offices, which allow our entry, have barely touched the exuberant interior. A mural (by Ernest Peixotto) in the marble-floored vestibule depicts the château at Vaux le Vicomte, which supposedly was the grandiose inspiration for all of this. With the (free) floor plan in hand, you should find the *trompe l'oeil* lattice arch in the solarium, the elaborate paneling and the parquet floor in the living room, more fancy woodwork and a checkerboard marble floor in the dining room, and an oval staircase that follows the curves of an ornamental skylight to the bedrooms and their carved marble fireplaces.

C · BEHR HOUSE
225 South Grand Avenue, on the southwest corner of South Grand and Columbia Street, South Pasadena
Reginald Johnson, 1919
Private residence

The Behr house is an Italian villa. A high, mottled gray-and-peach plastered wall, with orange trees peeking over its top, lines the sidewalks around its large corner lot. Openings on each street allow views of the peaceful mansion behind a mature formal garden. Tall pine trees, cypresses, shrubs and vines grow right up against the two-story rectangular volume of the house, so its burnt-sienna and red-ochre walls and low, red-tiled roofs glow through the dark green foliage.

The classic villa details are most visible from the new Grand Avenue entryway, a wrought-iron gate between statue-capped plaster piers. One of the house's two side wings, which have been slightly recessed and lowered to set off the main block, lies at the end of the driveway, whose large squares of rose-colored concrete are separated by crushed granite. The elaborate dark wood of the eaves plays against the plaster walls, which are punctured symmetrically by deep windows in small arches framed with Corinthian pilasters on the first floor and in large Palladian motifs on the second. Sometimes, classical music drifts down from these windows, mixing with the soft splashes of an unseen fountain, so perfect is the ambience.

XII 8 · LONGLEY HOUSE
1005 Buena Vista Street, South Pasadena
Charles and Henry Greene, 1897
Private residence

The Howard Longley house (8 A) is the earliest-known Greene and Greene structure still standing, a strange essay in eclecticism, built during the stylistic muddle of the 1890s before the Greenes had developed an architecture of their own. The fan-lighted, side-lighted, vaguely Palladian front door and the Classical moldings around some of the second-floor windows probably reflect the young Greenes' recent Beaux-Arts training; but the fledgling architects appear to have taken tentative steps in other directions as well.

Below a well-mannered, Mission Style pediment, French doors open onto a second-floor porch, whose shingled railing frowns down to become a mansarded entry roof; this is supported on the bulbous capitals of slender, fluted columns that mingle with the other elements in a manner mildly Oriental. The stepped, double-arched windows nearby look Spanish or Moorish, while the diamond-shaped panes nearly everywhere else seem to have been lifted from three sizes of English cottages. The shingled skin on this stout Richardsonian Romanesque volume swells out a little at the first-floor windows and eases forward on the right to form a hesitant, perhaps Second Empire tower beneath an Italianate roof. Its peak is capped by cryptic, metal pyramidal finials, which in no way presage Goodhue's on the L.A. Public Library. It is a fascination how this lurching architectural travelogue could have led to the surefooted genius of these architects' work not much later. This is a building to inspire hope in any designer.

The Longley house invites comparison with its far simpler next-door neighbor at 1001 Buena Vista (8 B), designed by the Greenes in 1904 for the widow of President James A. Garfield. As unprepossessing as the Longley house is possessed, this nearly symmetrical, three-story, shingled cube (a basement opens up as the site descends) lies mute beneath medium-steep gables. It was built during the Greenes' Swiss Chalet period; only the slightly rounded, mortised timbers around the entrance hint of the Oriental pleasures soon to come.

XII 9 · HOTEL GREEN
50 East Green Street; original entrance on South Raymond Avenue, Pasadena
Frederick L. Roehrig, 1899, 1903
Now the Castle Green Apartments, a private residence, but the grounds are open

During the years before World War I, the Green was one of America's most prestigious resort hotels, a grand reflection of its enthusiastic owner, Colonel G. G. Green, who built it with the fortune he had made in patent medicine. The hotel used to be even bigger than it is now. Another building (the original part of the hotel, built in 1890) was connected by a long pedestrian bridge across Raymond Avenue to the structure you see today; the earlier building was torn down in 1924, and the remaining part of the bridge now comes to an awkward stop above the sidewalk. Today it is hard to imagine that, during the reigns of Edward VII and William Howard Taft, this elevated promenade was the most fashionable place in town to sip tea and watch the Rose Parade as horses pulled the floats beneath. During that gilded age before the war, Benjamin Harrison, Grover Cleveland, Theodore Roosevelt, John D. Rockefeller and all the rest stayed in this American palace and enjoyed the best of the Southern California good life.

This six-story extravaganza has managed to combine freely the fanciest elements of that era's most treasured styles, especially Spanish, Moorish and Classical. The covered bridge, with its red-tiled roof, domed turret and strange balconies, has a style all its own as it slumps along on oddly buttressed limbs through thick foliage and tall palms, then enters the middle of the building above a long, fat-columned veranda. The central portion of the somewhat symmetrical, nearly flat façade of the hotel rises above the bridge to a pair of squat towers, which are topped by red domes and joined by a delicate arcade. On the south end are two more towers, round this time, which manage to clear the roof with their open viewing galleries.

The north end has been altered by a pale and precise 1903 addition, a block-long wing along Green Street. Though designed just four years after the rest of the building, and by the same architect, the sobriety of the newer part contrasts sharply with the lively confusion, everywhere else, of bi- or tripartite loggias, wrought-iron balconies and other protuberances, windows of every size and location, machicolated string courses, narrow layers of red-tiled roofs, and Classical balustrades, all interwoven with Sullivanesque ornament on Romanesquely massive walls of rough yellow-ochre plaster. If there is a theme to this playful collection, it is one of large, round things bulging even larger, from the bulbous columns to the distended domes and turrets and even to the first-floor lounges, where enormous curved sash windows reveal the extraordinary craftsmanship and grand luxe of everything here.

Today this once grande dame speaks sadly of having outlived her time: the magic of the gardens has disappeared; the yellowed plaster, grimy and morose, seems to hang from the heavy walls, while the flamboyant details now appear slightly sinister; and the windows, with their air-conditioner boxes, have turned inward from the traffic and the smoggy streets of this industrialized part of Pasadena. The palatial Hotel Green has become an apartment home for the elderly; it's now a castle, locked up, defensive and silent, except for a small fountain by the veranda that still splashes out a tune of long ago for residents who might have honeymooned here.

XII 9 · *Hotel Green*

XII 10 · PASADENA PUBLIC LIBRARY
285 East Walnut Street, at North Garfield Avenue, Pasadena
Myron Hunt and H. C. Chambers, 1927
Open Monday through Thursday, 9–9; Friday and Saturday, 9–6; Sunday,
*   1–5; closed on major holidays*

The pioneering Indiana Colony, which laid out the streets of Pasadena in 1873, allotted eight acres for a civic center. Here, fifty-four years later, the library became the first of three major public buildings to make a Beaux-Arts axis out of Garfield Avenue: the library and the Civic Auditorium (1932) closed off its north and south ends, while City Hall (also finished in 1927) became the focus alongside the midpoint of the two-block street. Although the post office of 1913 had been made to face around the corner onto Colorado Boulevard rather than onto the Garfield axis, it did establish a civic tradition of blocklike symmetry, red-tiled roofs and plain plaster walls that contrast with an elaborate entrance loggia of five arches. The quattrocento solidity of the post office relaxed, after fourteen years, into the gentilities of the library's Spanish Colonial Revival and was stirred into a blend of airy Beaux Arts meringue at City Hall; then, five years later, it was solidified back into the Renaissance at the Civic Auditorium, which looks like the kind of Italianate recollection that might grace a middle-size industrial city in Mexico.

The plain, cream-colored walls of the U-shaped library are three stories high at the central block and one floor lower on a pair of arms that reach out toward the street. An entrance courtyard in between, where tall Mexican fan palms wave, is enclosed by a one-story screen connecting the end walls, which is pierced by a set of five gateways. One-story additions flank this central portion, so the whole library seems to hug the ground—in deference, perhaps, to the San Gabriel Mountains, which on a clear day tower up behind. Attention focuses finally on five arched windows (as at the post office) high in the center of the main block, framed this time by Corinthian columns and cast-concrete ornament in an enthusiastic Italo-Iberian Classicism of acanthus leaves, scrolls, urns, griffins, keystones, putti and, of course, books.

The journey to the interior is enlivened by subtle changes of level and becomes a carefully modulated procession away from the bustle of the street to the calm of the grand hall. Wide steps rise slowly from the sidewalk to a small podium of a terrace. Then openings in the front screen lead through a shadowy shed-roofed colonnade and out into a sunny, brick-paved square atrium; in the center is a fountain modeled after the Mirador de Daraxa at the Alhambra; on each side lies a square that same size, but two feet higher and filled with plants. (The separation is now delicately underlined with a chain-link fence.) The covered colonnade, with its assortment of mysterious capitals, continues around both sides of this front court and, on the back, becomes the rusticated stone entry to the library; its three doors, reached by three more wide steps, lead to a low room that heightens the surprise of the last episode: the enormous main hall leaps up almost forty feet to the dark wood coffers of its ceiling, past a wainscot of Doric bookshelves and white plaster walls and vast volumes of silence.

XII 11 · PASADENA CITY HALL
100 North Garfield Avenue, Pasadena
John Bakewell and Arthur Brown, Jr., 1925–1927

The Pasadena City Hall is a piece of cake—a jubilant, flamboyant, frothed-up wedding cake, full of air on the inside; not a doughy lump of rooms here, but an airy courtyard, with trees and flowers and a grand central fountain splashing, entered through a spacious domed tower you can see right up through—a frothy delicacy with no calories at all.

The architects, Bakewell and Brown, seem to have had an uncanny sense of what they could do spectacularly well, and how they could fit that to the rather

XII 10 · *Pasadena Public Library*   XII 11 · *Pasadena City Hall*

special images of their clients in Pasadena. Thirteen years earlier, they had confected the San Francisco City Hall, a high-calorie special, robust and rotund, with classicizing details of the French Beaux-Arts persuasion handled with such verve and sophistication that they come off Baroque. For Pasadena, they whipped up the French neo-Classical-into-Beaux-Arts details they did so well into an aerial frenzy so dazzling and so dreamy that it was received as Mediterranean fantasy–Spanish—rather like Bertram Grosvenor Goodhue's Churrigueresque fantasies that had been such a triumph at the 1915 San Diego fair.

The other California fair of 1915, the Panama-Pacific Exposition in San Francisco, had offered up a parallel success: Bernard Maybeck's Palace of Fine Arts, which, like Goodhue's pavilions, is still there to see. Its details are different, more flowing and grandiloquent, but the confident gesture of throwing an empty space skyward to make a pavilion of air finds an echo in Pasadena.

The celebratory gusto of the Pasadena building is even more spectacular at night, when the walls are floodlit; since they rise in stepped-back planes, they afford excellent places for hiding the sources, so the building floats into dreams like a high-wattage Franco-Arabian nights, predating by some twelve years the next California World's Fair—Treasure Island, in San Francisco in 1939, which must be the closest humankind has come yet to an electrically illuminated dreamland.

There are rooms within, but they mostly open onto loggias, so they maintain an easiness, reflecting, as the guide pamphlet says, "the casual elegance of Pasadena."

XII 12 · POST OFFICE
Northwest corner of North Garfield Avenue and Colorado Boulevard, Pasadena
Oscar Wenderoth, 1913; Marston and Maybury, additions, 1938

This Italian Renaissance palazzo, which serves the people of Pasadena as a post office (12 A), speaks of the confident dignity of Old Money; indeed, the citizens themselves paid for the marble to make the government-issue building more agreeable. This two-story rectangular block, with a mild one-story addition behind, faces Colorado Boulevard with unswerving symmetry beneath an overhanging red-tiled roof. The cream-colored plaster walls, whose ends edge forward to frame the middle, become a spare contrast to the embellishments carved in the white marble of the first floor and the gray wood of the soffits. Plain windows on the second floor echo the rhythm of more elaborate openings below, particularly an entrance arcade of five identical arches that rises above a wide staircase.

This series of five arches, which is repeated again and again inside the building, forms the meter for a finely choreographed sequence of spaces. First, behind the entrance arches, comes a barrel-vaulted gallery, a sunny transition between inside and out that is made even brighter by white marble walls and white tiles overhead. The five entrance arches, which have grown into crossvaults, are duplicated on the opposite wall; three of these, at the ends and in the middle, have doors that lead to the next event, three tiny vestibules, each with another arch at its far end. Here a low ceiling and an even lower transom in this last arch have set you up for a thrill: this serenely reserved post office has suddenly exploded into a full-blown Farnese Palace of a courtyard with natural light glowing through a gold- and beige-tinted glass ceiling.

XII 12 A · *Post Office*

The sides of the great two-story lobby are all Classically detailed loggias that gleam in ocher and rose-colored terra cotta. On the second floor, piers and composite columns support basket arches that open onto narrow walkways. On the first floor, the half-round arches show up again, framing counters or doors or, on the north, entrances to the addition, which is a one-story anticlimax where the arches, now in plaster, have been reiterated once too often. But the main room is wonderful: it maintains your excitement long after the surprise wears off.

Across Colorado Boulevard from the post office looms Plaza Pasadena (12 B), praised by mild-mannered *Progressive Architecture* magazine as "a kind of landmark in contextual sensibility for new urban commercial centers of such scale." That means, presumably, that it's a rather docile bull in this china shop. Its stores mostly face into an enclosed pedestrian street, while the real streets bask in the sunshine. At the end of Garfield Avenue, the mall's many-layered triumphal arch marks the southern end of the library–City Hall axis. Through the corrugated glass walls of this vaguely Palladian window, which is said to recall the tunnels on the Pasadena Freeway, you can just see the Italian Renaissance City Auditorium (12 C), a palazzo with cheerful blue tiles on those same familiar five arches and with flamboyant City Hall finials on the roof. It used to mark the end of this axis, and still tries.

XII 13 · BOWEN COURT BUNGALOWS
539 East Villa Street, a block and a half east of Los Robles Avenue, Pasadena
Arthur Heineman (Alfred Heineman, designer), 1911
Private residences

Here, in one group, are some of Los Angeles' best-preserved bungalows, the Southern California phenomenon that became, from about 1880 through the 1920s, one of the most widely produced building styles in America. As Robert Winter describes it in his book *The California Bungalow,* the British in India picked up the idea from the Bengali *bangala,* low, open-planned cottages in the countryside; and the English Arts and Crafts Movement spawned rustic retreats surrounded by gardens in England and then New England. But it was in Southern California where a mild climate, plentiful land and waves of new people migrating to it all combined with a new middle-class populism and a flamboyant boosterism to create row upon row of simple, land-hugging, single-family houses, each in its own autocelebratory yard.

In one sense, the electric trains and then the automobiles were responsible for the vast sprawl of Los Angeles; but just as important were the commuters' destinations, these affordable little cottages, which, like the automobile, combined a certain amount of panache with a great deal of utility. Gone were the many tight Victorian rooms, replaced by a few moderately sized spaces, usually all on one floor, which flowed together and eventually outside to conjure up expansiveness on a low budget; but the price still included the most modern amenities in plumbing, lighting and kitchen gadgetry. Although the later bungalows were often plastered in Spanish or Pueblo ways, the Craftsman Movement, with some Japanese and Swiss longings, supplied most of the charms: gently pitched roofs, with an occasional low dormer, projected far over the dark, often shingled wood walls and rested on the tapered posts of ingratiating front porches; inside, the living and dining rooms were comfortably rustic, with wood paneling and cozy inglenooks, while the bedrooms, kitchen and bath gleamed in modern white plaster.

While Los Angeles must have the most bungalows anywhere on the planet and Pasadena sports some of the best, almost every city in America still has acres of them; even Frank Lloyd Wright designed a few. The Heineman brothers, two Los Angeles architects, seem to have designed most of the bungalows (at least locally), which were built either from their own plans or from prolific plagiarisms of them; anybody, it was said, could build a bungalow. Charles and Henry Greene, who had earlier designed many simple little ones, proved later in their careers that even high-art architects could build large and elaborate ones for the very rich.

The Heinemans designed Bowen Court, one of the first of its kind, as a pastoral haven for wealthy Easterners to vacation in. The Greenes, used to more room, described it as "hopelessly crowded." The density is even greater today, for the twenty-three holiday cottages have been divided into thirty-five apartments, but the place seems more beautiful and inhabitable than ever: the much ballyhooed natural setting has by now grown lush. A low, vine-covered brick wall undulates into a front gateway, announcing the separation of this miniature oasis from the rest of the world. A narrow walkway, lined with hedges and tiny lawns, runs down the center of this long, L-shaped forest, passing through sunny clearings and then green tunnels of dappled light. The close proximity of the bungalows begins to relax; the dark green and earthy red of the low wood walls, which seem lower still with their variety of horizontal texturings, is hardly discernible from the boughs and shrubs and vines that grow everywhere, although flowers and white-trimmed windows sparkle from the shadows.

Bowen Court holds another small place in history in that its plan developed into the first motel. In 1925 the same Alfred Heineman designed the first motel in America, the Milestone Mo-tel in San Luis Obispo (which still stands, on Monterey Street near US 101 North), though his concurrent copyright of the word Motel must have faded, by now, into the public domain.

XII 14 · BULLOCK'S
401 South Lake Avenue, between East Del Mar Boulevard and San Pasqual Street, Pasadena
Wurdeman and Becket, 1947

Bullock's department stores, as they have branched across Southern California, have managed to reflect both the times and a sure sense of what makes Southern California magical—Ramona up to date. By far the most striking is Bullock's Wilshire (page 147), of 1929, as stunning as an architectural monument as it is important in pioneering urbanism, facing at once the major street in front and a major parking lot on the opposite front. The two most memorable Bullock's stores built after World War II, in Westwood (page 207) and Pasadena, are much blander as urban design, with parking lots on both ends of the latter in a manner that was becoming standard. They are also much more recessive as architecture, though their slick, streamlined shapes are maneuvered with considerable sophistication and laid-back verve.

Bullock's Pasadena comes off as a richly landscaped oasis. Its architects took advantage of a site that slopes down to the south to allow entry from the south parking at the lower level of the store and from the north parking at a mezzanine level. Lake Street, which runs north and south, is separated from the building by a thickly planted berm, so grandly exotic planting provides the intricate ornament that the style of the forties denied itself; but what was allowed, and the architects helped themselves to it, was an extensive catalog of surface textures, from stainless steel to smooth concrete to rough flagstone to showcases of wood.

Inside is an equally convincing repertoire of spaces, sometimes vast, sometimes cozy, high or low, long or square. Their wall surfaces, cabinets, cash-register islands and display cases are finished extremely variously in mirrors, stucco, flagstone, brass, many kinds of blond wood veneers—even tapestries and murals—but a single attitude toward a kind of well-bred restraint holds it all together. The cosmetic department perhaps says it most clearly: the room is long, narrow and tall, with natural light from the north end. Behind the glass counters, which run along both long sides and into shallow alcoves, a wainscot of blond wood cabinets is topped by a muted mural of tropical foliage in tones of blue. The occasional columns are all mirrored, base to capital. There is no tension in all this muted elegance, but rather a relaxed drift through the good life.

XII 15 · OAK KNOLL
Southern edge of Pasadena

Oak Knoll was, from the beginning, one of Pasadena's fanciest subdivisions, with curving streets that preserved the knolls and the oak trees, and with sites that often brought out the best in some of California's finest architects. Here, across Hillcrest Avenue from each other, are two of Charles and Henry Greene's largest, most elaborate and carefully crafted works. Just down the same street from these, in a two-block stretch, is a collection of houses by a large number of other noteworthy architects. What boggles the mind is that, in this small area of Pasadena, there are blocks and blocks of streets almost as crowded with wonders as this one. Gebhard and Winter list many of them in their excellent *Guide to Architecture in Los Angeles and Southern California;* we have picked a few favorites.

A · ROBERT R. BLACKER HOUSE
1177 Hillcrest Avenue, Pasadena
Charles and Henry Greene, 1907
Private residence

Although most of its great lawns and Japanese-inspired gardens have been sub-divided, the two-story, dark-shingled Blacker house, the grandest bungalow ever constructed, is still imposing, commanding the most prestigious site in Oak Knoll. The nearly symmetrical front façade, with two overspreading end gables that become wings in the back, faces Hillcrest Avenue, while an elaborately timbered porte cochere erupts diagonally from the central entrance to claim the

XII 15 A · *Robert R. Blacker House*

corner of Wentworth Avenue as well. This foray is balanced, to a degree, by similar timbers on a long balcony that covers the living-room terrace on the left. The huge house presents a strong, spiky silhouette on the north front, but heavy roofs and strong horizontal lines manage to give it a land-hugging bungalow demeanor that belies its 12,000 square feet.

The dark walls are enlivened by the flowers and trees and rolling lawns of a flourishing, if now foreshortened garden. The Blacker house is perhaps the finest demonstration of the Greene and Greene philosophy of building for the warm climate and permitting a comfortable relationship between indoors and out. Deep overhangs of the roofs shield the sun, while openings in the Oriental latticework of the gables vent the high attic. Great banks of casement windows and French doors on the main floors allow cross-ventilation, views of the garden and immediate access to decks or to brick and red-tiled terraces that surround the house. Even the billiard room in the basement was uncovered by a southeast roll in the landscape to get its own garden door, its own terrace and natural light. And organic forms from the garden make their way inside, in plaster friezes on the walls and ceilings and in the Tiffany glass of windows and lampshades.

Although Mr. Blacker was in the lumber business, the house still cost over $100,000, twice as much as the Gamble house, enough to buy the full range of the Greene perfection at its peak. Orientally inspired intricacies abound: simple railings, curved corner braces and graceful copper drainpipes seem to grow out of the structure for reasons of their own; and a sinuous motif, which begins in the teak front doors, finds its way into a three-paned portion in almost every window of the house and then continues inside, carved into the teak or mahogany walls—even the lighting fixtures and switchplates match the wood of the walls.

B · CORDELIA A. CULBERTSON HOUSE
1188 Hillcrest Avenue, Pasadena
Charles and Henry Greene, 1911
Private residence

Across the street from what used to be the Blackers' enormous east lawn, the Culbertson house is another of the Greenes' most elaborate and expensive works, although looking at the modest front on Hillcrest Avenue you would never guess it. The one-story, splayed U-planned house, with one wing parallel to the street, focuses demurely on its interior courtyard and on what once was a magnificent garden down the steep slope at the back. The low, ocher-colored plaster walls, the blocks of rectangular windows and the simple gable roofs combine with a bright green lawn to seem, at first glance, more an upper-income ranch house than an estate. Although the walls are made of gunite, the lovingly joined and sanded beams are still present, becoming a spare, linear contrast to the new plastic medium, making up the roof overhangs, the garden trellises and the huge piers of a long pergola that shields the driveway from the courtyard. The Oriental theme is present, too, in the green roof tiles, in the tiled gate on the left, and in the entry, whose raised and overhanging roof, with the air of a pagoda, is supported, apparently, on its graceful copper downspouts.

The house was designed meticulously around the needs of the three daughters of James A. Culbertson, who had his own Greene and Greene masterpiece on Arroyo Terrace (page 318). On this site developed what must, for all its small size, have been one of history's most aggravated little chapters in the age-long search for perfection. Between the Greene brothers, already fussy to a fault, and three dazzlingly persnickety maiden sisters, the rush to perfect and multiply the rooms and the plaster friezes in them, and the lacquered wood trim and the well (if frenziedly) rubbed columns and furniture would have been headlong. The monomania must have rolled on outside, on wider and wider terraces, down the formal stone staircase and into the huge garden, past the arbor and the lily pond and over the brink: in just five years the Culbertsons sold their precise paradise because it had cost far too much.

HILLCREST MEDLEY
1200–1425 Hillcrest Avenue, Pasadena
Private residences

Almost next door to each other on two blocks of Hillcrest Avenue are about a dozen of Pasadena's most remarkable houses, designed by an array of famous architects. Most of these houses were built between 1909 and 1926, so they span the two great periods in this city's architectural history: the wooded Craftsman era (led by the Greene brothers) before World War I and the white-walled golden age of Spanish Colonial Revival in the mid-1920s. A few houses in this collection were built or bizarrely remodeled much later in this century and speak of another, lesser period after the smog arrived.

First, at 1200 Hillcrest, comes the International Style Hurschler house (15 C) (Gregory Ain, 1950), a strange next-door neighbor of the Culbertson house. Ain designed it when functionalism was at its most ardent, so it looks a lot like one of Neutra's elementary schools. The house's one-story intimacy takes away some of the earnestness, but more helpful still is the manner in which it is sited, nearly hidden behind a vast front lawn and a large Chinese elm.

Down the street are two splendid Spanish Colonial Revival houses, next door to each other. The first, at 1265 Hillcrest, is the Griffith house (15 D) (Roland Coate, 1925). This straightforward arrangement of white plaster and red tile is an unusually beautiful way to make a house. A one-story living room volume, in front of a two-story bedroom wing, provides an inviting, human-scaled entrance. At the same time, the almost blank front wall gives the entire house an importance without going to a lot of fuss: a gutter along the roofline becomes a handsome molding, while a simple frame turns the little front door into a grand welcome. Next door, at 1275 Hillcrest (15 E), an earlier Griffith house (Johnson, Kaufmann and Coate, 1924) is another straightforward and pleasing use of the Spanish idiom, but with a shingled roof instead of red tile. Set behind a large lawn, the two-story house forms an L around an entrance courtyard. Although a high wall protects the other two sides of this patio, an iron-grilled opening next to the front gate allows an enticing glimpse of the pleasures within.

At 1290 Hillcrest is another fine Spanish Colonial Revival house (15 F), built for the Elliots in 1925 by Wallace Neff, a celebrated master of this sort of thing. A driveway flanked by kumquat trees pierces a thick mass of foliage along the sidewalk and opens directly onto a flagstone courtyard; a fountain spews up cactus in the center while the two-story house curves around behind. A low garage continues the curve on the left, but it is nearly hidden, like everything else on the first level, behind dense foliage. In the middle, below a triple-arched loggia, a glassy entry lets you peek right through the house to more jungles in the back. Usually, two white cars are parked in the courtyard. (If you belong to the upper classes in Pasadena, you really have to drive a white car, and that is just all there is to that.)

The two-story Prindle house (15 G) at 1311 Hillcrest was designed in 1926 by George Washington Smith, who some say was the greatest practitioner of the Spanish Colonial Revival. This white-plastered assemblage of big and small things under an assortment of gable roofs is as lively as the spiky palm trees around it, but, in the hands of a man who really knew what he was doing, the house maintains the dignified demeanor alluded to by the manicured lawns in front. Smith demonstrates his mastery over huge leaps in scale: on the right side of the house, enormous corbels hold up a wondrously tiny porch, while to the right of the entry iron brackets support the balustrade of an upstairs window, easing the transition to the much fancier ironwork below; to the left of the entry, brackets show up again as machicolations along the top of a tower, but these are at the scale of the cornice moldings, which help bring the many red-tiled roofs together.

Across the street, at 1330 Hillcrest, is the huge Freeman house (15 H) (Arthur and Alfred Heineman, 1913). The Heineman brothers, who designed more bungalows than anyone else in the world (page 331), have made, this time, a considerable mansion from their repertoire of Craftsman cottage parts. Shingled roofs droop over vast white plaster walls, which have been scaled down by thick window frames and Tudor-like half-timbers. On each side of the generous entry, a one-story wing and a pretty bay window manage to add a little more charm to this big-time bungalow.

Hidden behind flowering hedges at 1344 Hillcrest, the Spinks house (15 I) is a big, simple barn of a house designed by the Greene brothers in 1909, two years after the Blacker estate. This dark-shingled, two-story volume beneath its straightforward gable roof does not even try to compete with the masterwork up the street, but just quietly enjoys its own tree-shaded lawns and mountain views. The chimney, however, reveals an attitude: a white stucco ghost chimney, which sticks up far enough to satisfy the building code, rises out of a brick one, which is the size deemed correct for the proportions of the composition.

The rest of the houses on this street seem less self-confident. At 1365 Hillcrest, the Landreth house (15 J) (Reginald Johnson, 1918) is a rather nervously grand Federal mansion, sort of Lana Turner Hollywood. At 1409 Hillcrest the pleasant Spanish Colonial Revival Osthoff house (15 K) (George Washington Smith, ca. 1923) has been heavily West Hollywooded (page 226), with thin shutters and plastic mullions. It shares the same hill and a similar hesitancy with its neighbor at 1425 Hillcrest (15 L), a sort of Tudor effulgence of the freeway era. Near here, Hillcrest Avenue ends at the Huntington-Sheraton Hotel, which has itself undergone a number of retrofittings but is still grand in places.

XII 16 · HUNTINGTON-SHERATON HOTEL
1401 South Oak Knoll Avenue, Pasadena
Charles Whittlesey, Hunt and Grey, architects; Frank M. Moore, paintings in the Picture Bridge, 1907, 1914

Like the Hotel Green (page 326), the Huntington was built in the early part of this century as a posh resort for wealthy people from farther east; also like the Green, this hotel is six stories high and has a central observation tower, red-tiled roofs and that same lugubrious dun-colored plaster on equally massive walls. Unlike the Green's, these walls are flat and plain and symmetrical, but they are so engulfed by vines that the long rows of identical windows seem lively enough. Indeed, the main element in the design now is the ivy, which manages to conceal almost everything. Along the southside, the vines have so overwhelmed a colonnade that it has ballooned into a topiary caricature of itself.

The Wentworth Hotel, as it was first called, got off to a shaky start until Henry E. Huntington, who owned almost everything else around here, bought it in 1911, renamed it and had his architects fancy things up. The Sheraton chain, after it bought the Huntington in 1954, added most of the one-story modernity on the north, the first thing you see, which includes a museum-quality 1950s lanai complete with red concrete pavement and aluminum awnings. All this replaced an earlier central entrance court, so a new porte cochere, a sort of lunar lander with white concrete legs, has locked onto the east side of the main building.

The Huntington's major attraction, however, is beyond all this, on the west side of the hotel: it is a long, covered footbridge that crosses an arroyo to a little compound of cottages. Though it has been given an asphalt walkway, the bridge is a beautiful composition of simple posts and railings, elegantly carved eaves and a red-tiled roof, which is just visible beneath pink mounds of wisteria that spill over in great boughs along the open sides. A walk across it provides contrasting views on each side as it cleaves through the Huntington's two distinct periods: on the north, a typical 1960s motel addition wraps around a turquoise swimming pool and bright green Astroturf; on the south, the arroyo seems nearly untouched as a tiny stream runs past a natural garden with dirt paths. But more important, the bridge's dark timbers act as romantic frames for thirty-nine exquisite little oil paintings of scenes in California, placed against the trusses of the roof so that they glow overhead in both directions. These dreamlike recollections of California's happiest places, with occasional thick daubs that give relief to the oranges and the surf and the mission walls, were painted by one Frank M. Moore in 1932, during the Great Depression, when the spirit of Ramona was as uplifting as it is becoming again in our own shadowed times.

XII 17 · *El Molino Viejo*

XII 16 · *Huntington-Sheraton Hotel*

XII 17 · EL MOLINO VIEJO

1120 Old Mill Road, San Marino
Padre José Maria Zalvidea, ca. 1816; Frederick H. Ruppel, restoration, 1927–1928
Now the Southern California Headquarters of the California Historical Society and a small museum; open daily, 1–4, except Mondays and holidays

El Molino Viejo, the old mill, was the first water-powered gristmill in Southern California, built by Father Zalvidea to service his flourishing San Gabriel Mission two miles south (page 63). The mill's relatively large size (twenty by thirty feet) for such an early date (about 1816) attests to the padre's agricultural acumen as well as his ability to coax work out of the Indians. Despite the permanence of the adobe walls, which are three and a half to five and a half feet thick, the simple horizontal waterwheels proved too slow, the storage room too damp, and the mill too far away from the mission; only seven years later, in 1823, it was replaced by a better mill next to the mission.

El Molino, quickly become Viejo, gradually became, in turn, a rustic retreat that charmed even the mountainman Jedediah Smith: a porticoed, shingle-roofed and leaned-onto residence, a clubhouse for the Huntington Hotel golf course, and then an abandoned ruin. In 1927 a Huntington heir hired Frederick Ruppel, who had restored Mission San Juan Capistrano, to rescue the old mill. Ruppel stripped off the accumulated wood additions and then re-created this romantic liturgy to California's Old Spanish Days that you see today.

Entrance is from the west through a gate in an adobe garden wall, near the base of a hillside forested with pines. A little stair leads down past an ancient black walnut tree to a patio of well-worn red tiles, and there, half covered in vines, is the old mill. From here it looks very small and only one story high (though it is two), for it is partially buried in the slope where the water once flowed. The earth-red plaster of the walls, made with the lime of burnt seashells, has faded and chipped to reveal variously hued layers of paint and, in some places, the adobe bricks underneath. The chunky handmade roof tiles are as patinaed with age as the walls, for they were salvaged from an old adobe in Santa Barbara. On the left, casement windows within a half-circle arch illuminate the office, which used to be the cistern. On the right, a small staircase leads up to a simply carved wooden door and the main level of the museum.

A walkway curves down to a larger patio where the lower level of the mill reveals itself. The long east wall is relieved by a few simple moldings and a small number of plainly framed, deeply set openings, including two arches at the base that open into the old wheelrooms. Huge cone-shaped buttresses at the corners kept the waterwheels and the earthquakes from shaking the mill apart. On the east edge of this patio a fountain splashes and a coppice of lemon and orange and tangerine trees casts its fragrances.

Inside, on the upper level, the confinement of the heavy walls is relieved by the loftiness of the roof. Its exposed beams and rafters were hewn out of local pine and sycamore, then fire-charred and scraped to preserve them without varnish. A hand-painted Indian pattern, which runs along the base of the cream-colored plaster walls, is reflected in the floor tiles, which have been worn and waxed and polished into lustrous shades of terra cotta. Narrow stairs, which were added by Ruppel, lead down to the naturally lighted wheelroom, where old photographs and a small model recall how it used to be; like many of California's Spanish landmarks, the old mill is much nicer now than it ever was before.

XII 18 · CALIFORNIA INSTITUTE OF TECHNOLOGY
Bounded by East California Boulevard, San Pasqual Street and South Wilson and South Hill avenues, Pasadena
Myron Hunt and Elmer Grey, original campus plan, 1908–10
Bertram Grosvenor Goodhue, expansion of the Hunt and Grey plan, 1915

In the 1930s, before technologists' hearts flew into outer space, this paradigm of science, then called Throop Polytechnic Institute, had become one of the most carefully considered, comfortable and inhabitable, yet grand and inspiring college campuses anywhere. A collaboration by some of that era's greatest architects, this collection of Spanish and Italian Renaissance buildings, united by long arcades along a narrow green, recalled at once Thomas Jefferson's masterpiece, the University of Virginia, and a semitropical version of the cloistered quadrangles of Oxford and Cambridge. By the 1950s, though, it appears that the scientists here had decided their buildings should reflect the sleek rockets and spiky satellites they were fixing to send into orbit. To this end, many of the old buildings along the green have been replaced by more up-to-date versions. Most noticeably missing is Throop Hall (Myron Hunt and Elmer Grey, 1909), a domed Beaux-Arts exuberance out of the Spanish Renaissance; it used to be the centerpiece before it was demolished and replaced by the shiny new Millikan library, a nine-story glass slab that conjures up the sinister black monolith in the movie *2001: A Space Odyssey,* or maybe the Ministry of Truth in *1984.*

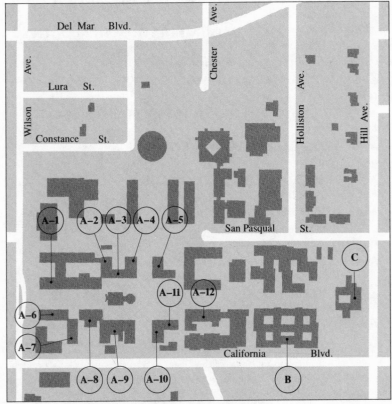

XII 18 · CALIFORNIA INSTITUTE OF TECHNOLOGY

Even more astonishing is the newer, north half of the campus, which has been turned into a dazzling showcase for a number of Modern Architecture's greatest outrages. Indeed, it boggles the mind how such a small area could contain so many specimens of the sleaziest and most inhumane building ideas of the last thirty years. Because of its staggering variety and depth, this collection could be said to beat out even Century City's (page 211), though that collection is considerably larger.

So, at Cal Tech, two campuses sit side by side, the older one serene and habitable and beautiful (except for a couple of intruders), the newer one redolent of Dr. Strangelove and thus perhaps valuable as a model of, if not for, our time.

A · LABORATORY BUILDINGS
The original arcaded buildings along the narrow common that opens off Wilson Avenue
Bertram Grosvenor Goodhue & Associates (except as noted), 1928–1939
On the north side, beginning at Wilson Avenue

A–1 · KERCKHOFF LABORATORY (BIOLOGY)
1928, 1939

A–2 · CRELLIN LABORATORY (CHEMISTRY)
1937

A–3 · GATES LABORATORY (CHEMISTRY)
1917 (Elmer Grey), 1927

A–4 · PARSON-GATES HALL OF ADMINISTRATION
1925; restored, 1983

A–5 · DABNEY HALL (ADMINISTRATION, HUMANITIES)
1928
On the south side, beginning at Wilson Avenue

A–6 · MUDD LABORATORY (GEOLOGY)
1938

A–7 · ROBINSON LABORATORY (ASTROPHYSICS)
1930

A–8 · ARMS LABORATORY (GEOLOGY)
1938

A–9 · BRIDGE LABORATORY (PHYSICS)
East wing, 1922; library annex, 1924; west wing, 1925

A–10 · HIGH VOLTAGE RESEARCH LABORATORY (NOW THE SLOAN LABORATORY OF MATH AND PHYSICS)
1923; interior remodeled, 1960

A–11 · KELLOGG RADIATION LABORATORY
1931 (office of Construction Engineer, Cal-Tech)

A–12 · GUGGENHEIM LABORATORY (AERONAUTICS AND PHYSICS)
1929

The entrance to the original campus is still on Wilson Avenue, where the narrow common begins. On each side of the plaza, next to the sidewalk, is a matching four-way symmetrical aedicula, with a large open arch in each of its tawny plaster walls, frugally voluted decoration at the edges and a blue-tiled dome on top. These little temples announce the beginning of long arcades, which, from

XII 18 A–1 · *Kerckhoff Laboratory*

the outside, are simple, one-story plastered walls regularly punctured by round arches, plain except for thin lines at the imposts and tall cypresses in between. Behind these rise the three-story laboratory buildings, which are similarly stark, squarish masses with flat roofs and regular rows of rectangular windows. But here the plain plaster walls and the insistent rhythm become a foil for a carefully plotted Churrigueresque insurrection that quietly unites some openings, surrounds others and then swarms into central panels with stylized symbols of each building's scientific activities.

The first floors of these buildings are raised above ground level to allow light into the basements, so a walk through the arcades along the front is enlivened by glimpses through two levels of windows and into entryways filled with low stairs. The colors and materials in these shaded walkways have become rich, with large terra-cotta floor tiles and ceilings of dark wood beams that are mixed, in that wonderfully undaunted tradition of Southern California, with dark-stained, wood-grained reinforced concrete. Seen from the inside, the repetitive arches recall the arcades on many of the California missions, or the ones in Europe the mission builders had remembered.

A caution: as you walk farther east, it becomes better for a while to keep your eyes on the terra-cotta floor tiles in order to avoid the glare of Millikan Library. You will know when to start looking down when you glimpse a Japanese garden (where Throop Hall used to be) that plunges another worthy tradition into degraded futuristic sleaze.

B · DORMITORIES
Backing on East California Boulevard, near South Hill Avenue
Gordon B. Kaufmann, 1931

With the library and its corporate Japanese-American trappings safely behind, the central brick walkway, lined with olive trees that strain to conceal new horrors along the north, passes, on the south, a building of great consequence. Here, beneath low red-tiled roofs, are beautiful cream-colored plaster walls trimmed in Classical stonework and pierced by great numbers of colonnades and arcades and winding stairs and long galleries and secret loggias; and all of them lead to or overlook sunny courtyards filled with pepper trees and orange trees and tall palms. This is just a temporary residence for fast-paced college students, but it speaks at length about inhabitability and sense of place and the romance of California.

At first glance this dormitory, with its many cloisters, looks more like an Italian Renaissance monastery built only for quiet reflection. The long front adheres religiously to the principles of symmetry and to Cal Tech's original arcade theme, though accomplished here with great verve as the red-tiled walkway passes through four pavilions, two colonnades and, in the center, one magnificent double-vaulted arcade on paired columns. The monastic configuration allows a degree of privacy as well as a sense of community, for the building is divided into four distinct quadrangles, each with its own entrance; though all the living groups are served by a common central kitchen, each has its own dining room, lounge and rows of rooms that face onto a separate courtyard.

But college students in Southern California do a lot of things that Italian monks don't; and on closer inspection, the livelier capacities of this place reveal themselves: the elaborate capitals of the staid columns are seen to be human torsos—grimacing fathers of science mixed in with more ordinary folk, even athletes throwing footballs and baseballs at each other. The other details, from Gothic tracery and brackets to Baroque broken pediments to colorful Spanish tiles and iron filigree gates, bring a cheerful individuality to each of the galleries, courtyards and balconies. The lounges and dining rooms, with their fireplaces and French doors, have a relaxed intimacy, while the more formal spaces become settings for impromptu gatherings and other student events.

Especially heartening is this building's ability, in a half-century of vigorous use, to accommodate people's need to change things around and to claim a territory with objects and actions of their own. Here, with surprising ease, columns support hammocks, brackets hold up flowerpots, a raised plinth becomes a lounge chair or a bicycle rack, and an old storeroom provides a quiet refuge where some future Einstein can play Space Invaders.

C · ATHENAEUM
Near the northwest corner of East California Boulevard and South Hill Avenue
Gordon B. Kaufmann, 1930

The faculty club, which is called the Athenaeum, is as wonderful as the dormitory. Designed a year earlier by the same architect, this great U-shaped palace, wrapped around a beautiful courtyard, speaks even more eloquently of the Italian Renaissance, with details that are lavish and serious. It sits at the end of the original common, with the same focal importance as Jefferson's library at the University of Virginia; but here the front columns hold up a delicate open arcade that runs between the ends of the two-story wings and bids welcome up a low flight of wide stairs. Open galleries, shaded by red-tiled roofs, surmount the tops of these plain plaster end walls; similar galleries under the roof of the three-story back wing look down onto the brick-paved courtyard, which is girdled with arcades, extensions of the one in front. Here lunch is served beneath an ancient olive tree and boughs of wisteria.

The main entrance, though, is on the south, through the arches of a monumental porte cochere, up a pair of grand stairs and past a heavy wood door. Beyond that is a finely chiseled travertine reception room with an ornately vaulted ceiling, a marble floor and large French doors that bring in light from the courtyard. On the right, through a travertine doorway, is an anteroom with a travertine stair curving up to the guest rooms. After this comes a baronial lounge, rich and strange, a somber festival in dark wood, from the high, beamed and coffered ceiling to the carved wood walls to the lustrous floors covered with Oriental rugs. But all this, including the mandatory walk-in fireplace, is lightened up by sunlight through enormous windows, partially shaded by the trees outside.

XII 18 C · *Athenaeum*

To the north is an equally sumptuous main dining room with more carved paneling and great arched glass doors that open, at one side, onto the interior courtyard and, at the other, onto a private arcaded patio. But the main story here, and especially in a smaller dining room beyond, is one of ceilings—magnificent, hand-carved, hand-painted, gilt-edged, coffered extravagances with enough modillions and pateras and rosettes and embellished moldings to satisfy even a Medici. The Athenaeum, unlike the dormitory, would be difficult to call home, but for a little while it does make you feel like a Nobel prizewinner.

XII 19 · SPANISH COLONIAL MASTERPIECES

San Marino, a tranquil residential town just south of Pasadena, is synonymous in Southern California with Old Money—families who built sumptuous houses here before the smog came. The favored style in the heyday of the city was the Spanish Colonial Revival, and four masterpieces by two of the masters of this idiom lie very near each other, almost at the gate of the Huntington estate. Two were designed by Los Angeles architect Wallace Neff, and two by George Washington Smith, of Santa Barbara, who was central to the conversion of that Edwardian town into a Spanish Colonial fantasy.

A · OSTHOFF HOUSE
**1779 Lombardy Road, San Marino, on the northwest corner of Lombardy
Road and South Allen Avenue**
George Washington Smith, 1925
Private residence

Behind large lawns and stands of palm trees, the rectangular volumes of this
two-story house form an elegantly simple composition of red-tiled roofs edging
over vast white plaster walls, which form a T in plan: the stroke of the T, with
the entrance near the middle, faces south along Lombardy Road, while an off-
center wing extends north, paralleling Allen Avenue, and creates a garden on
each side. Low tile-roofed garages nestle into the western garden, which is
screened from the neighbors by walls and foliage and, from the street, by a
thick, one-story extension of the house's south wall, which rises in gentle loops
to piers that flank the driveway. The garden on the east, which faces Allen, the
busier street, is the main patio of the house, enclosed by another one-story wall
that flows out of the east end of the front block toward the northern edge of the
property. Just visible above this wall, before it rises at the end, are the intricately embellished arches of an extraordinary tiled-roof arcade, which extends back
to the house to enclose the north end of the patio.

XII 19 A · *Osthoff House*

The plain white walls of the house and these extensions of it form the epic
narrative of the design, with fenestrated footnotes and fanfares deployed infre-
quently but surprisingly into the deep shadows with astonishing little flourishes.
The few windows are all small, sometimes covered with wrought iron, sometimes made noticeable by an oversize sill or faced by a handful of colorful tiles.
Faint lines of molding accentuate the eaves and frame a few more tiles around
the spare front door. The chief protagonists in this drama of ornament, though,
are the vivid monster plants whose shadows dance on the nonstop walls of
white; dragon's blood trees, yucca and palms rustle from languor into ornamental violence and back again.

Across the street from the Osthoff house, at 1750 Lombardy Road, is another
attractive Monterey Revival house (19 B), this one designed in 1929 by Roland
E. Coate, one of the masters of that idiom.

C · BALDWIN HOUSE
665 South Allen Avenue, San Marino
George Washington Smith, 1926
Private residence

The year after the Osthoff house was built, another George Washington Smith design, the Baldwin house, went up next door. This time exotic ornament picks up where the plants at the Osthoff house left off; a two-story façade of largely Spanish Colonial Revival persuasion gives way to a gate of Oriental provenance over the driveway, which in turn leads to a realm of Moorish arches. But Smith knew just how to keep it all under control. All this exotica is never weird, and never stuffy, always lively but adequately correct. The Baldwins' own vast lawn calms the house and the shadows of the Osthoff's trees stir its spirit. It is all so abundantly full of the good life in the California sunshine.

D · BOURNE HOUSE
1861 Lombardy Road, on the northeast corner of Allen Street, San Marino
Wallace Neff, 1927
Private residence

Across Allen Street from the two G. W. Smith houses is, for us, the radiant prize of this urbane group, Wallace Neff's Bourne house, which has, more than the others, all sorts of opposite qualities all at once: it is grand and intimate, chaste and flamboyant, modest and sumptuous. It sits private behind its white walls, but it also gives itself to the street and the passerby. A grand exterior stair sweeps up, in full view, to the second floor, as though we, gaping from the sidewalk, were in on the inner life of the house. The one-story wing to the right of the front door has an air of intimate domesticity to it, too, and of including the viewer, maybe because the architect has dared to place a part of the structure so humble (albeit so composed) right up front. A palm and lush dark green foliage tumbling over the garden wall to the left of the entrance help Ramona's children even more with the imagery of the good life in the sunshine.

E · SINGER HOUSE
2035 Lombardy Road, San Marino
Wallace Neff, 1925
Private residence

Here is one of the most satisfying examples of the Spanish Colonial Revival ever built. Its wings of white plaster and its concord of red-tiled roofs seem wedded, along with the fan palms, the olive trees and a huge live oak, to the spirit of this place and to this specific site. Sitting comfortably behind clipped hedges, lawns and a circular driveway, the two-story main volume extends one-story arms toward Lombardy Road on the south; a gable-roofed colonnade reaches out on the right and a shed roof slopes forward on the left. The ends of the wings become low plaster walls that curve forward to protect a flagstone courtyard; birds-of-paradise line the edges and flowers splash up from a stone wellhead which serves as a central fountain. Behind the fountain, the front door hides in a little vestibule that's been carved from the center of the main mass and outlined by a slightly pointed arch; directly above the arch, a tiny rosette window in a grand frame helps to amplify the soft-spoken greetings below.

To the right of the entry, a stairway rises along the main wall and disappears into the boughs of an olive tree. To the left are two small asymmetrical windows that introduce a two-story turret bulging from the corner; only one-quarter of

XII 19 E · *Singer House*

this giant cylinder is visible, so it does not overpower the tiny windows and the lacy fairy-tale balcony upon it. From here, another stairway, shaded by a huge live oak, curves down along the west wing to the point where, with a quick arched gate and a Mission Style wave, the building becomes a garden wall. As on the Osthoff house, the windows are few, small and deep-set, and some are covered in intricate wrought iron. Their placement, too, seems gracefully incidental to the great white walls, whose own liveliness is enhanced by the animated shadows of the trees. The playfulness of the shapes—the archways, the outside stairs and the fat turret in the center—speaks of the romantic fantasy of Southern California. The brio of this house, its easy exuberance, presages the Santa Barbara County Courthouse of some four years later, which capped this whole gorgeous idiom. Such a nice, clean framework the white walls and red-tiled roofs made; and with what lithe grace the rhythms spin within it. The spirit of the time was just too wonderful to last.

XII 20 · HUNTINGTON ESTATE
Entrances at 1151 Oxford Road and at the south end of Allen Avenue at Orlando Road, San Marino
Myron Hunt and Elmer Grey, architects of the mansion, 1910; Myron Hunt and H. C. Chambers, architects of the library, 1925; William Hertrich, superintendent of the ranch and gardens, 1904–1949
Now a library, art gallery and botanical garden
Open to the public Tuesday through Sunday, 1–4:30; closed Mondays and major holidays; call (818) 449-3901 for mandatory but free tickets on Sundays; $1 donation suggested

Henry E. Huntington was an urban planner on a grand scale. First he helped to shape the development of much of the western United States by working with his uncle, Collis P. Huntington, an owner of the Central Pacific and Southern

Pacific railroads. After his uncle's death in 1900, he moved to Los Angeles and invested his considerable inheritance in the Pacific Electric Railway Company, which, in ten years, would surpass every other interurban rail system in the world and, while the population trebled, would establish the framework for this area's famous sprawl. Because he was an urban planner who owned the networks, he possessed a remarkably lucid vision of which towns would boom, bought up the land beforehand, and made more fortunes. Henry E. Huntington quickly became the largest landowner in California and, consequently, one of its wealthiest and most influential citizens.

In 1910, at the age of sixty, Huntington retired officially from business in order to have the time to collect *things* as resourcefully as he had collected money. He had already become, in his spare time, America's largest collector of books. Easily a million dollars a year went to this passion as he bought up whole libraries at a time, but he was determined to amass one of the world's greatest collections of the literature and history of the English-speaking peoples. He succeeded, buying books so fast that now, over fifty years later, the staff is still cataloging them. When his mansion could no longer hold the burgeoning collection, he had Myron Hunt, who had designed his house, do a giant library next door.

Huntington had also become interested in art, as well as in his uncle's widow, Arabella, who was by then one of America's most eminent art collectors and wealthiest women. He married her in 1913. Huntington's palatial house, which overlooked his six-hundred-acre San Marino ranch, was complete by then, its vast rooms and elaborately framed walls ready to greet his new wife with her voracious—and contagious—appetite for art. Before her death in 1924 and his in 1927, they had filled the house with sculpture and paintings, most notably eighteenth-century English portraits. Just west of the library, the mansion reposes in a sort of opulent Georgian-Edwardian fulsomeness, symmetrical and white. Inside are art galleries, appropriately splendiferous, where the visitor can become acquainted with Lawrence, Gainsborough, Constable, Romney, Reynolds and the rest. In a large gallery added later—one of the most memorable rooms in the world, thanks entirely to the figures on its walls—"Pinkie" waves cryptically across the room at "Blue Boy" with "Mrs. Siddons" looking on.

Huntington's house acts as a kind of elegant signpost for a variety of gardens: on the south a sunny red-tiled terrace overlooks the vast greensward of an English landscape with trees and lily ponds beyond; on the west a vine-covered pergola extends out between rose and herb gardens on its way to gardens of the

XII 20 · *Huntington Estate, Cactus Garden*

XII 20 · *Huntington Estate, Rose Garden Gazebo*

Orient; on the north a long lawn slices a vista through palm trees, thick shrubbery and camellias to a large classical fountain; on the east, pointing toward a palm tree forest and mountains of cactus, is an enormous entrance porch that is nearly engulfed by one of the world's largest knots of cyads, the mysterious, slow-growing palmlike plants tht date from the Mesozoic era. Soon after Huntington bought the ranch in 1903, he and his foreman, William Hertich, began growing plants, thousands and thousands of them, in about a dozen distinct settings. Although the ranch has been reduced to 207 acres today, these much loved-over gardens are more flourishing than ever, with mor than one hundred thousand specimens representing about nine thousand species.

The Rose Garden and the two Camellia Gardens are botanical catalogs of their species. The highly cultivated roses grow from precisely rectangular beds within a vast lawn, while rambling and climbing roses clamber over white-painted arbors and trellises. The camellias bloom in thick natural clumps, penetrated by winding pathways of decomposed granite and shaded by California live oaks. The Shakespeare Garden, hidden behind hedges and trees, is a literary landscape with flowers and herbs mentioned in the playwright's works. The curving parterres are more Deco than Elizabethan, but the scents and colors and the splashing fountain do evoke, if you try hard, some of the magic in the plays.

Entrance to the Japanese Garden is beneath the enormous roof of a traditional gateway with guardian lion-dogs. The visitor walks down a path beside an ancient Buddhist bell in an open temple and through a wisteria-draped arbor composed of some of the world's most realistically molded concrete tree trunks. All the parts are here: vermilion bridges, one moon and one zigzag, extend across a still pond surrounded by shrubs and flowering trees and little lawns sprinkled with lanterns, pagodas, votive stones, water-holding stones, a buddha and an exquisite teahouse on a hill that leads to a Zen Garden; and all are brought together in a surprising historical mix that spans several centuries of Japanese garden art. The lush plants are a little odd as well: while many are traditional Japanese, most are actually from the Mediterranean. But the effect is convincing—authentic enough, at least, for the numerous movies that have been filmed here.

The acres of lawns and forests and thick shrubs that roll south down the hill from the house and the library have the natural yet contrived quality of an English landscape garden; here are exotic plants and trees from everywhere—the Chinese dawn redwood, the tremendous Argentine ombu, the South African cape chestnut with its pink flowers—all laid out in a geographical microcosm of the planet. A world traveler in this garden can still be smelling roses as he walks south through a subtropical garden on his way to Australia; after passing more than ninety species of palm trees in the tropics, he can easily step down to even thicker jungles and lily ponds fed by the waterfalls of alpine mountains, which are still within yodeling distance; or he can turn east, for the most astonishing transformation of all.

The Desert Garden is in a class by itself—the largest outdoor collection of desert plants in the world. The dense green and the cool shadows of the Jungle Garden end abruptly as the sun burns down on a bristling, bulging, writhing environment that looks like it might have crash-landed from Mars. Here are twelve acres of enormous, tightly packed mounds of spiky xerophytes—over 2,500 species of them. In their native, almost lifeless habitat, these plants, which include cactus and need very little water, are slow and meek; here, with careful nurturing and the benign Southern California climate, they thrive and blossom and seem about to leap out at you as you walk carefully down the center of the paths.

Near the north end of the estate, west of the Allen Avenue entrance, are the Huntingtons themselves planted, beneath a handsomely detailed classical temple, Ionic columns supporting a low dome, round in plan and bright white against encircling lawns and trees. The Huntington Mausoleum was designed in 1933 by John Russell Pope, architect of The National Gallery in Washington, who was proud of it.

XIII / SANTA CATALINA ISLAND

Casino

Early Spanish navigators, persuaded by the penetration of the Gulf of California into the west coast of North America, decided that California must be an island. That seemed poetically correct, as well, since islands are, in human experience, magic places, and that is what the mythical California was meant to be.

Further exploration demonstrated conclusively enough that California was not a magic island, but just off its shore were some real islands—one of which came close to the edge of magic. The Spaniards landed here as early as 1542, named the place Santa Catalina, and noted that the inhabitants were taller and much lighter than the Indians of the mainland and seemed to be regarded in the area as superior beings. (Some shreds of archaeological evidence even suggest a race dominated by Amazon warriors.) In any case, the Spaniards reasoned that the conversion and improvement of this fortunate race could only be accomplished by their imprisonment on the mainland. So this magic isle was almost

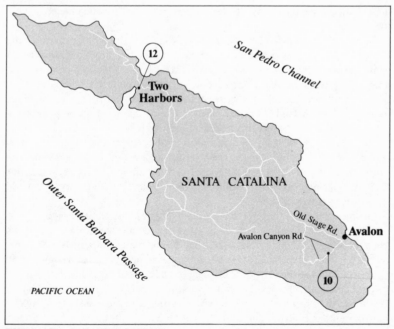

XIII/SANTA CATALINA ISLAND

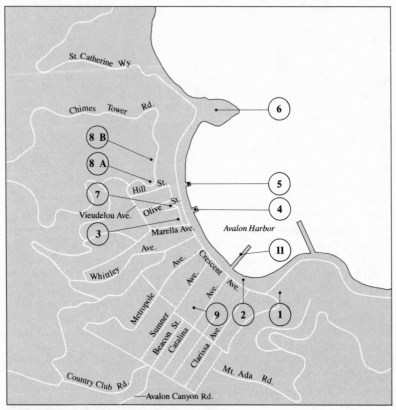

XIII/SANTA CATALINA ISLAND (AVALON)

unpopulated when the canny Yankees began to eye it in the late nineteenth century.

But it was still magic. Twenty-one miles long and twenty-two miles off the coast at Palos Verdes, cooled in the summer by the ocean breezes, warmed in winter by the temperate ocean, surrounded by an underwater paradise and graced by green hills that tumbled down around a perfect sheltered cove, at once dreamily exotic and right there, it was—as it remains today—the distilled essence of Ramonaland. But they called it Avalon, after the magic place King Arthur's sword Excalibur came from and went back to.

The subdividing of 1887, on a miniature grid beside the harbor, was not as exotic as the setting, but it began the layering on of a kind of tacky hominess, a gentle Midwestern sleaze that alternated with South Seas romance and native California splendor to make Catalina the complex and contradictory real-world magic island that it is today.

The most important layerer was William Wrigley, Jr., of Chicago and Pasadena, who bought Catalina in 1919 with part of a fortune made in chewing gum. He built a big white house there (Mt. Ida, visible only from a distance), a memorial botanical garden, a little tower and a casino, which joined the fine old St. Catherine Hotel at the end of the crescent of buildings along the harbor. The St. Catherine was occupied by the military during World War II so enthusiastically that it had to be torn down after the war; but the Casino remains. Mr. Wrigley's most important contribution, though, will probably turn out to be the protection of the open space on the island—which is practically all of it, past the edges of the two towns—with title now vested in a public conservancy and with access much restricted.

In the heyday of the popularity of this island paradise, between the two world wars, a fleet of great white steamers brought crowds of merrymakers who stayed in cottages and camps along the streets, danced to the big bands in the casino and partied in the grand hotel. All that is past now (except for an occasional band at the Casino), but boats and airplanes still come and numbers of unusually modest little hotels recall the easy days of long ago. The lingering nostalgia is an important part of the delight now: this is the best, and maybe the only place left where you can move to the rhythms of the Southern California of the 1930s. But it is more than that: the chaparral is more fragrant, the quail are plumper, the poppies are brighter; bougainvillea and copa de oro drape over porches and whole rooftops, geraniums of every color cover the hillsides in huge mounds, and the imported palms and eucalyptus have escaped from the little streets to form groves in the soft, grassy hills. It's Southern California's Southern California: there is, indeed, a magic island.

XIII 1 · HOLLY HILL HOUSE
Near the south end of Crescent Avenue
Peter Gano, 1890
Private residence

The first astonishment along the walk from the boat landing to the center of Avalon is Holly Hill House, originally called Look Out Cottage, which perches on top of a cliff entirely corseted in gunited concrete. A perfect preamble to the island, this house is both homey and bizarre: it offers comfortable, modest recollections of the wide-verandaed houses of the American past, while at the same time it is held absurdly aloft above this magic harbor by one of the most zanily monomaniacal applications of squirted concrete that high technology has yet provided. The house itself, at once almost desperately dramatic and sort of easy, was constructed by one Peter Gano with the help of his horse Mercury in a spasm of derring-do-it-yourself Queen Anne dazzle. Gano had built it for the woman he loved, but when he was done she refused to move to the island; by then, of course, he loved the house more than any woman, so he lived in it by himself for over thirty years.

A great circular tower shelters an array of walls with endlessly varying patterns of clapboards, simple shingles and fish-scale shingles, slipping and undu-

XIII 1 · *Holly Hill House*

XIII 2 · *Crescent Avenue*

lating around arched windows, bay windows, dormer windows and portholes. Crushed abalone shells and shiny stones ornament special places in the walls, and tiny white pebbles make up a sign above the entry that spells out LOOK OUT COT. The tower, which replaces one that burned in 1966, accommodates a wide-open viewing platform topped by a red-shingled conical roof, which is pierced by a red brick chimney and capped by a weather vane in the shape of Mercury the horse. Breezy, laid-back, wild-eyed and mad, the house presses totally gratuitous images of right-wing missionaries in Polynesia, and neatly brackets the range of island sights that are to come.

XIII 2 · CRESCENT AVENUE
Along Avalon's beachfront
Most of the buildings designed or remodeled by David M. Renton; landscaping by Ralph Roth, 1932 and after

Crescent Avenue traces the graceful arc of Avalon Bay as it forms a casual, hospitable boundary between the city and sea. This little roadway is the commercial and entertainment center of Avalon: one side is lined by sidewalk cafés, gift shops, hotels and restaurants, the other side by the palm-dotted beach, the Pleasure Pier and the Visitors' Bureau. There are very few cars on Catalina and most of those are tiny motorized buggies available for high-priced tourism, by the hour, so this, the most crowded street in Catalina, becomes a place for tourists and islanders to promenade.

The present sunny character of the esplanade was developed under the direction of Philip K. Wrigley, after his father's death in 1932. He imported white sand to cover the rocky beach and hired costumed troubadors to greet the steamers at the end of the walk. He planted mature palm and olive trees ferried over from the mainland and constructed and remodeled a number of buildings in Spanish Colonial Revival Style faced with colorful tile, locally made. The troubadors are gone now, but the rest remains. The tile gleams as brightly as ever and shows up again on a low wall, between pavement and beach, which slithers casually along, a friendly dragon in the sand with brick benches tucked into its curves. A vaguely Spanish fountain, which splashes water onto panels of more local tiles, forms the center of a cheerful little town plaza where Sumner Avenue arrives at Crescent and the shore. Here raised planters overflow with geraniums, honeysuckle and bougainvillea, as people on holiday pause and lick their ice cream cones.

XIII 3 · EL ENCANTO INTERNATIONAL MARKETPLACE
Corner of Marella and Crescent avenues, Avalon
Entrance archway, 1924; side wings, David M. Renton, 1934; Solomon's Landing Restaurant, 1980

At the end of the downtown part of the curve of Crescent Avenue is a low promontory with a Spanish Colonial Revival market that serves as a particularly pleasant terminus for the view along the street. The low building is triangular, like its site, with a low elliptical tower at the leading point that is pierced by an inviting shadowy tunnel lined with little shops. The tunnel comes out in a sunny patio, heavily planted and surrounded by more shops, with terraces beyond for an open-air restaurant.

The idiom is an intensification of the colorfully tiled cheerful Spanish of much of the street: the stucco walls are gleaming white, the conical roofs are red tile, the tunnel entrance is surrounded by a swirly frieze of a dancing señorita and a serenading don. The risers of the steps to the upper terraces and the sides of the fountains are resplendent with the bright tile of Catalina; even the garden walls sparkle with tile panels of toucans and parrots.

XIII 3 · *El Encanto International Marketplace*   XIII 5 · *Yacht Club*

XIII 4 · TUNA CLUB
Casino Way, Avalon
1916

The Tuna Club, built on piles over Avalon Bay, is, with the Yacht Club next door, one of the most poignant links to Catalina's past, which wasn't many years ago but now seems dreamily distant. The Tuna Club was founded in 1898 by Charles Frederick Holder of Pasadena as a gentlemen's club (ladies from nine to five only) to improve the standards of game fishing. It was named, according to Holder, "after the tuna, because it was a good and euphonious name, and its organization followed my catch of the first very large tuna." Voting membership requirements included having landed a hundred-pound tuna by the club rules. The members themselves built this clubhouse after an earlier one was destroyed by a fire in 1915 that consumed most of Avalon. The 1916 Tuna Club is foursquare, painted white, with a rather grand entrance of beveled glass through which the curious passerby can look to the bay beyond. Its simple windows are trimmed in dark green; the first floor is covered in clapboard, the second in shingles; the low roof has green asphalt shingles; and there's a squat tower at every corner. The mood is proper but relaxed seaside, full of sun and breeze and the aura of vacation.

XIII 5 · YACHT CLUB
Casino Way, Avalon
1924

Just beyond the Tuna Club, also built on pilings, is the Yacht Club, white clapboard with blue trim, gable-roofed with ends to street and bay, with shed-roofed extensions at the sides. The extension on the right opens up as a little entrance porch and later gives way to a lighthouse-shaped tower, square in plan with a railing on top around a little octagonal cupola, which is surmounted by an even smaller round one, whose gold dome is topped in turn by a weather vane. A deck goes around the building, and on the back side a glassy shed-roofed extension extends a previous shed-roofed extension. The extensive extensions and the modest nine-paned square windows, blue-framed below and blue-shuttered above, give the Yacht Club an even more relaxed air than that of its neighbor. Like the Tuna Club, it was constructed by its members. It's wonderful how shacky and ad-hoc a really self-confident upper-class building can be and still keep its aristocracy intact.

XIII 6 · CASINO
At the end of Casino Way, Avalon
Walter Webber and Sumner A. Spaulding, 1929

At the very end of the crescent walk along the bay, a sugarloaf-shaped peak used to mark the intersection of harbor and open ocean. It was leveled to make a base for the grand circular Casino, a high-spirited blend of Zigzag Moderne and Spanish Colonial Revival on a building that was extremely popular, and A.I.A. award–winning, in 1930. In the tiny city of Avalon it seems particularly gigantic, and it does represent an impressive feat of construction, with a clear span dome 178 feet in diameter over the upper-level ballroom and a span almost as long over the round movie theater on the lower level. The exterior is attractively finished with a red-tiled roof, a grand second-story arcaded balcony and a forty-foot-high entry loggia decorated with Moderne murals of the island's submarine gardens in elaborate zigzag frames. Inside, the lobby is still complete with original wood paneling, lounging sofas and Moorish fantasy murals.

Farther inside is surely the finest Art Deco cinema left in the United States. It seats 1,200 and is said to be the first ever to be acoustically engineered for

XIII 6 · *Casino*

sound movies; such luminaries as Cecil B. DeMille, Louis B. Mayer and Sam Goldwyn yachted across the channel to preview their motion pictures here. When the lights go up, the room is breathtaking, still in mint condition with the upholstery and carpet intact. The walls glow with friezes of island flora all around. Overhead, a gorgeous silver-leafed dome twinkles with stars. The tour guide will demonstrate the amazing range of the indirect lighting effects and of the four-manual pipe organ.

Two grand ramps climb up from the theater past a mezzanine lounge to the immense ballroom, where great dance bands of the 1930s—Kay Kyser, Benny Goodman, Jan Garber and the others—once broadcast to the nation and where name bands still come on occasion. The 15,000-square-foot dance floor is inlaid with six hardwoods over cork subflooring. One-fourth of the circumference is taken up by a bar, while the rest is rimmed by an overhanging outside balcony right out of the Alhambra. It's all very interesting and you should finish the tour, but it all seems anticlimactic after the movie theater, which will linger in your memory forever.

XIII 7 · MURDOCK HOUSE
103 Maiden Lane, at the west end of Crescent Avenue
Elmer Grey, 1927
Now called La Casa Gaviota; private residence

Here is a particularly striking instance of the Spanish Colonial Revival idiom in the service of hilltown picturesqueness. Set high on a corner lot overlooking the bay, this three-story white stucco block of a house is embellished with a number of romantic architectural elements. Next to the sidewalk a low wall with an iron filigree gate protects a little entry patio whose back is a simple colonnade that supports a second-story front porch. Tiled stairs on the right curve up to the porch and the front door, which is painted aqua and dark blue and set into a deep shell arch painted in corresponding colors. To the right of the door is a triple set of arched windows separated by two Byzantine columns, a motif that occurs again just around the corner; a dark wood Spanish balcony on the third floor wraps around the corner to shade both sets of windows. The third story is pushed slightly forward, its lower edge scalloped between exposed beam ends. Red tiles, naturally, cover the hip roof and underscore the authority with which the house sits on its hillside.

XIII 8 · WOLFE HOUSE
124 Chimes Tower Road, Avalon
R. M. Schindler, 1928

The Wolfe house (8 A), the first of R. M. Schindler's hillside houses, rests lightly on the chaparral- and geranium-covered cliffside above Avalon. Easily distinguished from the surrounding scatter of pastel-colored Mediterranean stucco boxes, this is one of Southern California's most notable pieces of Modern Architecture. Sheathed in white stucco with dark gray wood trim, this delicate, complex composition of slightly staggered solids and cutaway voids forms four garden terraces as it steps down the slope. Though built to the edges of its thir-

XIII 8 A · *Wolfe House* XIII 10 · *Wrigley Memorial*

ty-by-forty-foot lot, the house guards its privacy on the west with narrow vertical windows and on the street with a wood slot screen, which also protects an
outdoor ramp to the topmost roof deck. Floor-to-ceiling windows, shaded by
the deep overhangs of the terraces, look down on the town and the beautiful
bay.

Spread across an outcropping above the Wolfe house, near the end of Chimes
Tower Road, is the Zane Grey Pueblo (8 B) (1923), formerly the home of the
famous author. Now a hotel (added onto in 1979), the simple buff-colored volumes of lumpy stucco take specific inspiration from the Hopi but manage to
look sufficiently Spanish Colonial Revival to fit the setting.

XIII 9 · GOLF GARDENS
Between Sumner and Catalina avenues, northeast of Beacon Street, Avalon
John Frick, 1973
Open daily; admission fee

The miniature golf course is a landscape genre that is one of Southern California's true art forms (page 382). Golf Gardens is, hands down, the best. Here, as
at the others, each hole presents the player with a new golfing conundrum that
offers bizarre surprises along the way to its solution. Sometimes the hole involves a maze in which the ball might disappear down one of three holes on one
green, roll through a length of pipe, head off down a narrow incline, bounce
down a tiny set of steps, turn ninety degrees into another sloped tunnel and then
drop casually onto the final green. In some places you reach the green by rico-
cheting your ball off an ingenious arrangement of variously angled concrete em-
bankments. But here, uniquely, it is always the little colored ball that is
important, not the surrounding gimmicks: the ball rolls across tiny viaducts,
hurtles off obstacles, averts heart-wrenching perils, even disappears, but it never
loses center stage. Here, too, the landscaping, which is colorful and fragrant and
luxuriant, is an important part of the setting for every hole. You are really playing golf in a garden.

Part of the heartwarming appeal of Golf Gardens is that it was done by a
man who never built a miniature golf course before or since; he designed it in
eight days and built it in three months. But this sort of inspired do-it-yourself

enthusiasm has faded from the Southern California scene; most of the home-made miniature golf courses are gone. The new ones are factory-built products, far bigger and fancier than this, but with about as much built-in surprise as a Barbie doll. This one is Art.

XIII 10 · WRIGLEY MEMORIAL
Approximately one mile southwest of Avalon, on Avalon Canyon Road
Memorial: Bennett, Parsons and Frost, 1934
Garden: Ralph Roth, 1933 and after

The pale, narrow tower of the Wrigley Memorial, set against the soft, dark backdrop of its chaparral-covered canyon, has about it the brooding romanticism of a Maxfield Parrish painting. The precise geometry of the reinforced-concrete structure, with its pyramid roof, finely proportioned arched opening and pair of symmetrically curving stairs, contrasts dramatically with the wild slopes around it.

There is a fine view from the tiled observation pavilion at the base of the tower. The canyon below the monument contains a botanical garden with a thriving collection of cactus and succulents, and a fascinating display of flora native only to this island: Catalina currant, Catalina cherry, Catalina lilacs, Catalina ironwood and St. Catherine's lace.

XIII 11 · UNDERSEA GARDENS
Boats depart from the Pleasure Pier, Crescent Avenue; tours given daily, weather permitting

The best ride at Catalina is the tour of the Undersea Gardens; it allows even non-scuba divers to view the mysteries of the deep, seated in a big glass-bottomed boat. The first views are of beer cans and tires and boots, but after your boat leaves the harbor a tape prepared by the University of Southern California oceanography department is turned on and the exploration begins of a mile-and-a-half natural preserve along the coast just south of Avalon Bay. Catalina happens to be situated on the border between a warm and cool ecological zone, so the variety of underwater life here is especially abundant.

A magical landscape unfolds beneath you. Giant bulb and iodine kelp, though no more than limp twisted masses when they wash up on the shore, form the hauntingly graceful swaying trees of this garden. Below them grow the sea mosses whose names evoke their appearance: heather moss, coral moss, ruby moss, bridal veil moss and feather-boa moss. Delicate fish bone, chiffon and maidenhair sea ferns intertwine with ribbon, rainbow and sea-grape kelp and bright red and lavender algae.

The denizens of this watery wood carom, crawl and slither beneath you: there are bright orange garibaldis and sea hares and sheepshead and rock bass and silver, blue, green, gray and convict (striped black and white) perch; hiding in the foliage on the bottom are colorful starfish, sea urchins, abalone, sea cucumbers, lobsters and sea anemone; leopard shark, moray eels and bat rays provide hints of danger. The spectacular finale is the fish feeding, which accelerates the languid rhythms of the deep into oceanic frenzy.

XIII 12 · TWO HARBORS
Near the northern end of Santa Catalina Island

Though Catalina is over twenty miles long, it is almost entirely uninhabited except for Avalon, clustered around its crescent of a harbor on the southeast side of the island. There is a much smaller settlement called Two Harbors at a narrow isthmus near the northern end, a dusty frontier whose thatched-roofed beachside shacks offer only the barest essentials of holiday island life: marine supplies, basic groceries, fast food and a cocktail lounge.

But the settlement is not the attraction; the landscape is. The two harbors here are Isthmus Cove on the northeast and Catalina Harbor directly opposite, to the southwest. Between them only a narrow mesa about a half-mile wide separates the waters. From the isthmus, the land rises to rugged hills on one side and to a higher, broader mesa on the other. The native vegetation is scruffy, low chaparral with a few eucalyptuses, planted randomly in the 1920s, that provide shade and a pungent aroma. From the gentle rise near the center, you can gaze out toward the mainland or out to sea and feel the full fragility of this last little outpost of human habitation before half a world of ocean begins. How far from home the Spanish explorers must have felt when first they came to Southern California. How much farther they would feel if they could see Los Angeles now.

XIV / OTHER CONTINUING ATTRACTIONS

Magic Mountain

This chapter was at first meant to provide a home for places that were geographically or, especially, philosophically removed from our thirteen fairly linear rides through the vastness of Los Angeles. But it soon became apparent that the ones turning up here had begun to take on a coherence of their own and were lining themselves up as yet another ride. These places, some of the most special in Southern California, are for the most part miniature worlds, representations of life somewhere else or some other time or some other way, often created by the vision of one person and always directed toward some particular

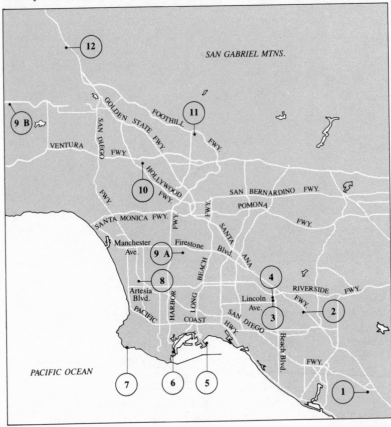

XIV/OTHER CONTINUING ATTRACTIONS

end or theme. Usually each is arranged as a ride or series of rides: the visitor pays some money and is taken through a show, a carefully structured one, where the sequence as much as the events themselves produces the desired atmosphere or response or thrill. The shows can be a complicated set of experiences, as in Knott's Berry Farm, which is not at the scale or refinement of Disneyland but has some of the same excitements, with a down-home Ramonaland warmth found nowhere else; or they can be less complex but more plentiful and more highly charged, as in the heart-pounding rides of Magic Mountain, which has an atmosphere different from that of Disneyland and Knott's but is still a collection of things to ride through and see and do. Some shows, such as movie studio tours and a miniature golf course, are arranged with precision, while the organization of others, like the *Queen Mary* and the funny little commercial buildings around Disneyland, is considerably more relaxed. Two shows, Marineland and Lion Country Safari, might just be ordinary animal acts except that here in Los Angeles the parks have been carefully choreographed and have become rides, too. A few might not seem like rides at all, but the rhythms in places like Watts Towers and Grandma Prisbrey's Bottle Village can be discovered and felt. The grandest and most extensive show of all, the famous L.A. freeway system, where admission is free, is obviously a ride; but its joys, like those of fine wine, often need to be learned. And so this chapter is a ride of rides, the quintessential stuff of which Los Angeles is made.

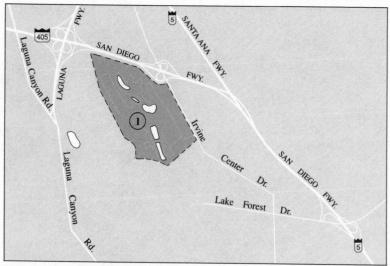

XIV 1 · LION COUNTRY SAFARI

XIV 1 · LION COUNTRY SAFARI

At the intersection of the San Diego Freeway (405) and Irvine Center Drive, Irvine
Duell and Associates, architects; Lang and Wood, landscape architects, 1970
Open daily; Safari Trails open 9:45–5 in summer, 9:45–3:30 in winter; admission fee; call (714) 837-1200

Lion Country Safari, where a sign says "No Trespassing—Violators Will Be Eaten," is a five-hundred-acre African game preserve with village that was magically set down on the grassy veldt of Orange County. This happy premise has had to contend with more than a few trespassers: some of the fastest-growing suburbs in America are approaching from almost every direction; several freeways pass close by; jets from the adjacent El Toro Marine Air Station often scream overhead; and the Irvine Meadows rock concert amphitheater has moved in next door. Still, the designers here have carried out the African wildlife theme with aplomb and with occasional brilliant invention. The park is divided into two discrete areas: a drive-through zoo called the Safari Trails, where wild animals are observed from car windows; and a themed amusement park called the Safari Camp, a richly landscaped African village with animal shows and exhibits and one very special ride.

The Safari Trails is the latest in that particularly Southern Californian phenomenon of drive-in everything, from hamburger and doughnut stands to car washes to banks to Sunday services. This time the genre has inverted the usual expectations of a zoo, so that the animals roam around at will and entertain themselves by observing the people inside their vehicular cages. The best time to take the trip is in the early morning of a cool day, when the animals are active and your cage, whose windows cannot be lowered more than an inch, won't become an oven.

After driving through a double stockade, you come out in an African plain, which doesn't look much different from anyplace else in Orange County except that it's undeveloped. But the voice on the tape cassette (should you choose to rent one) is quick to point out that the animals here are from the grassland, not the jungle. Then groups of antelope, impala, giraffes and flamingos come ambling by, and the magic begins to take hold. The only ones that seem at all concerned about the automobiles are the huge and smelly and very ugly ostriches, who spend a lot of time pressed up against side windows, peering through windshields; at these moments the enchantment is in danger of vanishing.

But soon you pass through a gate into a different, ostrichless section with zebras and gnus. The game preserve is separated into six areas, often by cleverly concealed ha-has, to keep the different species happy and breeding and, in particular, away from the lions. Young white hunters in little guard towers stand ready to close the gates should any miscegenation be attempted. More white hunters in zebra-striped jeeps are parked gallantly around the park in case anything else might go wrong. They help to calm any fears that some wild animal might smash through the glass, especially in Section 3, where the lions pad around and sometimes roar. The lions are often very near, enjoying the shade of a well-placed tree beside the road. The sight of ferocious lions just inches from your car door, even if some of them are draped across logs or curled up like kittens, can be a four-star gut-level thrill.

There is a big jump in scale in Section 4, with its Cape buffalo and white rhinos—the last very rare, each more massive than most automobiles. Section 5 has lovable but extremely dangerous grizzly and black bears, which are kept amused by long-armed African chimpanzees. Section 6 is the home of the elegant cheetahs, who can quickly accelerate to sixty miles per hour when pressed, but in this case they aren't. You turn around in Section 6 and return on the same road. Most people seem to go a little faster, thinking perhaps about the chance to cool off at the Oasis bar.

Past the Oasis, which is next to the entrance of the Safari Camp village, a walkway leads through the jungle and then divides to curve around a pretty lake with little African-style buildings tucked into the foliage along the way. Like the tour gardens in Japan or their eighteenth-century English equivalents, there are special views or events to be enjoyed as the visitor walks around the water. The events in this case are mostly animal shows, four major ones, which alternate throughout the day and feature lions and tigers and bears and birds and even a dog performing unbelievable stunts. In other areas you're allowed to feed the animals (the Petting Village) and ride them (the Elephant or Camel Ride). Or you can escape the wildlife altogether on the terrace of the Rondavel Restaurant, which is on an island at one corner of the lake. As in the early Ghost Town at Knott's Berry Farm (page 371), there is an appealing hominess to these buildings that overcomes any lack of architectural enchantment. And the landscaping is beautiful; when it matures a little more, any flaws will probably be forgotten.

Like Marineland (page 380), with its Baja Reef swim-through aquarium, Lion Country has one really splendid ride. This is the Zambezi River Ride, involving a flat-bottomed boat with a canvas canopy and a white hunter who steers you, along a track, down the waterways of darkest Africa to observe the wildlife alongside. It sounds like the Jungle Cruise at Disneyland (page 41), but it's not. The spirit of this ride is educational rather than melodramatic, presented conversationally rather than with memorized histrionics, and everything you see is alive; as in Disneyland, the exotic animals and even the many colorful birds always present themselves on cue, but here they are real rather than plastic, responding to the guide's food handouts rather than to electronic signals. The effortless choreography of strange and beautiful creatures darting in and out of view as the boat glides past, from leafy tunnels to sunlight and back, is mesmerizing. What a nice way to be in a zoo.

Clearly, what the designers of Lion Country Safari do best is to shake apart the usual notions of what a zoo ought to be like and then create altogether stunning experiences out of the parts. As seen in the Safari Trails and the Zambezi River Ride, their main device, even more than bringing you in close, has been to apply that particularly L.A. phenomenon of stringing independent attractions into a harmonious series, or a ride. The series of sights becomes an event that is more powerful and memorable than the parts alone. You don't just see it, you feel it with all your body.

XIV 2 · DISNEYLAND SURROUNDS
A tour of the streets around Disneyland, particularly South Harbor Boulevard, West Katella Avenue and West Ball Road

Walt Disney always regretted that he couldn't afford in the beginning to buy up and keep control over the orange groves surrounding the one that became Disneyland. Indeed, when he purchased the great chunks of Florida that became Disneyworld, one of the most secretive land acquisitions in history, Disney made certain there was more than enough of his own real estate around the park to maintain the carefully orchestrated enchantment and to prevent what happened in Anaheim. For here, as soon as Disney's fantasy had become a super-high-profit reality (which was almost instantaneously), an all-American free-for-all of roadside restaurants, motels, miniature golf courses, Go-Kart tracks, and campgrounds popped up all around. Quick to recognize a good thing, the builders of these places seized on Disneyland's themes, especially the futuristic ones, and transformed their everyday buildings into fantasy worlds of their own making.

There is much to be learned in this, as Walt Disney did, about the clutter that

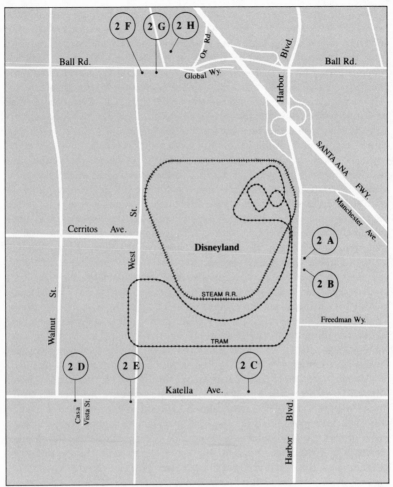

XIV 2 · DISNEYLAND SURROUNDS

laissez-faire commerce can produce, but there is a lot that is humorous and interesting in this particularly intense version of the Southern California streetscape. That most of these little buildings went up in the architectural blind spot of the 1950s and '60s and that most were inspired by Tomorrowland (page 51), Disneyland's quickly dated and now almost comical theme, makes a ride down these streets all the more enjoyable.

The most astonishing of the distractions are to be found on the many, many motels, which often begin and end with the signs out front, with names like Peter Pan or Jack and Jill or, more directly, Fantasy. Other allusions make it as far as the front wall. The Carousel Motel (2 A) (1530 South Harbor Boulevard), oddly, is not round, but sports a huge A-framed tunnel for a porte cochere. Next door, the Tropicana Motel (2 B) (1540 South Harbor) hides behind thick tropical foliage but has a Modern erector-set gift shop out front, a promise of South Seas romance smoothed out by the latest conveniences. One of the most heartfelt is the Alpine Motel (2 C) (715 West Katella), styled like a Swiss log cabin and covered year round by a heavy blanket of plaster snow with big icicles hanging from the eaves.

By far the most extraterrestrial motels are the seven created by a Mr. Al Stoval, who had been a well-known band leader of the 1930s and a legendary mining figure known as "America's Mr. Manganese" before he decided to leave his mark on Anaheim. He built almost all his motels during the early fever for America's space program. The Space Age Lodge (2 D) (1176 West Katella Avenue, 1963) was Stoval's first and most sincerely executed fantasy. Just an ordinary two-story motel building, sheathed in white stucco, it's been decorated at every turn with a variety of Tomorrowland objects, most of which look enthusiastically homemade. The sign out front is in the form of a silver rocket ship with blue fins and the words SPACE AGE written along the side. It's aimed at the street above a silver porte cochere supported on thin columns with sputnik capitals. Nearby, amidst brightly painted moon rocks, is a giant atomic sculpture made of silver-painted interlocking rings; smaller sets of rings, interspersed with more sputniks, are mounted along the edges of every roof to serve as finials for the pipe columns of the balconies. These columns, like the light fixtures and numerous sheet-metal panels, are riddled with different-size round holes—the result, perhaps, of a meteor shower. Other panels, most notably in the office, are made of glittery white plastic sprinkled with blue plastic star bursts that obviously were made from cupcake forms. Molded plastic furniture and the silvery geodesic dome of a poolhouse decorate a swimming pool, which is in the shape of America's first manned space capsules.

About a block away, at 1110 West Katella, is Stoval's fourth masterpiece, the Inn of Tomorrow (2 E) (1969). Here the futuristic trappings of what was becoming a standard Stoval format were soon overshadowed by Stoval's next enthusiastic avocation, also borrowed from Disneyland, the training of hundreds of *Eugenia myrtifolia* to look like animals; Stoval named it the Wonderland of Topiary Trees. Since 1972 Stoval and his assistants have shaped over eight hundred of these shrubs, which are displayed here and at various other of his motels. On a little plot behind the Inn of Tomorrow's swimming pool is a forest made up entirely of clipped green elephants, horses, camels, giraffes, hippos, ducks, rabbits, the Three Bears, the Big Bad Wolf and even Mickey Mouse. As in Disneyland, these more recognizable fantasies have managed to overcome the burdens of an outdated search for tomorrow.

A number of 1970s establishments, much more refined and bland, have joined in the parade: Delaney's (2 F) (1050 West Ball Road) is an English pub with a modern-day witch's roof and pastel-colored fake stones breaking through its stucco wall; the Admiral's Cove Motor Inn (2 G) (1028 West Ball) sports a miniature lighthouse; and the Sheraton-Anaheim Motor Hotel (2 H) (1015 West

XIV 2 D · *Space Age Lodge*
XIV 3 · *Knott's Berry Farm: The Bottle House*

Ball) is an enormous castle made of pre-used brick with a half-timber veneer. Like the themed McDonald's, the newer buildings seem designed by corporate decorators and have none of the cheerful ingenuousness or energy or seat-of-the-pants imagery achieved by Stoval and his contemporaries.

XIV 3 · KNOTT'S BERRY FARM
8039 Beach Boulevard, Buena Park
Walter Knott, 1940 to present
Open daily 10–12 (Friday and Saturday till 1:00 A.M.) in summer; Friday through Tuesday, 10–6 (Friday and Saturday till 9) in winter; admission fee; call (714) 827-1776

Knott's Berry Farm is the oldest historically themed amusement park in America and surely one of its most endearing places. A large number of 1970s thrill rides have been added to keep up with the competition that Knott's spawned, but much of the park still reflects the sort of homemade charm of its beginnings, in the early 1920s, when the grounds were all berry fields and the only building was a roadside fruit stand. In 1928 Walter and Cordelia Knott built their first permanent building, a little market with an attached tearoom where Cordelia served berry pies. In 1934, to bring in extra income during the Depression, Cordelia began serving chicken dinners, a hugely popular venture that soon required a three-hundred-seat restaurant; by 1940 she was serving as many as four thousand dinners a day. That same year, in an effort to entertain the hundreds of people waiting in line, Walter began to build a little ghost town next to the restaurant, and that uniquely Southern California phenomenon, the theme park, was born.

During the 1940s and early '50s, Walter Knott's Ghost Town grew into a sizable village of six little streets lined with ramshackle stores and saloons and assorted false fronts. Knott built most of them himself, often modeling them after famous Western buildings, but many, such as the schoolhouse, the hotel and several log cabins, are the genuine nineteenth-century article, purchased and brought here from towns around the Old West. Knott furnished the rooms with old-time paraphernalia and populated them with costumed mannequins or with costumed employees who sold trinkets and jars of jam or poured out glasses of boysenberry juice; some even cancanned in the Calico Saloon or acted out melodramas in the Bird Cage Theatre. Stagecoaches rattled in and out ot town, and an authentic Colorado mining train steamed up to a Victorian station. And there was no admission charge: this was, after all, just a pleasant place to wait for your chicken dinner.

The ingenuous sincerity of it all managed to overcome a thick layer of hokum, so everything looked—and smelled—very old and dusty and real. And it does still. The wild new rides have been placed in separate areas, called Fiesta Village and Roaring 20s, to the north and west of Ghost Town; except for minor additions, including a general admission charge, Walter Knott's original fantasy is unspoiled.

Visitors still leave their cars in what are surely Los Angeles' most pleasant parking lots, which are just grass and dirt shaded by giant eucalyptus, sycamores, pines and palms. The scale is brought down here, by the trees and the general layout, to the point that people can feel they've arrived at somewhere special. Near the parking forest on the east, across the street from the entrance, looms a full-scale replica of Philadelphia's Independence Hall, exact down to the Liberty Bell, a breathtakingly extensive statement about Mr. Knott's love of America. In the shadow of Independence Hall, a little to the north, is a wonderfully decrepit and amateurish playground for children called Jungle Island, which is surrounded by a lagoon and reached by a tiny covered bridge. The foliage is thick and tropical and penetrated by paths and little clearings with simple objects to climb around on; along the water's edge are a variety of primitive but carefully thought about water devices that allow participants to squirt streams of water at targets in the lagoon.

Entrance is through a white-plaster and red-tile Mission Style arcade. Directly behind is a circle of covered wagons around a grove of eucalyptus; a little Western town has grown up at one end, the stage for a Wild West Stunt Show. To the left is Ghost Town's first street, which includes a house constructed out of thousands of bottles, an exact replica of Judge Roy Bean's courthouse saloon and a fake adobe ruin like the one at Mission San Gabriel (page 63) but much more real, with giant boughs of ivy and purple bougainvillea hanging over the arches.

Across from here is a general store where some of the goods are old, for atmosphere, and some are new, for sale. There's a big potbellied stove around which visitors can sit comfortably on a winter afternoon and play checkers. Back at the beginning of this street is the most memorable building in Ghost Town, the Gold Trails Hotel (from Prescott, Arizona, 1868), a two-story rustic Victorian structure with peeling gray paint and a handsome cupola on the roof. Empty rocking chairs rock themselves gently and spookily on an upstairs terrace; inside is the simple and charming Covered Wagon Show, Walter Knott's first attraction, which is just a little room where lights on a desert diorama fade into nightfall as the taped voice of an old cowboy recalls how it all used to be.

Near the hotel is a sunken desert landscape where visitors are invited to pan for gold in water that seems to splash down from an earth-red plaster volcano; the most thrilling way to get there is along a mine tunnel that snakes eerily through the smoking mountain. And then comes Ghost Town's longest street, which zigzags diagonally past souvenir shops in every imaginable disguise; mixed in with them are mannequin displays, behind fixed windows, of a Chinese laundry, a gunsmith, a post office and a whorehouse, this last a big surprise

XIV 3 · KNOTT'S BERRY FARM and XIV 4 · MOVIELAND WAX MUSEUM

XIV 3 · *Knott's Berry Farm:*
Timber Mountain Log Ride

in a place that is so morally spotless beneath its layer of applied dust. Next to the loose women, also oddly, is the sheriff's office, and behind that an outhouse-size jail whose mannequin prisoner flabbergasts visitors who peer inside by mentioning their names. Farther along is the Bird Cage Theatre, copied from the one in Tombstone, Arizona, and a little red schoolhouse, built in Beloit, Kansas, in 1875 and filled with inkwell desks and McGuffey's readers.

It's interesting that Walter Knott didn't scale his buildings down, as did Walter Disney a few years later, yet achieved a similar intimacy with a lot of miniature things inside them or nearby, with displays in the windows and in the many Western dioramas. Knott also planted a great many pepper trees, which are the best possible trees for creating the kind of fine scale and dappled sunlight that makes it so wonderful in California and in particular in Knott's Berry Farm.

Across from the red barn a little walkway winds between a railroad trestle and a mountain stream. On the other side of the tracks is a gigantic stucco wall (the back of the Good Time Theatre) that is painted, like a movie backdrop, to look as if it were about thirty miles of mountains. The bottom part gradually becomes three-dimensional, turning into plaster rock formations and plaster Indians and real cactus. The path continues through a simulated Boot Hill (where the graves are fake but the tombstones are said to be real), passes a building made out of barrels, and ends at a gristmill (ca. 1865) brought here from England by way of Yuba City, California; its waterwheel still grinds flour, which is offered for sale.

North of here, just across the railroad tracks, is the Haunted Shack, an old and very simple and always astonishing exhibit. Groups of visitors are guided through a tumbledown cabin whose rooms have been cleverly tilted so that water appears to run uphill and people can sit down on the walls. The tour is particularly moving in that the experience is your own: you are participating, and it is your perceptions that are being played with; you are not just sitting and watching a show.

Nearby are two of Knott's Berry Farm's finest Old West rides. The older of the two, the Calico Mine Ride, takes visitors on a tiny, slow mining train through the inside of a giant plaster mountain, past thundering waterfalls and sparkling treasures and a few not too terrifying adventures. It's all very much like one of Disneyland's happiest earlier rides, a train trip through Nature's Wonderland, which was replaced by the neck-snapping Big Thunder Mountain Railroad roller coaster (page 48). The other ride, which takes place in and around an even bigger mountain of plaster, is called the Timber Mountain Log Ride, one of the most satisfying adventures in Southern California. Knott's Berry Farm's version of the ubiquitous water-flume ride manages to combine the exhilarating yet gentle movement of Magic Mountain's Log Jammer ride (page 393), which offers little to see along the way, with Big Thunder Mountain's beautifully crafted scenery, which goes by so fast you never get the chance to notice it; and then it adds a few layers of homey charms found only in Ghost Town. Much of the ride takes place in a dark tunnel, the old Disney device, setting up the surprise of bursting into the sunlight with boulders and waterfalls framing views of the trees below or of entering suddenly into large caverns where miners are working and more waterfalls are crashing. As in Thunder Mountain, the waiting line has become part of the ride, snaking up through rocky canyons past mining shanties and perilously poised equipment; only here it's even better, thanks mostly to the gushing water displays, which are everywhere; at one point visitors actually walk underneath a waterfall and can look out on the park through a shimmering window of water.

The north part of Knott's Berry Farm is occupied by Fiesta Village, a softly handsome, luxuriantly planted recollection of small towns in Mexico. A lot of people, however, seem to think of it as just a place to pass through on the way to the famous Montezooma's Revenge, a great long snake of a roller coaster with a coil near one end that allows riders to be upside down for a split second. Fortunately, the entrance to this ride is at the far end, as are the rest of the village's rides, which are only standard carnival attractions disguised mostly by their names—Tijuana Taxi, Mexican Whip and the like. Except for the screams and the occasional view of people hanging from their seat clamps, most of Fiesta Village is extraordinarily beautiful and almost peaceful.

The first half is a big lake that breaks up on the east into two ponds surrounded by jungle foliage and crossed by little bridges. Two more bridges, much longer ones, arch over the lake to an island pavilion in the center, a sort of World's Fair fantasy with a huge white canvas dome rising out of a series of gaily painted Mission end walls. Near the west shore, shaded by a row of eucalyptus trees, are exquisite models of the California missions, each one in a little adobe shed. Ducks and geese glide by as people stroll along the edges or sit on brightly colored docks that look like tiny boats. At night little lights outline the awnings of the boats and sparkle on the trees and flowers and reflect in the water; and the translucent dome of the pavilion, lit from within, glows orange and peach and vivid red, as if by sorcery. Beyond the lake is the Mexican village, whose simple white-plaster and red-tile buildings, arranged around two splashing fountains, are enlivened by multicolored arches and brightly hued tiles and signs and tourists.

Beyond the village comes the newest part of the park, thrill rides. Almost the whole western half of Knott's Berry Farm has been given over to the latest off-the-shelf roller coasters and centrifuges and general stomach-wrenchers; sometimes they've been given a thinly applied theme, something to do with a Roaring '20s air show, but they're always immediately recognizable as the kind found in amusement parks everywhere. Knott's now even has a revolving sky tower, just like all the rest, so visitors can look down on the flat roofs and air conditioners behind the false fronts; only at Knott's, though, can they also stare out at other visitors floating by in tiny parachutes. The architecture of the new part is slick and half hearted and suffers a prefabricated anonymity—a match, like the rides, for Magic Mountain, where they seem to have ordered everything except the trees from a catalog.

It's always a disappointment to see how Knott's Berry Farm finds it necessary to stop doing what they do so well and add more and more of the standard, sure-fire, commercially successful gimmicks in order to keep up with the competition. Disneyland has done it, too, though they at least make the attempt to disguise their roller coasters. But Disneyland is at its best when it lays on the hokum so thick that, as Noël Coward said about the phony in L.A., it becomes really convincing. Knott's is at its best when its hokum is homey and more transparent; but in the new stuff there's hardly any hokum at all. There is, however, one ride in the new part that merits a visit. It's called Knott's Beary Tales and stirs up memories of Disneyland's very old rides, like Peter Pan's Flight, where, for instance, flames are obviously red cellophane blown by a fan. The Knott's version features a ride through bright green two-dimensional forests with simple cartoon characters, painted in Day-Glo colors, moving to uncomplicated mechanical rhythms. In this era of computer games and video and Disney's sophisticated animatronics, such simpleminded corniness can be dazzling. This ride is a direct descendant of Ghost Town: like the Covered Wagon show and the Haunted Shack and just about all of Ghost Town, it displays so much evidence of someone caring that we go along with it and either ignore or find delight in the homespun techniques.

XIV 4 · MOVIELAND WAX MUSEUM
7711 Beach Boulevard, one block north of Knott's Berry Farm, Buena Park
1962
Open daily 9–9 (winter, 10–8), Friday and Saturday until 10 P.M.;
admission fee; call (213) 583-8026 or (714) 522-1154

Billed as the "Greatest gathering of stars in the world," this glittery place manages to live up to most people's expectations of what Hollywood ought to be like. The enormous white warehouse of a building is fancied up along its façade with eye-catching effects, so that by day it sparkles and by night it gleams. The interior, on the other hand, looks like a sound stage: everything is either pitch black or brightly colored under precisely aimed spotlights. In here the visitors can stroll past an extraordinary number of famous scenes from the movies, with lifelike wax movie stars posing in original costumes in front of original sets. Scratchy clips from the sound tracks accompany many of the tableaux: Shirley Temple sings "The Good Ship Lollipop" from *Bright Eyes*; gunfire interrupts Edward G. Robinson's snappy dialogue in *Little Caesar*; the Roman crowd cheers on Charlton Heston in *Ben-Hur*. Some effects are more elaborate: a perpetual downpour almost drowns out Gene Kelly in *Singing in the Rain*; cold air and rooms engulfed by artificial snow set the mood for *Dr. Zhivago*; a similarly icy feeling pervades a more recent insertion of the North Pole hideaway in *Superman*. New scenes from the latest box-office hits are added regularly. The newest attraction is called the Black Box, in which groups of people are ushered through remarkably realistic sets from the horror movies *Halloween*, *Altered States* and *Alien*.

The glitter and hoopla and the flagrant phoniness of the Movieland Wax Museum seem just the right approach for the subject at hand, the silver screen, which is by definition unreal. The wax figures deny movement, but they add three-dimensionality and allow us a strange sort of intimacy with our favorite movie stars—almost, but not quite, like getting to look behind the scenes. Though this particular piece of show business is usually less convincing than the movies, it is no less real, and it makes for an interesting retrospective, something like watching Parts I and II of *That's Entertainment.*

XIV 5 · QUEEN MARY

Pier J, Long Beach; take the Long Beach Freeway (7) south to the *Queen Mary* exit

Cunard Steamship Company, Ltd; Benjamin V. Morris, head architect; John Brown and Company, Ltd, Clydebank, Scotland, builder

Launched: 1934; maiden voyage: 1936; berthed in Long Beach: 1967

Open daily, 10–4; admission fee

Sometime after a bon voyage party in the late 1930s, Beatrice Lillie, the English comedienne, summed up most people's feelings about the *Queen Mary* when she inquired, "When does this place get to Europe?" For thirty-one years, on a thousand voyages across the Atlantic, the *Queen Mary* was one of the most special places in all the world. In an era when few things were as elegant and dashing as a luxury liner, this one was the grandest of the lot. She was certainly the biggest—the largest passenger ship ever built. The statistics go on and on: she was 1,019 feet long, displaced 81,237 tons, and had 2,000 portholes, 10 million rivets and 140 tons of paint on the exterior alone; each of her three 65-foot-high smokestacks could have accommodated three train engines traveling abreast; four turbines, capable of 40,000 horsepower each, drove four 35-ton propellers at a cruising speed of 28 knots; and she used up a gallon of fuel every 13 feet. With a crew of some 1,200, it cost, even in the 1930s, about $20,000 a day to keep her running.

But the expense was not a concern for each trip's 1,900 or so passengers, or at least not for the ones in first class, who included some of the richest and most celebrated people of two continents. The *Queen Mary* was a palace and an Art

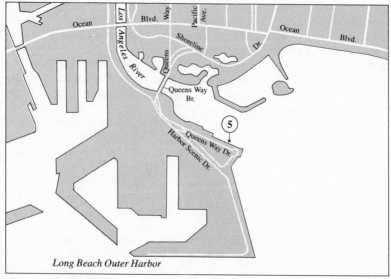

Long Beach Outer Harbor

XIV 5 · QUEEN MARY

Deco one at that, designed during the full flowering of that extravagant style. Her vast dining rooms and lounges and salons were resplendent with the work of some thirty artists, who covered every inch with vibrant murals and tapestries and inlaid wood panels and marble plaques and etched glass and molded bronze and streamlined nickel-silver railings. Their enthusiasms flowed down grand staircases and into the lobbies, and even the corridors and staterooms had sleek wood veneers. They used fifty-six kinds of wood in all, and the *Queen Mary* became known as "the ship of beautiful woods." But she was better known for something grander even than the opulent trappings: she was the pride of her builders and her crew and all of England, and that extraordinary love was reflected in every part, warmer than any wood. You felt it as soon as you arrived on board. As Beatrice Lillie implied, the *Queen Mary* was not just an elegant way to get somewhere; she was a destination—and she was almost a person.

But it's all very different today. The body of this once grand lady has been fastened permanently to a pier in Long Beach, her starboard side hemmed in by a breakwater, her port side by ramps and escalators and post-industrial towers. Visiting her now is a bit like going to a funeral: the familiar features are still there, rouged and made up as if she were alive, but you know it isn't true. The spirit and the magic have gone, replaced by the unguided efforts of various commercial enterprises to turn a proud ship into a tourist attraction.

Some of the grand rooms are intact: the King's Grille and the Queen's Salon and the Art Deco Lounge, which overlooks the bow, are still lavish affairs, the latter a gleaming Streamline Moderne spectacular. The bridge is dazzling, too, with its intricate array of steering wheels and compasses and engine-room telegraphs, all in highly polished brass. The rest, or at least the remaining parts of the three main decks that the visitor can wander about on, is a disappointment. There are a number of museumlike displays, usually behind big windows, of the captain's quarters, various table settings, a first-class suite, a barbershop, a radio room and a bunk room from the World War II days when the *Queen Mary* was a troop transport. They're all interesting, but they look like the exhibits they are, disengaged completely from what they used to be a part of. Most of the displays, in fact, were brought up from their original locations and were inserted into holes left over after the remodelers had gouged away equally grand places. The worst offenders are the numerous gift shops and restaurants and fast-food stands that have hacked their way into some of the ship's finest rooms and then try to hide the wounds with shopping-mall veneers. At one point someone turned about four hundred of the staterooms into a hotel and came up with a sort of Holiday Inn with portholes. At these moments the *Queen's* funeral begins to look more like her post-mortem, or maybe her scavenging by vultures.

The tour of the engine room, which is reached through a hole near the waterline, is at once one of the most fascinating and disheartening of the exhibits. It begins with another museum, whose objects get lost in the dark cavern that has been cut out for them, and goes down narrow stairs and steel catwalks to the astonishingly huge machinery, or what's left of it, that somehow made this small city glide through the water—so fast that German U-boats couldn't hope to get a bearing. The size and complexity of this maze of turbines and shafts and pipes and gauges is staggering, and yet nowhere else is it more apparent that the old lady's heart has stopped and that she is dead. Most of her engines have been removed and sold as scrap, three of her propellers now serve as trophies on shore, and lifelike steam jets make this cavity all the more ghoulish.

A new organization has recently taken over the *Queen Mary* and promises to change things for the better. It has a long way to go. What's happened to the *Queen Mary* recalls the endless 1950s and '60s remodelings of old and beautiful buildings where their most wonderful parts were mercilessly scraped off and replaced with hokum and commercial sleaze. Almost all the special qualities of this ship have been ignored or destroyed as it has been adapted for uncreative re-use into what will sell or rent or seem familiar to another generation. There's the unmistakable feeling here that the redesigners have never been on this ship, or even any ship. To take a first-class stateroom, with all the vanished splendor that the idea, at least, of a stateroom implies, and turn it into a motel bedroom is really a dreary idea; the result is the quintessence of everything that is so tacky and so commonplace that it can't possibly have any specialness or magic.

But the project was a perilous one from the beginning, based as it is on such an odd premise. Here, in a city where the real seems phony and the phony real and where *almost* anything can be turned into a ride, the people of Long Beach decided to turn a real ride, one of the most glorious rides of all time, into a fake one. It seems far easier to pull off when it's the other way around, as with Lion Country Safari (page 366), where a piece of Orange County was changed into a convincing habitat for ostriches and giraffes and lions. That the *Queen Mary* remodelers have made their fake ride unconvincing has only made matters worse.

Near the entrance to the *Queen Mary*, in a similar vein, is a make-believe sixteenth-century English shopping village, called Londontowne, whose little buildings have lots of small-paned windows and half-timbered walls and steep roofs with tall brick chimneys. It has exactly as much charm as one of the *Queen Mary*'s revamped staterooms, but it's hard to say precisely why. The place does look a lot like an English village. God knows we've been to a great many of the real ones and enjoyed them, but there's something macabre about this one. It has the smell of phoniness in the bad sense; it is not a place that makes you feel good. Comparisons come to mind with Main Street in Disneyland (page 39) and with Crossroads of the World (page 174), both of which do make us feel good. Part of the excitement of these places is that the theme is unabashedly eclectic: someone has had a wonderful time choosing shapes and transforming them. At Disneyland they transformed the scale and the building styles and a great many other things, too—the colors, the banners, the policemen's suits, the works. At Crossroads they had a wonderful time miniaturizing, massaging, making ambiguous, and changing around various pieces of the world's architecture with considerable wit. But at Londontowne there is the sense that whoever did these buildings did so because he was hired to and had to and it doesn't seem as though he enjoyed it very much. We can't put our finger on exactly why that is or what the tipoff might be, but we're sure it's the case. Whenever a place has been loved over, however temporary or cheap it is, it gives the same air of confidence that people do who have been loved over; and when a place has been deprived, it can act with the same hostilities as people who have been deprived often do.

A more recent installation (1983) next to the world's largest passenger ship is the world's largest airplane, Howard Hughes' *Spruce Goose,* which is housed inside the world's largest clear-span aluminum dome (415 feet in diameter). Hughes built this 8-engine, 319-foot-wingspan, all-wood flying boat during World War II as a prototype transport for the U.S. Government, but the war was over by the time it was done. By 1947 controversy over the project had reached a Senate investigating committee, which claimed among other things

that the plane couldn't fly. Hughes won that day by personally piloting his behemoth on a Kitty Hawk sort of maiden flight—one mile long, seventy feet
above the harbor; after that he removed it to a Long Beach hangar, where it
stayed, carefully maintained, for thirty-five years. And now it's here, all four
hundred thousand pounds of it, astonishingly big and beautiful and as mysterious as the man who built it—a billionaire's Watts Towers.

XIV 6 · PORTS O' CALL VILLAGE
**Berth 77, San Pedro; take the Harbor Boulevard exit from the Harbor
Freeway (11), turn right and follow the signs for half a mile**
*Vern Lechman and Cushman-Long (phases 1 and 2); Charles Ramm
Associates (phase 3), 1962 to present*
Open daily, 11–9

Ports O' Call Village is a long, very narrow and beautifully landscaped cluster
of shops and restaurants on a finger of land beside the main channel of San Pedro Harbor. It is one of the first specialty, or themed, shopping centers in
America and one of the most successful. Its theme, a none too serious evocation
of a New England fishing village, has been modified by the foliage into a sort of
sun-drenched tropical oasis and made vibrant by a very L.A. sort of juxtaposition: modern fishing boats are moored all around, huge tankers and freighters
pass close by and eerily colossal machinery looms up from shipyards across the
channel.

The village was built in three phases, beginning in 1962. The first phase

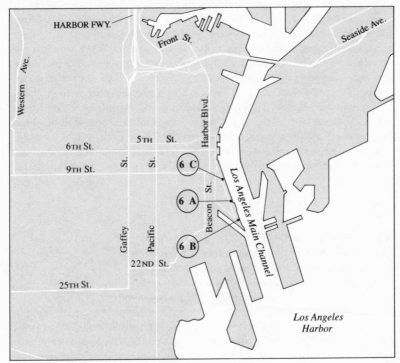

XIV 6 · PORTS O' CALL VILLAGE

(6 A), in the middle, is a particularly relaxed mixture of California Ranch board-and-batten and shakes, a somewhat Spanishy stucco, and a little Beverly Hills ornamented French, just like everything else in Los Angeles—especially in the early 1960s. The Polynesian-flavored Ports O' Call Restaurant, engulfed by palms and reached by bridges over jungle pools, echoes the 1950s love affair with the South Seas and offers pleasant views of the harbor. The next section (6 B), on the south, is the prettiest. After the spare landscape of New England was substituted for *Kon-Tiki,* an Old Nantucket whaling port theme was kept in mind and was carried out with considerable verve. The shops are mostly two stories, but they seem small and cute, arranged informally along winding brick streets or wooden wharves or intimate plazas. The buildings come in a number of persuasions, covered in clapboard or shingles or sometimes brick, but they all seem to belong here, united by certain details, like small-paned windows in white frames and by the luxuriant foliage and the care that went into them. Three full-size, square-rigged sailing ships, which go out on harbor and dinner cruises, are berthed at one of the wharves; their intricately rigged masts float above the little buildings at least as realistically as the Matterhorn at Disneyland does above Main Street (page 39).

The newest part (6 C), some distance to the north, was inspired perhaps by Pier 39 in San Francisco and other sorts of latter-day packing-crate phenomena. It's a much schlockier, more egregiously ad-hoc version of a fishing village, piled up out of shed-roofed factory forms covered in worn-out wood and rusty sheets of corrugated metal. Still, even this clunkier section is saved by its sea-washed location and by a row of big fishing boats tied up behind. More than anything, it's the sea that makes this part and all the parts of Ports O' Call come alive; in particular, it's the ever-present, weirdly dramatic view of those shipyards across the way, of giant and magnificent cranes that are somewhere between a piece of sculpture, of the bigger-than-Picasso variety but much better, and some monster out of the 1960s that could walk right over you.

It's interesting to compare this manufactured seaside village with the one we've just visited beside the *Queen Mary.* The two share a number of similarities, including being right up against some monumental feats of naval engineering, but Ports O' Call seems cheerful and alive while the other seems macabre and sinister and, like the Tin Man, without a heart. Part of the reason for the difference might be that the *Queen Mary* village introduces a shell, a sort of death mask of a once glorious ship and ride, now dead in the water, harnessed and gutted; Ports O' Call, on the other hand, is a place to watch great machines and ships that move and blow their whistles and go about the business they were built for.

XIV 7 · MARINELAND
6610 Palos Verdes Drive South, Ranch Palos Verdes
1945; 1978, remodeled by Pereira and Luckman
Open daily, 10–7, in summer; Wednesday through Sunday, 10–5, fall,
winter and spring; admission fee; call (213) 541-5663

First opened in 1954, a year before Disneyland, Marineland is one of Los Angeles' first theme parks. From the beginning, the sea-life theme has never really been helped along by the architecture. And then there was a mid-1970s remodeling by new owners, Hanna-Barbera, the famous makers of animated cartoons,

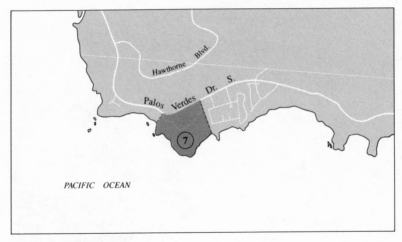

PACIFIC OCEAN

XIV 7 · MARINELAND

aided by Pereira and Luckman, the famous makers of skyscrapers. So now there are silly blowups of Yogi Bear and his friends plastered around everywhere, trying to liven up International Style boxes and monumentally futuristic amphitheaters, fish tanks and pedestrian ramps. The tropical landscaping, though overwhelmed by the buildings, adds to the sea-washed appeal of the site, which is the greatest asset of both the theme and the park. Marineland lies along the cliff edge of a particularly dramatic bulge of Los Angeles into the ocean; directly behind it are surprisingly barren and grassy hillsides that heighten a 180-degree sweep of the Pacific, focusing on an extraordinary view of Santa Catalina Island. The view from Marineland's new observation tower, the sine qua non of latter-day amusement parks, is for once worth the acrophobia; and, unlike most of the other parks, the tops of these buildings are no less attractive than their sides.

Many of the exhibits, usually the older ones, are just bigger versions of those in a standard zoo or aquarium: walruses and penguins flap around in lumpy plaster enclosures; unidentifiable fish swim by, barely visible through the dirty windows and murky water of enormous steel tanks, one oval and one round. But some of the newer exhibits are fascinating: the *Encyclopaedia Britannica* offers colorful displays of deadly sea creatures, and the Marine Animal Care Center demonstrates how sick and injured sea mammals and birds, found along the seacoast, are treated before being released. At the southeast corner of the park is a pool where visitors can lean over and throw balls for a remarkably friendly group of dolphins and sea lions. Nearby, a trail winds down a little ravine to Sea Lion Point, a natural sanctuary for sea lions on an offshore outcropping of rock; they are always there, dozens of them, barking and flopping around their little island, the only volunteers in this giant seaside circus.

The main attractions at Marineland are the seven live performances, staged in separate arenas and scheduled so that at least one is going on at any given moment. For the most part, they are the expected animal-and-trainer acts, though they are often thrillingly executed, from carefully choreographed sea lion high jinks to breathtaking leaps by dolphins and giant killer whales. But Marineland's most memorable show is its newest, the Baja Reef, where (for an additional fee) the spectator becomes the performer by donning a wetsuit and a face mask and swimming through a 240-foot-long, 12-foot-deep representation

of a reef along Baja California. The visitor is allowed to glide along at his own pace, completely unguided, through the clear water of an undersea world whose craggy walls and sandy bottom seem altogether real; tiny fish, in brightly colored schools, dart in and out of leafy plants and dark hollows, while bigger fish and fellow swimmers drift gracefully by. For a few minutes, the straitlaced buildings on the surface are forgotten, and Marineland becomes a magic place after all.

XIV 8 · CASTLE PARK
2410 West Compton Boulevard, just west of the San Diego Freeway, Redondo Beach
Take the Inglewood exit: turn north, then west on Compton Boulevard
1978
Open daily; admission fee for golf and water slide

This Castle Park, the first and biggest of three Castle Parks in Los Angeles, is included here to represent the numerous miniature golf attractions that have blossomed all around Southern California. The ones of recent years began as straightforward prefabricated versions of the owner-built (and endearingly amateurish, quirky and high-spirited) pee-wee golf courses of old, but lately have added such other features as electronic games, water slides and snack bars in an effort to become complete Family Entertainment Centers. This one, lying up against piers of the San Diego Freeway, is one of the best, or at least biggest, of the new breed.

In the middle is the cavernous, foursquare, turreted and fake-rocked castle surrounded by a moat where plaster tortoises either swim or hover depending on the water's depth that day. This fortress is the opposite of most historical ones in that the battles (the latest in video warfare) all take place inside, saving the rest of the grounds for less bellicose fantasies. The richly planted golf course wraps sinuously around the castle and then around a lake on the south, each hole enshrined by a small, apparently off-the-rack edifice—a gingerbread house or a California mission or the false front of a frontier town.

A stroll through these gardens, with or without a golf ball, is a pleasant one,

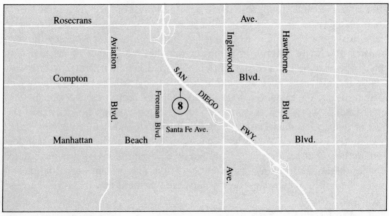

XIV 8 · CASTLE PARK

but there are a number of problems: first, the lake's heavy concrete edges and obvious shallowness dispel some of the naturalistic enchantment; second, the young plants haven't managed yet (and may never be allowed) to entangle each little architectural vision into a magic world. Some of the most moving parts of these miniature villages involve the mix-up in scale between tiny make-believe objects and full-size items from the real world. Since this sort of contrast is most easily achieved with large trees, Castle Park should improve when its foliage matures. In the meantime there is always the colossal San Diego Freeway rushing by, almost overhead, to help send the visitor's sensibilities flying.

The dumbest part, though, of a circumambulation through most of the miniature golf fantasies, new or old, is that the journey is conceptual rather than experiential; neither player nor ball goes through any special kinetic excitements like both do in the much simpler miniature golf course, Golf Gardens, on Santa Catalina (page 360). The much fussed-up little buildings are isolated objects with no decipherable reason for their position in the drama. Maybe it's pretentious and unfair to pit these delicate diversions against the garden masterpieces of seventeenth-century Japan or eighteenth-century England, but they tease you on (or at least they tease us on) to expect a pop version of the same rich and unflawed narrative of evocative pieces combined into a dramatic event, of the sort that enriches the Rikugi-en in Tokyo or Stourhead in England or Disneyland in Anaheim. Here the architectural or landscape events along the way don't seem part of any plot that builds to a conclusion beyond tallying up the score.

Adjoining, the newest and fastest thrill, which has numerous siblings, too, is the water slide. Here, at a cost of $3 per hour plus one day of subsequent muscular agony for every three years of age by which the headlong plunger exceeds fourteen, one can rent a thin mat and plummet (over and over) down one of four moistened chutes into a little pool at the bottom. The bonus is Participation, the Glory of Our Time. The penalty is skinned elbows and knees and the rude derision of the Adolescent Majority.

XIV 9 · TWO FOLK FANTASIES

There is a fascinating category of buildings that are built by what unsympathetic people might call monomaniacs, who—for one reason or another, but usually after suffering some disappointment—devote the rest of their lives or at least a great many years to making something. At the Cliff House in San Francisco there used to be a wax statue of some Oriental man that was made by the man himself, absolutely faithful; so complete was the transference of the man into the image that he plucked out all his hairs and jammed them into the wax. There are less scary phenomena that are made by people, often people of no special means, out of things that are at hand, like broken crockery or glass or bits of metal. Watts Towers is probably the grandest example in America of this sort of thing; Grandma Prisbrey's Bottle Village in Simi Valley is often placed high on the list as well. A special fascination develops for these works, as it does for anything that has been cared for and loved over and invested with so much human attention. In many instances the works may be untutored or uncomposed, but still it is the sheer energy and love that went into them that carries.

A · WATTS TOWERS
1765 East 107 Street, Los Angeles
Simon Rodia, 1921–1954
Administered by the Los Angeles Department of Cultural Affairs; no public access, but the towers are visible from all sides

The acts of love, in this case, were produced by one Sabbatino (Simon) Rodia, an Italian immigrant tile-setter who lived in a little house, since burned down, on this knife-edged triangular lot in Watts. He underwent, apparently, some personal misfortune and then spent three decades (1921–1954) building these amazing towers out of scraps of metal covered in plaster and decorated with bits of ceramic and glass and thousands and thousands of seashells. He did it all himself, suspended on a window washer's seat, adding pieces as the spirit of the thing moved him: "How could I have help?" he later said. "I couldn't tell anyone what to do . . . most of the time I didn't know what to do myself."

The towers are very high (the highest is 107 feet) and appear to be extremely fragile, as delicate and lacy as Christmas tree ornaments, so a large part of their fame comes from the extraneous fact that they are extraordinarily strong. Urban renewers from the City of Los Angeles tried to tear the towers down in 1957 in order to build a bowling alley or something, using as an excuse that they were structurally unsound because they were so thin. But, as Rodia had predicted,

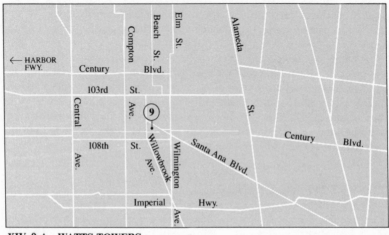

XIV 9 A · WATTS TOWERS

XIV 9 A · *Watts Towers*

his towers couldn't be pulled down, so money and support were marshaled to save them.

Much more important than the structural excitement, though, is the loving way in which each shiny shard has been chosen and placed into this freeform masterpiece of folk art; Rodia's work is so vivid and exciting and so much a world in itself that it doesn't matter how big or small it is. His towers are on a very ordinary little piece of ground, on a very ordinary street, in a very ordinary part of Los Angeles, but they are magic; they transcend place. And, untutored as the composition may be, it is extremely beautiful.

B · GRANDMA PRISBREY'S BOTTLE VILLAGE
**4595 Cochran Street, about a quarter-mile east of Tapo Street, Simi
    Valley; from the San Fernando-Simi Valley Freeway (118), take Tapo
    Canyon Road south to Cochran Street, then go east**
Grandma Prisbrey, 1955–1972

There are many more of these personal statements around the world, but there is only one more well-known in the Los Angeles area; it is about forty miles northwest of Watts, in Simi Valley, on a narrow third of an acre, surrounded— and, at this writing—threatened by advancing suburbia. Bottle Village is a collection of thirteen little buildings made up of hundreds and thousands of glass bottles and an astonishing variety of broken plates, ceramic tiles, tools, toys, television sets, automobile parts and anything else that might sparkle in a junkyard. It was all done between 1955 and 1972 by a Grandma Prisbrey, whose personal tragedies during that period were staggering—the deaths of six of her seven children and finally that of her husband. "I had to do a job to forget," she said.

It all started when Grandma Prisbrey, then sixty years old, needed a building to house her collection of seventeen thousand pencils, which had outgrown her tiny house trailer. Not having much money, she went to a garbage dump for materials and saw treasures there that the rest of us, save Simon Rodia and a few others, are usually blind to. And so the vision began to unfold, piece by piece, each one discovered in some mound of garbage, brought back in an old

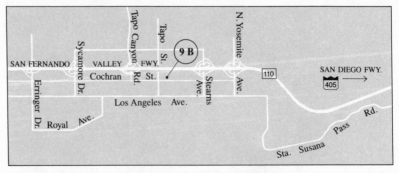

XIV 9 B · GRANDMA PRISBREY'S BOTTLE VILLAGE

truck and lovingly positioned in this new little world. The outsides of the buildings, especially today, often recall the junkyards they came from, but the interiors can become magical; sunlight gives every room a glow of its own as it filters
through or reflects against the different materials—the hundred and eighty
thousand green wine bottles of the Rumpus Room, the three thousand amber
beer bottles of the Little Hut, the thousand shells of the Shell House, or the
gold-painted Venetian blinds and telephone poles of Cleopatra's Bedroom.
Other buildings accommodate special collections: the School House contains a
thousand books and the Doll House some five hundred fifty dolls; and, of
course, there's the Pencil House, with space for two thousand pens. There are
objects in the landscape, too: a pyramid of automobile headlights, a wishing
well of bright blue milk-of-magnesia bottles, a TV Tube Walk lined with twenty-eight picture tubes, a mixed-media Leaning Tower of Bottle Village, and a
very spooky planter where little doll's heads on sticks seem to grow among the
flowers.

Until recently, Grandma Prisbrey gave lively tours through her miniature
world, but failing health forced her at last to move away. Without her attention
and love, the fragile village has deteriorated rapidly; a developer wants to tear it
down, while other people try desperately to save it, claiming that this is "one of
the most significant extant examples of twentieth-century American folk art."
Grandma Prisbrey, leading a tour, called it simply "my monument to show
biz." But there's something more than that, beyond the glittery surfaces and
Grandma's lighthearted descriptions of her life laid out here. There is a spirit to
this place that can be felt everywhere but is most revealed, perhaps, in the little
garden of plastic doll's heads, which seem at once so macabre or half-crazed
and achingly, heartbreakingly sad. There was once a rose garden here that was
tended by one of Grandma Prisbrey's daughters until she died. After the roses
died, too, she replaced them with colored bottles, which she thought of as im-
mortal blossoms.

XIV 10 · MOVIE STUDIOS

Even more than its beaches and balmy climate, Los Angeles is known throughout the world as the place where movies are made; Hollywood movie studios
and movie stars have always been the first item on the tourist's list. But things
are a little different today. During the 1950s, the movie companies suffered severe declines, brought about mostly by the growth of television. Many of them
left Hollywood and went on location or into partnership (or receivership) or

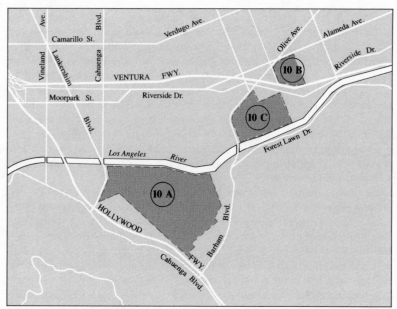

XIV 10 · MOVIE STUDIOS

into television themselves; mega-corporate economics were in, the star system and the studio tours were out. At the same time that this was happening, Walt Disney was picking up on the excitement of the studios, using movie magic to create images of other places and things to do within the images; and so Disneyland became the number one tourist attraction. There was, however, one noticeable difference: the magic in Anaheim was never explained; no one was ever allowed to peek behind the scenes.

Then, in 1964, in an L.A. sort of twist, Universal Studios decided to go into the tour business in a big way, using Disneyland as a model. They turned their old studio tour into a ride and lined it, increasingly, with replicas of movie sets and props. It's not at all clear whether this double-negative of fakery has created something that is real or is just ultra fake. On the other hand, there is the unheralded Burbank Studios Tour, the last of its kind, which allows visitors to see exactly how fake the real props are; but there is a lot of magic, too, as we witness how little it takes for skilled movie people to create their illusions. It's probably unfair to compare the two: both kinds of experience are fun. We can only point the way to Burbank, Hollywood's new home, and offer once again Noël Coward's observation that Los Angeles is, by nature, the place where the phony seems real and the real phony; the movie studios just add a few more layers of unreality to it all.

A · UNIVERSAL STUDIOS
Between the Hollywood (101) and the Ventura (134) freeways, Universal City; take the Lankershim Boulevard/Universal City exit from the Hollywood Freeway, or take the Cahuenga Boulevard exit from the Ventura Freeway and go south to Lankershim
1964 to present
Open daily except Thanksgiving and Christmas; call (213) 877-1311 for hours; admission fee

Universal Studios, spread across 420 acres in the foothills of the Santa Monica Mountains, is the largest motion picture and television production company in the world; and it's one of the oldest, founded in 1915. While most studios never allow visitors, Universal makes up for the rest with a thrilling half-day show that in places surpasses even Disneyland. The Universal brochures and billboards around town say "See the movies before they're movies," but that's not quite accurate: visitors here very rarely get to see anything being made. What is offered instead is a nicely organized entertainment package that combines a little education on movie technology, a little nostalgia from familiar sets and props, and a great deal of Hollywood razzle-dazzle; the Universal Studios Tour is much less a sightseeing expedition than it is a thrilling ride in a theme park —welcome to Movieland.

Like Lion Country Safari (page 366), the Universal tour is divided into two discrete parts: the Entertainment Center, where the theme park imagery really takes hold, is a richly landscaped little village with restaurants and exhibits and four live-action shows; the tour itself, a sort of three-dimensional movie, is a two-and-a-half-hour ride in what they call a GlamorTram—open tram cars with red-and-white striped roofs—through back lots and specially produced adventures with a stopover at a sound stage for more shows.

After visitors climb on board, the GlamorTram glides down a hill as a young tour guide, who doubtless thinks of himself as the next Steve Martin, begins his monologue. Then, abruptly, the tram is captured and swallowed up by an alien spacecraft that has landed on the road. Inside is a dazzling rendition of *Battlestar Galactica,* where a silver-suited actor destroys a number of mechanical villains in a laser gun fight and allows us to escape. After circling down past the false front of a house that bursts into flames on cue, the tram enters the bleak streets of windowless warehouses that are the sound stages. Visitors walk through a mock-up of a dressing room filled with famous costumes and then visit three sound stages where multi-screened movies explain how special effects are created, including the latest computer illusions. After each show a few members of the audience are allowed to become actors in full-size props, to fly like Superman on a hydraulic platform or to fend off aliens from the cockpit of a spaceship.

After reboarding the GlamorTram, visitors are driven past the well-known though surprisingly grungy false fronts of San Francisco, Chicago, New York (also known as Wilshire Boulevard), Old Europe, ancient Rome, the South Pacific, small-town America, big-town suburbia, Mexico and the Old West. Along the way come a number of Moviola perils, which are often interesting but never as vivid as they are on the screen: the tram lurches across a collapsing bridge, drives through the parting of an undistinguished Red Sea and endures a flash flood, a torpedo attack, a near train collision, an avalanche of foam rubber boulders and a close encounter with a very plastic-looking Jaws. The most realistic effect is at the end, where the tram enters a tunnel whose walls are a huge, translucent fiberglass drum, molded to look like ice; the drum begins to revolve, and soon it appears that the tram is spinning—not the walls—headlong into an infinite glacier.

The visitor is spared, though not always with his lunch, and he is let off at the Entertainment Center. Here, enveloped by tropical foliage, are souvenir shops dressed in movie-set façades, a real movie star signing autographs, and a little museum that displays old cameras and such prized artifacts as a script from *Gone With the Wind,* Errol Flynn's sword and Shirley Temple's teddy bear. The covered terrace of a nearby restaurant looks out through a perpetual rain shower along its eave line to a tropical lagoon where tiny ships do battle.

The main attractions, though, are the four stage shows, which are performed in giant amphitheaters: one features trained animals and birds doing tricks from the movies; another has cowboys slugging and shooting each other in front of an Old West town; Castle Dracula is an enormous horror-movie set with real actors and an array of eerie-giggly special effects. The newest and most entertaining show is the Screen Test Comedy Theatre, the closest thing to real moviemaking the visitor ever sees, only the actors in this case are fellow tourists. They are costumed and directed and videotaped in a number of apparently unrelated scenes on a stage filled with elaborate props and sets; at the end, the tape is quickly edited and then presented on big TV sets as a complete, though decidedly B-grade slapstick melodrama.

B · NBC STUDIOS
3000 West Alameda Avenue, Burbank; guest parking lot is off California Street
Open daily, 9–4, except major holidays; admission fee; call (818) 840-3572; for free tickets to TV shows, call (818) 840-3537

After Universal, NBC–Burbank, home of the *Tonight* show and one of the world's great clusters of TV studios, is the second, and almost only movie studio attraction in Los Angeles. The tour is much shorter (about an hour) and less precisely choreographed than the GlamorTram ride, and there are no specially manufactured excitements beyond the flashy sets themselves—which you *do* get to see, though once again the places where shows are being made are carefully avoided. Courteous NBC pages in blue blazers lead groups of about thirty people around the hangarlike interiors. They explain some of the mysteries of videotaping and answer questions as visitors walk through various sound stages and peek in on the wardrobe, makeup, special effects and set construction departments; occasionally they swing open one of the thick, two-story studio doors and reveal an astonishingly familiar set, usually for a game show, which most people in the group try to pretend is altogether unfamiliar. The climax of the tour is, of course, the Johnny Carson set, where visitors are allowed to sit down in the cool darkness and soak up the magic, much the way they do at Chartres or Notre Dame or Westminster Abbey.

C · BURBANK STUDIOS
4000 Warner Boulevard, Burbank; visitors' entrance is at the south end of Hollywood Way
Tours are given Monday through Friday, by reservation only; call (818) 954-1744; admission fee

Burbank Studios, a giant conglomerate of motion picture and television studios owned jointly by Warner Brothers and Columbia Pictures, call this the VIP tour—and they mean it. The tour is small (limited to fifteen people), relatively unpublicized (reservations are required) and expensive ($16.50 in 1983); a very knowledgeable young woman guides you through, it seems, every inch of the place, introduces you to production people and makes you feel rather like a big-time producer who's thinking about renting space here for his next film. The false-fronted streets are like those at Universal Studios, and the sound stages like those at NBC, but the approach here is altogether different. Rather than avoiding the places where people are making movies, this tour makes every effort to head straight for them. The itinerary is changed constantly so that visitors can get close to the stars and the action, and can see how repetitive and boring the movie business really is.

During the long periods between takes, you are ushered into sound stages where it's possible to touch the flimsy sets that looked so real last week on television; or you can amble into vast storerooms filled with props or brush past racks of familiar costumes, including the one Bette Davis wore as Queen Elizabeth. And all the while, all around, people are working—painting and sewing and adjusting lights and making wonderfully realistic things out of wood and plaster and fiberglass. The chief satisfaction in this apparently unplanned visit is your sense of being able to go anywhere, to talk with anyone and to linger as long as you please. The studio people seem glad you've dropped by and will often stop what they're doing to show how a vacuum mold can instantly create a gladiator helmet or a spaceship control panel or how small explosives can make bullets seem to rip through a car door; even in the hush of the dubbing room someone will explain how he's adding sound effects to next month's box-office hit.

XIV 11 · DESCANSO GARDENS
1418 Descanso Drive, La Cañada; take the Glendale Freeway to Verdugo Boulevard East, then turn right on Descanso
E. Manchester Boddy, 1937 to present
A botanical garden administered by the Los Angeles County Department of Arboreta and Botanic Gardens; open daily except Christmas, 9–4:30; admission fee

Nestled near the foothills of the San Gabriel Mountains, on the north side of the San Fernando Valley, Descanso Gardens is one of the most tranquil and beautiful outdoor places in Los Angeles. Part of the charm is that it once was a private garden, created by E. Manchester Boddy, who was the owner of the Los Angeles *Daily News.* He bought these 165 acres in 1937 and named them Rancho del Descanso, which in Spanish means rest or repose, which became the theme for his personal paradise. He then bought 460 acres of a high mountainside, just visible from here, to bring in a steady supply of water, built a Federalish white house on a hill and spread his garden out before it. Today it has become a forest. On his retirement in 1953 Boddy sold his garden to the County of Los Angeles, which has maintained it well despite someone's strong desire at one point to run a freeway through the middle of it.

Entrance to the garden now goes past a new administration and education center, a pleasant group of woodsy buildings (Barry A. Berkus, 1982) that try to recall a streamlined version of the Pasadena of Greene and Greene on a tight modern budget. A little bridge crosses over to a flower-bordered terminus for four paths; nearby, ducks and geese glide by in a shadowy pool. The path to the right leads to a five-acre rose garden, one half for All-American Rose Selections, the other for a History of Roses, where the plants are laid out chronologically, going back to the age of Augustus. The next path follows along a pretty creek and then heads up to a seven-acre hillside of native California plants, one of the most extensive native gardens in Southern California; close by it is a twenty-five-acre natural forest of California live oaks.

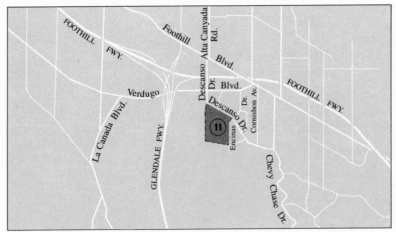

XIV 11 · DESCANSO GARDENS

The other two paths lead across bridges to what is said to be the largest collection of camellias in the world, over one hundred thousand plants of six hundred species. Off to the left, in a particularly cool and shaded part of this flowering forest, is a Japanese teahouse (1966) with a bright blue tiled roof. There are a few too many concrete foundations and tiki-telephone poles here, but even so, this is an especially restful place to sip tea and look out over a beautiful pond lined with rocks and ferns and Japanese maples and, if it's January or February, a million camellia blossoms.

XIV 12 · MAGIC MOUNTAIN
Take the Golden State Freeway (5) to the Magic Mountain Parkway, Valencia
Thomas L. Sutton, Jr., original architect; Emmit Wemple, landscape architect, 1970 to present
Open daily, 10 A.M.–midnight, in summer; weekends and school holidays, 10–6, fall, winter and spring; admission fee; call (805) 255-4111

Mention rides in Los Angeles, and most people will talk about Magic Mountain. This cleaned-up, expanded and exaggerated version of a carnival fun zone, spread across 260 acres on a grassy foothill of the San Gabriel Mountains, has only one real theme: transportation—the fastest, wildest and most heart-pounding means of transportation available on the planet. Packed inside, looping and careening through the grounds or through the air, are some thirty-five different ways to enjoy the thrills of motion or lose your lunch.

The rides can be categorized by the kinds of restraints involved. Some require none, such as the monorail, the railroad, the skyride gondolas or the trip up the 385-foot-high Sky Tower. The next group either requires seat belts or at least fits you tighter into the seat. This includes the three boat rides: two involve sliding happily down chutes in a hollowed-out log or a speedboat; the other, called Roaring Rapids, is one of the newest and most popular rides here, taking you in a rubber raft down mountains of white water through a realistic and very wet version of the Colorado River. The category where steel bars are lowered onto

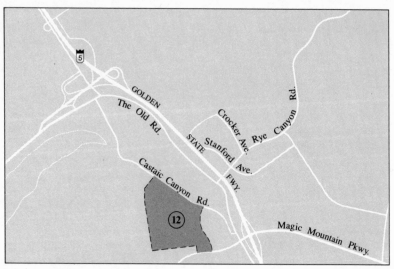

XIV 12 · MAGIC MOUNTAIN

your lap comprises the specialties of the house. There are a great many. Some of them are variations on roller coasters, while at least five are the real thing—the finest roller coasters anywhere. There's the Colossus: the largest, fastest, highest, steepest and scariest wooden roller coaster ever made. And it is surely the prettiest. It's an incredibly big and fluid and lacy mountain range of white sticks that glows magically at sunset. By day, though, the whole structure shudders as twin cars of screaming riders animate its top edge. Almost as famous is the Revolution, the world's longest steel roller coaster, which at one point causes you to be upside down. And then there's the Free Fall, where your little car is dropped off a ten-story tower, allowing you to consider a split second of zero-gravity before somehow sliding to a stop.

The concentration on the thrill rides, fortunately, has not interfered with the landscaping. Magic Mountain is surely one of the most gorgeously planted places in California. From the sky tower or the sky ride, the place looks less like an amusement park than it does a forest park, with flower-bordered footpaths winding through tunnels of big trees, past pretty lawns and fountains and streams that grow into large ponds. In many ways it's better even than Disneyland, more shaggy and relaxed (here, at least, they let you sit down on the manicured grass).

Nor have the thrill rides interfered with the other expected theme park attractions. There are Mexican and Oriental and American Northwest restaurants and lots of futuristic fast-food stands. There are themey places to buy things, most notably in Spillikin Handcrafters Junction—a blander, though lusher version of Knott's Berry Farm's Ghost Town. And there are numerous live performances in amphitheaters and pavilions scattered around the park. Live bands are playing, one place or another, throughout the day, while animal and dolphin acts and the world's largest puppet show are performed regularly. There's a colorful place for children, who are given watered-down versions of the adult thrills.

However, the concentration on thrill rides has had, for the most part, a disappointing effect on the architecture. Hardly ever is there a consistent theme to an area or a group of buildings. The designers are said to have not cared about such things, wanting the rides to speak, or shriek, for themselves. And perhaps we could accept that. Except that it's not true: over and over we find examples of their trying to create some enveloping allusion or setting, but the attempt is usually thin and halfhearted and unconvincing. It's as if they had really wanted to do the place up in Modern Architecture, but knew that that sort of thing didn't turn on most people; so they made historical forms instead, as plain and unemotional as they dared.

Therefore, there's the Animal Chatter pavilion, where a Spanishy wood pergola surrounds a space-age main structure. There's the Pacific Northwest Log Jammer flume ride with its half-timbered, half-Tudor façade: the open first floor, where you wait in an endless line, is all exposed concrete and dripping plumbing; the ride itself is in a plastic channel so brightly turquoise that it blinds the view of the supposed Oregon forest it slips through. And then there's the main gift shop, a big rectangular volume, where one side has a handsomely detailed Monterey balcony projecting from adobe-colored San Fernando Valley Apartment House stucco; another side has a white painted wooden porch, meant to be Victorian, but it's not. Of course, there's nothing inherently wrong with this abrupt juxtaposition of styles, witness the joys of Crossroads of the World (page 174). But that one was done with brio. The designers of Magic Mountain may have belonged to the wrong generation or have gone to the wrong architecture school, or both. In any case, they seem to have wanted it clean, and mute.

XIV 12 · *Magic Mountain Colossus*

Still, there are exceptions to the general lack of any architectural magic; these are found occasionally in small places, usually isolated from the rest, and made special by the bountiful landscape. The entrance forecourt, for example, is a regal affair of formal stone piers and wrought-iron bars that verges on Beverly Hills French but is made resplendent by its overflowing planters and the dappled light of overspreading trees. This leads to a thrilling water display, a sort of theme piece for the park, where waterfalls crash down artificial rocks into a big pool while big jets of water spout up, framing the amazing roller coaster loop where people travel around upside down. Off to the right are the totally undistinguished buildings of Children's World, which are saved by white-painted wood pergolas that connect them and march all around the asphalt, sometimes popping up into slatted pyramid roofs; they even begin to create a sense that this might be a special place. The designers are often very good at making pergolas and at having balls of petunias or geraniums or lobelia hanging down from them. Vine-covered timber pergolas fill the central space of Spillikin Junction, where most of the buildings manage to seem at home in their rustic outfits. They, too, are well shaded by trees, which become a forest at one end where little wooden bridges cross a particularly energetic, boulder strewn brook. Farther on, the brook becomes a shallow pool that was, like most of the waterworks here, apparently constructed by flood-control engineers; the crystal-clear water helps to point up the great quantities of concrete involved.

And then there's the one really evocative building in Magic Mountain—the Victorian railroad station, made of handsomely carved wood, painted earthy red with teal green trim. A dormered tower with an oversize wind vane rises up from the center as long gable roofs, bristling with ridge pieces, extend over open waiting rooms on each side. The station sits behind a beautiful circular plaza with a large island of flowers in the center. Enclosing the sides of the plaza are, not surprisingly, the park's prettiest pergolas, also made of red- and green-painted wood, with delicate arches and columns that curve around to little pavilions at the ends.

Though many of its attempts at enchantment are flawed, however, Magic Mountain can indeed become magical, for it does adhere mightily to its own particular theme—mechanized movement, as much as you can take, softened a bit by shrubbery. The theme vibrates through every inch of the grounds. You feel it most intensely when you're on one of the death-defying rides, but you also feel it as you glide along on one of the slower ones, watching all the other rides sliding in and out of view. And you feel it everywhere you walk, for the tracks and chutes and hurtling cars are always very near, often directly overhead. You even feel it sitting in the shade, as you listen to the constant rattling and the continual screams and the horrible thud of the Free Fall machine, which echoes through the park like a drumbeat.

And you can see it in the faces of the participants. The crowds here seem a little younger and leaner and somehow tougher than in the other places. (There are lots more tattoos.) This must be partly because Magic Mountain is one of the few amusement parks that serve beer. But, more than that, the crowd is drawn here by the thrills that these rides offer—and maybe, too, by their sense of accomplishment or relief when the tension of the waiting line and the horrors of the ride are over. Perhaps Magic Mountain can be seen, as much as anything else, as a test of nerve. If Disneyland can be thought of as a nonthreatening training ground for life's adventures, then maybe Magic Mountain is the final exam.

XIV 13 · FREEWAYS

One of the most characteristic parts of Los Angeles is the presence everywhere of its freeways (see figure 6, page xxiv), the kind of phenomenon called in the eastern United States the interstate, separating vehicular traffic from everything else and trying to make it possible to move continuously on elevated thoroughfares and sweeping ramps, at never less than fifty-five miles an hour. Los Angeles' first freeway—which, if it wasn't the first in the world, was surely one of the earliest—was the Arroyo Seco Parkway. Now the Pasadena Freeway (II), it was begun in 1934 to connect downtown Los Angeles with Pasadena. The Hollywood (101), San Bernardino (10) and Santa Ana freeways (101) were next, started during World War II. But it was during the fifteen-year period between the early 1950s and the mid-1960s that the fever really took hold, when most of the now some twenty-one freeways were begun. And the construction goes on, always about a decade behind the traffic.

Urban planners have long complained that these concrete ribbons have become walls that divide neighborhoods, but, granting that, the freeways in L.A. do manage to unite various parts of this spread-out city in ways that couldn't otherwise happen yet. The freeways of Los Angeles are usually elevated, so they also provide some of the best places for seeing the city as a whole rather than as a patchwork of separate little towns. And, for many of us, the freeways are Southern California's grandest public artworks. They seem to coincide with the ideas on beauty of Horace Walpole and other eighteenth-century English writers who spoke of "the line of beauty" or "the limp curve of humanism," the feeling you get when you sweep over hills in a carriage. It's that beautiful movement that seems to account for the magic of the freeways, at least for those of us who think they have any magic. Still, today that enchantment can evaporate abruptly. The line of beauty and the exquisite sinuous movement get messed up during increasing numbers of hours—from about seven to ten in the morning, and later in the day from about three to seven. At these times the movement becomes one of short jerks, matched by the jerks in other cars who are driving along in short jerks as well.

But once the traffic is moving, the special attribute of Los Angeles' freeway system, the quality that separates it from most other systems in the country, becomes apparent—it is, for the most part, raised high up in the air. The only other place that would afford this view of L.A. is the cockpit of an airplane. Going east on the Santa Monica Freeway (10) on a clear winter day, we can see snow-capped peaks rising up in the distance and all the houses tucked into the green Hollywood Hills and the clusters of skyscrapers that mark Santa Monica, Westwood, the Wilshire Corridor, Century City, Beverly Hills, the Miracle Mile, Hollywood and then, especially, Downtown. It's almost as if the highway engineers had planned it so that we would be at just the right distance as we drive along to see at once the whole thing and the unfolding sequences that it comprises.

Or we might choose another ride that gets us closer, to where the buildings have details and seem to move. The northbound Harbor Freeway (II), just south of the intersection with the Santa Monica, passes near Patriotic Hall (1816 Figueroa Street, Walter S. Davis, 1925), a perfectly ordinary building with its signs of habitation way up on the tenth floor instead of the first, as if it had anticipated the coming of the freeway by some thirty years. After we slip beneath the Santa Monica, the gleaming asparagus stalks of Downtown (page 1) begin to loom up and then are astonishingly close; the mirrored cylinders of the Bonaventure Hotel (page 15) flash by as the sequence of the city becomes a blur. In the distance is City Hall (page 11), gliding by more slowly. And then we sweep through the shadowy convolutions of the famous four-level interchange (page 13), where four freeways and countless on-ramps twist together; it now seems quaintly antique, but it is still a thrill to make it through. Beyond is the Pasadena Freeway (II), whose sharp curves were designed for a less hurried era; it winds along the Arroyo Seco, a dry riverbed, through old tunnels to that other world of Pasadena.

Some structures, because of their size or location, can only be appreciated from the freeway. Such is the case, for both reasons, with the old Samson Tyre and Rubber Company building (Morgan, Walls and Clements, 1929), which faces the east side of the Santa Ana Freeway (101), between the Atlantic Boulevard and Washington Boulevard exits, in the City of Commerce. Its awe-inspiring façade, nearly a third of a mile long, is done up in an Assyrian (or maybe it's Babylonian) style to look like an ancient walled city. Clearly, it is the only Assyrian tire factory that has ever been, and it must be one of the largest buildings, Assyrian or otherwise, that human hands have ever made. The scale is exactly right at fifty-five miles an hour. Other structures, even though they're visible from regular streets, can assume new dimensions from the freeways. Farther south on the Santa Ana, the snow-capped Matterhorn of Disneyland floats above the roofs of low-lying commerce. A little farther south, on the Garden Grove Freeway (22), we can glimpse the Crystal Cathedral (page 62), which looks strangely like the Matterhorn and is from here even more startling.

The most exciting moments along the freeways—and the favorites of freeway-experience collectors—are the intersections. These days, they're amazingly grand and sweeping and capacious places, where the rider is allowed to soar around in space from one freeway to another. Some claim that the best on-ramp is the one that takes you from the eastbound Ventura (101) to the northbound Glendale Freeway (22). It is one long, long graceful arc, very thinly supported and very high in the air, with airy panoramic views of the Verdugo Mountains; and it's never crowded, so no one ever gets stuck or panicked at the top.

There is another excellent new intersection, with high, dramatic supports, where the San Fernando Valley Freeway (118) joins the San Diego (405). And there are a number of old favorites on the Santa Monica Freeway (10) going east: the long ramp that swings overhead to the northbound San Diego (405) is one of the first of the really grand sweeps and is still one of the best; the one that connects the southbound Harbor (11) with the eastbound Santa Monica somehow manages to do a near-360-degree curve; then, after the Santa Monica becomes the San Bernardino Freeway (still 10), come some of the best of the new intersections, especially high and thin and thrilling: at the Foothill Freeway (210), between Covina and Pomona; Interstate 15, east of Ontario; and the Riverside Freeway (15 E), east of Colton, which may be the most dramatic of all because it seems to be in the middle of nowhere, next to the biggest truck stop in the world.

The straightaways are best used for sightseeing, for enjoying the fairly relaxed parade of the city going by, but the intersections, where there's not much time to look, are more gut-level thrills—a little like the roller coasters of Magic Mountain, but far more beautiful than they are frightening. If the freeways can be said to follow the line of beauty, then surely their intersections are highly potent developments of that line. They are, at least, fitting public monuments for this city of rides.

INDEX

ABOUT THE AUTHORS

CHARLES MOORE is one of America's most distinguished architects and writers on architecture. A principal in the Los Angeles firm of Moore, Ruble, Yudell, he also practices with the Urban Innovations Group. He is a professor of architecture at UCLA, a former Dean of the School of Architecture at Yale University, and the author of many books: *Home Sweet Home: American Domestic Vernacular Architecture* (with Peter Becker and Kathryn Smith, 1983); *Body, Memory and Architecture* (1977); *Dimensions* (with Gerald Allen, 1976); *The Place of Houses* (with Donlyn Lyndon and Gerald Allen, 1974). He is a fellow of the American Institute of Architects, recipient of the Brunner Prize, a Guggenheim Fellowship and more than forty design awards. Among his most recently completed projects in Los Angeles is the Beverly Hills Civic Center (1983).

PETER BECKER has collaborated with Charles Moore since 1981, working on architectural projects and co-editing *Home Sweet Home: American Domestic Vernacular Architecture* (1983). He received a Master of Architecture degree from the University of Colorado at Denver. At present he and Moore are working on a book about water and architecture.

REGULA CAMPBELL, who received her B.A. from Scripps College, is a partner in a Los Angeles landscape architecture firm. She has received an NEA grant to write about landscape design in southern California, and has written and lectured widely on subjects related to the landscape and the built environment.